The Last Frontier

Fighting Over Land
in the Amazon

Sue Branford and Oriel Glock

Zed Books Ltd.

The Last Frontier was first published by Zed Books Ltd.,
57 Caledonian Road, London N1 9BU, in 1985.

Copyright © Sue Branford, Oriel Glock, 1985

Cover designed by Andrew Corbett
Cover photographs by Sarah Errington
Frontispiece by Amaro Francisco
Maps by Sandra Oakins

Printed by The Bath Press, Avon

All rights reserved

British Library Cataloguing in Publication Data
Branford, Sue
    The last frontier : fighting over land in the Amazon.
    1. Amazon River watershed — Economic conditions
    I. Title   II. Glock, Oriel
    330.981'1   HC188.A5

    ISBN 0-86232-395-9
    ISBN 0-86232-396-7 Pbk

US Distributor
Biblio Distribution Center, 81 Adams Drive,
Totowa, New Jersey 07512

Contents

Tables

Maps

Illustrations

Glossary

abertura	the process of political liberalisation.
agente pastoral	church layworker.
alqueire goiano	measure of land used in most of the Amazon region, including Santa Teresinha and Porto Alegre, equivalent to 4.84 hectares. One hectare equals 2.47 acres.
alqueire paulista	measure of land used in south of Brazil, and some parts of the Amazon, equivalent to 2.42 hectares.
comunidade de informações	the whole intelligence network headed by the SNI.
garimpo	gold/silver mine.
garimpeiro	diamond and/or gold prospector.
gato	'cat', i.e. labour contractor.
grileiro	land robber.
jagunço	hired gunman.
latifundiário	big landowner.
latifúndio	large estate.
lei do posseiro	peasant's law.
lei do usucapião	law by which property rights are acquired through occupation.
minifúndio	smallholding.
município	district.
mutirão	collective act.
paranaense	person from Paraná.
paulista	person from São Paulo.
posseiro	peasant farmer without legal title to plot.
roça	cultivated plot.
sertanista	Indian specialist.
sertão	hinterland.
terra devoluta	unoccupied public land.
tori	Indian word for non-Indian.

List of Abbreviations

AEA	Associação dos Empresários da Amazônia/Association of Amazon Businessmen
CEB	Comunidade Eclesial de Base/Basic Christian Community
CEDI	Centro Ecumênico de Documentação e Informação/Ecumenical Centre of Documentation and Information
CFP	Companhia do Financiamento da Produção/Production Financing Company
Cimi	Conselho Indígena Missionário/Missionary Indian Council
CNBB	Conferência Nacional dos Bispos Brasileiros/National Conference of Brazilian Bishops
Contag	Confederação Nacional dos Trabalhadores na Agricultura/National Confederation of Agricultural Workers
CPI	Comissão Parlamentar de Inquérito/Parliamentary Commission of Enquiry
CPT	Comissão Pastoral da Terra/Pastoral Land Commission
CSN	Conselho de Segurança Nacional/National Security Council
Funai	Fundação Nacional do Indio/National Foundation of the Indian
GETAT	Grupo Executivo das Terras do Araguaia–Tocantins/Executive Group for the Araguaia–Tocantins Region
IBDF	Instituto Brasileiro de Desenvolvimento Florestal/Brazilian Institute for Forest Development
IBRA	Instituto Brasileiro de Reforma Agrária/Brazilian Institute for Agrarian Reform
INCRA	Instituto Nacional de Colonização e Reforma Agrária/National Institute for Colonization and Agrarian Reform
INPA	Instituto Nacional de Pesquisas Amazônicas/National Institute for Amazon Research
INPE	Instituto Nacional de Pesquisas Espaciais/National Institute for Space Research
Intermat	Instituto de Terras do Estado de Mato Grosso/Mato Grosso Land Department
IPEA	Instituto de Planejamento Econômico e Social/Institute of Economic and Social Planning

OAB	Ordem de Advogados Brasileiros/Order of Brazilian Lawyers
PDS	Partido Democrático Social/Social Democratic Party; formerly Aliança Renovadora (Arena)
PDT	Partido Democrático Trabalhista/Democratic Labour Party
PMDB	Partido do Movimento Democrático Brasileiro/Party of the Brazilian Democratic Movement; formerly Movimento Democrático Brasileiro (MDB)
PT	Partido dos Trabalhadores/Workers Party
PTB	Partido Trabalhista Brasileiro/Brazilian Labour Party
SEMA	Secretaria Especial do Meio-Ambiente/Special Environment Secretariat
SNI	Serviço Nacional de Informações/National Intelligence Service
SPI	Serviço de Proteção aos Indios/Service for the Protection of the Indians
STF	Superior Tribunal Federal/Supreme Federal Tribunal
STM	Superior Tribunal Militar/Supreme Military Tribunal
Sudam	Superintendência do Desenvolvimento da Amazônia/Superintendency for the Development of the Amazon
Sudeco	Superintendência do Desenvolvimento do Centro-Oeste/Superintendency for the Development of the Centre-West
Sudene	Superintendência do Desenvolvimento do Nordeste/Superintendency for the Development of the Northeast
UNI	União das Nações Indígenas/Union of Indian Nations

Preface

All books are the result of collaboration, but this one more than most.
With so little written information on land struggle in the Amazon, many
of the facts – and much of the analysis – were the result of long talks
with peasant families, settlers on the colonisation projects, cattle-
rearers, Indians, Church workers and government officials. Particular
thanks should go to: Jussara Ribeiro de Oliveira, who accompanied us
on our longest trip and spent many an hour transcribing tapes; Antônio
Carlos Queiroz, who visited Fazenda União on our behalf in April
1982; Dona Geralda and Sr Amado in Fazenda União; Fernanda and
Cascão in Porto Alegre; Teresinha and Tadeu in Santa Teresinha;
Mariano Klautau de Araújo in Belém; Hermínio Ometto and
Hildebrando de Campos Bicudo who took us on plane trips around the
ranches and answered our questions with impressive frankness; the late
Dr Paulo Botelho de Almeida Prado in Conceição do Araguaia; Odair
Cordeiro in Porto Velho; Jan Rocha who went on one of the trips; Nick
Terdre who held our home together while I travelled; my daughter
Rebecca who came with us on a couple of the trips and formed an
immediate point of contact with women from many different walks of
life; and Ralph Smith.

Tragically, Oriel died before the book was completed. After months
of long – and at times heated – discussions over what was happening in
the Amazon, I missed her sorely during the last stages of the
preparation of the manuscript. I should like to thank Bob del Quiaro for
his support during this period. I undertook the last trips to the Amazon
by myself, which accounts for the awkward transition from 'we' to 'I' at
points in the text. There is perhaps no better tribute to Oriel's warmth
and spontaneity than the deep grief over her death shown during these
last trips by many of the peasant families whose lives we tell in this
book.

Sue Branford, May 1985

North-easterners in the Amazon

Woodcut: Amaro Francisco

x

Introduction

Moda	Ballad
Vou falar para o governo,	I am going to tell the government,
eu quero proteção sua,	I want its protection,
prá fazer minha mudança,	so that I can move away,
não posso ficar na rua.	I can't live in the street.
Vou fazer baldeação	I am going to move
de cima deste torrão	away from this little plot
morar na terra da lua.	to live in the land of the moon.
O governo vendendo as terras,	The government, selling the land,
fez uma grande loucura,	made a great mistake,
a pobreza está passando	poor people are going through
numa triste desventura.	a dreadful misfortune.
Precisa morar nas trevas,	They can only live in the shadows,
bem entre o céu e a terra	midway between heaven and earth,
no espaço das alturas.	high up in the sky.
Quem inventou venda de terra,	Whoever invented this selling of land,
com a mesma mão se matou,	at the same time killed himself,
conheceu que neste mundo,	and let free in this world
ia ser um grande horror.	what was going to be a terrible horror.
Morreu e deixou o laço,	He died and left the problem
para o governo no palácio,	for the government in the palace,
seus assentos não esquentou.	not staying for more than a moment.
Por esta venda de terra,	Over this sale of land,
aquí neste Brasil,	here in this Brazil,
Por esse projeto,	for this whole project,
vai entrar uma guerra civil.	a civil war will be waged.
Se acaba tudo em fogo,	Everything is ending in flames
e pode ser que este povo,	and this may be the heaven
vá gozar num céu de anil.	awaiting our poor people.
A terra toda vendida,	The land all sold,
para os ricos tubarão,	to the rich sharks,
os pobres não pode mais,	the poor cannot work any more
trabalhar prá ter o pão.	to earn their daily bread.

1

Agora com mais o INCRA,
e o imposto tá de riba,
prá acabar com a geração.

Now with INCRA as well,
the land tax is so high,
that it'll be the end of all of us.

(Saturnino, a ballad singer in Mato Grosso)

A terra é toda dos ricos, tem título e assinatura,
o pobre perdeu direito, só tem o da sepultura.
(All the land belongs to the rich, who have it all signed and sealed,
And the poor have lost their rights, to all but the grave.)

(Verse from ballad composed by Mato Grosso musicians)

The Amazon region was a bewildering succession of powerful images for us, two English women, on our first trips to the region in the mid 1970s. The natural beauty was breathtaking: the swift waters of the Araguaia river running beside white, sandy beaches, at times dotted with huge and unexpectedly agile turtles; the graceful Brazil nut trees, often a hundred feet high, towering above the rest of the luxuriant tropical forest; and the views from a small plane as we first cruised over the dense, dark green tropical forest and then followed the course of a lithe, transparent river which ran over wrinkled dunes of white sand and patches of black mud, forming impressive designs of abstract art.

Human settlements in the Amazon can possess the same tranquil beauty. We remember well a procession of chanting peasant farmers bearing candles and lanterns, and wending their way at dusk up the hillside along a rough path hacked out of the thick tropical forest, to take part in a simple ceremony in a holy sanctuary to express gratitude to God for their continued survival as a community, despite persistent harassment by a powerful landowner. On another occasion, we listened to a group of old peasant men and women, sitting out on wooden benches in front of their mud-and-daub huts as the sun disappeared behind the forest in the quick tropical sunset, while they recounted contentedly for the hundredth time the story of their struggle for survival in the early pioneer days: the encounters with lethal snakes – *sucuris*, rattlesnakes, *urutus*, coral-snakes and others – jaguars and wild boars; the tragic deaths of children, succumbing to untreated illnesses such as malaria, or killed by scorpion stings; the long struggle during the rainy season when the floods isolated the community for months from all outside contact and created serious food shortages. Another day we stood and watched a group of Indian boys, laughing with infectious hilarity as they played in the water, spearing fish with amazing dexterity and weaving their way in canoes along rocky, fast-flowing rivers.

But our dominant impression from the settlements we visited on our first trips was not of peacefulness and beauty, but of rapid change and great brutality. We were prepared for the transformations which the region was undergoing, but not for the violence. Before we made our first trips, we had heard much talk in São Paulo of the government-sponsored 'March to the Amazon'. As a result, we were impressed, but not surprised, by the remarkable speed with which the region was being opened up. New roads were being built in a matter of months. Thousands of land-hungry peasant families were moving in, settling on the virgin land beside the roads. Large areas of forest were being felled by gangs of labourers employed by the cattle ranches. Towards the end of the dry season, in August and September, these areas were set alight to clear the felled vegetation so that grass seed could be sown. The fires raged for several days, making it difficult for the little planes run by the ranches to land and take off. The frontier region was bustling with activity, as we had anticipated.

We were not expecting, however, the scale of the lawlessness and violence accompanying the occupation, its cost in human suffering. People everywhere – in buses, bars, pensions – spoke of murders, brutal beatings, threats, bullying. Very often the violence was the result of land disputes, with powerful landowners and land thieves sending in gunmen to clear peasant families off the land.

Every day on our journeys we heard complaints from peasant farmers that they had been evicted, brutally and illegally, from their plots of land. One old man told us that everywhere he had settled he had planted fruit trees, yet never had his family eaten fruit from his trees. At times he had moved on because the fertility of the soil had been exhausted, he said, but not infrequently he had been evicted by gunmen. The dispossessed farmers told us that it got them nowhere – and could even be dangerous – to complain to the local police force which, they alleged, was corrupt, working hand-in-glove with big landowners. Some of the evicted farmers told us they had spent their savings on a trip to Brasília to report the incident to the federal authorities, but again they had achieved nothing.

The difficulties faced by the ranch labourers were equally serious. We heard reports of isolated camps in the heart of the forest, holding hundreds of unskilled labourers, employed by labour contractors to fell the forest and clear the land for the formation of pastures. We visited a couple of these encampments and found gunmen at the entrances and a few labourers, ill from malaria, shivering under four blankets despite the tropical heat. The sick men, untreated, lay in hammocks in rough, open huts built by the men themselves out of tree trunks; the roofs were made of banana or palm leaves or thick plastic sheeting.

On another visit we were shown around by the farm manager, who – possibly to impress us – picked up at the forest camp a labourer, seriously ill with malaria, to take him back to the ranch headquarters. The sick man clearly mistrusted our requests that he travel in the covered cabin on a padded seat. He insisted on riding in the back among a load of tree trunks, although he was jolted roughly as we drove along a dirt track. He accepted the cups of water we brought during stops on the journey back, but obviously found our behaviour strange. So did the manager, and we were angered and embarrassed by his amusement at our 'Florence Nightingale' gestures. We realised that the manager, and even the labourer himself, felt it to be improper and somewhat ludicrous that two white, well-educated women should be concerned about the welfare of an illiterate black worker.

The labourers were frequently caught in a vicious circle of exhausting labour and reckless pleasure. During our first evening in São Félix, a little town on the banks of the Araguaia river, we were startled by the number of reeling drunk labourers, who were making the rounds of the local bars and brothels. We were frightened to see that many were armed with long knives, axes or hatchets. The town was plunged into darkness at 10 p.m. when the local electricity generator was shut off – a routine procedure that no one had thought to tell us about. Scared that we might be attacked by one of the armed drunks in the street, we found it a nerve-racking experience to stumble our way back to our small hotel in the noisy, unlit and unfamiliar town.

When we got back to our hotel, we were told that a local ranch had 'let free' a few hundred labourers in the town earlier that day. After several months in a camp in the forest, without alcohol or women, the men were out celebrating. Unwilling to leave their work implements in the pensions for fear they would be stolen, they carried them around with them in the bars. Not infrequently, through drink, prostitutes and thieves, in that first night on the town the men lost all the money they had earned from several months of hard physical labour. They ran up bills in the pension and were then 'sold back' to a ranch by the lodging-house owner in return for payment of their debts.

We saw little evidence that the police were making an attempt to force the ranch owners to respect Brazil's labour legislation or to put an end to the illegal evictions of peasant families. On our first trip, we travelled by lorry along a half-finished road, from Conceição do Araguaia to Marabá. The road went through Redenção, a little town that did not exist in 1970 but had 5,000 inhabitants by the time of our visit at the end of 1974. The lorry driver told us that Redenção had grown so quickly that it lacked even a token police force. All affairs were settled by the town's 'strong man' and his gunmen, who were getting very rich from land speculation (urban plots which had cost Crs 40 (£2.80) a hectare in 1971 were Crs 40,000 (£2,275) a hectare by 1974).

We noticed that many of the huts in Redenção had walls made of roughly-hewn planks of mahogany, though the roofs were made of the customary palm leaves. The driver told us later that some of the violence arose from disputes over the mahogany, which was found in fairly large quantities in the region. This timber, previously considered worthless, had suddenly become a valuable commodity when the opening of the new road made it possible to market it. A wild west atmosphere pervaded this town more than anywhere else we visited. Amused by our nervousness, the lorry driver introduced us to the gunmen, with pistols and revolvers stuck in their holsters, who, he confided to us later, would kill anyone for Crs 40,000

(£2,160). The local barman told us that very few of the people buried in the unexpectedly large local cemetery had been 'killed by God'. There was at least one murder a day in Redenção, he added. As if to drive the point home, we heard shots as we drove out of town; a few minutes later we came upon the still-warm corpse of a young man.

On our early trips, we saw few pure Indians (though it was clear from the slanted eyes, high cheekbones and straight black hair of some of the local inhabitants that a number of them had Indian ancestors). The little direct contact we had was not encouraging. On one of our visits, we stayed on a ranch owned by Bradesco, Brazil's largest private banking group. After having been shown around the ranch for several days, a ranch employee asked us if we would like a trip by motor boat to visit some Indians called *Caras-pretas* (black faces). We agreed, with some reservations, for we knew nothing about any such Indians and were aware that unauthorised visits of this kind were against the regulations of Funai (National Foundation of the Indian), the government body in charge of Indian policy. Just as we were about to leave, a US linguist employed by the Summer Institute of Linguistics arrived by plane. He had come specifically to visit the *Avá-canoeiros*, which, we learnt, was the Indians' proper name. During the boat journey, the linguist and the ranch employees told us the history of the group.

They had earned the nickname *Caras-pretas* because of the little black beard many of the men had – a rarity among Indians, for most show an aversion to facial hair. It was thought that these Indians had been living in the area for a considerable time, perhaps as long as 30 to 40 years. As they did not cultivate crops and carefully avoided contact with outsiders, even learning to speak very softly, they had successfully avoided any confrontation. However, a few years earlier, they had started to raid the company's cattle, wild prey having become scarce because of the large-scale forest clearings that had been carried out in the region by cattle companies.

The ranch had contacted Funai, which had sent in a young man, Apoena Meirelles, the son of Chico Meirelles, a famous worker with Indians, to establish contact with them. However, the gradual, peaceful contact planned by Meirelles turned out to be exceptionally difficult in practice because of the skill in evasion shown by the Indians, who then numbered between 30 and 35. According to the ranch employees, Meirelles lost patience and brought in 30 Xavante Indians (a very different group). They surrounded the *Avá-canoeiros'* camp one night and kidnapped five Indians, believing them to be leaders. With their legs and arms bound, these Indians were taken to the ranch. Four other members of the group, believed to be close relatives, joined the captured five a few days later.

The nine Indians were transferred across the river to the island of Bananal, a habitat strange to them, and left in a hut constructed for them by Funai employees. When we visited them – just a month after the transfer – they were dejected, apathetic and wracked by bad colds. The Funai officials, who had supervised the move, had left them in the charge of two

Javié Indians, who knew little about the group and its problems. No attempt was being made to help the group adapt to its new circumstances. The visit by the US linguist was the first endeavour even to identify the group's language family, a task which was not made easier by the *Avá-canoeiros'* habit of speaking extremely softly. The group seemed well on the way to extinction. (Six years later, by the time we came to write this book, the entire group had been wiped out by disease, despite later efforts by anthropologists and Cimi, the Catholic Church's missionary council, to help them.)

During our first trip in 1974, the buses we travelled in were stopped by groups of heavily-armed soldiers and thoroughly searched. This happened most often when we were in the region of Marabá, a town on the Transamazônica highway. We were startled at the strength of the military presence – we were variously told that there were 5,000, 10,000 or even 15,000 soldiers in the region. Everyone knew that the soldiers were fighting the 'terrorists', a small group of rural guerrillas who had been discovered in the region. While still in São Paulo, the most populous and developed city in Brazil, far to the south of the Amazon, we had heard vague rumours of army activity in the north. In those days the military dictatorship still imposed rigorous censorship which kept all news out of the press. We were not prepared for the extent of the army action. We asked ourselves what was going on. Was the guerrilla threat much more serious than we had been led to believe?

We were told on several occasions that peasant farmers had been tortured by the army to force them to collaborate. We tried cautiously to confirm some of these reports by talking to peasant farmers in the region, but we met a solid wall of silence from the scared families. We later learned that at least three peasant farmers had died under torture, for refusing to collaborate.[1] Another peasant farmer had asked a fellow prisoner what was the strange thing that had made him 'jump like a frog'; electric shock torture had been this man's first contact with electricity.[2]

Our first trips to the Amazon thus raised many more questions than they answered. Where did all the thousands of peasant farmers come from? How long had they been moving into the region? When did the cattle companies first arrive? How much government money was going into the cattle projects?

Surely the federal government must be aware that the landowners were systematically bribing the local police forces and violently and illegally evicting peasant farmers on a large scale? This widespread disregard for the law was creating a situation in which the peasant farmers and labourers had no authority to which they could readily turn to redress the wrongs they had suffered. It seemed to us a potentially explosive situation, for sooner or later it could lead them to form their own organisations to defend their rights, using violence if necessary. Why was the government allowing this time-bomb to tick away? Why was it not bringing some law and order into this wild west?

Many peasant families had told us that the only people who cared for them and helped them in their difficult struggle against the landowners were Catholic priests and lay workers. We had seen that the church was carrying out work of great importance, helping the peasant families to organise and unite in their struggle. How had the Catholic Church become involved in such a radical task? How was the church hierarchy reacting to this new role being carried out by the church workers?

And the Indians: why was the government doing so little to protect the Indian people when so many were dying as a result of their initial contact with the encroaching society? Was it already too late? Were the Indian people doomed to destruction?

This book is an attempt to answer the questions thrown up by the initial visits. We decided to look at the history of peasant migrations to the Amazon, to find out why and when the big companies had first arrived, to trace the growing conflict between the peasant families and the ranches and to look at the government's response to it, to look at the work carried out by the Catholic Church, and to examine the impact of the occupation process on the Indians. Above all, we decided to get to know a few peasant communities that had been involved in long struggles with cattle companies and to ask both sides – peasant families and company employees – to tell us in their own words how the conflict had emerged.

Notes

1. According to the Catholic priest, Humberto Railland, in an interview published in *A Guerrilha do Araguaia* (História Imediata, Editôra Alfa–Omega, São Paulo, 1979), p.61.

2. According to ex-guerrilla José Genuíno Neto, in an interview published in ibid., p.44.

1. The Peasant Families Arrive

About midnight the wind, for which we had long been waiting, sprang up, the men weighed anchor, and we were soon fairly embarked on the Amazons. I rose long before sunrise to see the great river by moonlight. There was a spanking breeze, and the vessel was bounding gaily over the waters. The channel along which we were sailing was only a narrow arm of the river, about two miles in width: the total breadth at this point is more than 20 miles, but the stream is divided into three parts by a series of large islands. The river, notwithstanding this limitation of its breadth, had a most majestic appearance. It did not present that lake-like aspect which the waters of the Pará and Tocantins rivers affect, but had all the swing, so to speak, of a vast flowing stream ... A chain of blue hills, the Serra de Almeyrim, appeared in the distance on the north bank of the river. The sight was most exhilarating after so long a sojourn in a flat country.
(Extract from *The Naturalist on the River Amazons* by Henry Walter Bates, a British naturalist, who lived in the Amazon region from 1848 to 1859).

The Amazon

The Amazon is a vast area of about seven million square kilometres – roughly the size of Australia. Most of it is situated in Brazil, but the river's tributaries spread out across a huge area: to Bolivia in the south; Peru, Ecuador and Colombia in the west; and Venezuela and Guyana in the north. The Amazon itself rises in the snows of the Peruvian Andes just a short distance from the Pacific. It travels across the heart of the South American continent – a distance of 6,570 kilometres – to flow out into the Atlantic Ocean near Belém on the Equator. It has about 15,000 tributaries, some of which, like the Madeira and the Araguaia, are mighty rivers in their own right. It has a heavier flow of water than any other river in the world, depositing each year about a fifth of the fresh water that pours into the world's oceans. It is the world's second longest river, being slightly shorter than the Nile (6,690 kilometres) but longer than the Mississippi–Missouri (6,211 kilometres).

The Amazon region has the world's largest tropical forest, which contains a bewildering abundance of plants, insects, reptiles and fish. It has no large mammals, but many smaller animals, such as monkeys, sloths, armadillos, anteaters and jaguars. It has remained virtually unchanged for one hundred million years, for it did not pass through an Ice Age. It is estimated to contain about a tenth of the plant, insect and animal species on earth.

Until a few decades ago it was assumed that only extremely fertile soils could support the Amazon's luxuriant forest. Since then, however, it has been shown that the riotous vegetation is the result of a delicate balance which permits nutrients, predominantly held in the biomass, to be recycled within the ecosystem. A decaying leaf falling off a tree is almost totally reabsorbed into the forest by a mass of creepers and roots before it reaches the ground. Thus the Amazon forest depends very little on any supply of nutrients from the soil and the exuberance of the undergrowth cannot be taken as an indication of soil fertility.

Because the Amazon soils on the whole contain so few nutrients, the water in the rivers which run off the Amazon forest is very pure; it is equivalent to 'slightly contaminated distilled water', according to Harald Sioli, formerly director of the Max Planck Institute of Limnology in West Germany, and a renowned Amazon specialist.[1] This explains the famous 'meeting of the waters' in Manaus where the clear water of the Negro river, which rises in the Amazon forest, runs for several miles beside the muddy water of the Solimões river, which comes down from the Andes. Brazilians call the river Amazonas (the Amazon) after this meeting.

Although about three-fifths of Brazil lies within the Amazon region, the country's basic farming and industrial development took place until recently in the narrow band of fertile land running along the Atlantic coastline, particularly in the south-east near Rio de Janeiro and São Paulo. For centuries the vast Amazon region was neglected, with only occasional and temporary forages to plunder its wealth such as the spectacular rubber boom in the late nineteenth century.

It was only in the 1960s that the government made serious efforts to integrate the Amazon into the rest of the country and to develop its economy in a sustained fashion. By then, the traditional isolation of the region had already been partially broken by the steady influx of land-hungry peasant families moving in on their own initiative without assistance from – or, at times, even the knowledge of – the federal government.

This chapter contains a brief description of the early phase, followed by an account of the crumbling of the region's isolation and its growing involvement, in many different ways, with the rest of Brazil.

The Discovery

The original inhabitants of Brazil were the Indians, of whom there are about 180,000 today, but some five million at the time of the discovery of Brazil for the Portuguese by the explorer Pedro Cabral in 1500. Though today more than three-quarters of the Amazon belongs to Brazil, it was not originally intended to turn out in this way. Under the Treaty of Tordesillas signed in 1494, the Pope divided up the huge, and at that time largely unknown, area of South America between the expanding colonial empires of Spain and Portugal. If his demarcation had been respected, Brazil would have had very little of the Amazon. But through the steady expansion westwards of explorers, traders and settlers, it gradually imposed its territorial claims on most of the region in a long process which was only completed at the beginning of this century. However, even in the 1960s some government officials, particularly military officers, were not confident of permanently retaining the Amazonian frontiers and argued that Brazil could only be sure of keeping the Amazon once it had been fully integrated into the rest of the country. Geopolitical considerations were undoubtedly important in the government's recent endeavours to open up the region.

The first European to reach the mouth of the Amazon was a Spaniard, Vicente Yáñez Pinzón, in 1500. In 1541, Francisco de Orellana, another Spaniard, made the first 6,000 kilometre descent of the Amazon in an extraordinary trip chronicled by his chaplain, Gaspar de Carvajal. Orellana fought with a group of Tapuya Indians and noted, with amazement, that the women fought alongside the men. It is thought that Orellana called the tribe 'Amazons', after the ancient legendary nation of female warriors described by the Greek writers Herodotus and Diodorus, and in this way indirectly named the river.

The occupation of the Amazon region by the Portuguese settlers took on different characteristics from those elsewhere in Brazil. This was largely because the timid attempts by the early settlers to farm the region failed completely in the face of the immense and unknown tropical forest. Only in the delta itself was large-scale tropical farming possible, with the setting up of sugar plantations using African slaves. The rest of the Amazon forest was plundered, not developed. The only important economic activity carried out by the settlers was the collection of natural products, mainly cocoa, cloves, cinnamon, Brazil nuts, sarsaparilla and precious wood from the forest, turtle, turtle eggs, *manacuru* (cow fish) and others from the river. Because these natural products were dispersed irregularly through the forest, human settlement could not be organised around them. Rather, settlement was determined by the rivers which provided all-important access to the products. Thus, the settlement of the Amazon region become 'more of an adventure than the setting up of a stable and organised society'.[2] The isolation and distinct characteristics of the Amazon region were recognised by the Portuguese Crown in 1621 when King Philip IV created a separate state of Maranhão and Grão-Pará which dealt directly with Portugal.

Because of their undisputed expertise in collecting forest products, fishing and travelling by river, the Indians had greater prestige and influence here than elsewhere in Brazil. Nevertheless, they were fundamentally regarded as sub-human, as particularly skilful animals which could be peddled like expensive cattle. Their capture for sale as slaves became a key factor in the exploration of isolated regions. Imbued with what today seems unbelievable cultural arrogance and inhumanity, the Portuguese explorers also carried out the infamous 'punitive expeditions' or 'just wars': horrific incursions into the jungle with the specific intention of massacring Indians. In the 17th Century, the famous explorer Pedro Teixeira boasted that, after 30 years at the head of expeditions along the Negro and Amazon rivers, he had been responsible for the death of two million Indians. At times the Indians fought back courageously, despite the inequality in armaments, but were almost invariably overwhelmed and massacred. The famous stand made by the Rio Negro Indians who, under the leadership of the Tuxauá Indian Ajuricaba, resisted from 1723 to 1728, ended in crushing defeat with the death of about 15,000 Indians.[3]

The Jesuits arrived in 1653 and, for 30 years, enjoyed a monopoly in the catechisation of the Indians. They set up their famous *aldeamentos* (villages) in the forest where, as well as receiving the catechism, the Indians were expertly organised into becoming efficient collectors of forest products. The Jesuits became extremely prosperous, earning particularly large incomes from their sales of cocoa beans from the Madeira river and rosewood from the Tapajós river. One traveller cynically observed at the beginning of the 18th Century, that the Jesuit colleges and chapels 'look more like custom halls than praying houses'. By the end of the colonial period in 1822, the vast Amazon region contained only 85,000 inhabitants of European origin, most of them concentrated in the delta. No sustained economic activity had been organised on a significant scale.

The Rubber Boom

The region was largely peaceful throughout the 19th and early 20th Centuries, with only very gradual changes. The calm was broken by the extraordinary *Revolução dos Cabanos*, a local revolt of poor *mestiços* (people of mixed race, especially Portuguese and Indian) against their Portuguese overlords. One of their slogans was '*Volta ao Indianismo puro*' (return to pure Indianism) by which they meant, among other things, that the land should belong to those who occupied it. Th *cabanos*, the name given to those taking part in the revolt, occupied Belém for a year in1835-6 and were only completely subdued by the end of the decade after about 35,000 people had been killed.

Various attempts to set up large-scale commercial agriculture were made throughout this period, but none of them prospered. One of the problems was shortage of labour, a difficulty which became particularly marked after the abolition of slavery in 1888. Estate owners frequently complained about the way white workers, brought in from Portugal, would abandon their jobs on the estates, attracted into subsistence farming by the abundance of available land.

It was, however, the rubber boom which finally killed off commercial farming. Following first Faraday's discovery of electricity in 1831 and then the invention of the motor car in the 1880s, rubber came to be in great demand on the world market. For a while, the Amazon basin, with its vast number of native rubber trees, was the world's only source of this important commodity. Thousands of poor rural workers, mainly from Ceará in the north-east, were brought in to tap the rubber.

The area between the Juruá and Purus rivers was exploited first, partly because these were the most easily navigable of the Amazon's tributaries. Towards the end of the century, however, a much bigger area was used, with thousands of migrants settling along the Xingu, Tapajós, Madeira, Jutaí and Negro rivers. The population of the Amazon region rose from 333,000 in 1872 to 700,000 in 1900 and 1.1 million in 1920.

By imposing very strict control of the market network, the 'plantation owners' (who neither set up plantations, for they exploited the native rubber trees, nor in most cases owned the land, just occupied it and provided the capital) were able to hold the rubber-tappers in a stringent form of debt–peonage. In many regions, the tappers were even forbidden to cultivate subsistence crops, so that all goods had to be purchased at exorbitant prices from the plantation owner. While the owners made tremendous profits, the tappers themselves frequently had to work extremely long hours in a vain attempt to pay off their debts. Although enormous fortunes were being made by a few, living standards actually fell considerably during the period. Diseases, such as beri-beri, unknown in the region until then, became commonplace, largely because of the lack of fresh vegetables.

Rubber production increased from 2,600 tonnes in 1860 to 44,000 tonnes in 1911. However, nearly all other economic activities suffered greatly from the obsession with rubber. As early as 1854, the president of the Province of Pará complained of 'the almost exclusive use of labour in rubber extraction and rubber manufacturing, to such an extent that we have to import from other provinces basic foodstuffs that earlier we produced ourselves, and even supplied to other provinces'. In 1884, for the same reasons, the writer Barbosa Rodrigues spoke of the 'pernicious rubber industry'.

The towns of Belém and Manaus developed rapidly as a result of the rubber trade, but their prosperity was very precarious as it was highly dependent on rubber. Other economic activities were seriously neglected. Such was the extravagance that during one period families in Belém imported planks of wood from Europe, although vast quantities of timber were available on the outskirts of the town.

Productivity was low on the so-called plantations, for the rubber trees were scattered over vast areas. The boom was exclusively the result of the Amazon's monopoly on world production. When this was broken, as inevitably happened, the bubble burst. In 1876, an Englishman smuggled some seedlings out of the Amazon and raised them in Kew Gardens in London. These were then used to set up huge plantations in Malaya. As the trees were organised in a much more compact fashion, rubber could be produced at incomparably lower costs than in the Amazon. As a result, the price of rubber on the world market fell from twelve shillings a pound in 1911, to seven shillings in 1921 and to just one shilling and sixpence in 1932.[4]

This was the second time that the Amazon's natural wealth had been plundered, to the great benefit of another region. A century earlier, farmers had taken seedlings from cocoa trees, another of the Amazon's native species, to Bahia in the north-east. Grown on plantations there, Bahian cocoa had quickly driven the Amazonian product off the market. Today cocoa is one of Brazil's leading export products. After a gap of a century and a half, cocoa has been reintroduced into the Amazon region, this time to be cultivated on plantations.

The breaking of the monopoly in rubber production had much more serious social and economic consequences for the Amazon region than the earlier loss of its exclusivity in cocoa cultivation. From 1913, a process of involution took place from which the region only began to recover slowly in the 1940s. Although thousands of the rubber-tappers returned to the north-east after the crash, thousands of others stayed, trapped by their accumulated debts. Even as late as 1970, it was estimated that no fewer than 100,000 tappers were still working for a pittance in the Amazon forest.

The collapse of the rubber market was alleviated in some areas by an increase in the commercial importance of Brazil nuts, another native product. The collection of nuts was organised on similar lines to rubber-tapping, so some of the rubber plantation owners switched over to the new product. As is to be expected from the name, Brazil had – and still has – a world monopoly in this product. About three-quarters of the Brazil nut trees are to be found in the valley of the river Itacaiúnas, a tributary of the river Tocantins.

Throughout the 1930s and 1940s, many peasant farmers migrated from the north of Goiás, the west of Maranhão and the lower reaches of the Tocantins river valley to the Itacaiúnas region during the Brazil nut season. Most of them spent the rest of the year cultivating crops for their own subsistence, collecting babassu nuts for their oil, which they sold on the market for a low price, and rearing cattle. Many were employed under the *partilha* (share) system of cattle-rearing, by which the owner of the cattle (who frequently did not own – but merely occupied – extensive stretches of natural pastures) did not pay the herdsman a money wage, but allowed him to keep a proportion, usually a fifth or a quarter, of the calves he reared. In this way, collection of Brazil nuts offered the peasant families a rare chance to increase their cash income, if only by an amount that would seem risible to us.

The peasants' employment as Brazil nut collectors was, however, extremely insecure. The size of the harvest varies wildly each year, apparently as a result of natural factors not yet properly understood by botanists. It is not infrequent for the harvest to fall to one quarter of its level in the previous year, then to recover magnificently to a bumper crop in the following year. The peasants thus migrated to the region with no guarantee of employment at the end of their journey.

All the economic activities practised by the sparse population were precarious and essentially unstable. Even rubber-tapping, which brought the country a great deal of wealth for a short period, was essentially plunder that did not create solid foundations for prolonged economic prosperity. It is this history which led Caio Prado to conclude in his book, *Formação do Brasil Contemporâneo*, first published in 1942: 'Thus we still do not know what form the settlement of the Amazon valley will take'.[5] Forty years later this statement is no longer true, at least for large areas of the Amazon basin. What changes have occurred in the intervening years, and what form is the settlement of the region taking?

The Peasant Families Move In

From the beginning of the 19th Century, an increasing number of poor cattle-rearers had begun to move into the region from the east. Cattle-rearing had arisen originally in the 16th Century to supply with bullocks, beef and leather the sugar plantations established in the north-east by the Portuguese. As a subsidiary activity, it had been driven inland to leave the best land for sugar. But, with the decline of the plantations in the second half of the 17th Century, cattle-rearing had become an independent, predominantly subsistence activity, with the sale of some leather on the market.

This front moved slowly westwards across Maranhão. In the first decade of this century, this migratory flow was boosted by peasant farmers from Ceará and Piauí in the north-east, who had been driven out by the huge and unproductive estates (*latifúndios*), which were taking over most of the land. Unlike the plundering activities of earlier times, this penetration led to a modification of the Amazonian landscape and, for good or bad, it began to integrate the region into the rest of the country.

By the early 20th Century, this front had reached the Tocantins river. It started to move more slowly for several reasons: it reached better quality pastures that could support the cattle for longer periods, it encountered more numerous and more aggressive groups of Indians and, in some regions, it came up against the natural barrier of tropical forest.[6] The wave of migration gained impetus after the collapse of the rubber boom, which meant the end of rubber-tapping as a source of employment for the excess population. A few of the families gradually advanced into Pará in the 1930s and 1940s, forced further westwards by the exhaustion of the soil in their small plots or, still infrequently in this period, after eviction by a powerful landowner, claiming property rights over their land.

With the worsening of the agrarian crisis in the north-east in the 1950s, hundreds of thousands of families migrated south to the big industrial centres, particularly São Paulo. It was the beginning of the famous urban explosion. But thousands of others took a less-publicised route, travelling westwards in the wake of the early migrants. When in 1962 Sudene (Superintendency for the Development of the North-East) decided to set up a colonisation project in the valleys of the rivers Pindaré and Alto Turi in west Maranhão in order to settle some of the landless peasants from the north-east, it discovered that the region had already been occupied by peasant families acting on their own initiative. No fewer than 50,000 people were already living in the region.

During this period, migrants from the north-east also moved into Goiás, the state lying to the south-west of Maranhão. They were attracted to mineral prospecting after the discovery of diamond and rock crystal, and to the collection of the babassu nuts. They joined up with peasant families which had moved into the region earlier as part of the old penetration front of cattle-rearers.

As a result of the heavy influx, the available land soon began to run out in Maranhão. The plots set up by the first migrant families were divided between children and relatives until they became too small to support a family adequately. The number of farms of less than 10 hectares in size in the state of Maranhão tripled from 75,000 in 1950 to 230,000 in 1960. Moreover, the average size of these farms fell from 2.5 hectares to 2.3.

Though thousands of peasant families were moving out of the north-east, the land shortage continued to intensify in that region. While the *latifúndio* maintained a political and economic stranglehold over the region and kept vast areas out of productive use, more and more peasant families divided up the small slice allocated to them. Farms of less than 10 hectares rose from 53 per cent of the total in 1950 to 62 per cent in 1960. The farms became too small to support the population living on them. It has been claculated that no less than 37 per cent of the economically active population in the countryside in the north-east was unemployed or underemployed in the 1960s and 1970s.

Events in Goiás evolved in a somewhat different fashion. Farmers from the south of Brazil had been attracted to the state since the beginning of the century, encouraged by the construction of railways during the first two decades and compelled, in some cases, by the exhaustion of coffee plantations in the bordering state of Minas Gerais. From the 1950s onwards, however, with the greatly increased pressure on land in São Paulo and Minas Gerais, Goiás received a much larger agricultural overspill from the south. This led to a redistribution of the rural population, with more modern, better-off farmers from São Paulo and Minas Gerais buying out long-established Goiás farmers, who then moved up to more remote areas in the north of the state to carry out their traditional activities of cattle-rearing and rice cultivation. They, in turn, displaced peasant families from the north-east, some of whom had originally been attracted to the state to work as mineral prospectors and had stayed on as subsistence farmers.

In the 1950s many peasant families began to push on further west, crossing the Araguaia river into north Mato Grosso, in the wake of the few

The main migratory flows

hardy frontiersmen (and women) who had preceded them in earlier years. This decade marked the beginning of large-scale migration to the regions in north-east and north-west Mato Grosso where we carried out our case studies.

As we shall see later, the lives of these migrant families, who have faced remarkable dangers and hardships in their constant search for unoccupied land on the agricultural frontier, yield epic tales of self-reliance and courage. They tell stories of encounters with wild animals and Indians, of tremendous difficulties in slashing and burning the tropical vegetation to hack out a small plot on which to build a rough shack and plant rice, maize and manioc, of illness, disease, the *grileiro* (land robber), the *jagunço* (hired gunman), of eviction and moving on to start the cycle all over again. Many of these families have travelled 2,000 kilometres or more in their long trek westwards.

These migrants have created a mythic language in which to express the aspirations aroused by their recurrent journeys. All over the region we heard people speak of a 'land of freedom and plenty' which lay to the west of Araguaia river, the river which marks the approximate end of natural pasture and the beginning of tropical forest. A few of the families to whom we spoke had crossed the Araguaia in search of this land which, they claimed, was referred to in a prophecy by the mystical leader, Padre Cícero, who preached in the north-east in the first decades of this century.

The Early Migrants

There is a marked difference today between the older communities to the east of the Araguaia river in the states of Goiás and Maranhão, which were established during the slow, peaceful migrations of the first half of this century, and the more recent settlements to the west of this river, in the states of Pará and Mato Grosso, which were largely formed during the faster and more violent wave of occupation in the 1960s and 1970s. Carrying out our case studies in the younger communities, we met settlers who had considerable experience of the outside world, if only through their contact with cattle companies. Here we did not meet a single old peasant who had lived on the same plot for his whole life. To give an idea of the older communities we will tell one tale out of hundreds of similar cases.

In the early 1970s, about 100 families were evicted from their plots lying to the east of the river Tocantins in Goiás. Although these families did not possess official deeds to their land, some had been living in the region for more than 60 years and had paid land tax to the government since 1930. (In contrast, none of the peasants to whom we talked in Mato Grosso and Pará had been living on their plots for more than 20 or, exceptionally, 30 years.) This long-established, uncontested occupation of the land by the peasants of Goiás gave them clear-cut property rights in Brazilian law. None the less, like thousands of others, this isolated community was pitilessly destroyed by the landowner from the south, despite the remarkable efforts made by the peasants to defend themselves.

Like many of the migrant farmers to whom we spoke, these peasants in Goiás, whose life histories were recorded by members of the Catholic Church's Pastoral Land Commission, initially showed total faith in the goodwill and justice of the government. In moving fashion, they naively believed that General Emílio Garrastazu Médici, the authoritarian and inaccessible President who ruled Brazil from 1969 to 1974, had taken a personal interest in their problem. This ingenuous trust was later transformed into bitterness in the face of glaring evidence of the corruption and bad faith of the authorities. Unlike many of the younger, more adaptable migrants we interviewed in Mato Grosso and Pará, these peasant families, who had lived in a very closed, isolated community for decades, were experiencing great difficulty in relating to the modern world.

Dona Ana, a 63-year-old peasant woman, who had been evicted from her land and was squatting on a miserable plot beside the Tocantins river, told her story to the land commission workers. She recalled that, since the mid 1960s, the community had received threats from outsiders who purported to own the land, and she described the complete disarray into which this unexpected intrusion had thrown their life. She remembered that in 1969 one of the peasant families had been quite certain that they had heard on their transistor radio a personal message from President Médici confirming their ownership rights and telling them all to stay on their land. Dona Ana said that they had all been jubilant and that many of the families had planted three times as much rice in 1970 and 1971 as they were confident that they would be able to stay and reap it.

However, their heartfelt relief was short lived. The intimidations soon began again. When it became clear that, unless they moved out on their own initiative, the 'landowner' would send in gunmen to evict them, they sent a representative to Goiânia, the state capital, to speak to the head of the state's Department of Justice. Dona Ana said that at first their representative was told that they could all stay as they had clear property rights to their land. A day or two later, however, probably because by then the 'landowner' had had time to apply pressure, the official story was changed and their representative was told they they must all leave as soon as possible.

Dona Ana commented:

> I was born and bred here. If I don't have rights here, then I don't have them anywhere. My father died here, my mother died here, my husband died here. They were all buried in the cemetery here . . . Ah! How it hurts to think that I've suffered so much injustice. And it's worse because it's all happened now that I'm old. To see my children suffering, lacking everything. Everybody wants this land now, because now it's easier to live here, it's been tamed. There are roads. It seems that just us, who were born and brought up here, just us don't have any rights.

Her son, Zé, carried on:

> In the old days, there weren't any roads at all. Just jungle. But then the landowner arrived. We were treated worse than wild animals . . . it seems that we aren't people, that the law isn't for the likes of us. Just for those who have money. It can't go on like this.

Dona Ana added:

> All the authorities were against us: local police, judge, state police, governor . . . everyone. And here we are, in the state that you see us. And this little grandson of mine, we haven't even got milk for him. All of us are going hungry.

According to the church report, the landowner promised one of the larger families Crs 70,000 (£4,850) in compensation and finally paid Crs 30,000 (£2,080). Two years later, it said, the new 'landowner' sold half of this plot for Crs 1m (£69,000).

A New Phase

The occupation of Goiás was greatly accelerated by the construction in 1960 of the 2,000 kilometre Belém–Brasília highway, which cut through the heart of the state. The building of the road marked the beginning of a new phase because, for the first time, the road network superseded the rivers and cattle tracks as the main route for the peasant families' penetration of the region. The building of the road also constituted the first serious government endeavour to open up the Amazon region. This policy emerged during the government of the democratically elected Juscelino Kubitschek de Oliveira from 1956 to 1961. Under the slogan of '50 years in 5', Kubitschek took on as one of the main priorities of his government the expansion of Brazilian development into the interior. In 1957 he decided on the construction of a new federal capital, to be called Brasília, about 900 kilometres inland. Though Brasília was only 1,015 kilometres from São Paulo – and 2,118 kilometres from Belém – it was the first step in a new government policy of integrating the Amazon. From then on, the Amazon would be increasingly affected by decisions taken by the federal government.

Though in the long term the building of the Belém–Brasília highway greatly hastened the occupation of the region, its immediate impact was, paradoxically, to provoke a rural exodus, as some of the isolated communities began to break up. We spoke once to a 24-year-old peasant woman in Goiás who was sitting by the side of one of the access roads to the highway with her eight children. Speaking in a rough form of Portuguese, peppered with regional expressions typical of the *sertão* (hinterland), she told us her story:

My name is Iracema. I'm going to Gurupi to meet my husband, Zé. Imagine, it used to take three days. Now it is only a few hours. We had a *roça* [plot of land] near here. We sold the hut and the cleared land for two thousand cruzeiros. They say that they're going to put cattle to graze on it. Imagine, two thousand cruzeiros. I'd never seen so much money in my life. Zé says that we are going to live in a town now.

While she was chatting, Iracema was also busy feeding the youngest child which, in typical *sertão* fashion, was tightly bound up in swaddling clothes despite the oppressive heat. Although the baby was only two months old, Iracema had already stopped breast-feeding. She was giving it a paste made from finely-grated manioc and water. Iracema explained:

All these children grew up on manioc. The three youngest have never had cow's milk. The older children once drank milk when their father brought back a tin from Gurupi. But they can't remember the taste. We eat manioc in so many different ways – as a porridge, or boiled, or fried, or as a meal. It tastes quite different.

It was heartbreaking to imagine the hardships and disillusionment that lay ahead for this hard-working yet carefree woman who had confidently walked to the nearest road to hitch a lift to Gurupi with all her children, and who, with her husband, was optimistically facing the modern world with $50 in her pocket.

In their book on the Belém–Brasília,[7] Orlando Valverde and Catharina Dias have pointed out that an initial rural exodus often occurs in the wake of the construction of a new road across a hitherto isolated region. But it is generally ignored by sociologists, for its existence is often not reflected in census results, as it is obscured by the much larger population influx which occurs simultaneously or a little later.

The population inflow assumed massive proportions in the case of the area around the Belém–Brasília road. As well as providing migrant peasant families with access to fresh land, much of which was out of reach by river, the road also meant that cattle-rearers could reach the important markets of Belém and, more significantly, Brasília (and thus the whole of southern Brazil). The result was an enormous influx of land-hungry peasant families, cattle-rearers and opportunist land thieves. It has been estimated that, between 1960 and 1970, 170,000 people moved into the region, occupying the land on either side of the road.

This influx was reflected in the 1970 census results which showed that the population of the centre–west (Goiás, Mato Grosso and the federal district of Brasília) had grown by 72 per cent from 1960 to 1970, reaching 5.2 million. This was the highest growth rate recorded by any of the five regions of Brazil during the decade. By 1970, 32 per cent of the people in the centre–west were 'immigrants', that is, they were born in another region. Again, this was the highest rate of any of the regions. The average for Brazil as a whole was 11.6 per cent and only one state – Paraná, with 37 per cent – had a higher rate than Goiás and Mato Grosso.

The sudden access of markets for farm produce meant a rapid increase in the value of land which was being penetrated. As a result, the construction of the Belém–Brasília marked the beginning of the phase of very violent confrontations in the fight for control over the land in the region. The number of clashes between the various pretenders to the land increased enormously in eastern Amazonia in the 1960s.

The normal pattern all over the Amazon region has been for the peasant family to be the first of the outsiders to settle, arriving by river or along cattle tracks, to face alone all the hardships and privations that make up the frontier life. As for Iracema and her husband, the main crop for these farmers is wild manioc, which forms the mainstay of their diet. Although an extremely hardy plant, well-suited to the peasants' primitive farming methods, manioc exhausts the soil rapidly. The need to find fresh land for manioc farming has been a driving force behind the peasants' itinerant form of agriculture.[8]

Once a road has been built, which may occur after a few months or a few decades, many more peasant families move in, but this time they are accompanied by a new group of market-oriented entrepreneurs, be they timber companies, cattle-rearers or land speculators. Some of these newcomers are 'sharks', as the peasant families call those outsiders who come to the region to steal their land or the products from their land. In the case of the Belém–Brasília road, the influx of sharks quickly changed the system of land tenure. George Martine commented in an article on the settlement beside this road:

> Whereas the initial easy access to the land resulted in a patchwork pattern of subsistence agriculture, the itinerant form of occupation, the absence of government support and the lawless and uncontrolled nature of the occupation process, coupled to rising land values in the area, led to the expulsion (sometimes violent) of the small farmers and the legal and illegal concentration of lands into unproductive *latifúndios*.[9]

It was pointed out in a study on the impact of the road carried out by a multi-disciplinary team from Brasília university that, in a classic case of what elsewhere had been dubbed 'sub-imperialism', the relatively large money income going to the landowners was not spent within the region and thus did not contribute to any improvement in the living standards of the local population. The study commented: 'The dynamic effects of the road are being transferred to São Paulo. The region is becoming poorer and poorer, on the verge of chaos.' Particularly harsh criticism was made of the sawmill companies, many of them from Paraná and Minas Gerais, which were moving into the region temporarily, pillaging its timber and then pulling out. The new phase of the occupation did not, unfortunately, mean an end to the plundering of the Amazon.

The Lost Chance

While the centre–west was experiencing a rapid influx of peasants, the north (Amazonas, Pará, Rondônia, Acre, Roraima and Amapá) was taking in very few migrants. Even as late as 1970, as many as 96 per cent of the inhabitants had been born in the region. Its traditional isolation had not yet been broken.

When INCRA (National Institute for Colonisation and Agrarian Reform) carried out its survey into land use in 1966-7, much of the Amazon region was not only unoccupied (significantly, the Indians are ignored in these statistics), but, of equal importance, had no owner on paper. The results showed that, out of the total area of 487 million hectares, only 124 million were in the hands of private landowners with some kind of title to their land. The degree of property concentration was high. Over half (54 per cent) of the 198,000 farms were classified by INCRA as *minifúndios*, that is, too small to support a family adequately. These *minifúndios* covered only 2.6 per cent of the area in the hands of the private sector and had an average size of 30 hectares. In contrast, 211 *latifúndios* covered a remarkable 19.5 million hectares, or 16 per cent of the total. They had an average size of 92,400 hectares. Only 1,800 farms, which is less than 1 per cent of the total, were classified as 'rural companies', that is, farms run on rational, commercial lines. INCRA also calculated that, as well as the 198,000 small families on *minifúndios* who had some kind of legal rights to their land, there were 246,000 peasant families who were squatting on their land (*posseiros*) or had made a share-cropping agreement with the owner. In all, these figures suggest a peasant population of about two million in the Amazon region in the mid 1960s.

In a confidential study carried out in 1971[10] INCRA officials concluded that:

> the Amazon region possesses a system of land tenure that is acting as a brake on development. The *minifúndios* are unproductive and indicate the presence of a sector of the rural population that is poor, dependent and not in a position to create better conditions for its integration into the market economy. The *latifúndios*, which are partially or totally unproductive, restrict control of the land to a small sector of the population, make access to ownership extremely difficult and keep vast areas of land in stagnation.

The INCRA team strongly recommended that the government carry out a programme of agrarian reform to provide the squatters and share-croppers with permanent access to the land, to break the hold over the region exercised by the *latifúndio* and to prepare the region for development. They pointed out that the occupation of the region around the Belém–Brasília was an example of what should *not* happen, a recipe for violent conflict in the future. They said that, if the government wanted to prevent the eruption of further conflicts, it should take urgent measures to plan and control the occupation process.

But, though the government pushed rapidly ahead with the opening up of the Amazon, it ignored this advice. The opportunity for an orderly and rational occupation of the eastern region of the Amazon was lost for ever. To understand why this chance was thrown away, it is necessary to look at political changes at a national level. This is the first time that national developments had a crucial impact on the form of the occupation of the Amazon.

Kubitschek, who left the presidency in 1961, was succeeded by two vacillating and ineffective civilian Presidents, Jânio da Silva Quadros, who resigned after seven months in office, and then João Goulart, who resorted to increasingly left-wing rhetoric as he felt his political support slipping away. In 1964 he was removed from office by a military *coup* which ended two decades of uninterrupted civilian rule. Though the military had for many years exercised a veto over civilian governments, this was the first time it had intervened with the intention of actually taking over the government.

The military rulers began to see the occupation of the Amazon as an important objective for two main reasons. First of all, they wanted to fulfil the military goal of territorial occupation. There is no doubt that military officers had been alarmed by a proposal made by the Hudson Institute in the United States in 1967 that a large part of the Amazon river valley should be flooded to allow multinational mining companies easy access to the region's mineral wealth, much of which was to be found in isolated areas around the outskirts of the valley. Military officers had reacted angrily to this plan, which they felt was no more than a veiled attempt by the industrialised countries to plunder the Amazon valley. They began to lobby for Brazil to occupy the region itself so as to make such a scheme impossible.

The second reason for the new military concern with the region was connected to a far more real threat – the *de facto* occupation of the region by thousands of peasant families who were moving in on their own initiative as the result of land shortages elsewhere in Brazil. The military officers believed that this vast and potentially rich region could not be simply handed over to peasant families who had neither the resources to pay for the land nor, in their opinion, the expertise required to develop it properly. Though residual areas could be left for peasant families, the military considered that the bulk of the land should be occupied by wealthy and sophisticated economic groups.

So the military devised a two-pronged strategy to promote the type of occupation it thought desirable. In the first place, it worked out a scheme by which it could attract the big groups into the region to carry out what we shall call pre-emptive occupation, that is, a holding operation by which it could keep out peasant families and reserve the land for capitalist farming. As the region was still too isolated for commercial farming to be economically viable, the government, which was far more intimately linked to the big companies, both national and multinational, than it would have been in a democratic regime, agreed to subsidise the initial losses of the cattle companies. Not infrequently, members of the families of top government officials benefited directly from the subsidies. Details of the scheme will be given in the following chapter.

In the second place, the military undertook an ambitious road-building programme in the Amazon in the late 1960s and the early 1970s. Five of the roads built were particularly important: one ran from Cuiabá to Porto Velho in Rondônia and was later extended even further west to Acre (the BR–364); another ran beside the Araguaia river, joining Barra do Garças in the south first to São Félix and later to Conceição do Araguaia and Marabá (the BR–158); another linked Manaus to Porto Velho, thus giving this old town, built on rubber wealth, its first road link with the rest of Brazil (the BR–319); another linked Cuiabá to Santarém on the river Amazon, midway between Belém and Manaus (BR–163); and the fifth, the famous Transamazônica highway, ran from the north-east right across the heart of the Amazon jungle until it met the BR–319. These five highways, which add up to about 10,000 kilometres of new road, cut through an enormous area of hitherto inaccessible land to the south of the Amazon river.

They were all originally constructed as earth roads except for the Manaus–Porto Velho, which had to be tarmacked because of the long stretches of swampy land it crossed. For five or six months of the year they became heavily water-logged, with huge troughs of mud forming in low-lying stretches. The wooden bridges were frequently swept away in the torrential flooding. Yet communications rarely broke down altogether. With remarkable tenacity, truck drivers struggled through, at times waiting days or even weeks in the heart of the tropical forest for a stretch of the road to dry out sufficiently for them to get by.

Though the roads were primarily constructed to allow the big cattle companies to move in (see Chapters 2 and 3), they also greatly increased the speed of peasant migrations into the region. As a result, the population of the Amazon region more than doubled from 1960 to 1980 (see Table 1.1). The occupation front, which until then had moved fairly slowly, gained an enormous impetus. This was to have profound consequences for the region. The big states of Goiás, Mato Grosso and Pará and the territory of Rondônia were most affected. The outlying areas – Amapá, Roraima and Acre – recorded the smallest increases in absolute terms, for the occupation front only reached them at the end of the 1970s and the early 1980s.

In marked contrast to the full financial, economic and political support given to the cattle companies, the authorities provided the peasant families with very little assistance during this difficult and tumultuous period. Far from carrying out a programme of agrarian reform as INCRA had suggested, the government did not even provide the peasant families with any guidance as to where they could legally settle. Just as in the case of the occupation of the region around the Belém–Brasília, the families were left to settle in spontaneous and chaotic fashion. As a result, the number of land conflicts rose dramatically. Very often the cattle companies were slower to move in than the peasant families and discovered settlers on their land when they arrived. They then took measures to evict them.

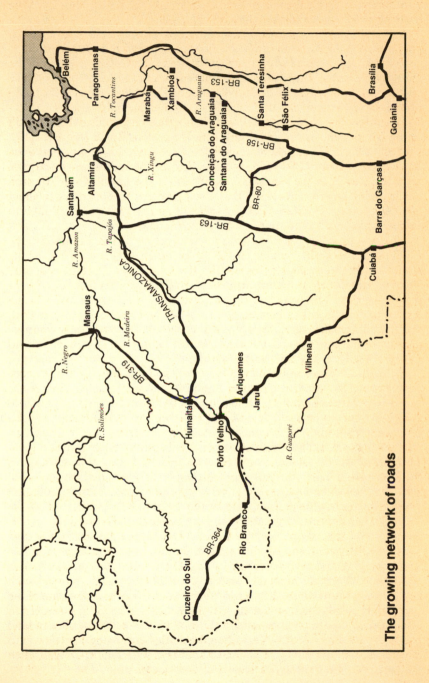

The growing network of roads

Table 1.1
The Peasant Families Move in

	Total population			
	1950	*1960*	*1970*	*1980*
Goiás	1,214,921	1,913,289	2,938,677	3,864,881
Mato Grosso	522,044	889,539	1,597,090	1,141,236
Mato Grosso do Sul[a]				1,368,803
Pará	1,123,273	1,529,293	2,167,018	3,411,235
Amazonas	514,099	708,459	955,235	1,430,314
Rondônia	36,935	69,792	111,064	492,744
Acre	114,755	158,184	215,299	301,628
Roraima	18,116	28,304	40,885	79,078
Amapá	37,477	67,750	114,359	175,634
Total	*3,581,620*	*5,364,610*	*8,139,627*	*12,265,553*

[a] Mato Grosso do Sul was created as a separate state in 1979; until then it formed part of Mato Grosso.

Source: *Anuário Estatístico do Brasil* (FIBGE, 1980).

In the beginning, the peasants were particularly vulnerable to attempts to dislodge them. Many did not understand the concept of property in the modern world. As no one in their families had ever paid money for the land they tilled, they did not attribute value to the land itself, but only to the labour they had expended in clearing the forest and building their huts.

However, although the peasant farmers were bewildered by the logic of capitalism, landowners understood all too well the values of the peasants' world and frequently took cruel advantage of their ignorance. We often met baffled peasant farmers who had been offered what they had to admit was fair compensation for their crops, huts, barbed wire and so on; and yet they instinctively felt that they had been tricked and deceived. They knew that they had lost something – their land – which was essential to their life. Yet, as they had been brought up to consider land to be a gift of God, like rain and sunshine, they did not immediately realise that they had indeed been robbed, and that, in the modern world they were entering, land was a commodity to be bought and sold like sacks of rice. Most old farmers never fully grasped the new concepts and bitterly resented the break-up of the traditional system of values. Others, particularly the young farmers, learnt very quickly, often through bitter experience, to make the difficult transition to the capitalist way of looking at the world.

It was clear to us from our trips that the number of evictions grew steadily throughout the 1970s, though they appeared to stabilise in the early 1980s. Yet it was impossible to calculate the number with any accuracy. When pushed, an employee at Contag (National Confederation of Agricultural

Workers) made the rough – and unofficial – estimate that in the late 1970s about 30,000 families – or 150,000 people – were being evicted each year in the Amazon region, out of a total peasant population of about 800,000 families, or 4 million people.

The Rush to Rondônia

Whereas in the 1950s and 1960s nearly all the families moving into the Amazon came from the north-east, in the 1970s more and more of the migrants came from southern Brazil where cheap farming land was beginning to run out. Unlike the families from the north-east, those from the south recognised land as a commodity and were prepared to pay for it. During the 1950s many of the landless families from the south moved into the state of Paraná which was undergoing a rapid process of occupation as its rich farming lands were brought into use for coffee cultivation and subsistence farming. However, by 1960 most of Paraná's land had been occupied. The size of the farms dwindled as the families tried to adapt to the land shortage by subdividing their plots among their children and by taking on tenant farmers. The proportion of farms of less than 20 hectares rose from 3.4 per cent of the total in 1950 to 12.5 per cent in 1960.[11]

Many settlers rapidly became dissatisfied with the new turn of events in Paraná and were ready to move on again. Some were attracted to the Amazon region, particularly Rondônia, which had become readily accessible with the completion of the BR–364 highway in 1965. This road, which provided the capital, Porto Velho, with its first land link with the rest of Brazil, made available a large new area of virgin forest. The news travelled rapidly to the south and many small farming families, particularly in Minas Gerais and Espírito Santo, who had been considering migration to Paraná, changed their minds and went to Rondônia.

In the mid 1960s Rondônia was very sparsely populated and the authorities had an excellent chance to settle the region in an orderly and rational fashion. Martine observed:

> When the first national cadaster of rural properties was carried out in 1967 (at a time when the first speculators had already made a few incursions) nine people claimed to own tracts of more than 100,000 hectares each. Their total claims alone would have added up to some 12% of the territory's land area; however, INCRA's final analysis established the existence of only 155 legitimate claims, comprising as little as 7% of the total land area. In sum, 93% of Rondônia's surface area was still owned by the Union [i.e. the federal government] in 1967.[12]

In the beginning it seemed as if good use would be made of the opportunity. In 1969 the Rondônian government carried out a study in which it discovered – predictably enough – that the small farmers in the territory were far more productive than the large ones. Though only 35 per cent of the occupied land was in the hands of small farmers, they were responsible for 96 per cent of the territory's agricultural output. The big farmers, occupying 65 per cent of the land, were contributing only 4 per cent of output. So the government drew up a plan, *Sistema Agrícola de Rondônia para o Pequeno Produtor* (Rondônia's system of agriculture for the small producer), in which it based its occupation model on the small farmer. It then deliberately set out to attract migrant families and brought the federal government's colonisation institute, INCRA, into the territory to set up large colonisation projects.

The government's plans were too successful. Peasant families – and land speculators – poured in. The influx was so disorderly that it is difficult to make an accurate estimate of the numbers involved. Yet numerous odd scraps of information give an idea of the scale of the inrush. For instance, the arrival of 900 families was counted at a single checkpoint along the BR–364 road in just one month in 1976.

To quote Martine again:

> The Rondônian government was, with good reason, frightened by the size of the flows; a monthly inflow of some 900 families would require that the government provide, each month, for the demarcation of 90,000 hectares, the construction of 225 km of jungle roads, the provision of seeds and utensils for those families, the building of 900 houses, as well as the undertaking of other infrastructure jobs and the contracting of technical backstopping. In addition, and at the same time, the government would have to make similar expenditure in order to absorb thousands of families who had arrived earlier and were still awaiting the opportunity to settle on a piece of land.[13]

The size of the influx reflected the growing seriousness of the agrarian problem in Brazil as a whole. According to the 1975 agriculture and farm husbandry survey, only 0.8 per cent of all Brazilian farms covered 1,000 hectares or more, but they accounted for 43 per cent of the occupied area. At the other end of the scale, 52 per cent of the farms were 100 hectares or less in size and they accounted for just 3 per cent of the land.[14] This highly-concentrated system of land tenure, one of the most skewed in the world, meant that only a small proportion of the huge areas of farming land was being used properly.

Because the government had not forced the big estate owners to sell part of these unproductive lands to small farmers, Brazil was, paradoxically, facing a serious land shortage. Small farmers had repeatedly subdivided their plots to fit in more members of their families, but eventually some were forced to leave. In the late 1970s this land shortage was aggravated by two additional factors – the mechanisation of agriculture in southern Brazil, which meant that fewer labourers were required; and the switch away from labour-intensive coffee cultivation to mechanised crops, particularly soyabeans. This change was particularly marked in Paraná after serious frosts damaged the coffee harvest in the mid 1970s. Whereas in 1975 Paraná had 876 million coffee bushes, occupying an area of 1,050 million hectares, by 1982 it had 554 million bushes, occupying an area of 540 million hectares. About one million people are estimated to have left the countryside in Paraná in the 1970s. By the late 1970s, there were believed to be about eight million landless migrant families in Brazil.[15]

Many of these families travelled to the cities, where most of them ended up as underemployed shanty-town dwellers. Others moved to the Amazon where they settled on any available plot of land. Official statistics show that, in Brazil as a whole from 1970 to 1975, the number of farmers with legal titles to their land fell, though the land in their possession increased. During the same period, the number of share-croppers also dropped, along with the area of land they occupied. The only category of farmers to increase, both in number and in area occupied, was the peasant farmer who had no legal title to his land (*posseiro*).

However, by the late 1970s, even this option was becoming exhausted as the big companies took over large areas of the states of Goiás, Mato Grosso and Pará and were increasingly careful to protect their lands from peasant invasion. Many of the families, unable to find land, settled in the rapidly expanding towns and tried to eke out a living by opening small stores or by finding seasonal jobs on the ranches. Others, particularly those from the south who had some capital behind them and could thus afford to buy a plot of land, moved in larger and larger numbers to Rondônia.

The problem was too serious for the Rondônian government to handle by itself. Its officials drew more and more plots on their maps but, all too frequently, when they travelled to the region, they found that they were already occupied. Very often families, desperate for land, settled on any available plot, hoping it was *terra devoluta* (public land). However, in pratice the plot was often claimed by an absentee landowner.

Numerous conflicts flared up between peasant families, land speculators, cattle companies, Indians and cassiterite (tin ore) prospectors. No one knows how many Uru-Weu-Wau-Wau Indians were killed. The Uru-Weu-Wau-Wau, of whom there are about 500 today, inhabited an area of about one million hectares to the south of the BR–364 highway, part of which is today in the district of Jaru. In 1978 a number of landowners sent in gunmen to kill a group of these Indians. Though this massacre is common knowledge in the region, no action was taken by the police.

It was not until 1980 that Funai, the government's Indian agency, sent in a team to attempt to establish peaceful contact with the Uru-Weu-Wau-Wau. Apoena Meirelles, the Funai delegate in Rondônia at the time, said that the work was made much more difficult by the years of persecution, which had made the Indians very wary of outsiders. Peaceful contact was finally made in March 1981, though communication was difficult because the anthropologist working with the Funai team found it impossible to classify the language spoken by the Uru-Weu-Wau-Wau.

Equally serious conflicts arose between peasant families and landowners. Particularly violent clashes occurred with Nova Vida ranch, in the district of

Ariquemes. Though people in the region disagree about the number of people killed, most estimates are in the hundreds.

Overwhelmed by the invasion, the Rondônian government first tried to reduce the flow. It distributed 'disincentive' pamphlets in the main areas of Paraná, Mato Grosso, Minas Gerais and Espírito Santo from which the migrants were proceeding. Martine cites one of these pamphlets circulated at the end of 1977:

> Rondônia has soils of excellent quality for agricultural exploitation. But, for all practical purposes, these lands are already occupied. Therefore, only a limited number of plots is available for sale. Moreover, a large part of the land (more than two million hectares) is located either in official colonization projects or in areas which have been turned over by INCRA, at public auction, to farming and cattle ranching companies.

Despite these warnings, the migrants continued to move into the territory in ever larger numbers.[16] Colonel Jorge Teixeira de Oliveira, a hard-line military officer and an expert in counter-insurgency warfare in the jungle, became governor in 1978. He began to take tougher action against disorderly settlement by forcing peasant families, whenever he could, to wait in reception centres until plots became available. At the same time, he obtained World Bank financing for the paving of the BR–364, the 1,100 km. road running from Cuiabá to Porto Velho. This loan, for $240 million, was personally authorised in 1979 by Robert McNamara, the president of the World Bank at the time. Since then, further World Bank finance has been obtained, largely for the construction of 1,000 kms. of feeder roads.

At the same time, the state government, with the federal government body INCRA, reorganised the land settlement scheme beside the road. By the end of 1983, about 50,000 families had been settled onto an area of 4.5 million hectares. Relatives were attracted to the plots, so some families are believed to have as many as eight or nine members. As a result, it is estimated that about 300,000–350,000 people have been settled on the land. It has become INCRA's largest programme, but even so it has clearly failed to meet the demand. In early 1984, it was estimated that there were at least another 30,000 families still waiting for plots.

The colonisation projects have changed the system of land tenure in Rondônia. According to a table compiled from the ten-yearly censuses by Eliano Sérgio Lopes, an economist living in Porto Velho, medium-sized farms (200 to 500 hectares) virtually disappeared from the region during the 1970s. These farms, which accounted for 44.4 per cent of the farming land in 1970, covered just 7.4 per cent of the area in 1980. Meantime, smaller farms (those under 200 hectares) increased their share spectacularly, from 12.9 per cent in 1970 to 47.8 per cent in 1980. The area covered by large farms (those over 1,000 hectares) also rose from 38.3 per cent of the total to 41.7 per cent. The change appears to be the result of the incorporation of new land, not from modifications in the ownership of existing farms. The land under cultivation rose from 1.6 million hectares in 1970 to 5.7 million in 1980. The attention paid to the colonisation projects has tended to obscure the importance of big farms (over 1,000 hectares). In 1980 these covered 2.4 million hectares, almost as much as the 2.7 million hectares occupied by small farms (under 200 hectares).

Largely as a result of the colonisation projects, where settlers are generally given plots of 100 hectares, farms of 100 to 200 hectares were the largest single category in 1980, accounting for just over a quarter (26.4 per cent) of the land in use. But this is not expected to be the case in 1990. Many people studying the colonisation projects have noted a trend towards concentration. Many of the settlers who move in with little or no capital are highly vulnerable. They cannot survive if they are hit by an unexpected difficulty, such as a heavy hospital bill or the failure to market their crops because the roads are impassable. As a result, many are selling their plots, often to more successful neighbours, though this is supposed to be forbidden. The families who lose their land often become tenant farmers for former neighbours.

Much of the land is not being farmed properly. The migrants arrive with little understanding of the ecology of the land they are occupying. They cut down the forest indiscriminately, often hacking down rubber and *guaraná* trees and then later replanting these very same trees in the form of seedlings purchased from a transnational seed company. They plant coffee in straight lines, though it is widely known that erosion would be greatly reduced if the bushes were planted in curved rows. They clear the forest, not only close to the roads, which exposes crops to the harmful effect of dust, but also beside rivers, which increases the dangers of leaching and erosion. They throw vegetation into the rivers, turning them into excellent breeding grounds for mosquitoes. This may be one reason why malaria is on the increase. One is reminded of the comment, made several years ago by Paulo de Tarso Alvim, scientific director of Ceplac, Brazil's cocoa research institute: 'I think Brazilians are suffering from a novel disease, which I should like to call ecological masochism.'[17]

In part, this negligence is the result of ignorance, but it also stems from the nature of the occupation. Many of the settlers are aware that their hold on their plots is precarious, so they farm with an eye to increasing the market value of their land so that they can make as much money as possible if they are forced to sell. In both the first and second years, they clear 10 out of the 100 hectares they have been given by INCRA. Then in the third year, instead of fertilising the cleared land, they plant it with grass seed and move onto a new area. Government officials warn that they will ruin their plots in this way, for without fertilisers their land, which is not particularly fertile, will quickly become barren. But their cautions are not heeded. The settlers have powerful reasons for acting in this apparently irrational way. Petrol for their motor-saws is cheaper than fertilisers. Even if the land they have cleared becomes very rough pasture, mixed with secondary growth, they will obtain a higher price for their plot, the more of it they have cleared.

Recently ecologists have expressed fears that the scale of the ecological damage is far greater than had previously been imagined. Philip Fearnside, a US scientist working at the federal government's research body INPA in Manaus, said in mid 1982: 'At the present rate of destruction the last tree in Rondônia will be used as a Christmas decoration in 1988.' At first sight, his observations do not appear to be supported by the evidence provided by the US satellite Landsat. This indicated that, by early 1982, only 600,000 of Rondônia's 24 million hectares had been cleared. But Fearnside believes that the satellite pictures are deceptive: 'Areas of the forest which showed up quite clearly as clearings in the 1976 pictures reappeared as "virgin forest" in the 1978 pictures', he said. The explanation, Fearnside believes, is that many of the cleared but abandoned areas are showing up in the photographs as virgin forest because of the secondary growth which has sprung up. The land, though, has lost its protective cover of tropical forest and has been exhausted.

By 1982 the population of Rondônia was estimated at 600,000 to 700,000, compared with 111,000 in 1970. The federal government recognised Rondônia's new stature and, at the beginning of 1982, upgraded it from a territory to a state. The migrants continued to pour in. In 1983, 92,723 people were registered as new inhabitants of Rondônia at the official entry post at Vilhena on the BR–364 road. This compares with 58,052 in 1982, 60,218 in 1981, 49,205 in 1980, 36,791 in 1979 and 12,658 in 1978. In 1983, 29 per cent of the migrants had previously lived in Paraná, 11 per cent in Mato Grosso, 9 per cent in São Paulo and the rest in the other states in Brazil. Officials said that each year fewer came directly from the north-east and far more from the south, particularly São Paulo, and from the easterly states of the Amazon. This last trend is a clear indication that land is beginning to run out in that region.

At the same time, there are signs that, such has been the pace of occupation, Rondônia's own capacity to absorb peasant families will shortly become exhausted too. According to a study carried out by the Rondônian government in 1982, Rondônia could at that time take a further 20,000 families with the existing system of land tenure. If the Guaporé valley, a large part of which belonged to the Nambikwara Indians (see Chapter 5), was included in the stock of land available for colonisation, then the study calculated that the state could absorb a further 72,000 families. This means that nearly all the available land outside the Indian areas must be occupied by now.

As yet, however, there has been no sign that the influx is slowing down. During the first quarter of 1984, 35,021 new arrivals were registered at Vilhena, an all-time record. In early 1983, Eucatur, a transport company which runs three coaches a day from Cascavel in the state of Paraná to Porto Velho – a distance of 3,000 kilometres – reported a steady increase in demand since the end of 1981. According to Assis Gurgacz, the managing director of Eucatur:

About 99 per cent of our passengers are small farmers, with little capital, who are moving up to Rondônia so that they can go on working on the land. If they sell their tiny plot in Paraná, they can get for the money a piece of land up to 200 times the size in Rondônia. And the quality of the soil is almost as good.

For the state authorities at least the sky seems the limit. At the celebrations at the end of 1981, the state governor said triumphantly: 'Rondônia is the same size as the state of São Paulo, so there is no reason why we should not soon have the same population – 20 million people.' And this same uncritically expansionist attitude has prevailed until the present.

The Missed Opportunity in Acre

Even before Rondônia was showing signs of saturation, some families had pushed on even further west, to Acre, on the border with Bolivia and Peru. This route was only opened in 1971, when Acre was finally given a road link with the rest of Brazil with the extension of the BR–364 highway from Porto Velho to its capital, Rio Branco. Though it took several years for the occupation process to get properly underway, it was clear that isolated and stagnant Acre was soon to be jolted into the modern world. Once again, the government initially did little to ease the birth pangs.

Even before the present disruptions, Acre had had a turbulent history. Thousands of poor north-easterners had moved into the state in the late 19th Century, making long and arduous journeys up the tributaries of the Amazon to work on the rubber plantations. They had been attracted to this remote region by wildly exaggerated stories of the huge fortunes which could be made overnight. The spontaneous invasion which resulted had enabled Brazil finally to wrest the region out of the hands of Bolivia after years of acrimonious wrangling.

As elsewhere in the Amazon, Acre stagnated after the rubber boom ended. Thousands of rubber-tappers, virtually imprisoned in the forest, had had little option other than to carry on working on the plantations, however low the remuneration. During the 1960s Acre sank into even deeper decline, with an average annual growth rate of only 1.4 per cent, compared with 5.8 per cent for the Amazon region as a whole. Per capita income, already the lowest in Brazil, dropped even further in absolute terms, for economic growth did not even keep up with the low rate of population expansion, of 2.4 per cent a year.

The new economic prospects which emerged with the building of the roads delighted the state government. 'Now that we have a road link with the rest of Brazil, investments in Acre are the most profitable in the world', declared state governor Wanderley Dantas in 1971. Unlike his fellow governor in Rondônia, Wanderley Dantas did not want peasant families to move in. He was anxious to attract only big companies from the south, which, he believed, alone had the capital to develop the state. He hoped to take advantage of the export boom underway at that time in southern Brazil and coined his own slogan: 'Acre, the natural route to the Pacific.' The idea was to open up big ranches in Acre and to export large quantities of beef to Japan and other Asian markets, while Brazil at the same time should channel all its exports to these markets through Acre rather than through the Panama Canal or the Straits of Magellan.

Dantas's strategy was based on two factors: first, the state's relative proximity to the Pacific (Rio Branco is only 800 kilometres from the Peruvian port of Callao, but 2,000 kilometres from Belém on the Atlantic); and secondly, the fertility of the soil. Acre is one of the few extensive areas of rich soil in the Amazon; Radam, a radar survey carried out by the federal government, showed that 13 million of its 15 million hectares were fertile. The state government undertook a big campaign in the press in the south of Brazil to attract investors. One of its advertisements had this heading: 'A new Canaan – without the droughts of the north-east, nor the frosts of Paraná.'

From the state government's point of view, the campaign paid off handsomely, for it sparked off an unprecedented land boom. Many big companies, including the huge sugar cooperative Copersúcar, the insurance group Atlântica Boa Vista, the soluble coffee company Cacique, the meat-packing group Bordon and the coach company Viacão Garcia, bought vast tracts. Some of Brazil's wealthiest landowners, such as José Tavares do Couto and Mário Junqueira, were also attracted to the region. In 1971 three-quarters of the land in Acre was *terra devoluta*; by 1975, four-fifths of the land belonged to investors from the south. It was another lost opportunity for developing the land in a productive and socially responsible way.

The state government did little to sort out the question of land ownership, though the situation was further confused in Acre by the existence of some valid – and many forged – land titles issued by the Bolivian government in the second half of the 19th Century. Peasant families began to occupy land which appeared not to have an owner but which had, in fact, been sold in this land fair to companies from the south. Many of the new owners did not even bother to visit their new estates; they were either waiting for transport links to improve before opening up ranches, or, as was frequently the case, for prices to rise before reselling their virgin land. As a result, there were a growing number of conflicts. Even government officials admitted to feeling alarm. Assis Canuto, who resigned as INCRA coordinator in 1971, commented after he had left his job: 'The government must be made to understand that Acre will not embark on the road to true development until it has sorted out its land question.'

Some of the new landowners set about opening up ranches. They cut down thousands of hectares of forest and sent in gunmen to evict the rubber-tappers. The violent switch from a labour-intensive activity (rubber-tapping) to one employing very few workers (cattle-rearing) caused great hardship to the local inhabitants. With nowhere else to go, thousands of summarily evicted rubber-tappers swarmed to the state capital. By 1981, about 30,000 people – a quarter of the city's total population – were living in terrible conditions in shanty-towns. Even highly conservative government officials were shocked at the turmoil caused by the land boom. Amir Francisco Lando, head of INCRA's land discrimination commission for Acre and Rondônia, commented: 'We do not defend the archaic structure of the rubber plantations; but we believe that man is the main agent of the production of wealth. There is no point in bringing in capital if it expels man.' Rio Branco could not provide employment for more than a small fraction of the evicted tappers. Dom Moacyr Grechi, Bishop of Acre-Purus, estimates that about 40,000–50,000 tappers moved into Bolivia and Peru in search of work in the second half of the 1970s.

However, the businessmen – who soon became known as *paulistas* (people from São Paulo) whatever their origin – made a serious mistake; they failed to build up a local political base. They soon faced stiff opposition from the local community. Rural workers' unions and local community groups organised by the Catholic Church began to mobilise the population. However, the conflict did not become the classic confrontation between the landowners and the government on one side, and the unions and the Catholic Church on the other. In the late 1970s, the state goverment itself began to feel hostility towards the *paulistas* and to monitor more carefully their activities. As a result, the number of violent confrontations decreased, as the landowners were unable to rely on the automatic support of the authorities and thus felt much less confident about infringing the law.

Joaquím Falcão de Macedo, the state governor at that time, began to have second thoughts about the form of occupation undertaken by Wanderley Dantas. He put an end to the most blatant forms of land speculation and set up the state's own colonisation project, which began to settle in an orderly fashion the families arriving in the state. His successor, Nabor Telles, who was elected to office for the opposition party, Partido do Movimento Democrático Brasileiro (PMDB), in November 1982, is pushing ahead with similar policies.

As yet, the influx of migrants has not been very heavy. The government in Acre will face a much more difficult challenge over the next few years as Rondônia's capacity is exhausted and many more families move on to Acre. The problems will not be easy to solve, for the Acre government has few resources and it has inherited a concentrated form of land tenure from the government of Wanderley Dantas.

Notes

1. In a speech given at the Conference on Development of Amazonia in Seven Countries, Cambridge, 23–26 September 1979.
2. Caio Prado Júnior, *Formação do Brasil Contemporâneo* (Editôra

Brasiliense, São Paulo, 1942), p.152.

3. Márcio Souza, *A Expressão Amazonense do Colonialismo ao Neo-colonialismo* (Editôra Alfa-Omega, São Paulo, 1978), p.46.

4. See Martin T. Katzman, *The Evaluation of the Brazilian Model of Regional Planning*, mimeographed paper.

5. *Formação do Brasil Contemporâneo*, p.216.

6. For a detailed account of peasant migrations into Maranhão and Goiás during this period, see Otávio Guilhermo Velho, *Frentes de Expansão e Estrutura Agrária* (Zahar Editores, 1972).

7. *A Rodovia Belém–Brasília* (IBGE, Rio de Janeiro, 1976).

8. Although manioc is an easy crop to cultivate, a long and arduous preparation is required to extract its poisonous juices before it can be eaten.

9. *Recent Colonization Experiences in Brazil: Expectations versus Reality*, mimeographed paper.

10. INCRA, *Condicionantes Institucionais do Uso e Posse da Terra*, 1971. The specific area referred to in both this study and INCRA's 1966-67 survey into land use is 'legal Amazonia' as defined on p.43.

11. Milton da Mata, Eduardo Werneck R. De Carvalho and Maria Thereza L. L. Castro e Silva, *Migrações Internas no Brasil: Aspectos Econômicos e Demográficos* (IPEA/INPES, Rio de Janeiro, 1973), p.65.

12. Martine, *Recent Colonisation Experiences in Brazil*, p.28.

13. Ibid., p.31.

14. See José de Souza Martins, *Expropriação e Violência* (Editôra Hucitec, São Paulo, 1980), pp.45 and 46.

15. Ibid., p.47.

16. Much of the recent information on Rondônia and Acre was provided by the journalist José Roberto de Alencar e Silva.

17. Quoted in *O Estado de S. Paulo*, 6 May 1979.

2. The Big Companies Move In – Part One

The deal was closed very quickly and I suddenly found myself the owner of 450,000 hectares of virgin forest. I knew that it was a good investment, but I hadn't the faintest idea of what I was going to do with all that jungle.

(Nicolau Lunardelli, describing how his group moved into the Amazon in 1963)

The First Big Landowners

By all accounts, nearly all the 'big men' moved into the Amazon region several decades after the arrival of the first peasant families. Whereas the latter were self-sufficient in almost all their basic needs and were thus satisfied with minimal links with the outside world, the landowners wanted to market their produce which even in these early days was largely cattle.

Virtually the only wealthy people to move into the region in the 1930s and 1940s when it was still very isolated were men wanted by the police in other parts of Brazil. The US anthropologist Charles Wagley, who was in the region in 1939 on his first field trip to visit the Tapirapé Indians, met one of these men. He spent a night at the ranch of Lúcio da Luz, a cattle-rearer living beside the Araguaia river. Some of the early inhabitants of Santa Teresinha, where we carried out one of our case studies of land conflict, came into the region to work as cowhands on da Luz's estate. Here is Wagley's account of his visit:

> We spent the night at the ranch of Lúcio da Luz, a man who lived isolated on the Araguaia because he was wanted for murder both upriver in Goiás and downriver in Pará. But on his ranch he was law and order, for he had surrounded himself with a group of cowboys who were well armed and who served as his henchmen and bodyguards. He told me he had ordered the execution of a man and woman who had run off together leaving their respective spouses. Lúcio later played an important role in Tapirapé history

37

as he expanded his ranching activities into their territory. He was hospitable, kind and friendly to his young foreign guest. He told me of his growing herd of cattle, but complained that he could not sell them because of the lack of 'understanding' of the outside authority (the police) and the great distance to any market.[1]

It was only in the late 1950s, when access to the region became easier, that landowners began to explore this region in its own right to assess its economic potential, particularly for cattle-rearing. In these early days the landowners did not think of turning to the government for financial support for their initiatives. They were all attracted by the cheap price of land and expected to make a profit, either quickly through land sales, or over a much longer period, when transport links improved and it became possible to market their produce.

Unlike the peasant families, most of whom moved to the Amazon region from the backward and impoverished north-east, the landowners reached the region from the south-east, the heart of Brazil's farming and industrial wealth. This front formed part of a natural progression from São Paulo to Minas Gerais and then on to the south of Mato Grosso and Goiás. As these areas became partially occupied, the next step was to move into the vast areas which lay in the north of Mato Grosso and south of Pará.

The landowners did not travel unprepared into these wild and sparsely populated areas. They always sought out the scant but invaluable knowledge built up by the real pioneers – the peasant families and the *garimpeiros* (diamond and gold prospectors). The old experienced landowners we met spoke freely of their debt to the latter. It was only the land speculators and businessmen, who moved into the region later as the result of the government's tax rebate scheme, who spoke to us in grandiose fashion as if they had been the first intrepid explorers to have penetrated the region.

João Lanari do Val, a friendly and tough-minded farmer now in his late sixties and living comfortably in São Paulo, spoke to us about his first trip to the south of Pará. In the late 1950s, he said, he was running his ranch in the adjacent state of Goiás and he frequently heard intriguing talk of rich farming lands which lay to the west of the Araguaia river, particularly around the little town of Conceição do Araguaia in the south of Pará. The main bearers of the information, he recalled, were itinerant peasant farmers and above all the *garimpeiros*, who were always on the move and alert for news of fresh mineral discoveries.

Fascinated by these conversations, do Val contacted a land company, Prospec, which made its money from seeking out *terras devolutas*, registering them in its name for virtually nothing and then selling them still fairly cheaply to landowners from the south. Prospec itself rarely visited the land it sold, which was frequently located in inaccessible regions. Unlike the speculators who were soon to enter the region, do Val was in search of good, cheap land which he himself could farm; he was not after large empty areas which could be acquired for a trivial sum and later resold at a huge profit (though he has undoubtedly made much money through the rapid appreciation of land prices in the region).

Do Val found out from Prospec where it had land for sale near Conceição do Araguaia and then brought together a small group of tough horsemen to ride into the region with him to locate and evaluate the area for sale. The group travelled for three weeks, cooking on open fires and sleeping in hammocks slung between trees. They used a compass to keep themselves travelling in roughly the right direction and relied on the sparse local population of peasant farmers to indicate the best route through the forest. Do Val still recalls very vividly the isolation and poverty of these peasant families. He remembers how women and children, particularly if they were alone in the hut, would run off and hide themselves in the forest, startled by the arrival of visitors.

When he finally reached the lands, he liked them. 'Some of the land was of particularly good quality, particularly to the west', he told us. As the land was very cheap, he bought an extensive tract – 360,000 hectares – in the region to the north of Conceição do Araguaia where the town of Redenção was later to be founded.

He moved in soon afterwards to open his ranch.

> And that is why I've had very few peasant families invading my lands. As I was actually living there I was able to spot invaders quickly and evict them. That is the number one rule – don't let any of them stay on your land. If a family moves in, you must evict it immediately, with or without violence. And usually violence isn't necessary. Most peasants settle on virgin land in good faith, believing it to be *terra devoluta*. The serious conflicts occur when an absentee landlord turns up years later and finds much of his lands occupied by peasants who have put down roots. But if you're there from the beginning and never let anyone invade your land, then you have few problems.

He said that, like most landowners in the region, he had set up – and still had – his own police force to patrol the ranch and keep out invaders.

When land prices rose, do Val sold off part of his land for a good profit. Though he no longed lived in the region, he still had a 200,000-hectare farm with 12,000 hectares of pasture and 15,000 head of cattle.

Some years after do Val and a handful of other farmers had moved into the region and begun gradually to open their ranches, a few astute property dealers from the south discovered the money-making potential of this new frontier region. A colourful example of this new trend was Carlos Ribeiro, who has become something of a mythic figure among the landowners. Born into a very poor family in São Paulo, he worked first as a trapeze artist in a circus and later as a waiter. A great talker and inveterate schemer, Ribeiro was by all accounts a man of great daring and imagination who could shrewdly detect an excellent business opportunity and tenaciously follow it through. Although he was widely regarded as a cunning rogue who could talk himself out of any predicament, many of the farmers remember him today with respect and even affection.

In the 1950s Ribeiro was working as a waiter in the north of Paraná, a region which was undergoing rapid expansion as its rich agricultural soils were being brought into productive use for the first time, mainly for coffee-farming. Some of the farmers had piled up huge fortunes over a few years and were looking for a new investment. Ribeiro felt sure that there must be some way in which he could take advantage of this easy flow of money. Through his numerous contacts as a waiter in one of the leading restaurants in Londrina, the heart of the coffee-growing region in Paraná, Ribeiro heard talk of vast stretches of extremely cheap forest land which lay to the west of the Araguaia river. After visiting the region himself, he realised that he had been presented with a golden opportunity to make money.

In a short while he had started a flourishing property business. He took wealthy Paraná landowners up to Mato Grosso and then, on commission, arranged for them to purchase the areas they wanted. Often he arranged for the resale of these lands, just a few months later, at considerably higher prices. A further fat commission fell into his lap after these deals. Ribeiro grew rich very quickly, first buying a tiny twin-engined plane in which to carry his clients and later moving on to a small jet.

The powerful Lunardelli family was among his clients. A penniless but determined Italian immigrant, Geremia Lunardelli had built up his family's fortune from nothing in the early part of this century. In doing so he became a kind of folk hero among the large community of poor young Italian immigrants who arrived in Brazil in the late 19th Century, many of whom were equally determined to make their fortune. While the vast majority failed, it is surprising how many of Brazil's self-made men in this period were Italians or sons of Italian immigrants. Some of these families played a significant role in the opening up of the Amazon.

Geremia Lunardelli was just a year old when he arrived in Brazil in 1886. He came with his parents, who were brought across the Atlantic in the hold of a ship under the Brazilian government's free immigration scheme. As a young boy, Lunardelli worked as a cart driver and rural labourer on a farm in the state of São Paulo. As part of his work, he learnt how to deal with all the phases of coffee cultivation.

Through skilful land-dealing, Lunardelli quickly built up the family's fortune. By 1927 he had become known as the *rei do café* (coffee king), and was reputed to be the biggest coffee-farmer in the world, owning at least 18 million bushes. His 9 children and 24 grandchildren have increased the family's wealth. Nicolau Lunardelli, one of his sons, said: 'My father died in 1964. And perhaps it was the call of the blood which made me take on the wild north of the country.'

In the first instance, however, Nicolau Lunardelli seems to have misinterpreted this call. He described how he was made to change his mind:

It was very amusing. In 1963, after Carlos Ribeiro had been very insistent, I agreed to go up and visit a huge area of the Amazon. We flew over the region for a long time in a small Cessna plane. We touched down on a small landing strip in a region where Santa Tereza ranch, belonging to my friend João Lanari do Val, is situated today. By then it was very wild, it was just beginning. By the time we'd landed, I'd taken my decision: I would never buy land there. I simply didn't like the look of it.

The next day, after Lunardelli had told Ribeiro of his decision, they took off to fly back to São Paulo. Apparently because of an error in take-off, they had to make an immediate crash landing. Lunardelli described the incident: 'The plan dragged through the undergrowth and we only survived because there was a lot of vegetation which deadened the impact.' It was in January and the region was heavily flooded. With the front of the plane damaged, the only solution was to wait at least three days while one of the employees on the ranch undertook the long journey to Conceição do Araguaia to rent another plane.

But while I was waiting, my walks around the region showed me that this land in Pará was simply excellent. I changed my mind – and I became so enthusiastic that I made a point of buying the area which had been offered at the price asked by the owner, though Ribeiro told me that he could have got a discount of as much as 50 per cent. The deal was closed very quickly and I suddenly found myself the owner of 450,000 hectares of virgin forest. I knew that it was a good investment, but I hadn't the faintest idea of what I was going to do with all that jungle.

Jeremias Lunardelli, Nicholau's son, told us with a laugh that his father had later discovered that 'accidents' and 'breakdowns' had occurred on other occasions in Ribeiro's planes, always when he was carrying dissatisfied customers. Today he believes that his father may have been the unsuspecting dupe of yet another of Ribeiro's original, if risky, sales techniques.[2] Just a year after buying the land from Ribeiro, Nicolau Lunardelli bought up another large area where the ranch Companhia do Desenvolvimento do Sul do Pará (Codespar) was being set up. 'At that stage the ranch merely consisted of 250 hectares of pasture which was not even fenced. But I decided to take on the enterprise because the ranch was properly established in legal terms and this would make it easier to start work.' The Lunardelli family subsequently purchased large tracts of forest land all over the Amazon region (exactly how much it owns it will not reveal, though it is said at one time to have owned well over one million hectares) and has made a great deal of money from land transactions. Today, the family runs six cattle ranches and still owns large, unoccupied areas. Jeremias Lunardelli, Nicolau's son, is today president of the Association of Amazon Businessmen (AEA), the powerful lobby of businessmen with interests in the Amazon.

The early occupation of the Amazon by businessmen was dominated by a few powerful families, the fortunes of most of which had been built up by a powerful individual, usually an Italian immigrant or the son of Italian immigrants. Apart from Lunardelli, two other family names – Ometto and da Riva – are to crop up repeatedly in the story of the occupation. More is said about these families in the following chapter.

In the early 1960s, a few big farmers began to move on from the Araguaia river valley, where land was beginning to appreciate with the gradual influx of cattle-rearers. They travelled further west, moving into remote areas by the Xingu river. José Ramos Rodrigues, known as Zezinho das Reunidas (Zezinho being the popular diminutive form of José) because he was one of the owners of the large Reunidas bus company in São Paulo, was one of these pioneer cattle-rearers. He bought up a large area of land along the Xingu river in the early 1960s 'for nothing', as he later said. In 1968 he sent in a group of men to open up a rough track, 280 kilometres long, so that he could reach the land he had bought.

Thirty labourers took four months to do the job. They carried 30-kilo packs on their backs with food, pans, firearms, axes and topographical instruments. They were unable to take animals with them as there was no pasture on which they could graze. Now and again they made clearings in the forest so that sacks of food could be dropped to them from the air. At times the pilot miscalculated and the food was lost. Then the labourers had to live off animals they hunted in the forest. The labourers finally reached the area where the ranch building was to be constructed and cleared a landing strip for a small plane. Vegetation was cut down and burnt and grass seed sown. After two years the first cattle were brought in. Zezinho opened up nine ranches in similar fashion in the Xingu area.

In 1971 Zezinho became involved in a violent controversy which had international repercussions. At that time, the São Paulo construction company, Camargo Corrêa, had begun to build a new road (BR–80) which was to run along the northern border of the famous Xingu Indian Park and to link up with the Cuiabá–Santarém highway at Cachimbo, thus forming part of the Manaus–Brasília connection. About 130 kilometres of the road had been built when Zezinho, who owned some ranches in the region, took up in his plane some government officials from Sudeco, the regional development agency which was financing the road.

He pointed out to them that the road would be 200 kilometres shorter if it cut across the park instead of skirting it. Zezinho suggested that the land lying to the north of the new route for the road, which consisted of an area of about 800,000 hectares, should be sold to the cattle companies, while a stretch of land of comparable size should be added to the southern border of the park. His proposal was not as disinterested as it might have appeared: part of the land which it would make available to farmers was exceptionally fertile, whereas the Indians would gain an area of poor soils.

Zezinho's suggestion was accepted by Sudeco, despite the cost involved in this late change of plans. The construction company stopped work on the old route and the abandoned stretch of road, which quickly won the nickname of 'Perdidos' (the lost) from the local inhabitants, was kept open in precarious fashion for the peasant families who had settled on its margins.

The government was bitterly criticised at the time by anthropologists at home and abroad for this decision. As they predicted, the Indians suffered greatly through the re-routing of the road, which led to the contamination of several groups. Moreover, one Indian group in particular never accepted its transfer as permanent, but insistently returned each year to its traditional lands. In 1984 this group's smouldering resentment flared up into a conflict which was to have a profound impact on the government's Indian policy (see Chapter 5).

The Big Boom

The gradual process of occupation by big companies, which was occurring outside government control, was greatly accelerated in 1966 by the launching of the Operação Amazônica (Amazon Operation) by General Humberto de Alencar Castelo Branco, the first President after the military *coup* in 1964. It was a project fervently supported by nationalist military officers on the left and on the right, for whom the occupation of the country was one of the Permanent National Objectives drawn up at that time by the Escola Superior de Guerra, the leading military college, as part of the armed forces' geopolitical strategy. The project was very important too for the landowners and business community in the developed south-east; it meant that for the first time government money – and a lot of it – was available for their endeavours to open up the Amazon.

The cornerstone of the new policy was Sudam (Superintendency for the Development of the Amazon), a special federal government agency to promote the development of the Amazon region, just as Sudene was supposed to advance the interests of the poor north-east region. The term 'legal Amazonia' was adopted to define the region to benefit from the incentives to be administered by Sudam. It consisted of the states of Acre, Amazonas and Pará, the federal territories of Rondônia, Roraima and Amapá, the area of the state of Maranhão west of 44° longitude, and the areas of the states of Mato Grosso and Goiás north of 16° and 13° latitude respectively. In all, it was a vast area of five million square kilometres, about 60 per cent of Brazil's territory.

Sudam was based on a tax rebate scheme. Under law 5,173, of October 1966, which set up Sudam, companies were allowed to deduct up to 50 per cent of the income tax payable on all their operations throughout Brazil, provided that the money was invested in an approved industrial or farming project, or in infrastructure, within 'legal Amazonia'. These rebates could not make up more than two-thirds of the total cost of a project.

The procedure for cattle-rearing was as follows. A group of businessmen would present a project for a cattle ranch to Sudam. They would detail their planned expenditure over a period of four or five years. Once the project had been authorised, Sudam would pay out the tax rebates to the ranch in yearly instalments, always respecting, on paper at least, the stipulation that the rebates could not cover more than two-thirds of the ranch's predicted expenditure. The big companies, like Volkswagen, could earmark the tax rebates from their big industrial operations in the south specifically for their own ranch in the Amazon. Small companies, most of which did not have their own ranch, were allowed in the early days to select the ranch to benefit, but were later obliged by Sudam to pay the tax rebates into a general fund administered by Sudam. Apart from receiving the tax rebates, Sudam-approved projects were also exempt from income tax and other government charges for ten years. Later, customs duty on equipment imported for Sudam-approved projects was also cut drastically.

The ranches were not limited to one cycle of tax rebates. Many of the projects were 'reformulated' and a further series of tax rebates was then duly approved. Some companies 'reformulated' their projects three or four times, always with a much larger volume of tax rebates. Because the scheme involved large volumes of 'free money', it was enthusiastically welcomed by businessmen in the south. Groups which had previously never dreamed of setting up a ranch in the Amazon decided to take advantage of the opportunity. From mid 1966 to December 1978, Sudam approved 358 cattle projects and authorised almost half a billion pounds in tax rebates for these ranches. A number of industrial projects, mostly in Belém, was also approved.

Sudam turned down very few projects. The Institute of Economic and Social Planning (IPEA), a research body linked to the ministry of planning, commented in a study: 'Sudam operates by attracting as a great a volume of investment as possible, whatever form it might take or to whichever sector it is directed.'[3] Not even basic precautions were taken to minimise the disruptive impact of the big new projects in the region. Though on paper Sudam insisted that each ranch obtained a certificate both from the *prefeitura* (local council) to testify that there were no peasant families living on the land on which it wanted to set up its ranch, and from Funai to testify that there were no Indians inhabiting the area either, in practice it did not supervise these procedures. As it was well known that both local councillors and Funai officials were frequently bribed by the ranches, Sudam was effectively conniving in practices which were very likely to provoke serious conflict in the future.

Moreover, a project was never rejected because it was considered harmful to regional development. The IPEA study observed: 'The approval or not of a project depends basically on the undertaking being considered economically feasible. Projects with good prospects of being profitable in private terms are, almost certainly, declared to be of regional interest.'[4] Yet, as soon became clear, many of these big projects from outside did a lot of harm to the local economy. Armando Mendes, an economist from the university of Pará, rang the alarm bells in 1971 and 1972. He wrote a series of articles in which he pointed out that the transport facilities provided by the new roads, which were largely being built to support the new projects, would severely damage the small, vulnerable industries already established in the region. He warned that local manufacturers would be unable to compete with goods brought up from the south, where economies of scale were possible and production costs lower, and, as a result, many could go bankrupt.

Moreover, he cautioned, the old way of life would be destroyed. 'The new activities will break up the area, destroying the earlier internal structures, without putting anything else in their place', he wrote.[5] He pointed out that traditional farming activities had already been severely affected and that this was likely to lead to a serious decline in the local supply of foodstuffs. Mendes suggested that, despite the government's rhetorical commitment to the development of the Amazon, the initiative was in fact bringing far more benefits to the companies in the industrialised south than to the Amazon region itself. He wrote:

> A substantial part of the tax rebates given to the new projects returns directly to the south as payment for equipment, construction material and so on. The multiplier effect is felt much more in the rest of the country than in the region itself, which retains the wages paid to the local labour and little else.

Despite the criticisms, the cattle boom continued. The high points were 1969 and 1970 when altogether 125 cattle projects were approved. The businessmen, who were mainly from São Paulo, were happy with the easy flow of funds, particularly as Sudam was very lax in its supervision. It did not examine the ranches' budgets critically to make sure that they were not overestimating their expenditure. Nor did it check that the rebates were really invested in the ranches. Indeed, it was common knowledge in the region that on some ranches much of the money went on personal consumption. One government offical cynically told us that some corruption was the price of development, for without it the big companies could not be enticed into the region.

The most popular region was the largely uninhabited land to the west of the Araguaia river. As we have seen, this area had been sparsely occupied by poor peasant families, who had moved in from the north-east travelling up the rivers. Then, under Sudam, cattle companies began to penetrate the region from the south, using as a base the little town of Barra do Garças, which, though it would not normally be classified by geographers as belonging to the Amazon region, was artificially tucked in by placing the limit to 'legal Amazonia' in Mato Grosso (but not Goiás) as far south as the 16th parallel. At the same time, the government encouraged some of the companies to leapfrog over the north of Mato Grosso and to move directly into Pará, using the old, established town of Conceição do Araguaia as their base.

Though the four *municipios* (districts) to the west of the Araguaia river (Barra do Garças and Luciara in Mato Grosso and Santana do Araguaia

Table 2.1
The Cattle Boom Hits the Amazon

Year	No. of new cattle projects approved by Sudam	Value of authorised tax rebates, including those for reformulated projects (£ million at current exchange rate)
1966	4	£4.4
1967	47	£30.4
1968	44	£19.7
1969	67	£26.6
1970	58	£25.8
1971	50	£28.1
1972	40	£28.8
1973	10	£27.6
1974	11	£40.4
1975	12	£62.2
1976	11	£77.3
1977	3	£31.9
1978	1	£40.7
Total	*358*	*£443.9*

Note: The figures for tax rebates may slightly inflate the true value, for a few of the projects were not completed with a full disbursement of the tax rebates before the reformulated project came into effect. Sudam officials were unable to provide the complete figures for disbursed tax rebates.

Source: Sudam.

and Conceição do Araguaia in Pará), covered an enormous 221,000 square kilometres, this area was only 4 per cent of the whole of 'legal Amazonia'. Yet these districts received tax rebates worth £203.1m, close on half of the total. Barra do Garças, the largest and most southerly district, which alone covered about 50% of the total area of the four districts, received about 50% of the tax rebates. Well over half of the 149 ranches were set up by groups based in São Paulo.

The other 209 projects were distributed over a huge area: some were located beside the Belém–Brasília road, just south of Belém, in the north of Pará; others were situated in Goiás, on the eastern bank of the Araguaia river; yet others were located to the north of Cuiabá, in the north-westerly corner of Mato Grosso state; and a few were situated far over on Brazil's north-westerly frontier, in Rondônia and Acre.

Yet huge areas of 'legal Amazonia' were left virtually untouched: Amapá, Roraima, Amazonas (except for a cluster of projects around Manaus) and extensive tracts in the other states and territories. The occupation frontier had not yet reached these areas and even with the bait of the tax rebates the companies were unwilling to move in. Most of the ranch

Table 2.2
The Most Popular Area for the Sudam-backed Ranches: the Four Districts
to the West of the Araguaia River

	Area in sq. kms.	No. of cattle projects approved by Sudam	Value of authorised tax rebates (£ million at current exchange rate)
State of Mato Grosso			
Barra do Garças	121,936	76	100.2
Luciara	49,653	18	33.7
State of Pará			
Santano do Araguaia	21,284	22	39.9
Conceição do Araguaia	28,572	33	29.3
Total	*221,445*	*149*	*203.1*

Source: Sudam.

managers to whom we spoke said that they needed a road – or at least an earth track which could take lorries during the dry season – within a few hundred kilometres.

Despite the corruption, the rebates became by far the most important source of cash flowing into the region mainly because very large sums of money were involved and, before that, the region had had a very low level of investment. As a result, the Sudam scheme completely transformed the earlier slow process of penetration.

From the beginning, as well as distributing resources to a fair number of medium-sized ranches, Sudam concentrated some of its funds into four very big projects. The largest of all was Suiá-Missu in the district of Barra do Garças which, in four stages over a decade, received tax rebates worth £19.7m. Suiá-Missu, which was set up by the Ometto family from São Paulo, was later sold to the Italian company Liquigás. The other three big ranches were Campo Alegre in the district of Santana do Araguaia owned by the large São Paulo construction company Cetenco, which in five stages received tax rebates of £7.1m; Codeara in the district of Luciara with its sister company, BCN Agropastoril, owned by a São Paulo financial group, Banco do Crédito Nacional, in which Barclays Bank has a small share, which was awarded tax rebates worth £8.1m; and Vale do Rio Cristalino in the district of Santana do Araguaia, owned by Volkswagen do Brasil, which received tax rebates worth £12.4m. These four 'super ranches' were together awarded tax rebates of £47.3m, about a tenth of the total going to the 358 ranches. By concentrating resources in this way, the government hoped to create poles of development from which progress and prosperity would radiate. Developments on these large ranches are discussed in the following chapter.

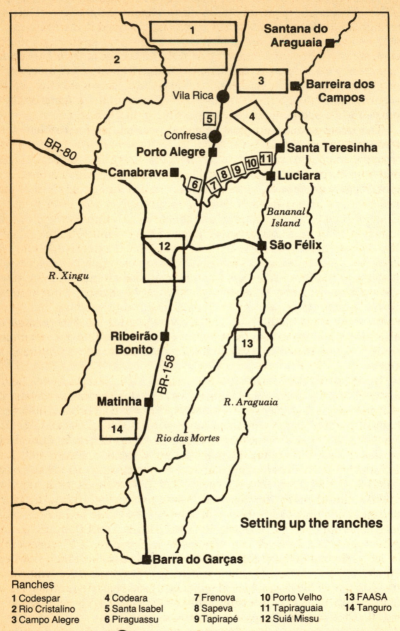

Setting up the ranches

Ranches

1 Codespar	**4** Codeara	**7** Frenova	**10** Porto Velho	**13** FAASA
2 Rio Cristalino	**5** Santa Isabel	**8** Sapeva	**11** Tapiraguaia	**14** Tanguro
3 Campo Alegre	**6** Piraguassu	**9** Tapirapé	**12** Suiá Missu	

Colonisation projects ●

The ready flow of free money acted like a magnet, attracting many different types of people into the Amazon. Some of the new arrivals were traditional cattle-rearers who had successfully farmed in the south but had had no experience in the Amazon. Others came from big industrial companies in the south which wanted to take advantage of the unprecedented opportunity to set up a successful ranch but did not want to put much of their own money into the undertaking. Yet others – and there were many of these – were sharp-witted businessmen who wanted to get their hands on the tax rebates while spending as little as possible in the Amazon.

The boom opened up great financial possibilities for the few cattle-farmers with experience in the Amazon. They were in great demand, both from the companies which seriously intended to set up a successful ranch, and from the profiteers, who wanted to present Sudam with a project which lookly highly impressive, on paper at least, so that they could squeeze out as much money as possible. One such Amazon expert was Hildebrando de Campos Bicudo, who, though he was only in his mid thirties when we spoke to him in 1979, had already spent about 18 years farming in the Amazon. Bicudo comes from a well-to-do family which owns extensive farming land in the state of São Paulo and Minas Gerais and can trace its origins back to Dutch and Portuguese settlers who arrived in Brazil in the 16th Century. He attributed his urge to farm in the Amazon, even though there were far easier options available, to the spirit of adventure which has always characterised his family. He referred with pride to his *bandeirante* ancestors who, in the 17th Century, took part in expeditions into unknown territory in the Brazilian hinterland to explore the land and capture Indian slaves.

Bicudo first visited the region in the late 1950s in search of good land for cattle. He finally purchased a farm, which, at 10,000 hectares, was small by the businessmen's standards. It was situated in Mato Grosso on the western bank of the Araguaia river, to the south of the island of Bananal. He paid just Crs 2,000 (£38) for the land in 1962. He told us that there were already peasant families in the region, mainly from Maranhão, Ceará and Goiás. He bought up the plots of three families who were living on his land, paying Crs 200 (£3.80) for each of them. To illustrate just how rapid the appreciation of land prices has been, Bicudo told us that, without taking into consideration the pasture he had planted and the cattle he had reared, the land in his farm was alone worth about Crs 10m (£190,000) by 1979, about a hundred times the price in real terms he had paid for it 17 years earlier. Bicudo said that in those early days he had opened up his ranch slowly and carefully. Scarce resources, lack of farming experience in the Amazon and the isolation of the region had all militated against hasty decisions. He said that, though he had made mistakes, he had managed to correct them in time and that his farm had been a modest success.

Bicudo's life changed with the creation of Sudam. He told us that he presented his own project to Sudam, commenting with a laugh that his ranch, called Fazendas Associadas do Araguaia SA (Faasa), must have been the smallest enterprise ever to have received tax rebates. His original project involving a total investment of Crs 1.9m (£160,000), of which Crs 1.4m (£118,000) was to come from tax rebates, was approved in July 1970. A reformulation of this project, with a total investment of Crs 4.7 m (£324,000) of which Crs 3.4m (£234,000) was to come from tax rebates, was approved in December 1973. Total tax rebates amounted to £352,000 – a hefty injection of capital for a ranch covering 10,000 hectares.

More important than this, however, was Bicudo's realisation that he had a valuable and scarce commodity to sell on the labour market: his expertise in rearing cattle in the Amazon. With so many companies anxious to jump on the Sudam bandwagon but with little idea of how to start a ranch in the wild, largely unoccupied region, Bicudo's know how was in great demand. His first consultancy job was with Laboratórios Fontoura, a São Paulo pharmaceutical company. First of all it asked him to locate the land it had just bought to the north of Barra do Garças and then to draw up a cattle project for this land. On his return Bicudo bluntly recommended that the firm should not go ahead with the proposed cattle project as he considered the soil to be too poor to support pasture. However, in its eagerness to get its hands on the tax rebates, the company decided to terminate, not its project, but its contract with Bicudo. It pressed on alone, opening up Tanguro ranch. The Tanguro project, with a total investment of Crs 2.9m (£277,000), of which Crs 2.1m (£200,000) was to come from tax rebates, was approved by Sudam in June 1969.

As Bicudo had predicted, the ranch did not prosper. A part of the land was eventually sold in 1972 to Coopercana, a cooperative from Rio Grande do Sul, which opened one of the first colonisation projects in the region. The rest of the area continued in name to be run as a cattle ranch though little real effort was made to open it up. In October 1976, when a team of researchers from the government's National Institute for Spatial Research (INPE) visited the ranch, they found it in a pitiful state. In the original project it had presented to Sudam, Laboratórios Fontoura said that it would be clearing 800 hectares a year for the first six years. Instead, after seven years of activity, it had cleared a total of only 50 of its 20,000 hectares. The ranch had a herd of only 517 head of poor quality cattle, most of which were being raised on natural pasture. The ranch had eight registered employees. The government had achieved negligible results from its investment of Crs 2.1m (£200,000).

Though his first deal did not work out well, Bicudo had learnt his lesson. He realised that, if he wanted to make money, he should not concern himself unduly about the long-term viability of the projects he was putting together. If asked, he would give his honest opinion; but if the company merely wanted a project which looked good on paper but was in fact quite impractical, he would provide that too. In 1967 he set up a project bureau in São Paulo. He offered São Paulo businessmen a package deal: he would locate the land which they had bought as a mysterious rectangle on a map in a São Paulo property office, send in a team to hack its way through the forest to the land to set up a rough shack as a ranch headquarters, and then work out a suitably impressive cattle project which they could confidently present to Sudam. Bicudo made it clear that it would not be his responsibility if the project was not fully implemented at a later stage.

Bicudo did not sell his services cheaply. He told us that on average it took him two to three months to elaborate a project, for which he charged a fee, over and above his expenses, of Crs 100,000 – Crs 150,000 (£10,000 to £15,000). His scheme worked out very well for him. By 1979, he had drawn up about 70 projects. He told us that several groups had asked him to do a series of projects on adjacent lands and that in these cases he had given a discount as each project required less time to formulate in these circumstances. One of Bicudo's most important clients was a group of São Paulo businessmen headed by José Augusto Leite de Medeiros. João Carlos de Souza Meirelles, an eloquent spokesman for São Paulo businessmen with investments in the Amazon, who in the 1970s was president of the powerful businessmen's lobby, the Association of Amazon Businessmen (AEA), was involved in some of the transactions carried out by the group.

Medeiros and his partners had a quick eye for a good business opportunity but little farming experience. Many farmers spoke of them in very scornful terms, for they believed them to be the worst kind of profiteers to have been thrown up by Sudam. They bought up extensive tracts of land beside the Tapirapé river, a tributary of the Araguaia, in the mid 1960s and early 1970s. Some of the land was purchased from Miguel Nasser, a businessman from Campo Grande in the south of Mato Grosso, who had bought up for virtually nothing a huge area of 1.2 million hectares of land in the region.

Nasser gradually sold his land in the 1970s for a big profit. We were told by several businessmen that Nasser sold his first plots for Crs 2 (17p) a hectare in 1970, but was charging Crs 1,000 (£28) a hectare by 1978. Apart from the Medeiros group, his clients included the big São Paulo Banco do Crédito Nacional, which, in the early 1970s, bought up the large area which it later turned into Codeara ranch.

As they had little farming experience, Medeiros and his partners found it difficult to draw up their first project for Sudam, which was for the Tapiraguaia ranch, to be situated at the confluence of the Tapirapé and Araguaia rivers. This project was duly approved by undemanding Sudam in June 1967. It entailed a total investment of Crs 3.4m (£520,000), of which Crs 2.5m (£380,000) was to come from tax rebates. While working on this project, the partners realised that they would be in a better position to take full advantage of the tax rebates if they found an experienced farmer to draw up impressive – and expensive – projects. So they contracted Bicudo to do this work for them. Over the next two years, he drew up projects for six ranches, to be set up side by side on the northern bank of the Tapirapé river. The results achieved on these ranches are examined in the next chapter.

As more and more companies from the south realised that they could get their hands on 'free money' through the tax rebate scheme, the inefficient Sudam bureaucracy was overwhelmed with project proposals. Most of the businessmen who moved into the region during this period were not interested in farming for its own sake. João Lanari do Val told us:

> There emerged a basic distinction between the businessmen in the region – those who knew how to open a pioneer cattle ranch, and those who knew how to open bank coffers. There is no doubt that the latter variety was both more numerous and more successful in these early years.

Sudam itself was largely responsible for the pervasive climate of graft and double-dealing. Many of its officials were notoriously corrupt. It was well known that on their tour of inspection to see how work was progressing on a ranch, most officials had little interest in anything other than the fat bribe paid to them to ensure a highly favourable report. The evasive answers and defensive attitudes of the Sudam officials to whom we spoke in Belém on several occasions were a clear indication that much was being concealed.

Several ranch managers, who were making a genuine effort to set up a viable ranch, complained to us of the tremendous waste of government resources. Moreover, because of the prevailing climate of corruption, Sudam officials did not provide the technical advice and support which might have prevented serious and costly mistakes. Amílcar Rodrigues Gameiro, manager of Codeara ranch, told us during our visit in November 1976 that he found the conniving, ingratiating attitudes of some of the officials extremely irritating. At times, he said, he had become so exasperated that he had forced them to make a real tour of the ranch, though they expressed no interest whatsoever.

Job Lane, an American running Swift-Armour's ranch near Paragominas in Pará, estimated that only 90 out of the 358 cattle projects approved by Sudam actually got off the ground. Hermínio Ometto, who set up the Suiá-Missu ranch, reckoned 'a hundred at most'. Many remained tiny clearings in the forest, the absolute minimum necessary to maintain the façade of a 'project in implantation' and thus to keep the government funds flowing in. João Lanari do Val estimated that, at the beginning, 80 per cent of the tax rebates went straight into the businessmen's pockets. Like other serious farmers, he believed that the tax incentive scheme had led to a profoundly harmful flippancy about money: 'If you blundered and lost all your money, it didn't really matter because you were losing very little of your own money. If things worked out and you made money, it was an extra bonus.' He believed that this had encouraged businessmen to embark on foolhardy gambles in which they would never have risked their own money and was responsible for much of the ecological damage caused at this time.

A few individuals, particularly those with long experience in the Amazon, realised from the beginning that the cattle-ranching offensive was technically unsound. Dennis Creswell Allan, a semi-retired Englishman, who had earlier been president of the large meat-packing group, Anglo Frigorífico, a subsidiary of the UK Vestey group, was opposed from the outset to the reckless haste with which the farms were being set up. On numerous occasions he warned the authorities of the permanent damage which would be caused to the land unless proper care was taken to protect the fertility of the soil. In 1971, David Lilienthal, a US agronomist who set up the Tennessee Valley Authority, visited the Amazon at the invitation of the Brazilian government. He later contributed to a survey of Amazonia carried out for the government by the French company Serete. On several occasions, he and another US agronomist, Frank Venning, warned the government that, with existing farming practices, the expected useful life of the pastures would be at most five or ten years.

Allan told us that Anglo Frigorífico, which is one of the biggest landowners in Brazil, had been keen to move into cattle-rearing in the Amazon and had spent three years in the early 1970s looking for a suitable project. He said that the company had decided that, to be acceptable, the project must be viable as a business undertaking in its own right, without taking into consideration the tax rebates or the gains to be made through land appreciation. Anglo had finally given up when none of the proposals they had studied passed this test.

Allan told us in 1975 that even Sudam officials had in private admitted that only about 100 of the cattle projects had been technically sound when they were presented, and that some of these were facing serious problems because of inadequate cattle management or through failure to take proper measures to maintain the fertility of the soil. He said that Sudam's cattle projects had become 'a skeleton in the cupboard' which would have to come out into the open one day.

For a long time we puzzled over why the government had provided such massive support for the cattle companies, even though, from the very beginning of the Sudam scheme, it had been clear to informed observers such as Allen that not only were the ranches unlikely to be economically viable in such a remote region, but, worse still, they represented a serious threat to the ecology and could cause permanent damage to the soil. Though graft could in part explain the businessmen's eagerness to become involved, it was an inadequate explanation for why the scheme had been set up in the first place. It seemed to us that, despite all the government's talk of the 'economic occupation of the Amazon', the fundamental reason for the initiative had been political, in that it stemmed from the heart of the struggle over the possession of the land. Sudam was set up when peasant families – the only group willing to take on the hardship and the isolation of the Amazon forest on their own initiative – had begun to move into the region in a big way. If the government had done nothing, these families would have taken over large areas. By setting up Sudam, the government created a bait which attracted businessmen into the region by the dozen. As a result, they had taken over vast tracts of land and were carrying out an enormous holding operation, reserving the land for capitalist farming. It was pre-emptive occupation. If the businessmen had waited until the region was more accessible and prospects for commercial farming much brighter, great violence would have been required to expropriate the millions of peasant families who would have settled by then. Possession of some large areas might even have been lost.

The businessmen's main role was simply to be there. For a few years at least, the government was prepared, not only to cover the ranches' losses, but also to allow the businessmen to make a big profit, although they were producing very little. It appeared an excellent deal for the businessmen, for in the longer term they seemed virtually assured of an ever larger profit through the appreciating value of the land.

Conditions on the Ranches

In the early days, to prepare the land, all the companies used the traditional slash-and-burn method. Many have carried on with the same practices on at least part of their ranches until the present day. Labourers cut down the vegetation during the first months of the dry season, from May to July. It is left to dry out for a couple of months and then burnt in August and September. During the burning season thick layers of acrid smoke hang over huge areas of the Amazon region, making it difficult for the ranches' small planes to land or take off. Grass seed is sown in October and November, sometimes by plane. It sprouts quickly in the tropical heat, often growing by as much as a centimetre and a half in a single day. It gives the impression that the soil must be rich, though ecologists have been quick to point out that this apparent fertility is no more than the temporary result of the humus left from the burning of the forest.

The pastures formed by the slash-and-burn method look extremely rough to European eyes. Huge gaunt trees, too thick for the labourers to chop down, jut up from the land like lonely sentinels. They are charred by the burnings and will die slowly over the years. The ground is littered with the trunks of smaller trees which have been cut down but incompletely burnt. The cattle, usually hump-backed zebus, pick their way over the littered ground, often stopping to scratch their backs on the tree stumps.

Labour relations are primitive. The ranch makes an agreement with a labour contractor to have a certain area of the jungle cleared for a fixed sum per hectare. The contractor goes off to a heavily-populated poor area, often in the north-east, or to one of the rapidly-growing towns in the Amazon region, where he contracts unskilled labourers to carry out the work. The labourers are brought to the ranch in the back of cattle trucks or, very occasionally, by plane if the area to be cleared is extremely remote. The contractors have become generally known as *gatos* (cats), possibly because of the cat-and-mouse games they play with the labourers who are easy prey. The labourers are held as virtual slaves in the forest, as they can only leave when the *gato* provides transport. They are often very badly treated, forced to work extremely long hours and obliged to buy foodstuffs and work tools at exorbitant prices from the store run by the *gato*.

The cattle companies usually turn a blind eye to these abuses. Their most common ploy is to claim that the labourers are not their employees and are thus not their responsibility. In August 1974, when we were at Suiá-Missu ranch, which was then owned by the Italian company Liquigás, we were repeatedly told that the company had just 220 employees, despite the huge size of the ranch. It was only by chance that we discovered that there were at least another 400 labourers working in the forest for *gatos*.

The labourers usually stay in the forest for three or four months. They are then paid, usually much less than they anticipated because of heavy deductions for their purchases at the store. It is very easy for a *gato* to rob illiterate labourers in transactions which are almost never supervised by the cattle company. The labourers are taken by lorry to the nearest town. Throughout the dry season little towns such as São Félix, beside the Araguaia river, receive a constant influx of exhausted and momentarily rich labourers. The sad scenes of frenzied riotous living, as they drink cheap white rum and hire prostitutes for the first time for several months, can be readily imagined. It is not uncommon for a labourer to spend all his earnings in just a couple of days of heavy drinking and whoring. He then lives on at the local pension until the next *gato* appears with another attractive proposal.

Sometimes the *gato* receives payment for the service carried out and then decamps, not handing over to the labourers their share. We talked to a labourer in hospital in Afonso in the north-west of Mato Grosso in September 1976. He and his workmates had been employed for several months on a cattle ranch to clean up the pastures. Then, at the end, the *gato* had fled and they had received nothing. A few hours later, after they had complained in vain at the ranch office in Afonso, a brawl had broken out between the labourers themselves, and the man we met had been knifed by one of his workmates. He felt no resentment towards the friend who had injured him, instinctively understanding that the latter had been expressing pent-up bitterness towards the *gato* and the exploitative system in general. From his hospital bed, the injured man confided to a visitor, whom he later to his consternation found out to be the local priest: 'The only solution is to become a gunman (*jagunço*). They kill at will and are never afraid of being caught. We work our guts out and then don't get anything for it.'

It is estimated that in the early 1970s there were anything from 250,000 to 400,000 labourers working on ranches in the Amazon region during the dry season. Such was the lack of control over the occupation process that no one in the government could give us a reliable figure.

The Maranhão state government estimated on a somewhat surer basis that in 1975 there were about 100,000 men from that state alone working on cattle ranches in the Amazon. João Muniz Pereira, mayor of São Bento, which was one of the *municípios* worst affected by this annual evacuation, said that this migration was 'extremely harmful',[6] though he admitted that there was little other work in the region. He explained that many of the labourers never went back to their homes, leaving wives, children and parents, and that this created a serious social problem in the region. The mayor said that he had ordered the arrest of the leading *gatos* in his district, but that this had achieved very little, as there were another 100 of them operating in neighbouring districts.

Conditions on the ranches were uniformly bad in the early days. After close questioning, even well-intentioned managers admitted to us apologetically that they had employed *gatos* on their ranches, at least during the first few years, as it was the easiest way of solving the labour shortage in a remote area. Moreover, as far as we could ascertain, very few managers, even on the better-run ranches, had taken practical measures to supervise the way the labourers were treated by the *gatos*. Unless pushed on the point, nearly all the managers to whom we spoke completely ignored the existence of the labourers.

A few managers admitted that they considered the labourers to be inferior human beings. Roberto Kacinski, a leading São Paulo businessman and director of a large car parts factory, Cofab, is a case in point. He spent part of his time setting up a ranch for his company in Mato Grosso. While taking part in one of the guided tours of the Amazon sponsored by the government he clearly expressed his opinion of labourers to a São Paulo journalist:[7]

> It's true that the labourer has a difficult job, that he lives in a wretched hut, eats just rice, beans and wild boar, when he's lucky. But he is a social outcast. He doesn't have a family. He doesn't have a moral code. He doesn't have a clean police record. At times, he doesn't even have any identity documents. He's the worst race that exists.

At times labourers would escape from ranches, running the risk of being shot dead by the gunmen who guarded the exits or of dying from starvation in the jungle. They told terrible tales of arbitrary killings for insubordination, clandestine cemeteries, mass executions and so on. Very few of their denunciations were published in the press, partly because of the heavy censorship in force in the early 1970s, and partly because the leading newspapers showed little interest in what was happening in the Amazon.

Lawyers who defended labourers and peasant families were frequently harassed and intimidated. Florisvaldo Flores, a lawyer in Barra do Garças, the stronghold of reactionary landowners, told us of threatening telephone calls he had received when he had represented labourers in court. Another lawyer, João Guarino, showed us a note in execrable Portuguese, which he had received from a ranch administrator, when he had helped some labourers while working as a lawyer for INCRA:

> Fale para esti adivagado do Incara este tal de João que eu mandei falar com eli que eli é um viado. Eli é um Fedaputa. Que eu mandei falar com ele, que eu

sou o dimistrador da fazenda de Ribero Burim eu cero que ele vem ca, que eu cero da um tiro na cara deli

Antonio Soubri
dimistrador Aantelma

Tell this lawyer from Incra, this so-called João, that I sent someone to speak to him to tell him that he is a queer, that he is a bastard. That I sent someone to speak to him, that I am the administrator of the ranch Ribero Burim, that I want him to come here, that I want to put a bullet in his face.

Antonio Soubri
administrator of Aantelma

The government's failure to enforce the law during the early stages of the occupation of the Amazon region provoked strong criticisms, first from individuals, and later from institutions. One of the first individuals to wage, almost single-handedly, a campaign to improve conditions was Paulo Botelho de Almeida Prado, a São Paulo lawyer and farmer from a well-established, traditional family. He had come to the south of Pará in the late 1960s to administer a Sudam-backed ranch. He had been so shocked by the conditions in the region that he had resigned from his job and, although an elderly man, had spent the next ten years practising as a lawyer in the region in a quixotic attempt to defend the rights of labourers and peasant families. When we visited him in 1974, he was living in a simple hut, without running water or proper sanitation.

Paulo Botelho had an impressive faith in the power of justice. He believed that many of the region's problems would be solved, if the federal government found out what was going on and sent in officials to enforce the law. At the end of 1972, he and a colleague, João Carlos Ramalho, both living in Conceição do Araguaia, wrote a letter to a leading São Paulo newspaper,[8] denouncing the terrible exploitation of the labourers on the ranches. They claimed that the latter were treated like slaves and kept in conditions of imprisonment on the ranches. If they tried to escape, they said, they were shot dead or recaptured and tortured.

Botelho had been bitterly angered by the corruption of the local courts of justice, which almost invariably ruled in favour of the rich and powerful. He told us that he had once been visited by a French priest, François Jentel, who was similarly disturbed by the lawlessness of the region. Jentel, who is a major figure in our case study of Santa Teresinha, had come to consult him over a serious legal matter. Botelho's advice had had an important impact on Jentel's thinking and had indirectly affected key developments in Santa Teresinha. Botelho died in 1980, bitterly disappointed that the government had done so little to improve conditions in the Amazon.

The Catholic Church was the first body to protest to the government about what was going on in the Amazon. It has been more vigorous in defending peasant families and Indians than labourers, largely because it has found it much easier to work in the more established Indian and peasant communities. Very often church workers have not even been allowed to visit the labourers in their camps on the ranches. The church's work with peasants and Indians is discussed in a later chapter.

The political parties and the press have failed almost completely to make any real effort to investigate conditions on the ranches. Though in the late 1960s and most of the 1970s the government was systematically censoring out of the press 'alarmist' stories about rural violence and was firmly discouraging any investigations, this scarcely seems an adequate justification for their inaction. Only a few courageous individuals, particularly journalists, have tried to lift this blanket of silence. Though they were endowed with very little power and were frequently intimidated for their efforts, the local union bodies and the regional federations of rural workers have been more active than the political parties and the press, particularly in some areas. Contag, the agricultural workers' union, has usually upheld the criticisms made by the local bodies, though it, too, has suffered repression.

The government does not ever appear to have taken action, publicly at least, to punish a ranch for maltreatment of its labourers. At best, it may have privately warned individual companies to eliminate the worst abuses so as to avoid further negative publicity. However, a few individual members of the government have felt compelled to make public criticisms, even if moderate ones. For instance, a federal police officer, Calvis Moreira, criticised the whole *gato* system in 1973. He admitted that many abuses were occurring in the region and that, as a result of the conditions of semi-slavery on some of the ranches, many labourers had tried to escape. He said: 'I believe that many have died in these attempts, due to the conditions that they have had to face in the wild and dangerous forest.'[9]

Colonel José Meirelles, at that time commander of the 9th BEC (Engineering and Construction Battalion) which built the Cuiabá–Santarém road, went much further in his criticisms. In 1973, he complained to the press about the government's conspicuous failure to work out a coherent policy for the Amazon region. He said:

> Economic groups, backed up by tax rebates and other favours, are growing stronger every day. But the authorities, I ask, when is their presence going to be felt in the region? Only they can prevent the local inhabitants from becoming involved in a process of marginalisation. Will the authorities wait until the minds of the local inhabitants have become an easy prey for subversive ideas?[10]

The most serious attempt to improve conditions on the ranches, not through legal action but indirect pressure, was made by José Smith Bráz, a civil servant at the ministry of labour. He was president of a special Amazon work group, consisting of himself and four others, which was set up by the labour ministry and sent on a special mission of investigation. Though this group was not provided with its own aircraft and was thus dependent on the ranches for transport – which clearly limited its freedom of action – enough was seen to shock profoundly all the members of the group. Smith Bráz admitted that he had discovered secret cemeteries 'along with other horrors', and denounced the conditions of the semi-slavery on some of the ranches. He called in vain for the appointment of hundreds of ministry of labour inspectors to supervise conditions all over the region, as he considered this to be the only way in which real improvements could be made.[11] On another occasion, he commented: 'Work conditions on the pioneer fronts in the Amazon are worse than anything you can imagine, although Brazil has signed all the international conventions which condemn the type of labour conditions to be found in this region.'[12]

Despite his occasional impassioned outbursts, Smith Bráz never made a detailed public exposé of what was happening. It is not known whether he made a report to the ministry; none was published. One of his suggestions was the creation of a 'special, provisional work document' which would only be valid in the Amazon region and could be issued with a minimum of bureaucracy. At the time, nearly all the labourers were working illegally, without documents, and this made any form of government control even more difficult. Smith Bráz's proposal was half-heartedly adopted in 1975 but was never applied properly – once again because of lack of government supervision. Despite Smith Bráz's own personal goodwill and commitment, his work group did not succeed in improving conditions. When we went to see him in 1981, he refused to speak fully about his experiences. By then, his special work group had been disbanded and he had been placed in a safe bureaucratic job in Brasília.

The Transamazônica Highway

In 1970 the government's Amazon policy suffered a violent – if temporary – transformation. Until then, the occupation had taken place largely outside government control (even though the government was providing substantial financial assistance for one of the protagonists). Despite the sporadic denunciations of slave camps buried in the heart of the forest and the growing number of violent clashes between cattle companies and peasant families, the government had deliberately kept out of the region. It was as if it had decided that violence was an integral part of the occupation process and that nothing should be done about it.

However, in 1970 the government unexpectedly decided to take a more active role in the region. Its decision did not mean that the government had been goaded by its critics into taking measures to enforce the law and reduce the violence. On the contrary, its new policy was not even based on a realistic analysis of what was happening in the Amazon, but was formulated in response to another violent tragedy which was occurring in another huge, abandoned region of Brazil – the north-east.

'I saw all this with my own eyes ... Nothing in my whole life has shocked and upset me so deeply. Never have I faced such a challenge.'[13] This was President Emílio Garrastazu Médici's emotional reaction on 6 June 1970 to the starvation and misery he saw in the huge, poor north-east region of Brazil, which was being assailed by one its periodic droughts.

There is no reason to doubt the authenticity of General Médici's feelings. The head of what was the most repressive of the five military governments which ruled Brazil from 1964 to 1985 had become painfully aware of the suffering and despair of a sizeable sector of the population. One conclusion which the President did not reach, at least publicly, was that the military regime over which he presided could be held partly responsible for the severity of the suffering of the north-easterners. Yet numerous economists and journalists had pointed out that the peasant families would have been in an unquestionably stronger position to withstand the onslaught of the prolonged droughts if the government's priorities had been different and a radical programme of agrarian reform had been carried out, together with the provision of extensive technical and financial assistance.

Even under the emotional impact of the drought, President Médici did not propose radical changes in the system of land tenure in the north-east, for agrarian reform would have been bitterly opposed by the large landowners (even Médici himself referred in his speech to the 'powerful of the land' who had tried to stop him seeing certain aspects of the region). Any type of radical reform would thus have required massive political mobilisation to organise popular support to overcome the resistance of the landowners. This was inconceivable. The government would never have declared open warfare on the large landowners, faithful and important supporters of the regime.

Instead, the President searched for some kind of *deus ex machina*, an emergency solution outside the region which would mean that future droughts would cause less suffering and would be less likely to stir up politically dangerous hunger riots and demonstrations. At the same time, it was essential that the existing social and economic set-up was not seriously disturbed. The rapid construction of the Transamazônica highway – a huge 5,000 kilometre road across the heart of the Amazon jungle beside which millions of peasant families from the north-east could be settled – seemed to be the answer. The planned colonisation on both sides on the Transamazônica highway marked a departure in official action in that it allocated a fundamental role to the government itself in settling an area. As we have seen, the earlier large-scale settlement of small farmers had occurred spontaneously.

The Transamazônica highway was in fact first planned by the National Department of Roads (DNER), a federal government body, in 1968. In March 1969 Eliseu Resende, the national director of DNER, spoke of a new 5,000 kilometre road which was being planned to cross the heart of the Amazon forest and to span Brazil from João Pessoa on the north-east coast all the way to Benjamin Constant on the border with Peru. He stressed that the road by itself would not bring development to the region and suggested that, to make full use of the opportunity, a comprehensive colonisation project should be carried out in careful consultation and coordination with other governmental and private bodies. The settlement of poor north-easterners beside the road formed part of this original project. Resende commented at the time:

> It is certainly true that the DNER does not have sufficient resources available to be able to carry out at the same time all the construction work for all the stages of the Transamazônica. Even if we had these resources, this would not be advisable from a macro-economic point of view, for there are other roads which are unquestionably more urgent in economic terms.[14]

However, in June 1970, shortly after the President's visit to the north-east, the National Integration Plan (PIN) was unexpectedly announced. The plan was not debated in Congress but was produced as if out of a hat by decree-law 1,106. Congress was empowered to vote on the plan as a whole, but could not suggest amendments. In practice, given the repressive political conditions of the time, the plan was certain to be approved. Through PIN, which was announced as a master-plan to solve the problems of the north-east, the government planned to invest Crs 2bn (£178m) in irrigation, and the construction of the Transamazônica. The resources were to come from a compulsory deduction of 30 per cent from the tax rebates handled by Sudene, the north-east development agency. Sudene officials made vehement protests at this drastic and unexpected cut in their budget.

But this slash in their budget also provided Sudene with a convenient excuse for the disappointing results it was achieving in its work. As they had been prevented by the government from carrying out effective agrarian reform, Sudene officials had been attempting to build up regional industry. But, caught in a vicious circle, the officials had found it impossible to set up factories which used local raw materials and which would thus have had a beneficial multiplier impact on the regional economy, because the latter were prohibitively expensive owing to the backwardness of the primary sector. As a result, Sudene had been forced to bring in technologically-advanced assembly plants, which merely took advantage of the cheap local labour. In this way, Sudene had created isolated, artificial and incongruous islands of sophisticated manufacturing activities which had done virtually nothing to improve the living standards of the mass of illiterate and impoverished north-easterners.

The federal government expropriated a band of 10 kilometres each side of the new highway. It said that it would be carrying out a massive colonisation programme on this land. Transport minister Mário Andreazza explained the basic philosophy behind the plan:

> On the one hand, the north-east, ravaged by periodic droughts, with a huge sector of the population lacking even the basic conditions for survival, sees

many of its inhabitants emigrate to the centre-south where the large cities are not in a position to absorb this unskilled labour. On the other hand, the population of Amazonia, which is a vast region with fertile valleys and important mineral deposits, is concentrated in tiny hamlets beside the navigable rivers.[15]

The solution, Andreazza continued, was to let the two regions solve each other's problems. The catch phrase became: 'The land without people for the people without land.' (It was a slogan which in typical fashion completely ignored the 10,000 Indians and the peasant families already living in the Amazon.) Andreazza predicted that two million people would be settled along these roads within two years.[16] Eventually, he said, the number would increase to ten million.

The project was widely used in government propaganda throughout the country. It was presented as a fearless, patriotic undertaking, carried out by a government in a hurry to develop the hinterland and to bring progress to the poorer sectors of the population. It was used with some success to divert attention away from the violent political repression of that time and to present the Médici administration as an effective government which was rapidly developing the country.

All the leading ministers and top officials dutifully expressed great enthusiasm for the project. Eliseu Resende forgot his earlier reservations. Agriculture minister Cirne Lima displayed remarkable ignorance of previous research carried out by his ministry, which had shown it to be a very expensive business to settle people successfully on farming land, and commented in simplistic fashion: 'It is an initiative which, to tell the truth, does not demand much investment for the land in these areas is very cheap.'[17] Indeed, no separate budget was even drawn up for the ambitious colonisation project, as it was seen to form part of the road construction programme.

One middle-rank civil servant dared to challenge the facile assumption that the Transamazônica would help to solve the problems of both the north-east and the Amazon. José Sérgio de Paz Monteiro de Castro, director of the Amazonas state road department (DER–AM), gave an interview to a leading São Paulo newspaper, *O Estado de S. Paulo*, in June 1970. He seems to have been the first person publicly to have warned the government, with sound technical arguments, of the drawbacks to the Transamazônica project. He said that he could see no good reason for building more roads in the Amazon region at that moment. He believed that it made much more sense to consolidate the occupation of areas already served by roads by setting up carefully-planned colonisation projects and by improving the infrastructure and the standard of public services.

He commented:

> The simple fact of building roads does not mean that we are creating conditions for the occupation of an empty area. As well as roads, we must

provide the settler with technical and financial assistance so that he can produce and establish himself on the land.[18]

The engineer estimated that for a colonisation project to be successful it alone demanded an investment twice that required for the road.

However, as well as these convincing arguments against a large road-building programme for the Amazon region in general, Monteiro de Castro had specific reasons for believing that the Transamazônica was a particularly unsound project. He said that some of the other new roads, such as the one which ran from Manaus to Porto Velho, made economic sense because they linked areas with a high consumption of raw materials (the industrialised south) to an area which required manufactured goods (the Amazon). 'But', he said, 'this is not the case with the Transamazônica, for the north-east consumes very little of what we produce and it produces very little of what we consume.' He predicted that the road would carry very little traffic and that this in its turn would act as a deterrent; drivers would be unwilling to make a long drive along a deserted road as they would be afraid of being stranded for days if their vehicles broke down. Monteiro de Castro also questioned the assumption, glibly made by the government, that hundreds of north-easterners would want to settle in the Amazon. 'Migrants have always travelled in search of a labour market and better living conditions', he explained. 'They won't find them in the Amazon.'

The interview had considerable repercussions in Brazil. The engineer's observations were widely praised, even by well known conservative figures such as the economist Eugênio Gudin. However, in keeping with the dominant climate of political repression, the government could not tolerate criticism, however well founded the observations might be. Monteiro de Castro was forced to make an unconvincing retraction in which he denied even talking about the Transamazônica project with the São Paulo paper. In an evident attempt to do enough to save his job but no more, Monteiro de Castro published a letter of retraction in an obscure Rio de Janeiro evening newspaper.

It was, however, discovered by a sharp-eyed reporter from *O Estado de S. Paulo*. In a subsequent article the newspaper had no difficulty in demolishing the engineer's retraction. Moreover, it justly observed that it was really irrelevant who made the criticisms; what mattered was that the government could not answer them.

The engineer did not have to wait long for the vindication of his gloomy prediction. Although the road itself was constructed in the record time of just over a year, serious problems soon arose with the grandiose colonisation project. This had been given to INCRA, the civilian institute attached to the agriculture ministry, to administer. Though INCRA had many hard-working and committed employees, particularly at the lower levels of its administration, it was corrupt, under-staffed and inadequately financed. Within a year INCRA had given up its original plan of settling millions of illiterate and impoverished north-easterners. Its officials began to recruit better-off settlers from other regions, hoping that they would be better able to fend for themselves as they had at least had a little experience in cash crop farming, in the use of machinery and in contracting bank loans. It was shown in a research project carried out in 1972 that north-easterners made up only 34, 39 and 42 per cent of the settlers in the main projects carried out in Altamira, Itaituba and Marabá.

However, even with better-prepared settlers, the project floundered badly. Several writers have suggested that the unprecedented degree of government intervention was more of a hindrance than a help and that the settlers would have fared better if they had been left alone to choose their own plots of land and farm them. But this is probably no more than an indication of the enormity of the government's blunders; what the settlers undoubtedly required was government backing of the right kind.

The colonisation project was virtually halted in 1974, just two years after the completion of the road. From October 1970 to June 1974, only 4,969 families were settled along the road, instead of the 100,000 originally planned. Sudam officials have calculated that four families moved into the region spontaneously for each INCRA-sponsored family. This would indicate that about 25,000 families settled in the region, which is a somewhat higher figure than the estimate of 15,000 which we were given by people working in the region in 1974. Whatever the true figure, it is clear that nothing like the number of families suggested in the original high-flown plans actually moved into the region. As Brazil has approximately eight million or nine million landless peasant families, the Transamazônica scheme, for all its publicity, cannot be said to have contributed significantly to the solution of this problem.

The INCRA-sponsored families we visited in 1975 were facing serious problems. They were housed in flimsy, prefabricated little wooden houses with corrugated iron roofs, which looked incongruous in the midst of the tropical forest and, according to the settlers, were less suited to the humid climate than the traditional wattle-and-daub huts. Many complained of failures in the government's back-up programme: little technical assistance, highly expensive farm inputs (pesticides, fertilisers, sprays, etc.), inadequate marketing facilities and so on. One settler told us that the road should really have been called the Transmisery highway. Another told us what he thought INCRA really stood for: Instituto que Nada Conseguiu Realizar na Amazônia (institute that did not manage to achieve anything in Amazônia).

A few stretches of the road, generally those which fitted into north–south routes, were being heavily used. For the most part, however, the road had very little traffic, as had been predicted by Monteiro de Castro. As a result it had been dubbed 'the road which links nothing to nowhere' by a Brazilian journalist. Predictably enough, the earth road, which was coated with a thin layer of fine gravel, had not stood up to the torrential rains which beat down on Amazônia from November to April. A heavy outlay was required each year to repair the wooden bridges, fill in the pot-holes, replace the broken drainage pipes and so on. Parts of it had been abandoned.

Much of the critical press coverage of the Transamazônica fiasco was censored out of the left-wing newspapers by the government, which was unwilling to face up to the mistakes and inconsistencies of its policies. When pushed hard, government officials referred to 'technical difficulties' as the main reason for the collapse of the colonisation scheme. But the main factor underlying the numerous setbacks was political. However great the personal commitment of a few INCRA officials, the project was glaringly at odds with the main thrust of the government's Amazon policy, which was to open up the region for the benefit of a small elite of big farmers, industrialists and bankers. As a result, the government lacked the political will to solve technical problems, most of which were quite surmountable.

From our conversations with businessmen in São Paulo, it became clear that the decline in government interest in the colonisation project was partly the result of pressure from businessmen from the south, powerfully represented by the Association of Amazon Businessmen (AEA), who were pleased enough for the government to build the Transamazônica but were resolutely opposed to the idea of more than token settlement of peasant families along this road. The interests of this group were ably represented in the Médici government by João Paulo dos Reis Velloso, the planning minister. Before long, he and other government oficials were able to force through an important change in government policy.

Notes

1. Charles Wagley, *Welcome of Tears, The Tapirapé Indians of Central Brazil*, Oxford University Press, New York, 1977.

2. Carlos Ribeiro was killed in a crash in 1975 when he was taking some passengers to Volkswagen's ranch in south Pará. Ribeiro had never learnt to fly the plane properly and did not have the appropriate licence. According to businessmen who knew him, he used to bribe an Air Force brigadier at Rio de Janeiro airport to sign the papers as if he were piloting the jet. It is believed that, not familiar with the routine emergency procedures, he made a crucial error while flying to Volkswagen's ranch in Pará. Two visiting West German directors from the parent company and the ranch manager of English descent, Oscar Thompson Filho, who was agriculture minister during the first military government after the 1964 *coup*, also died in the crash.

3. *Análise Governamental de Projetos de Investimento no Brasil: Procedimentos e Recomendações* (IPEA/INPES, 1972), p.66.

4. Ibid., p.58.

5. *O Estado de S. Paulo*, 29 November 1972.

6. *O Estado de S. Paulo*, 24 August 1975.

7. *O Estado de S. Paulo*, 12 September 1973.

8. *O Estado de S. Paulo*, 31 December 1972.

9. *O Estado de S. Paulo*, 19 July 1973.

10. *O Estado de S. Paulo*, 14 October 1973.

11. *O Estado de S. Paulo*, 22 December 1974.

12. *O Estado de S. Paulo*, 7 February 1975.

13. *O Estado de S. Paulo*, 7 June 1970.
14. *Jornal do Brasil*, 28 March 1969.
15. *O Estado de S. Paulo*, 14 November 1970.
16. *O Estado de S. Paulo*, 11 October 1970.
17. *O Estado de S. Paulo*, 28 September 1970.
18. *O Estado de S. Paulo*, 28 June 1970.

3. The Big Companies Move In – Part Two

> The government's aim is the economic occupation of the region, not its settlement. And this will be achieved more through capital and technology than labour.
>
> (Raymundo Nonato de Castro, under-secretary at the interior ministry, *O Estado de S. Paulo*, 10 November 1974)

The Government Sorts Out its Amazon Policy

By 1972 government policy for the Amazon was in a mess. In spectacular fashion the government had built the costly Transamazônica highway, but it was becoming clear that the project's only success was as a public relations exercise. It had done nothing to solve the perennial problems of poverty and malnutrition in the north-east. Though the government continued to pay lip service to its commitment to provide millions of peasant families with cheap land in the Amazon, it was not supplying INCRA with the back-up it required to carry out this policy properly. It was becoming increasingly evident that the government had never been serious in its colonisation project.

Nor could the government draw much comfort from Sudam's record. Though each year Sudam was pouring large sums of money into the region – £27m in 1969, £26m in 1970 and £28m in 1971 – there was little indication that the region was about to take off economically and enter a period of self-sustained growth. The government had been prepared to subsidise the companies during the early years in which they prematurely took over possession of much of the land and kept out the peasant families, but it had expected that the companies would eventually stand on their own feet.

Moreover, Sudam was chaotically administered. Partly because of the large number of projects under its control, there were longer and longer delays each year before the tax rebates were paid. This created serious difficulties for some of the smaller companies which were genuinely attempting to set up a ranch and did not have the backing of a powerful São Paulo group which would advance funds to them to tide them over a difficult period. Corruption had become ever more rife. Though the strict press censorship imposed at the time kept the scandal out of the press, it was an open secret to business circles in São Paulo, Rio and Brasília. It became an embarrassment to the government and in August 1972 President Médici finally moved in to sack General Ernesto Bandeira Coelho, the superintendent of Sudam, who had become renowned for his inefficiency and corruption.

The team which moved in with the new superintendent, Colonel Câmara Sena, was determined to put the house in order and to sort out the government's policy, not only for Sudam, but for the Amazon region as a whole. The new officials felt that it was time to prepare for a switch in the government's official Amazon policy away from what they considered to have been the pseudo-populism of the Médici government, which, they thought, was in contradiction with both the government's policies elsewhere in the country and with what was really happening in the Amazon.

At the same time, they felt that the government could not revert to its policies of the late 1960s. Though they shared the earlier administration's anxiety to keep out the peasant families, the new officials believed that Sudam had been too indiscriminate in the type of businessman it had attracted into the region. In particular, they were critical of many of the smaller and medium-sized companies, which, they felt, lacked both technical and financial resources. A few of the officials began privately to voice suspicions that, far from bringing progress to the region, some of these companies might actually be retarding development by causing serious – and possibly irreversible – ecological damage. It was clearly time for a rethink of the whole policy.

As a first move, the officials drew up a confidential document, called 'Studies for the Amazon Development Plan', which was later endorsed by the new superintendent. The study was to be the basis of government action under the administration of President Ernesto Geisel (1974–9). Though it was not published, in the course of our research we managed to obtain a copy. Perhaps because they were writing a confidential document, these technocrats expressed with unusual frankness their commitment to the 'model of economic development' then openly governing Brazil's economic policies in all parts of the country except the Amazon. Typical of many of the top government officials in power at the time, they clearly believed that all the government's energies should be channelled into building up the country's productive forces and achieving high rates of economic growth. They approved implicitly of both Brazil's enormous disparities in wealth and the low priority in the government's plans for social goals such as improving state education, the public health service and so on, as necessary measures to free resources for investment in big economic projects.

They believed that the government's main goal for the Amazon should be to incorporate the region into the rest of the country so that its economic potential could be taken advantage of as quickly as possible. They argued that any attempt to combine this with a grandiose and paternalist land settlement scheme for millions of poor peasant families was bound to fail. The technocrats did not hide their scorn for most INCRA officials whom they considered to be woolly-headed idealists who were trying ineffectually to carry out an egalitarian programme of land settlement which ran counter to the main thrust of Brazil's model of economic development and was thus doomed to failure from the outset.

The technocrats showed a complete lack of sympathy for the peasant families moving into the region:

> This spontaneous current [of peasant migrants] is composed to a large extent of settlers without any capital of their own, with a low level of general knowledge and, at times, addicted to notoriously poor farming methods, handed down from generation to generation.
>
> On the other hand, the Region cannot offer them in the required proportions the rich soils they dream of. So, dealing with chemically-poor soils, which they cannot handle correctly as they have no money, and faced by a government which is not in a position to increase the physical-chemical support conditions of the soil (even if this were the objective of its programmes), the majority carry out the only dangerous activity which they know how to do: the destruction of the forest and the exhaustion of the soils by the cultivation of extremely poor subsistence crops, according to the well-known system of itinerant agriculture, responsible for the formation of ever-larger deserts.
>
> Beside this predatory aspect, these unfortunate migrant families tend to establish a morbid system of exchange of disease with the local inhabitants, contracting some illnesses which they have not encountered before (malaria, virulent fevers and so on) and introducing others which were previously unknown (schistossomosis).
>
> The indiscriminate migration of these populations, thus, far from making a contribution to the development of Amazonia, creates every year a growing problem of how to absorb in productive employment the labour which manages to settle legally in the area and demands enormous resources in education, rural extension and training . . .
>
> Summing up the question in simple terms, direct and indirect incentives to migration from the north-east merely result in a geographical transfer within the country of a problem already established in another region, taking to Amazonia the responsibility of recuperating the so-called surplus population of the north-east . . .

So the technocrats called on the government to halt the influx of peasant migrants and to adopt a very different occupation strategy which they called the 'model of corrected, unbalanced growth'. They suggested that, instead of generalised measures to benefit all Amazonia, as had occurred under Sudam's earlier tax rebate scheme, a selection should be made of specific products, located in particular geographical areas, where the region had special advantages and could thus compete successfully with producers in the rest of Brazil and abroad. Their list of products to receive special incentives was made up of some minerals, some timbers, cattle in some regions, a few species of fish, a few industries and some cash crops, such as cocoa, African palm oil and coffee.

The technocrats believed that in this way they could create new centres of modern development which would have a dynamic impact on the whole region. They recommended that:

> the new model should be installed as rapidly as possible so that niches of old-fashioned forest activities, traditional agriculture and so on, will be spontaneously abandoned and the productive agents will move into more modern and more productive jobs in the new system.
>
> It is necessary and useful, both socially and economically, to tolerate old activities. But this tolerance must be *regressive*, that is, geared to phasing out an obsolete activity so that better advantage of the labour can be taken in more sophisticated activities.

This document served as the basis for the section on the Amazon in the *Segundo Plano Nacional de Desenvolvimento*, the development plan drawn up by the Geisel government which took office in March 1974. Couching the idea of 'unbalanced growth' in less controversial language, it is stated in the plan that the development of the Amazon will occur 'through the development of selected (and thus discontiguous) areas, through the choice of the most fertile land and through concentration of action'.

In this way the official Amazon policy, which had been bizarrely out of step with the rest of the country during the Transamazônica adventure, was brought into line. It was made to match the government's overall national strategy where, since the end of the 1960s, a clear policy of 'unbalanced growth' had been applied. Key sectors, such as manufactured exports, had received remarkable incentives, while most industries producing for the home market had been neglected.

The official switch to the policy of elitist, unbalanced growth for the Amazon only occurred in 1974 at the beginning of the Geisel government but well before then the key sectors of the government had moved in that direction. On several occasions, the planning ministry, in association with the Banco de Amazônia, took groups of top businessmen on guided tours to help them select areas for investment. The groups were shown extensive areas of fertile land recently made accessible by the construction of the Transamazônica and other highways, and were encouraged to set up large cattle ranches or colonisation projects.

About a hundred businessmen went on the first of these trips, called *O Sul vai ao Norte* (the South goes to the North) which took place in April 1973. On this occasion, Jorge Babot Miranda, president of the Banco de Amazônia, made a speech in which he defended unequivocally his commitment to the role of big business in the Amazon. He said:

> There is no point in carrying out the huge works of infrastructure now being undertaken in the area, if big new companies, which alone can take rational

advantage of the Amazon's huge potential, do not set up in the region. Brazil has decided in favour of free enterprise. The development of a country which has made this option will only occur with the total participation of businessmen, who in the last analysis are the only agents able to mobilise idle resources and turn them into wealth.[1]

In view of the success of this first venture, another trip was organised later. About 20 leading businessmen visited the region in August 1973 in the company of four ministers. The group included Sebastião Camargo, who had built up from nothing the huge Camargo Corrêa civil construction company; Amador Aguiar, another highly successful self-made man who headed Bradesco, Brazil's largest private banking group; Wolfgang Sauer, the West German president of Volkswagen do Brasil, the country's largest car manufacturer; Ariosto da Riva, one of the largest landowners, who has made a fortune through land deals in the Amazon; and Roberto Kacinski, director of Cofap, a big car parts manufacturer. Nearly all of the group already owned land in the region and some subsequently branched out into further projects.

On this occasion, civil servants from the planning ministry firmly defended the need for big projects: 'We must consider the need to develop economies of scale in the Amazon. For this reason support must be given to activities that demand heavy investment and are thus inaccessible to the settlers brought into the region by INCRA.' Taking an indirect dig at INCRA's endless headaches with its Transamazônica projects, they added smugly:

> The success of these large projects no longer depends on the federal government. The planning ministry has now done its part by bringing businessmen from the centre–south to priority areas and showing them the economic possibilities of each one. Except for works of infrastructure – which are the government's responsibility – the success of these enterprises now depends on private initiative.[2]

The planning minister, João Paulo dos Reis Velloso, was enthusiastic: 'With the mission, a new phase in terms of economy of scale is beginning in the Amazon region.'[3] He received the full backing of the interior minister, General José Costa Cavalcanti, who commented about this time: 'The future of the Amazon lies in the hands of businessmen, whether Brazilian or foreign, for Brazil has lost its fear of foreign capital.'[4]

Though some sectors of the agriculture ministry, to which INCRA is subordinated, stood up to the pressure from the technocrats until the end of the Médici government, others succumbed much earlier. At the beginning of 1973, INCRA gave up its earlier exclusive concern for small peasant families and began the so-called second stage of its colonisation project by which it sold plots of up to 2,000–3,000 hectares to medium-sized farmers. Unlike the first stage, which consisted of the sale of plots of about 100 hectares to small peasant families and in which the social aspect was dominant, the explicit objective of the second stage was to form a rural middle class. According to INCRA, the 'economic aspect' was predominant in this second stage. In the third stage, which was organised jointly with Sudam in July 1973, plots of up to 50,000 hectares were sold. Only big companies had the resources to buy plots of this size. INCRA justified this radical change in its policies by saying that it was necessary to attract capital and farming expertise to the region. It was partly in connection with this third phase that the visits of the leading businessmen to the region were organised.

By the end of the Médici government, only José Francisco Moura Cavalcanti, agriculture minister, and Walter Costa Porto, the president of INCRA, remained firmly opposed to the swing towards the big company. These two repeatedly pointed out to the rest of the government that, with the occupation of the Amazon, it had a unique opportunity to alleviate some of the country's pressing social problems and thus to protect the long-term interests of the regime. They said that the social unrest that was spreading to Brazil's cities through the migration of millions of underemployed north-easterners was largely the result of the archaic structure in the north-east. There was enough land for these families – but it was unavailable. They warned that, if the government allowed the big landowners to occupy the Amazon in similarly inegalitarian fashion, it would be cutting off an important safety valve for these north-easterners and other landless families and would be storing up explosive social problems for the country in the future.

However, their advice was completely disregarded. The swing towards the big company was firmly consolidated when the Geisel government took office. Care was taken to ensure that the top men in the agriculture ministry favoured the new line. In April 1974, Lourenço Tavares Vieira de Silva, the new president of INCRA said: 'INCRA was never against the presence of the big company. It was just opposed to the creation of the *latifúndio*.'[5] Alysson Paulinelli, the new agriculture minister, was a fanatical defender of capitalist farming. He said in May 1974:

> It is not enough to divide the region into small areas and distribute them among a large number of people. This would not be the most efficient formula for an economic victory. We know that no country can just have managers . . . and that it is impossible to turn every rural worker into a businessman.[6]

As a result, Paulinelli did not believe in distributing plots of equal size: 'This would hold back the most gifted while we would have to protect artificially the least gifted. We live in a capitalist country and we must therefore offer a chance for competition.'[7]

The government's radio programme, the 'Voice of Brazil', which goes on the air at peak listening time each day on all stations and expresses official thinking, reflected the new approach. In marked contrast to its more populist

line in 1970 and 1971 when it made great play of the government's
endeavours to settle hundreds of thousands of landless families alongside the
Transamazônica, in May 1974 the radio gave a sombre and hard-headed
account of its policies for the region:

> The heavy investments carried out in the opening up of the Amazon have
> transformed virgin land into available factors of production. It is thus
> legitimate for the Brazilian people to expect that these investments will have a
> multiplier effect on the national economy in the form of an increase in national
> agricultural production and the creation of a solid agribusiness sector.
>
> It would thus not make sense to sell plots of land to people without the
> technical and financial capacity to make use of them in such as way as to bring
> results compatible with the size of national needs in the agricultural sector.
>
> Without ignoring the problem of the landless peasant farmer, it is
> imperative that entrepreneurial agriculture be brought to the Amazon as it is
> the only type of farming which can produce an agile response to the need to
> increase national production of foodstuffs.[8]

The policy option of 'unbalanced growth' announced in the second
National Development Plan took concrete form in the highly-selective
Polamazônia – the Amazon Programme of Farming, Cattle-rearing and
Mineral Poles, which was passed by presidential decree on 14 September
1974. It set up 15 poles of development in which investment was to be
concentrated. For the first time, mining activities were given a dominant
role in a global development plan of this nature. This emphasis was to
become more marked by the early 1980s.

Pole 1, the Xingu–Araguaia, in the north-east of Mato Grosso and south
of Pará, and pole 3, the Araguaia–Tocantins, in the northerly tip of Goiás,
were areas of Sudam-backed cattle-rearing. The resources were to be
largely used to expand the road network and to help set up beef-processing
plants and colonisation projects. Mining activities were stressed in three
poles: pole 4, Trombetas, to the north of the Amazon river, where important
bauxite reserves had been discovered; pole 2, Carajás, a mountain range in
south Pará, where an extraordinarily rich mineral complex had been found;
and pole 14, Aripuanã, where various mineral discoveries had been made.
Of particular importance for some São Paulo businessmen, especially João
Carlos de Souza Meirelles, was the decision to include the construction of
the road AR–1 (Vilhena–Humboldt) among the works to be financed as part
of this east pole. The businessmen had bought up fertile lands in Aripuanã
for a song on condition that they set up a project within five years. As an
access road was essential, they would have had to pay for its construction
themselves, if it had not been financed by Polamazônia. The text was
remarkably explicit in its account of the way in which the funds were to be
used in this pole: 'The objective of the programme in this area is to provide
the necessary infrastructure and support for the development of the large
projects which are being carried out by private initiative.'

Nearly all the investment, fixed at Crs 2.5bn (£135m) for the three-year period 1975–7, was geared to large projects, particularly cattle-rearing and mining. Only Crs 24m (£1.3m), just 1 per cent of the total, was earmarked for so-called subsistence crops (rice, cassava, maize and beans) which are mainly cultivated by peasant farmers.

The Ranches Face Problems

As we have seen, the businessmen from the south were not greatly harmed by the government's decision to construct the Transamazônica highway or by the subsequent vacillations in the government's Amazon policy. Though they clearly perceived the project as a threat – it represented a very different way of occupying the Amazon – they continued to receive their tax rebates throughout the period.

However, they were eventually affected by the later change in official policy. Gradually in the mid 1970s the government began to withdraw the indiscriminate financial support it had given all the cattle projects during the earlier period. It did so for two main reasons: first, because of the country's worsening economic situation, partly created by the world oil crisis; and secondly, because it began to realise that the boom in beef production in the Amazon, which it had dreamed of in earlier years, was not going to take place as effortlessly as had been imagined; many of the ranches, particularly the smaller ones, were facing an unexpected threat – ecological disaster.

As we have seen, the move into cattle-farming took place extremely quickly, without any prior analysis of its ecological or economic viability. The cattle companies did not even make use of the limited knowledge of tropical farming that was available, but set about clearing the land as if they were dealing with the rich soils of São Paulo. In the mid 1970s, they (or, more accurately, the government, which was financing almost all the cattle projects) began to pay heavily for such high-handedness.

At first, neither government officials nor cattle-rearers would tolerate any suggestion that the large-scale move into cattle-rearing might threaten the ecology of the region. Mário Andreazza, who was transport minister during the Médici government, made several angry and irrational attacks on ecologists in the mid 1970s. For instance, he refused to take seriously the points raised by R. J. A. Goodland and H. S. Irwin in their study, *Amazon Jungle: From Green Hell to Red Desert?*, which was one of the first attempts to draw attention to the frightening ecological risk of the government's Amazon policy. Because the two writers were both Americans, Andreazza tried to dismiss their work as the product of 'international greed', part of a plot 'to halt the Brazilian effort to open up its virgin lands'.[9]

Many of the cattle-rearers refused in similar fashion to accept that ecologists might have anything to teach them. Mário Thompson, the manager of Volkswagen's ranch in the south of Pará, had perhaps some cause for resentment, for his ranch had been unfairly criticised in the mid 1970s by ecologists, including the internationally renowned Burle Marx, for cutting down 'half a million hectares of virgin forest' when in fact it had cleared only 10,000 hectares. Yet Thompson had clearly over-reacted. When we visited his ranch in November 1977, he told us with rancour that ecology was 'a new-fangled profession, recently invented by out-of-work intellectuals who have nothing new to say'.

More dangerous than this, however, was the willingness of leading government officials to give credence to half-baked pseudo-scientific views which by chance justified their development policies. The planning minister, João Paulo dos Reis Velloso, for instance, gave great support and publicity to the wild ideas of a scientist called Henrique Pimenta who was employed by Radam, the government body carrying out a radar survey of the Amazon. In novel fashion, Pimenta argued that the Amazon forest was senile and was being gradually suffocated by creepers. In his view, the only hope of saving the forest was to cut down the old vegetation so as to create space for young plants.

In an extraordinarily convenient way, he thus advocated the wholesale destruction of large areas of the forest, as this alone, he claimed, would lead to a marked increase in the production of oxygen with the regeneration of the plants. He dismissed completely the suggestion that this might cause a big climatic change:

> The climate in the Amazon does not depend on the forest. The latter is the result of the former . . . It would not be enough to cut down the forest to change the climate. We would have to knock down the Andes as well.[10]

Pimenta concluded:

> If we exchanged the forest for grass, for example, we would have more oxygen than now, as well as another advantage – grass consumes less water.[11]

On another occasion, when Pimenta was giving a talk to an audience which included two ministers, he was even more direct: 'Either the businessmen conquer the forest or it will disappear by the force of its own nature.' He scornfully dismissed what he dubbed 'the myth that the whole-sale destruction of the forest could have serious ecological consequences'.[12]

Pimenta's conjectures were too eccentric even for some government officials. Joaquim de Carvalho, president of the Brazilian Institute for Forest Development (IBDF), commented drily: 'Pimenta's ideas are, at best, anti-scientific.'[13] Many ecologists openly laughed at Pimenta's views and expressed astonishment that the government had the audacity to flaunt such barefaced nonsense. Yet Pimenta's theories became adopted as part of official thinking. As late as 1979, João Carlos de Souza Meirelles, president of the Association of Amazon Businessmen (AEA) said: 'The Amazon is a senile forest and it would be better to cut it down rather than let it flourish.'[14]

The conservationist lobby has not been without its exaggerations and inaccuracies too. Misinformed politicians and journalists have made wild allegations about the extent of forest destruction. They have damaged their credibility by falsely accusing ranches of clearing enormous areas of forest. They have made confused claims about the damage caused by chemical defoliants. Yet events were to show that they were essentially right in alerting the government to the disastrous consequences of large-scale destruction. It may be useful at this stage to describe briefly what happens after clearance to the infertile soils that lie under most of the Amazon forest.

The Amazon forest, with its dense canopy, provides excellent protection for these poor soils. When it is cut down, the fragile support system is broken. By planting grass, cattle-rearers are displacing a complex tropical forest, made up of at least 500 different species of flora, by a much simpler ecosystem, which contains only four or five species and demands a much greater supply of nutrients from the soil. The impact of this violent transformation can be catastrophic. After two or three years, the residual nutrition is exhausted and the acidic, lateritic soils, which predominate in the Amazon, are battered during long hours of exposure to scorching sun and torrential rains. Unless corrective measures are urgently taken, the soils end up hard, brittle and infertile.

Most ecologists are opposed *a priori* to the destruction of the forest ecosystem. With an arsenal of powerful arguments, they point to other options for economic development which permit either the preservation of all the forest or almost all of it. They have proposed the cultivation of perennial crops (such as rubber, oil palm, coconuts, Brazil nuts, tea, coffee and cocoa), native forestry and even plantation forestry. They have pressed the government to carry out research projects into the various options. Until adequate research has been carried out, many ecologists believe that the development drive should be deflected to the *cerrado* region of Brazil's central plain, where the vegetation is sparse and little ecological damage can be done. Mário Guimarães Ferri, a well-known Brazilian botanist, has made this proposal on several occasions. Goodland and Irwin repeat it in their study:

> There is mounting pressure to exploit Amazonia; much of this pressure could easily, and should be, diverted to the contiguous *cerrado* region which is spread over 1.5m sq.kms . . . Conventional agriculture in the *cerrado* is even now at least as successful as in the Amazon and provokes infinitely less environmental damage.[15]

The ecologists' attempts to divert the occupation were, however, a resounding failure. Government officials and cattle-ranches only began to listen to their arguments when some of their earlier predictions of ecological disaster began to come true.

By the mid 1970s some of the first Sudam-backed ranches started to face very serious problems of soil leaching, that is, the washing out of the nutrients in the soils by the heavy rains. The difficulties were particularly severe in the cluster of ranches around Paragominas in the north of the state of Pará where the soil was particularly infertile. Some of the businessmen in this region had been mainly concerned in laying their hands on the free money, but others had made a genuine attempt to farm the land and had been defeated by the scale of the problems. Such was the case of José Carlos Vilela de Andrade, an enormous 20-stone man, known affectionately as Big Vilela (Vilelão) to his friends.

We first spoke to him in his smart office on the Avenida Paulista in São Paulo in 1975. Lolling back in his plush leather armchair, he looked strangely out of place, as though temporarily confined and anxious to be back out in the open. He told us that he had been one of the first farmers to take advantage of the Sudam scheme. In 1966, he had bought 40,000 hectares of virgin land near the town of Paragominas. He said that the land had been so cheap that it had scarcely counted as a cost.

Vilela moved in quickly, clearing the land in the traditional slash-and-burn fashion, and set up a ranch called Rio Jabuti. To guarantee a flow of tax rebates he brought in as a partner the big São Paulo engineering company, Villares. Vilela recalled the early days with nostalgia:

> There were few people in the region when I arrived. Those who were there were migrants from Maranhão and the north-east. They were subsistence peasants, living in a closed economy, with little contact with the outside world. I remember their astonishment when we brought in the first tractor. They all gathered around in amazement when it was stationary, but ran off scared when I revved up the engine.

Vilela carried on much as though he was farming rich soil in São Paulo state, planting guinea grass without bothering about legumes or fertilisers. He sprayed defoliants to kill weeds. At first, the grass grew well and he brought in his first cattle. 'Can you imagine it? There were people in the region who had never seen cattle. I remember a woman looking at us with horror when she first saw us milking a cow. She had brought up all her children without even knowing what cows' milk was.'

Visitors to the ranch appear to have realised before Vilela that very serious problems were arising. Mark Hutton, a leading Australian agronomist, visited the ranch in April 1973. Shocked by what he saw, he wrote a letter to Luiz Dumont Villares, a member of the family owning the engineering group in São Paulo. In this letter (of which we obtained a copy) he expressed particular alarm at the use of defoliants: 'I regard as tragic the widespread spraying of defoliants as it will set back the use of improved legume-grasses by 20 years or more.' He warned that, unless this practice was stopped and legumes planted, the useful life of the pastures would be reduced to five or ten years.

This advice was not taken, but Vilela soon discovered the truth of the agronomist's gloomy predictions. When we saw him in 1975 he told us ruefully that very serious problems were emerging: 'A cattle ranch up there is like marriage. It all goes well the first year or two but then the problems begin.' He told us that the pasture was deteriorating at an alarming rate, with bush invasion, soil leaching and weeds. He felt sure that the land could still be saved, but that the whole process would be very expensive. 'With the high price of fertilisers and sprays and the low price of beef, we just cannot afford this level of investment'.

When we went back to see Vilela in 1979, he was a broken man. The state of the ranch had gone from bad to worse and he had been forced out. For a while Villares had tried to recoup the farm under new management, but finally had decided to put it up for sale. Not surprisingly, there were no takers.

Part of the blame for the failure of men such as Vilela should be placed on the government which encouraged the ranchers to move into the alien habitat of the Amazon but then provided no guidance as to farming techniques. Many of the ranch managers complained to us of the hit-and-miss methods they were forced to adopt under pressure from the company in the south to set up the ranch as quickly as possible.

The confusion which existed in the early days over the best way to clear the land was typical. When we visited the Amazon for the first time in the mid 1970s, many of the big companies were moving away from the traditional slash-and-burn method of jungle clearance. Instead, they were using machinery or chemical defoliants. Particularly popular at that time was the *correntão* (big chain) method, in which a huge 100-metre chain, usually an old anchor line, was pulled by two giant imported tractors, usually supplied by the Japanese company Komatsu. It was an awesome sight to watch these tractors crawl through the forest, toppling all in their path including 100-foot high trees. With this system, an area which would take 200 men a month to get through could be cleared in just a few days.

As the managers told us that to clear the land with the *correntão* was twice as expensive as using manual labour, we were perplexed at first as to why some of the big ranches preferred this system. Amílcar Rodrigues Gameiro, at that time manager of Codeara, a large ranch near Santa Teresinha, gave us one reason: 'In the early days, 200 or even 300 of the 600 labourers working on the ranch were at times down with malaria. How can you draw up a work schedule with this kind of instability? It created a real crisis in our planning.' Other ranch managers told us that the *correntão* cleared all the vegetation, including the tallest trees, so that it was possible to produce neat pasture. In constrast, the labourers left the land dotted with huge, charred trees and rotting tree trunks which made it very difficult to work. Many of the ranch managers felt that the employment of illiterate, unskilled labourers belonged to an early, primitive stage, which should be eliminated with the progressive modernisation of the ranch. In 1981 Volkswagen produced a glossy publication in English about its ranch in which it stated:

Between 1974 and 1975, close to 9,000 hectares of vegetation were cleared. The entire manual effort required the services of 900 men. There were periods during which many of them had malaria and consumed the quinine stocks. The following year, as the disease lost its force due to preventive medicine, the machete was substituted by the motor saw, which in turn was replaced by the large machines of today.

However this simplistic idea of progress is not always accurate. It has been shown that in many parts of the Amazon the more sophisticated techniques for clearing the jungle are not the most efficient in the long term. Suzanne Hecht, a US soil scientist who has carried out research in the Amazon, told us that the dangers of compaction increased with machine-clearing, because of the much greater upheaval in the soil, particularly if very heavy tractors were used. She said that soil compaction, which led to the formation of brittle, barren clods of earth, was probably the most serious ecological threat in the Amazon.

Her remarks were supported by Paulo de Tarso Alvim, a well-known Amazon expert. He told a local newspaper in 1979 that the managers at Jari – the huge farming and mining complex set up north of the Amazon river by the US millionaire Daniel Ludwig – had been forced to give up using the huge, 80-tonne tractors it had brought in to clear the land.[16] Though the tractors had done the job efficiently, he said, they had compressed the soil so firmly that virtually nothing would grow on it. Ironically Jari, which had come to symbolise modern, foreign development in the region, had been forced to revert to the traditional slash-and-burn method.

The ranches also experimented with chemical defoliants, particularly Tordon, which was sold by the US company Dow Chemical and contained Agent Orange, obtained cheaply from the huge stocks left over from the Vietnam War. Tordon was extremely powerful and rearers complained to us during our first visits in the mid 1970s about its heavy residual impact in the soils. They said that it made it impossible for them to plant legumes for several years afterwards. As far as we knew, no investigation was made at that time into the harm caused by this defoliant to the soil and possibly to the inhabitants of the region. Workers, who were applying Tordon to individual plants from huge canisters strapped to their backs, complained to us on several occasions that they felt sick after working with it for several hours. After a few years, Dow Chemical withdrew this defoliant from the market and replaced it with a milder version, also marketed under the brand name of Tordon. Some rearers then complained that the new version was ineffective; one farmer even threatened to sue Dow Chemical for misleading its customers in its advertising material.

The government's failure to provide the ranches with technical assistance, or even to supervise their activities despite the large sums of public money invested, clearly increased the failure rate. As many ranches began to face serious problems of bush invasion and soil leaching, it seemed to some that the region was on the verge of serious ecological disaster. Goodland and Irwin, for instance, wrote: 'The Amazon forests are being swiftly obliterated and the exposed land subjected to preposterous abuse for derisory short-term gains, which will rapidly be supplanted by desperate, long-term problems. This is a frightening prospect . . . '[17]

After visiting many ranches, we shared much of these authors' concern. It seemed ludicrous to us that the Amazon jungle, with its rich abundance of largely unknown flora and fauna, could be destroyed merely to increase beef production. We became increasingly apprehensive about the long-term impact of the destruction of the forest on both the local ecology and world climate. We became strongly opposed to the cattle boom which the government had been promoting. Yet, after talking to agronomists, we did not share Goodland and Irwin's conviction that cattle-farming was necessarily doomed to failure in the Amazon. Though by the mid 1970s some of the ranches appeared to be beyond recovery, we felt that many of the rearers had brought the problems upon themselves: either through ignorance or negligence. If they had been prepared to invest – and to invest heavily – many of the difficulties could have been avoided.

According to Suzanne Hecht, the cattle companies' first error had been to permit over-grazing. She told us that the pastures in the region could generally support only 0.8 animals per hectare, which is an extremely low ratio. Their next mistake, she said, was to fail to preserve and enrich the pasture.

Colonião (guinea grass), which is the most popular grass in the region, grows exceptionally well during the first two or three years, producing about 24,000 kilogrammes per hectare per year. However, this grass rapidly sucks the nutrients from the soil and, unless preventive measures are taken, yields fall off dramatically to about 5,000–10,000 kilogrammes per hectare in the fifth and sixth years. Hecht said that there was a solution: to fertilise with slowly soluble phosphates, sulphur, potassium and micro-nutrients, and to grow legumes along with the guinea grass. Legumes are able to absorb nitrogen from the air and are thus a cheap and natural way of increasing the nutrient content of the soils.

Her suggestion, which is gradually winning acceptance from the rearers, was to take advantage of native legumes. We discovered later that a few of the more imaginative farmers, such as Hildebrando de Campos Bicudo, had already worked out this solution for themselves. The first brush that sprouts after the jungle has been cleared is made up of about 30 or 40 per cent legumes. It is only after repeated burnings that a more spiny vegetation which contains only about 5 per cent legumes becomes dominant. Hecht recommended farmers to make a selective cut of this first brush so as to leave many of the native legumes, which would be readily eaten by the cattle and would greatly help to maintain the nutrient content of the soils. The drawback, from the rancher's point of view, is that it limits their use of defoliants to rid the pastures of weeds. While defoliants do little harm to guinea grass, they kill legumes, along with the weeds. This means that to save the legumes the ranchers cannot carry out indiscriminate application of defoliants from planes. At most, they can go on with the manual application of defoliants, with labourers picking out individual weeds to be destroyed.

Hecht's experiments suggest that, if the pastures were carefully handled, their quality could probably be maintained. However, the cost of these measures is high, particularly as fertilisers still have to be brought up by lorry from the distant south-east of the country. Moreover, the quality of the pasture on some ranches is now so poor that it would be prohibitively expensive to bring the ranch back into order. Though technical solutions are being found for the problems, it is likely that ranches will continue to be abandoned over the next few years, simply because the companies are unwilling – or unable – to make the heavy investment required for recuperation.

In the mid 1970s, the price of beef in Brazil and abroad did not merit this high investment. As a result, it gradually became clear to government officials that most of the companies were only maintaining their ranches because of the heavy influx of government funds and the hope that land appreciation would eventually turn the ranches into valuable properties. It was becoming increasingly evident that cattle-rearing was not creating a solid base for sustained economic growth in the region.

Paradoxically, the fact that many of the ranches have turned out to be financial disasters may mean that the forest – or part of it – will survive, for the time being at least. If the ranches had proved great money-spinners, the pace of destruction would have accelerated and the worst fears of the ecologists would have been realised. It was as if the jungle, horrified at man's mad escapade, had hit back in self-defence and created such ecological problems that many would-be devastators were scared off.

Yet the change in official policy occurred very slowly, largely because of the pervading climate of corruption which meant that it was in the best interests of all involved to turn a blind eye to the problems. The first serious difficulties began to appear in 1974 and 1975. By 1976 it was clear that some of the ranches were in dire trouble. Yet Sudam went on funding not only the well-administered and well-planned ranches but also some of the most neglected farms. The ranches set up by the group headed by José Augusto Leite de Medeiros are a case in point.

From June 1967 to October 1971, Sudam authorised tax rebates worth £3.7m for the seven ranches set up by this group along the northern bank of the Tapirapé river in the extreme north-east of Mato Grosso: Tapiraguaia – Crs 2.5m (£383,000 at the exchange rate of that time); Tapirapé – Crs 3.1m (£475,000); Porto Velho – Crs 6.2m (£950,000); Sapeva – Crs 6.2m (£593,000); Frenova – Crs 4.5m (£492,000); Piraguassu – Crs 7.0m (£483,000) and Codebra – Crs 3.7m (£312,000). Three of these ranches were later sold by the Medeiros group to other companies: Tapirapé to a São Paulo bank, Banco do Noroeste; Porto Vehlo to a São Paulo fertiliser company, IAP; and Piraguassu to the São Paulo subsidiary of a Japanese engine manufacturer, Yanmar.

From 1974 to 1976, Sudam authorised reformulated projects with further tax rebates for five of these ranches: Frenova – Crs 26.2m (£1.5m); Sapeva – Crs 23m (£1.3m); Codebra – Crs 15.9m (£900,000); Tapirapé – Crs 27.1m (£1.5m); and Piraguassu – Crs 50.1m (£2.7m). This brought the accumulated value of the tax rebates to £10.6m.

In 1976, all seven ranches were visited by a team from the government's research group INPE. In a special project, INPE selected an area in the north-east of Mato Grosso and attempted to identify the Sudam-backed ranches located there from the images of deforested land that it received from the Landsat satellite in its research centre in São José dos Campos in the state of São Paulo. It then sent in a team to check the satellite information and to obtain additional information. It is possible to use their results to assess the development of these ranches.

The ranches together covered 336,055 hectares, an area the size of Shropshire. As they had all been set up between 1967 and 1971, they should have been well underway by 1976. Yet, between them, they had only cleared 30,404 hectares of land and planted 24,020 hectares of pasture. They had altogether 44,860 head of cattle and provided just 267 permanent jobs. Moreover, the quality of the cattle was generally poor and, from the scant information that the team was able to obtain from the ranch managers – five of whom had only had primary education – it seemed that the ranches were being run on old-fashioned, unproductive lines. There was no indication that the ranches were about to overcome a difficult, initial phase and greatly increase their productivity. On the contrary, it appeared from a few cautious remarks in the report that some of the ranches could expect more serious problems in the future with the further degradation of the pasture.

Yet, despite this, Sudam continued to support these ranches. Three of them – Tapirapé, Codebra and Sapeva – were given authorisation for a further reformulated project in 1977 or 1978. This added a further £3.4m (Tapirapé – Crs 60.3m [£1.9m]; Codeara – Crs 23.9m [£580,000]; and Sapeva – Crs 39m [£947,000]) to the total government support, bringing it to £14m. By almost any standards, the government was obtaining a very poor return on its investment.

The poor results obtained on these ranches do not seem to have been untypical. The INPE team was told by Sudam that there were 85 of its ranches in the region under study, yet it was unable to locate 13 of them on its satellite pictures. The INPE team did not follow up this discrepancy, as it lay outside the terms of reference of its research project. It is possible that a few of the omissions stemmed from technical problems with the satellite pictures. Yet, as one of the researchers admitted to us, it seemed probable that most of the ranches could not be located simply because they had made so little progress that nothing showed up on the satellite pictures.

The INPE team obtained detailed information on forest clearance from 31 of the ranches it visited. It found that by the time of the visit, 19 of them had carried out less than half of the clearance work that they should have done in accordance with the timetable they had presented to Sudam. Moreover, they discovered that on many ranches the pasture was not being cared for adequately or used in the proper way. As a result, they calculated that on 90 per cent of the farms the pastures were being used to raise only 50–60 per cent of the number of cattle which they could have supported if they had been used properly. On average, the ranches had only 36 per cent of the number of cattle they should have had if they had kept to the projects they had presented to Sudam.

The cattle companies were also neglecting the commitment they had made to Sudam to provide primary schools for the children of their employees. The research team found that 77 per cent of the ranches had failed not only to provide their own school, but also to make arrangements so that the children on their ranch could study at a school on a neighbouring ranch.

Though little public attention was paid to the results of this survey, it may have contributed to the gradual awareness among government officials that their Amazon policy was not working out. A more important factor was probably the serious ecological problems which many of the ranches near Paragominas were facing. Though Sudam continued to pour money into unviable existing projects, it all but stopped approving new projects after 1976. By the late 1970s, it was giving the go-ahead for very few reformulated projects. By then it was convinced that only very big companies, such as Volkswagen and Liquigás, had the resources to solve the unexpectedly serious problems which were arising on the cattle ranches. But even with these, the government reduced its direct financial assistance.

The threat to the tropical forest did not disappear with the change in government policy. But the new, more cautious approach meant a reduction in the pace of destruction, which had reached a horrifying speed in the early 1970s.

The Move into Colonisation

With the running down of the tax rebates, many of the cattle ranches, particularly those headed by businessmen rather than farmers, began to look for other uses to which their large tracts of land could be put. Some were attracted to the successful experiences in land colonisation which had taken place. They gave the companies a chance to realise a quick – and very large – profit. Moreover, they were particularly appealing to companies which had a dubious claim over their lands and were anxious to establish firm *de facto* possession to pre-empt possible legal battles. One of the first to take advantage of colonisation in this way was Enio Pepino, who set up the Sinop project.

Sinop

Pepino bought an area of land beside the still unfinished Cuiabá– Santarém highway in the late 1960s. Taking advantage of the lack of

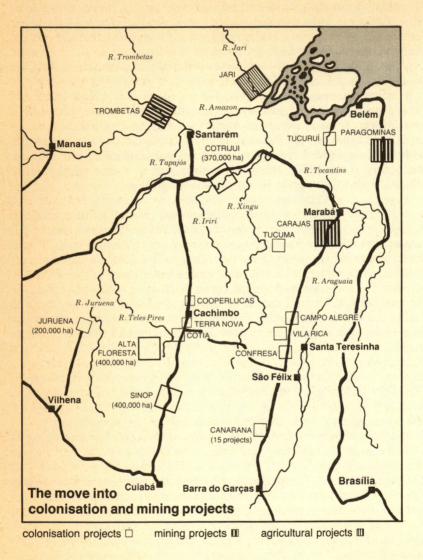

The move into
colonisation and mining projects

colonisation projects ☐   mining projects ▥   agricultural projects ▦

government supervision, he gradually incorporated into his estate areas for which he did not have land titles until he became the 'owner' of an enormous stretch of land, about 400,000 hectares in size. He initially decided to set up a colonisation project, selling off small plots of land to settlers because he knew that this would strengthen his claim to the land. A friend of his told us in confidence in 1979 that Pepino had calculated that if he settled enough families, he would be safe. He had realised, his friend said, that, if he did so, the government would be loath to move against him because if he were deprived of his rights to the land, the well-being of thousands of families would be put in jeopardy. It was an audacious gamble but it paid off.

His first company, Sinop Terras, was set up in 1973. A large number of people moved into the region buying plots from Pepino. More colonisation projects were set up as Pepino gradually took over more land that he did not own. Several towns were founded. In 1979, Sinop became a local district, with its own legally recognised separate administration and council. According to the 1980 census, the district had by then a population of 19,886, with 8,566 people living in the town itself.

Pepino did not rely solely on his *fait accompli* tactics, but was also careful to treat the authorities with the greatest respect. It has often been claimed, though never conclusively proved, that to oil the wheels of the government machinery and to avoid unnecessary problems Pepino bribed government officials. During our research at INCRA's headquarters in Brasília, we went through his file and found a letter, dated 25 March 1979, in which he most courteously requests Paulo Yakota, head of INCRA, for the land titles to Gleba Celeste, an enormous area of 2 million hectares beside the Cuiabá–Santarém. The letter amounts to an open admission from Pepino that he is not the legal owner of a vast stretch of land on which, according to INCRA's own statistics, he had by then settled 3,300 families. Though there is no record in the file, Pepino's request must have been granted, for his colonisation project became a showcase for the government. On 3 July 1980, Pepino received President João Baptista Figueiredo, five state ministers and the Mato Grosso governor at Sinop. It was the highest level group ever to have travelled to a project in the Amazon.

We visited Sinop in February 1979 and were impressed by the climate of enthusiasm and bustling growth. The vast majority of settlers had come from the south, mainly Rio Grande do Sul and Paraná where farming land had begun to run out. The project had not been the simple success story that one would infer from Pepino's own accounts. One of the earliest settlers told us: 'In the beginning it was difficult. The land in the region is not good and the subsistence crops we planted, without fertilisers, did not produce high yields. Many of the poorer settlers had to move out, selling up their plots for a song.' Some of them travelled further north along the Cuiabá–Santarém highway and settled precariously, without land titles, on more fertile soil in the extreme north of Mato Grosso or the south of Pará. The settlers told us that on the whole only families with some capital behind them, who could afford to use fertilisers, survived this first difficult stage.

Other businessmen, including some with Sudam-backed ranches, were quick to follow Pepino's example and, if not to move directly into colonisation, at least to reserve land which could later be used for this end. Like Pepino, many of these businessmen used their political and economic leverage over the authorities to obtain control over land to which they had no legal right, though not all were able to carry off the *coup* with Pepino's smooth assurance. Not surprisingly, the businessmen made their greatest efforts to gain possession of the rare stretches of very fertile lands such as those at Aripuanã.

Aripuanã

The rich lands of Aripuanã were originally occupied by Indians. According to Shelton Davis,[18] there were once about 100 Indian villages containing some 10,000 inhabitants in the area. The biggest groups were the Suruí and Cintas-Largas. None the less, in the early 1960s the Mato Grosso land department sold an area of over half a million hectares, some of it occupied by Indians, to peasant farmers. The farmers, who were given many years in which to pay for the land, were provided with provisional land certificates, perfectly legal documents to authorise occupation. In 1966, the state's land department was dissolved, but the continuing validity of its land titles was never questioned.

At the same time, mining companies began to send in gunmen to evict the Indians as rich reserves of cassiterite (the ore from which tin is extracted) had been discovered on their land. In 1963, a small plane was sent in to drop dynamite on one of the Cintas-Largas's villages. The incident, called the 'massacre of the eleventh parallel', became internationally known after a report by Norman Lewis in the *Sunday Times*.[19] The Aripuanã Indian Park was created in 1968, but it did not mean the end of the Indians' problems because the government did little to ensure that mining and colonisation companies respected the limits to this park. The numbers of the Indians declined throughout the 1970s.

Not even the peasant farmers were safe. Acting under pressure from large landowners who had become aware of the economic potential of the rich Aripuanã soil, and probably in his own interest too, state governor José Fragelli suddenly announced in early 1973 that the titles supplied by the defunct land department were no longer valid. A few months later, on 3 December 1973, he passed law 3,458 which made it obligatory for the state government to sell at Crs 50 (£3.45) per hectare 'public lands considered excessive'.

Armed with this outrageous new legislation, Fragelli formed a new land department and arranged for the sale of two million hectares to four large companies. The beneficiaries included Juruena Empreendimentos, owned by João Carlos de Souza Meirelles, which bought 200,000 hectares, and Indeco, a colonisation company set up by Ariosto da Riva, which bought 400,000 hectares. According to rumours at the time, Fragelli also managed to annex another 45,000 hectares to his own ranch, Taboco, by means of the new law. One of the arguments used by the government to justify the extremely low price was the condition in the contract that the new owner should set up a project on his land within five years despite the difficulty of access. It was thus argued that the large companies would be forced to carry out heavy investments in infrastructure and thus develop the region much more quickly than if the occupation was left to the small farmers.

The offensive against the peasant farmers at the legal level was backed up with tough practical measures. In early 1974, patrol platoons, each consisting of 32 specially trained men from the state's military police, were formed. According to a newspaper report at the time, Major Euro Barbosa, head of the state's military police, said:

> The main function of these platoons will be to protect the large properties in the north of the state, particularly Aripuanã, which have been bought by businessmen from the south. Many of these have been invaded over the last few weeks by peasant families arriving in search of land.[20]

On another occasion, the major said that the platoons represented 'the right of the state to protect its own lands and private property'. Reflecting the dominant attitude among the state authorities at the time, he described the 'invaders' as 'no more than land squatters who want to occupy illegally land that does not belong to them'.[21] The idea of the formation of these platoons is attributed to Gabriel Muller, president of Codemat, the state government's land company. He openly stated: 'The task of these platoons is to evict all those who wish to settle illegally in the Amazonian part of the state of Mato Grosso.'[22] As so often happened, some members of the Catholic Church had a different version of events. According to them, the platoons were being used on a large scale to evict peasant families who had been living for years in the region, both those with the old provisional land titles who were refusing to move out, and others who had been living on their plots for decades.

The new legislation, so clearly devised to benefit a few powerful groups, was too blatant to last long. The deal attracted the attention of the national press and became known as the 'Aripuanã scandal'. José Garcia Neto, who took over as state governor from Fragelli in March 1975, did not want his administration to be associated with the malpractices of the earlier government. He commented in September 1975: 'Government legislation should not force anyone, not even the state, to sell its land, much less at ridiculous prices which greatly damage public interest.'[23] Garcia Neto revoked the law but, significantly, respected the sales which had been made under it and took no measures to pay compensation to the evicted peasant families.

After this turbulent start, Ariosto da Riva, one of the key businessmen in this occupation story, was able to achieve an old wish and finally set up his own colonisation project, Indeco. Indeco was destined to become one of the most important projects in the region. Da Riva, the son of poor Italian immigrants, is another of the Amazon's self-made men. His father earned a living as a bandleader in a small town in the interior of the state of São Paulo. Da Riva left home when he was 18 years old to earn money to help bring up his younger brothers and sisters. Like nearly all of Brazil's self-made men, he belittles his achievement. He told us: 'If you are determined and prepared to work hard, it is not difficult to make money in Brazil. There are so many opportunities.'

In the beginning, da Riva led a rough, nomadic life as a *garimpeiro*, searching for semi-precious stones in Bahia, Piauí and Espiríto Santo, and for diamonds in Minas Gerais. And, unlike most prospectors, he apparently made quite a lot of money. Later he turned to land settlement schemes. 'All my life I've enjoyed founding new towns', he said. He worked for Geremia Lunardelli on several projects, including the setting up of Naviraí in the south of Mato Grosso. In the early 1970s, da Riva made a considerable amount of money through land deals in the Amazon, including the Suiá-Missu ranch about which more is said later.

By the time he set up Indeco, da Riva was a wealthy man and could have delegated the work, but he chose to become involved in the day-by-day running of the project. His excitement over all the new developments in the region was contagious. When we spoke to him in 1979, he said that the key to the success of his project was the quality of the land, for it formed part of the narrow band of rich, structured soils which spans Brazil from Rondônia through Mato Grosso and Pará to Maranhão. 'With the quality of these soils, how can we fail?', he asked. By then, the project was well underway. His company, Indeco, in which two sons and two sons-in-law were employed, had constructed a 180-kilometre access road to the Cuiabá–Santarém highway. Two towns – Alta Floresta and Paranaitá – were being built. About 1,500 families had already moved in and another 1,500 were expected to travel there later in the year.

Da Riva was very confident. He told us that by 1984 there would be about 200,000 living in the region and that Alta Floresta, with a population of about 50,000, would have become one of the state's leading towns. He predicted that by then exports of agricultural products from his project alone would be worth an amazing US$500m a year. 'I believe that I am acting as the fuse which will set off an explosion of growth and prosperity in the heart of the Amazon forest', he said.

Though most of the settlers to whom we spoke during our rapid visit in 1979 were well satisfied, many said that the going had been difficult in the beginning. They said that Indeco's prices were high and the company was rigorous in demanding payments on time. We learnt that a few of the settlers, nearly all of whom came from São Paulo or Paraná, had had to sell up and move out.

By 1982, the project was doing very well, though da Riva's goals had not been achieved as quickly as he had anticipated. A third town, Apiacás, had been founded. Alta Floresta itself had become a district in 1980 and had reached a population of 23,113 according to the census carried out that year. By the beginning of 1982 the settlers had planted 32 million coffee bushes and 10 million cocoa trees. Many of the farmers had begun to plant *guaraná*, the berries of which are used to make a popular soft drink which is selling well abroad. However, the settlers had had their problems. They spoke badly of Ceplac, the cocoa research institute, which, they said, had provided them with very poor technical assistance. They said that it had given them diseased banana trees to grow between their cocoa trees for shade, and another type of tree that did not grow tall enough to provide adequate shade. In the end Indeco itself had set up its own research unit to help the cocoa-farmers.

Indeco had ambitious plans. By early 1982 a small hydroelectric station was being built on the Apiacás river. With the new cheap energy, Indeco was planning to set up agro-industrial projects in Alta Floresta. Indeco had begun to sell off a further 200,000 hectares for cattle-farming. This land had been divided into 1,000-hectare plots and Indeco was charging on average Crs 40,000 (£163) per hectare.

By 1984, the region was expanding rapidly. Alta Floresta itself had a population of 45,000 and was still growing. Fernando Antônio Vieira, Indeco's sales manager, said in July 1984 that, despite their efforts, they could not keep up with the demand for plots. 'We're even having *garimpeiros* [gold-panners] arrive here to invest the money they have made in a lucky find of a gold nugget in the purchase of a plot of land.' But as before, the main demand came from the families of small farmers in Paraná, Santa Catarina and Rio Grande do Sul, who could no longer find cheap plots in their state of origin. The birthplace of many of the new settlers was reflected in the name of one of the towns – Paranaitá.

By then Indeco had set up its own marketing company, called Caiabi Empresa Agro-Industrial Ltda, to help the settlers sell their produce. Vicente da Riva, one of Ariosto's sons and a director of Caiabi, said in July 1984 that the firm expected that year to earn about Crs 2.5bn (£1.2m) from the export of just four products – cocoa, coffee, *guaraná* and Brazil nuts. Although this is a considerable achievement for such a short period, it suggests that total exports in 1984 will fall very far short of the ambitious target established by Da Riva in 1979.

It is clear that, even if profit was not the main reason why da Riva set up the project, the undertaking had brought in a very good income. While he had bought this land at Crs 50 (£3.45) per hectare in 1973, he was selling it at Crs 6,000 (£120) per hectare in 1979 and Crs 300,000 (£150) per hectare in 1984. Even allowing for a substantial investment in infrastructure, that is a phenomenal profit. Da Riva said that in 1974 he had been offered Crs 320m (£18.2m) for this land, which had cost him only one thirteenth of that sum just a few months before. But his family had jointly decided to turn down the offer and go ahead with the project which they found challenging and rewarding. They also appear to have made a somewhat larger profit by developing it themselves.

The other beneficiaries of the Aripuanã deal did not make such rapid progress, though, like da Riva, they had all made an undertaking as part of the conditions of the sale to develop the land within five years. João Carlos de Souza Meirelles had done very little to set up Juruena Empreendimentos by the time the period ran out at the end of 1978. He was trying to avoid the expense of building his own access road by waiting for the completion of the new AR–I road, which, probably as the result of pressure from Meirelles himself, had been included in the Polamazônia programme.

We felt during the several long conversations we had with Meirelles that, unlike da Riva, he had no great driving passion to found his own town and to develop a region. Just as in the early days of the Sudam scheme, Meirelles had been quick to spot a good business opportunity and had bought up the land in Aripuanã because of the enormous profit eventually to be made. His main concern seemed to be to keep his own investment in the project to the minimum needed to maintain possession of the land. As a result, in early 1979 he hurriedly cleared a few hectares of land and built a few huts, which was enough to convince the government that he would eventually be going ahead with the project.

Cotriguaçu, a huge but badly managed cooperative from Iguaçu in Paraná in southern Brazil, which had bought one million hectares of this controversial land, made no similar symbolic effort. Though the government could therefore have reclaimed this land, it was loath to move against the cooperative as it was a powerful political force with 30,000 members, most of them well-to-do soya bean farmers. Though Cotriguaçu was running out of land in Paraná, it had neither the resources nor the will to invest in the 700-kilometre access road required to open up the project.

After lengthy negotiations, a solution was finally reached. In June 1982, the national monetary council, the federal government's main decision-making body in the economic sphere, came up with a highly favourable package for Cotriguaçu: it cancelled Crs 1.64bn (£5.5m) of its debts, rescheduled another Crs 2.03bn (£6.8m) and made an additional loan of Crs 1bn (£3.3m) to provide it with working capital. The timing of the announcement was conveniently fixed, five months before the elections, to allow the government to gain maximum political advantage. The cooperative then contracted three experienced colonisation companies – Indeco, Juruena (a surprising choice, perhaps, in view of its own poor record) and Andrade Gutierrez, a big Rio de Janeiro construction company which is setting up its own colonisation project in Pará – to run the colonisation project. Cotriguaçu has remained the owner, but its only contribution in practice is to provide the settlers.

Now that the legal problems have been sorted out, this project is likely to become one of the largest in the Amazon. About 15,000 families should be moving in over the next decade. There will be no shortage of takers, as Cotriguaçu has 35,000 members, four-fifths of whom own plots of less than 20 hectares. For each hectare the family sells in Paraná, it will be able to buy at least 50 in Aripuanã. About 5,000 of Cotriguaçu's members lost their land in 1981 and 1982 with the construction of the reservoir for the huge Itaipu hydroelectric power station which has been built jointly by the Brazilian and Paraguayan governments on the border between the two countries. Many of these families have expressed interest in moving north to Aripuanã.

In their different ways, Enio Pepino, Ariosto da Riva and João Carlos de Souza Meirelles were quick to realise the great potential of Amazon land for colonisation projects. Other businessmen only moved into this area of activity a few years later, when the cattle ranches were facing their first serious problems. Paradoxically, some of these businessmen were brought into land colonisation by an ex-Lutheran minister, Norberto Schwantes, for whom many of them were later to feel great hostility. They were initially attracted to Schwantes because of the great success with which he developed his first colonisation project, Canarana.

Canarana

In the early 1970s, Norberto Schwantes, still a practising minister, set up Canarana, the first colonisation project to be established by a cooperative in the Amazon region, in response to social problems which had arisen 2,500 kilometres away. In 1971, Schwantes was working in Rio Grande do Sul in the extreme south of Brazil and became deeply concerned about the poverty of the families in his parish. When we spoke to him in 1979, he recalled that there were 5,360 families farming in the tiny district of Tenente Portela (99,000 hectares) where he lived. This meant that 80 per cent of them were farming plots of ten hectares or less in size. Every available scrap of land was used. Some of the families were ploughing the land by hand before planting soya beans and wheat, as no tractor could get up the steep slopes.

No radical, Norberto Schwantes did not organise a campaign to carry out a programme of agrarian reform within the state of Rio Grande do Sul – a solution advocated by some opposition politicians and some members of the Catholic Church. Instead, as in the case of the Transamazônica, a solution for a social problem was sought *outside* the region in question. His first plan was to set up a colonisation project in the Dourados region of south Mato Grosso where land was still cheap, at Crs 100–150 (£7–10) per hectare, as compared with Crs 1,000–2,000 (£70–140) in Tenente Portela. A scheme was drawn up to transfer 300 families and to supply each one with 100 hectares of land.

The project was presented to the Lutheran Church which had expressed interest in financing such a scheme. However, after more than a year of prevarication, the church finally turned down the plan as 'economically unviable', by which time the price of land in south Mato Grosso – a region which was being occupied extremely rapidly – had increased five- or six-fold. This mean that by then the land was far beyond the means of the small farmers and another scheme had to be worked out.

A new area was found, 300 kilometres to the north of Barra do Garças beside the precarious BR–158, the road leading to São Félix. The land was to be purchased from Fontoura Laboratórios, which, as we saw earlier, had pushed ahead with its cattle ranch against sound technical advice and was encountering serious problems. The land, known to be of poor quality, was going cheap, at Crs 40 (£2.75) a hectare.

Most of the cooperative members in Rio Grande do Sul were however, dissatisfied with this new solution. They felt that the new land was too far away and too isolated. They were reluctant to give up all public services and amenities, including hospitals and schools for their children, to move to a wild, remote region. At one stage, only 60 out of the 400 families remained in favour. But Schwantes pushed on with the scheme and in May 1972, the cooperative arranged to purchase 40,000 hectares of land from Laboratórios Fontoura to settle 80 families. The cooperative contracted a former INCRA employee, Sérgio Ludovico Bertoni, to run the project as its members had no experience of tropical farming. In August they managed to obtain a subsidised loan from the Bank of Brazil for the purchase. This was an unprecedented action by the bank which, because of the alleged high rate of risk, had never before agreed to finance a private land settlement project.

The first 40 families moved in in August and September 1972. These *gaúchos*, as people from Rio Grande do Sul are called, were very different from the local inhabitants, most of whom were illiterate migrants from Goiás, Maranhão and Ceará, used to the difficulties and isolation of life on the agricultural frontier. In contrast, many of the *gaúchos* were literate, accustomed to mechanised farming, and knowledgeable about such intricacies of modern life as bank loans. Furthermore, although poor, they were experienced consumers, used to buying a wide variety of goods from furniture to gas stoves and ready-made clothes. Though hard up and thus excluded from the world they wanted to enter, they were never the less firmly imbued with modern consumer values. The *gaúchos* saw the initial rigours of their life as pioneer farmers as a phase that had to be endured but which would pass. In contrast, for the migrants from the north-east the isolation, the primitive conditions and the lack of medical facilities were permanent, a part of their way of life.

We visited the project, called Canarana, towards the end of 1976. We were impressed by the progress that had been made in four years. There were by then 500 *gaúcho* families in the area. With the support of the cooperative, they all had access to bank loans and were purchasing tractors and other farm equipment and fertilisers. The landscape of the region was changing quickly with the cutting down of the shrubland and the planting of dry-land rice. Although the quality of the soil was poor, yields were fairly high, thanks to the use of fertilisers.

By then the settlers had fine wooden houses, gas stoves, furniture, schools and fairly good medical assistance, so they enjoyed recalling the first few tough months that they had spent in the region. We spoke to Margarida Zeich, a 25-year-old woman who called out to her two children in an archaic form of German. Like many of her neighbours, both she and her husband were blue-eyed and fair-haired descendants of German immigrants who arrived in the south of Brazil in the mid 19th Century. Though they had never left Brazil, they considered themselves almost as much German as Brazilian.

Sitting comfortably on a sofa in the living room and sipping maté tea from a *chimarão* (a special little teapot from which you suck with a metal straw) in true *gaúcho* fashion, she told us what it was like in the beginning:

> We were the third family to arrive, in August 1972. We spent a fortnight in our lorry travelling the 2,500 kilometres from Tenente Portela. There was no proper road the last 100 kilometres, just a rough track across the shrubland. I was feeling quite scared, clutching my two-year old son, César Icarus. We were jolting up and down so much that more than half the eggs we were carrying got broken. Believe it or not, we crossed 45 bridges in that last stretch. Nearly all of them were just two rough planks across the stream. My husband had a lot of trouble manoeuvring our lorry over them. When we finally got here, we then had to build ourselves a hut before we could go to bed. It was a pretty simple shack, I can tell you – just a tarpaulin stretched over four poles. We spruced it up a bit the next day. And that was our home for the next five months while we settled in.

Margarida said that her mother had been very concerned and had warned her: 'Going up to the Amazon with a young child, you're mad. Just think of the heat, the snakes, the mosquitoes and the piranhas.' Margarida laughed:

> Life was tough in the beginning, but not in the ways my mother imagined. The climate here is in fact better than in Rio Grande do Sul. It's warm, but not stifling hot. What worried us most in the beginning was the lack of transport facilities. The nearest airstrip was 140 kilometres away. And it took more than 30 hours to get to the nearest hospital by road. I was constantly worried that César Icarus would become seriously ill, or that I would have some problems during my second pregnancy. There were numerous minor discomforts too – no running water, no electricity, no new supply of Calor gas when the bottle ran out and so on.
>
> But for us, it has all been worthwhile. We have 460 hectares of land and we are buying a tractor and other equipment with bank loans. Up to the present, we have just cultivated rice which is a good reliable crop that grows well anywhere. But next year we are going to diversify into more profitable products, such as maize and soya beans. It's certainly hard going, but things are working out.

Some of the farmers told us of their concern about the size of their debts. They were afraid that, despite their hard work and the high yields they were obtaining on their farms, they might not have enough money to pay back their bank loans. They said that they were worried for many reasons: the low price of rice on the domestic market, the heavy freight charges they had to pay, the crops they lost because lorries got stranded on the rough earth roads which became impassable during the rainy season, and so on. Some of the farmers blamed the cooperative, which, they said, had unwisely encouraged them to take out very big loans.

None the less, we left the project in 1976 feeling optimistic. We felt sure that, despite the problems, the very determination of the settlers would make the project succeed. We spoke to Schwantes in Rio de Janeiro in early 1977 and he said that, when he went back to buy more land at the end of 1972, the price had already doubled to Crs 80 (£5.50) a hectare. By the end of 1976, it had increased to no less than Crs 1,400 (£65.85) a hectare, but Schwantes still considered it fairly cheap. By then he had purchased 360,000 hectares and was setting up seven more colonisation projects in the same region. 'We have made no effort to publicise the projects, but there are thousands of peasant families anxious to get away from the overcrowded conditions in the south. The demand seems insatiable.' By the beginning of 1977, about 500 families had been brought up from the south and there were plans to move up a further 500.

Schwantes was very excited by the prospects for more colonisation projects. He thought that many new opportunities were opening up because the Sudam cattle companies were facing such problems of soil leaching, inadequate transport facilities and shortage of skilled labour. He said that he had been talking to some of the companies, showing them how they could solve many of their problems if they sold a third or a quarter of their land to him to set up a colonisation project. He added:

> My most telling argument is to point to the rapid appreciation of the remaining land in the ranch, as a result of the improvements brought into the region by the settlers from southern Brazil. My experience suggests that within two or three years land values will reach a level that would have taken 15 years or more without the colonisation project.

He said that for once there appeared to be no conflict between a good business deal and social justice. 'This may be Brazil's only chance to resolve a pressing social problem in a painless way and at the same time to prevent the Amazon forest from becoming an enormous desert.' He was hopeful that, over the next few years, he could set up dozens of colonisation projects and bring thousands of small farmers up from the south.

At the end of 1976, Sérgio Ludovico Bertoni and Schwantes formed an independent company, Conagro, which, they hoped, would be the vehicle for setting up numerous colonisation projects all over the Amazon region. In their turn, the settlers in Canarana formed their own cooperative, Coopercana, which was to handle their immediate problems of technical assistance, farm inputs and marketing. Because of his earlier contribution and his administrative skills, Schwantes was elected president of Coopercana, despite his commitments elsewhere.

However, the future did not work out as either Schwantes or the settlers had envisaged. Some of the settlers faced near bankruptcy in 1979 and 1980, because of accumulated heavy debts with the banks. Though their crops were good, the low price of rice on the domestic market meant that they earned far less than they had anticipated. The settlers became very dissatisfied with Schwantes, whom they believed to be siphoning off money from their cooperative to help other projects in an even worse state, particularly Terra Nova. Some of the settlers even accused Schwantes of embezzling money for his own personal fortune.

In June 1980 the cooperative members voted Schwantes out of office as president of Coopercana and replaced him with Orlando Hoover. When I visited the region briefly in late 1981, the settlers were confident that the project would go from strength to strength under the new management. By then, 15 more colonisation projects had been set up. It was estimated that the new settlers had opened up about 700,000 hectares.

But once again events took an unexpected turn.[24] Most of the settlers had planted dry-land rice, a crop that they knew well from their farming experience in south Brazil. But the soil in this part of the Araguaia is not as rich as in their home state of Rio Grande do Sul. To cultivate it permanently on their new farms the settlers needed to use fertilisers. Many of the settlers knew this, but found that, with the high price of farm inputs, the price that they were receiving for their rice barely covered their costs, let alone allowed for an additional outlay on fertilisers. Oswaldo Masson, president of the agricultural workers' union in one of the new little towns, Nova Xavantina, complained: 'It is shameful that we only get Crs 2,500 (£5) for a 60-kilo bag of rice, yet we are paying out Crs 130 (£0.27) for a litre of diesel.' A few of the settlers tried to obtain subsidised Bank of Brazil loans to cover the outlay on fertilisers, but encountered serious bureaucratic problems. Most just hoped for the best.

In the event, the ecological problems turned out to be even more serious than they had feared. By 1983 the soil was exhausted and output on most farms had fallen sharply. Some families were forced to leave their plots. Others diversified into cattle-rearing, though the soil was not suitable for pasture either. The settlers estimated that, of the 700,000 hectares they had opened up, 250,000 had been abandoned, another 300,000 converted into pasture and only 150,000 were still used for crop farming. Many of the crop farmers had gone back to subsistence farming, hoping merely to cover the needs of their families. This ran completely against the original spirit of the cooperatives, which was to produce only market crops. It was estimated that fertilisers had been used on only 15,000 hectares.

The mayors in the little towns that had sprung up – Canarana, Agua Boa, Nova Xavantina and others – appealed to the settlers to stay, promising to obtain financing for fertilisers so that the soils could be replenished. Germano Zandona, mayor of Agua Boa, said: 'I'll do anything to keep the families here for another three years. By then, we should have managed to bring productivity back to its old level.'

Agronomists in the region agreed that it was possible to recuperate the soils, but said that heavy investment would be required. Ermeto de Cássio, from Coopercana, said: 'But it won't be enough to apply fertilisers. Farmers will also have to diversify into other crops beside rice. Soya, for example, is viable here.' Petrônia Aquino Sobrinho, from the Production Financing Company (CFP), added: 'Only those who are efficient, can run their farms properly and can obtain high levels of productivity will survive.' By then, the bigger farmers were beginning to buy up the land cheaply from the poorer settlers. It was the end of Schwantes's dream of reconciling social justice with capitalist farming.

The rift with the businessmen

Schwantes's other ventures also failed to work in the way he had confidently predicted when we spoke to him in 1976. His alliance with the businessmen lasted little more than a year. At the end of 1976, he and Bertoni formed Confresa with two businessmen mentioned earlier – José Augusto Leite de Medeiros and José Carlos Pires Carneiro – and some other business groups in São Paulo. As the first of what was planned to be a series of joint projects, Confresa bought 50,000 hectares near Porto Alegre in the north of Mato Grosso from the cattle company Frenova in which both Medeiros and Carneiro were directors. Confresa paid Crs 400–500 (£19–23.50) a hectare for the land.

However, after just a few months, the partners clashed and separated. Schwantes told us about it in Brasília in December 1978:

> We soon realised that Medeiros only wanted to absorb our know-how about colonisation projects to use it against the people. His only real interest was in making money, speculation. As we couldn't possibly get involved in something like this, we had no option but to pull out.

When we spoke to Medeiros in January 1979, he was less open about the reasons for the quarrel but hinted that Schwantes had made unreasonable financial demands. He said that he and Carneiro were carrying on with the colonisation project alone and would be setting up a town, Tapiraguaia, which would rapidly become one of the largest towns in the region. Medeiros said that they were already selling plots: 'We are fairly demanding in the type of settler we accept. We don't want subsistence peasants, but educated, modern farmers who will quickly learn how to cultivate crops like cocoa and coffee. We don't want failures.'

Most of the plots in Tapiraguaia were 400 hectares in size. Medeiros said that at a first stage only a relatively small number, about 60, would be sold. The land was not cheap, at about Crs 3,000 (£73), particularly as Confresa had paid only Crs 400–500 (£19–23.50) about 18 months before. 'We have invested heavily in infrastructure, setting up a school and a hospital', Medeiros explained.

Schwantes was sceptical about their chances of success: 'They don't know anything about setting up a town. It isn't easy. They won't succeed without us.' He said that Medeiros was hoping to make a great deal of money through the appreciation in the value of land around the town, Schwantes said that he had shown great interest in the way land prices had rocketed around Canarana. 'But for a town to act as a magnet, attracting well-to-do settlers, it has to be really well run and to be prosperous. I don't think that they can do this', he said.

In the event, while the Confresa project was not quite the disaster that Schwantes had predicted, it was by no means as successful as Medeiros had hoped. I visited it briefly at the end of 1981, by when about 70 families, all from Rio Grande do Sul, had been settled. Several of the families complained of the Confresa management, which, they claimed, had not provided the services it had promised. A few of the settlers told me that Frenova had collected bank loans for them and had then delayed for months before handing over the money. They said that in the meantime they thought that Frenova had speculated with the money on the financial market, which would have brought them a hefty profit given the extraordinarily high interest rate in Brazil. Despite the problems, most of the settlers said that they were making progress, thanks to their own hard work. The little town of Tapiraguaia was growing slowly.

However, much more was at stake in the conflict between Schwantes and Medeiros than the future of Confresa. As became clearer in 1979 and 1980, the two men stood for very different – and essentially irreconcilable – schools of thought over the way the Amazon should be occupied. Schwantes was completely indifferent to the fate of the thousands of peasant families who had migrated to the Amazon from the north-east. At times, it seemed that his lack of concern concealed a feeling of social – or even racial – distaste for the illiterate and impoverished peasant families. Yet, for all his shortcomings, he had provided hundreds of small farmers from Rio Grande do Sul with cheap land. Schwantes had great respect for the hard work and efficiency of the small farmers from the south and passionately defended their right to land in the Amazon. It was the small farmer who had given him his power base and whose interests he ultimately defended. Though he was prepared to form a tactical alliance with big landowners, he had no love of the unproductive *latifúndio* and did not believe that it should be allowed to proliferate in the Amazon.

On the other hand, Medeiros was a firm defender of big business. He told us on several occasions that the huge Amazon could only be tamed by businessmen who had at their disposal resources of comparable dimensions. Though he believed that small farmers from the south had an important role to play, he said that their part in the development process had to be coordinated under the umbrella of big business. He wanted the businessmen to be involved in – and to make money out of – every phase of the development process. In the last analysis Schwantes, who could successfully settle families on the land without the mediation of big business, represented a much more serious threat than INCRA, whose projects had almost always ended in failure.

The conflict between the two schools of thought blew up into a major conflict over government policy for the Amazon. One of the main issues was the destiny of the lands on either side of the Cuiabá–Santarém highway. The businessmen in São Paulo had had their eyes on this stretch of unusually fertile land (including Aripuanã) for several years. In 1976, João Carlos de Souza Meirelles, at that time president of the Association of Amazon Businessmen (AEA), had presented the government with a highly ambitious project under which the association would be responsible for the development of an enormous 10 million hectare area running for 100 kilometres each side of the Cuiabá–Santarém from the division between the states of Mato Grosso and Pará right up to the port of Santarém.

The association, which had become the main lobby for São Paulo businessmen with interests in the Amazon, proposed that the area be divided into 20 separate but interlinked projects each covering 500,000 hectares. These projects would cover many different activities: cattle-rearing, colonisation with big, medium-sized and small plots, forestry, agribusiness and so on. Meirelles told us in 1978 that, if his project got the go-ahead, it would within eight years create jobs for 3.2 million people and lead to the setting up of about 60 towns. By its fourteenth year, he said, the area would be producing goods worth £3bn. Meirelles made a point of stressing that only big private companies could successfully undertake a project of this size. 'Canarana was useful in its time', he said. 'It showed us the way. But cooperatives do not have the organisational structure nor the resources to carry out big projects.'

Schwantes and other people linked to his cooperatives vehemently opposed the businessmen's proposal. One of Schwantes's main allies was Colonel José Meirelles, commander of the 9th Engineering and Construction Battalion of the army when it built the Cuiabá–Santarém highway (and no relation to the businessman with the same surname). Colonel Meirelles was convinced that the government should use the vast empty space beside the Cuiabá–Santarém to solve some of the country's social problems. He said to us in 1979:

> This is the government's last chance to save the country. By resettling thousands of small peasant farmers along this road – which is one of the last empty fertile areas in Brazil – the government can prevent rural discontent from reaching boiling point. If not, these people will be all too easy prey for communist propaganda.

The colonel saw the colonisation of the Cuiabá–Santarém as part of a geopolitical strategy. He thought that the government should rebuild the BR–80 which runs from Cachimbo on the Cuiabá–Santarém to São Félix on the Araguaia river. This road, he said, had been built far too quickly and shoddily; but if it were kept in good condition small farmers from the south –

and even some from the north – could be settled along it 'to form a spearhead of prosperity and stability' as the first step in what he called the 'reconquest of the north-east of Mato Grosso', the region around São Félix. Largely because the authorities had failed to establish a firm presence in this pioneer region, he said, it had been lost to the 'communist' bishop Pedro Casaldáliga who had gained great sway over the local population. Because of the poor transport links with Cuiabá, this region had come to depend very heavily on the state of Goiás, so his strategy would also give the state government the additional boon of bringing the area back into its own sphere of government. Norberto Schwantes came forward with similar arguments:

> I can't believe that the government can give the go-ahead for a project like this. The speculation is just too obvious. The businessmen would make huge profits, while contributing little that others could not provide. If you let João Carlos de Souza Meirelles have his way, he'll gobble up all the Amazon.

The government procrastinated for several years over what to do with the lands on either side of the Cuiabá–Santarém. While it did not give the businessmen the go-ahead for their massive, integrated project, it allowed a few individual companies to move in. At the same time, Schwantes was praised for his work by some powerful sectors of the government. However, the latent conflict came to a head over a new colonisation project called Terra Nova.

Terra Nova

Given the government's tendency to use the Amazon region as a convenient safety valve to reduce social tension in other regions, it is no surprise that Terra Nova was created in response to a conflict over 2,500 kilometres away. In May 1978, the Kaingang Indians in the Nonoia reserve in the state of Rio Grande do Sul had attracted the attention of the national and international press. They had armed themselves with guns, spears and even bows and arrows and had burnt down buildings belonging to outsiders on their lands. A peasant farmer had been killed in the conflicts and the Indians had warned that others would die if they were not given back all their land.

This dramatic and violent action came at the end of a long history of government failure to resolve the Indians' serious problems. About two-thirds of the 14,910 hectares officially designated as their lands had been occupied by over 1,000 very poor non-Indian families, some of whom were even paying rent to Funai. Moreover, Funai had gone as far as selling to timber companies an area of forest land within the original limits of the Indians' reserve. This made it difficult for them to collect pine nuts, a traditional source of protein in their diet. As a result, the Indians' health had deteriorated markedly. A survey in the mid 1970s had shown that many suffered from tuberculosis, and that some of the children had muscular dystrophy, both being illnesses previously unknown.

The Kaingang had done all they could to win back their lands without resorting to violence. They had complained numerous times to Funai. They had written to the interior minister, to the President, to Congress. They had spoken to the settlers themselves. They had also warned the authorities that they were beginning to feel desperate. As early as 1975, a Kaingang woman had written a letter to the president of Funai in which she said:

> The blood of our people can no longer be contained in our veins, seeing our tiny reserves, the remains of eight million square kilometres of this our beloved Brazil, over which the Indian people had full dominion and right of occupation, being usurped by disorganised and destructive white people, disguised as farmers, but with the spirits of vandals. Today, my people see their lands invaded, their forest destroyed, their animals exterminated and their hearts lacerated by this brutal weapon that is civilisation.
>
> For the white and so-called civilised people this may seem like romanticism or something like it. But for our people, no. For us it is a way of life. It is our reason to live and therefore reason enough to die.

A few years later, a Kaingang man, called Candetê, said at an Indian conference:

> To tell the truth, the Indian has to risk his life to get the white man off his lands. Because it isn't just now that we are under attack. This has been going on for 15 years. The violence is continuous, nearly every month. We have to have some rights, some law that will protect the Indians.

As has happened in many other cases, Funai only moved swiftly after the outbreak of violence. With the death of the settler in May 1978, it arranged for 150 military policemen to be sent into the area to prevent further killings, and negotiated an agreement with the Kaingang by which the settlers were to be given one month to leave. The Kaingangs' victory played an important part in the emergence of a coherent inter-tribal movement among Indians in Brazil. It was yet another demonstration that the best way of guaranteeing their physical and cultural survival was through firm collective action, including the use of violence if necessary.

The evicted settlers were housed in an exhibition stadium near Porto Alegre, the capital of Rio Grande do Sul state, while the federal and state governments desperately looked for a solution. Rather than hand over the problem to INCRA, which clearly should have been entrusted with the resettlement of these families, the then interior minister, Maurício Rangel Reis, called in Norberto Schwantes for consultation. This move was in itself an admission by the government that it had no confidence in INCRA and yet further evidence of INCRA's fall from grace.

After talks with other Conagro officials, Schwantes agreed to resettle the small farmers on 100,000 hectares of land ceded by the army from a training area beside the Cuiabá–Santarém highway. Conagro was given a service contract in which it undertook to set up a cooperative, provide technical assistance and help the settlers in other ways to adapt to their new life. INCRA was called in to work out a fair price for the plots and to draw up a repayment scheme.

The arrangement was badly received by much of the press in Rio Grande do Sul, which believed that the solution to the problem should have been found within the state, through the expropriation of a few big estates. Like the earlier critics of Schwantes, some politicans and journalists claimed that the key issue – which they saw as the need for agrarian reform in the state – had been evaded by the government coming in from outside and magically transporting the farmers to another region thousands of kilometres away.

When Schwantes went to Rio Grande do Sul to talk over his proposal with the settlers, he found that very few of them were prepared to move to an entirely new region. It was only gradually – after Schwantes had had several opportunities to talk to them and it had become clear that the authorities were not going to offer any other solution – that most of them came round to accepting the move.

The first families arrived in August 1978. By the time of our visit in January 1979, 578 families had moved in. On one level the settlers had been given a good deal – the soil was fertile and initial studies by agronomists suggested that high yields would be obtained with such crops as coffee and cocoa. The settlers, most of whom were very poor, would be paying just Crs 1,000 (£24) per hectare of farm land, plus a contribution of Crs 178,000 (£4,340) to the cooperative. Both payments could be staggered over 12 years, with 5 years' grace. This outlay included all structural costs, such as road-building and fencing, and the clearance by tractor of a small area of each plot so that planting could be started quickly. It also paid for the establishment of a large collective forest reserve.

Schwantes told us in 1979 that this new colonisation project was different from the one at Canarana. There, he said, the settlers were better educated and, though not well to do, most had the resources to tide themselves over the initial difficult period and to make a down payment for some farm inputs, such as machinery and fertilisers. By contrast, he said, most of the settlers in Terra Nova were poor and illiterate (or semi-literate). The soil was rich, he added, but few of them had any idea of how to make good use of it.

Colonel José Meirelles was remarkably enthusiastic about the project when we spoke to him in 1979. He told us that a marvellous new town, also to be called Terra Nova, had been specially designed for the project by West German architects. Hermínio Ometto, owner of the large Cachimbo cattle ranch beside the project, had donated 2,000 hectares of land so that the town could be strategically situated on the crossroads between the Cuiabá–Santarém and the BR–80, the road which ran eastwards to São Félix. Colonel Meirelles said that Terra Nova was to be made up of a series of modules, each with 30 to 40 houses, which would radiate from the centre. Each module was designed to maximise green areas and to minimise pollution. As the town grew, new modules could be added.

The project was attractive in itself but quite divorced from the social reality of the Amazon region. It was designed as an answer to urban problems besetting heavily industrialised countries: overcrowding, lack of green areas, pollution, traffic jams. These concerns seemed bizarre, incongruous and above all irrelevant to the typical undernourished, impoverished Amazon family. The project was naively – but not for that reason less perniciously – Eurocentric.

We asked Colonel Meirelles what arrangements would be made for the poor migrant families who would be attracted like bees around a honey pot to the bustling centre of Terra Nova, if the project developed as he predicted, for it was clear that they would be unable to afford to buy their own plots. We were discouraged by his reply:

> They will have no place here. If forced to, we will build a satellite town for them and concentrate all our efforts on their children, to prepare them for a new world. Our project is not for the present generation but for their children.

The project had a strongly authoritarian flavour. Some of the Conagro officials said that the hierarchy and discipline were necessary because of the low cultural level of nearly all the settlers who, in their opinion, needed to be given firm guidance if the project was to be an economic success. We found it extremely difficult to talk freely to the settlers during our visit as Colonel Meirelles insisted on accompanying us everywhere. On the few occasions we managed to slip away, some settlers told us that they were unhappy with some aspects of the project. In particular they disliked the extraordinary shape of their plots – 200 metres by 5,000 metres – as it was so difficult to farm such elongated, thin strips of land. We were not convinced by Meirelle's explanation: that the bizarre shape enabled every settler to have an outlet on the road.

The directors foresaw a brilliant future for the project. Colonel Meirelles told us:

> Within 20 years, Terra Nova will be the second largest city in the state, after Cuiabá itself. Within a few years, large quantities of export products – coffee, cocoa, pepper, *guaraná* and who knows what else – will be cultivated on each side of the road. These products will be exported through the port of Santarém. Within four or five years the road will have to be asphalted. The government should already be building up Santarém as a manufacturing centre so that export lorries can take advantage of the ride back to bring in fertilisers, machinery and other farm inputs.

Terra Nova greatly exacerbated the tension between the cooperatives and the business community. At Terra Nova, the cooperative was charging Crs 378,000 (£9,220) for a 200 hectare plot of farm land at the beginning of 1979. Just 110 kilometres away in Alta Floresta, settlers were paying

Indeco Crs 1.2m (£29,270) for a plot of the same size. It was evident that, if Terra Nova were successful, it would provide the government with a much more equitable alternative to the businessmen's schemes and one which had the added attraction of helping to relieve social pressures elsewhere in the country.

Colonel Meirelles was well aware of the political issues at stake:

> This is the first time a cooperative has been given public land to develop. By successfully developing Terra Nova we are showing the government that not all socially-oriented colonisation projects are bound to fail like INCRA's. We are demonstrating that there exists an alternative to the businessmen's elitist, expensive projects, the only concern of which is to make as much money as possible. I have nothing against competitive free enterprise, but I do not believe that the allocation of land should be carried out on this basis.

However, Meirelles's optimism was premature. Although I did not visit the project when I went back to the region at the end of 1981, I heard what had happened. By the end of 1980, about 1,000 families had been brought in. The cooperative did not provide adequate support and some families had not even enough to eat. Though the businessmen kept a low profile, they made sure that government officials and journalists were well informed of all the problems. The news of the settlers' difficulties caused a furore in Rio Grande do Sul, where politicians and journalists claimed that the settlers had been very badly treated. José Augusto Amaral de Souza, the governor of Rio Grande do Sul, visited the project and then issued a firmly worded protest about the conditions.

Finally, in the middle of 1981, the federal government took discreet but firm action. Conagro was told that its services were no longer required and officials from INCRA and Sudeco took over the running of the project. The plans for the modular town were immediately scrapped and the plots redrawn. By the end of 1981, the project was reported to be making satisfactory progress, though some settlers appeared still to be facing serious financial problems.

The outcome in Terra Nova, partly caused by Conagro's mismanagement, strengthened the businessmen's hand in their negotiations with the government. Schwantes fell from favour and became involved in politics, joining the Partido Democrático Trabalhista (PDT), a small opposition party. Though the cooperative he founded at Canarana has not been adversely affected, he is unlikely to be setting up any more land colonisation projects.

The Compromise

However, the big companies did not obtain all that they were demanding. The government appears to have accepted tacitly some of the points made by Schwantes and Meirelles and to be trying to impose a compromise solution. In principle, it is encouraging cooperatives to set up projects in the more accessible areas beside the main roads, and the businessmen to move into more isolated areas, where heavier investment in infrastructure is required.

In practice, this arrangement is not working out particularly well, partly because Brazil's cooperatives do not have the flexibility to adapt successfully to Amazonian conditions. As we have seen, Cotriguaçu only recently got its project off the ground. Cotrijuí, the largest cooperative in Rio Grande do Sul and one of Brazil's largest grain producers, has been even less successful. INCRA sold it an area of 369,150 hectares beside the Iriri river near the Transamazônica in 1974. At Crs 64 (£3.60) a hectare, the land was cheap. However, some of the area was occupied by the Arara Indians, who began a long and violent struggle to defend their lands (see Chapter 5). Finally, in July 1980, Funai withdrew its authorisation for the colonisation project. Cotriguaçu is reported to be looking for an alternative area but no arrangement has yet been made.

Despite these difficulties, the government is still keen to attract cooperatives to the region. It has given its support to a special private consultancy company, Hecta, which was formed in 1980 to provide cooperatives with technical assistance for setting up land settlement projects in the Amazon. Hecta's first project has been with members of Holambra, a cooperative set up with Dutch settlers in Campinas in the state of São Paulo. Like many other cooperatives in southern Brazil, Holambra was anxious to expand but found local land prices exorbitantly high. For a while, it considered buying up land beside the Cuiabá–Santarém but in the end desisted. Some of its members, however, were keen to go ahead by themselves. They set up their own cooperative, Cooperlucas, but then found it difficult to find the capital to buy up a large tract of land. In the end, INCRA agreed to sell them a smaller area of land in the very north of Mato Grosso, along the Cuiabá–Santarém road. The first 51 families, each of which is buying 200 hectares, travelled to the region in 1982. Another 150 moved in during 1983. Hecta has been helping the new cooperative to get itself established legally and to set up a flexible administrative structure. In September 1982, Cooperlucas signed an agreement with INCRA to provide technical assistance to another 200 families who, like the settlers at Terra Nova, had been evicted from their plots in the Nonoia reserve of Kaingang Indians in the state of Rio Grande do Sul. These families are being re-settled by INCRA on plots very close to Cooperlucas's project.

A federation of cooperatives established by descendants of Japanese immigrants in Cotia in the state of São Paulo has also bought a large area of land beside the Cuiabá–Santarém. This area borders on Indeco's lands in Aripuanã. A manager from Indeco told me: 'Ariosto brought the Japanese into the region. If he couldn't go into this area himself, at least he was going to make sure that he had good neighbours.'

At the end of April 1982, Cotrisa, the second largest cooperative in Rio Grande do Sul, said that it would be setting up a colonisation project in the

Amazon. It said that it planned to cultivate perennial crops such as coffee and rubber on this project. It had taken this step, it said, to help its members break away from their present excessive reliance on soya beans and rice and to allow expansion, which had become difficult in Rio Grande do Sul because of the land shortage.

In the main, the cooperatives seem to coexist happily with the big companies. Unlike Schwantes, they do not have ambitious plans for the region, nor do they see themselves as an alternative to the businessmen. To a large extent, the two activities are complementary, with the cooperatives bringing in relatively skilled labour and the big companies providing some capital.

Though the businessmen complain of insufficient support from the government, they are gradually gaining the ascendancy in the region. Several more cattle companies have moved into land colonisation, while carrying on with cattle-rearing. Particularly notable is Campo Alegre, owned by the São Paulo engineering group Cetenco, which set up its colonisation project in the late 1970s. By 1981 the town of Campo Alegre in south Pará had 5,000 inhabitants. It is located on the BR–158, the road running from Barra do Garças in Mato Grosso to Marabá in Pará. The town gained a further boost at the end of 1982 with the opening of the Atlas meat-packing station. Several large ranches – Codeara, Suiá–Missu and others – may also set up colonisation projects shortly.

Andrade Gutierrez, Brazil's largest civil construction company, has had road-building and engineering activities in the Amazon since 1963. Though it has not moved into cattle-rearing, the company is now setting up a large colonisation project, called Tucumã, near São Félix do Xingu in Pará. After considerable delays, the company managed in 1982 to have Tucumã approved as part of the huge Carajás mining complex, making it eligible for substantial tax rebates. Unusually the company does not own the land, but has a service contract to set up the project on *terras devolutas*. Eventually about 3,000 families will settle at Tucumã, which covers an area of about 400,000 hectares. In 1981 the land was being sold at Crs 20,000–30,000 (£100–150) a hectare, with Andrade Gutierrez providing loans if required. Another unusual aspect of the project is the special arrangement to sell 10 per cent of the land to very poor families who cannot provide the initial down payment generally required.

Andrade Gutierrez has been accused by the Xicrin Indians of invading their lands to set up the colonisation project. Lúcio Siqueira, a doctor working with the Indians, told the press in 1980: 'If Andrade Gutierrez goes on clearing the land as it is at the moment, it will leave only a small plot for the Indians.' I was told in 1981 that a compromise solution had been worked out between the Indians and the company.

Unlike the cattle companies, the colonisation projects have been highly viable commercial undertakings. By taking advantage of the land shortage in other areas of Brazil, the colonisation companies have been able to sell plots of land for very high prices. However, their profit has been achieved through a merely financial transaction, not by putting the land to productive use. The real challenge of the occupation – which is to prove its economic viability through the success of its farming – has been almost completely transferred to the settlers. Though the going has been difficult at times and some families, particularly those with no capital behind them, have been forced to sell up, some of the settlers have begun to win the battle and establish themselves as successful farmers. This has been achieved through long hours of work in the fields and through endless lobbying of the local government bodies and political parties to achieve some improvement in the infrastructure, particularly roads.

The owners of the colonisation projects have established a firm distinction between the peasant families, towards whom they generally show considerable hostility, and the small farmers, mostly from the south of Brazil, to whom they sell plots of land. The latter have proved their credentials as good capitalists by being willing, unlike most peasant families, to pay for their land. In this way, the colonisation schemes play their part in reserving the land for capitalist farming.

Most of the colonisation projects go to considerable lengths to bar the entry of outsiders. Settlers at Indeco, Ariosto da Riva's colonisation project at Aripuanã, told us that a security check-point was staffed night and day at the only bridge over the river which has to be crossed to reach the project. No unauthorised visitors are allowed across the bridge.

How the Big Ranches have Fared

The shake-up in Sudam affected all the ranches, even the largest. After 1979 none of them had obtained authorisation for a further round of tax rebates, though they continued to receive the incentives negotiated earlier. Moreover, beef prices, which had been very high when most of the companies moved into the region, fell heavily, making it more difficult for the ranches to become profitable. The Amazon was no longer the treasure trove it had been in the early days.

As we have seen, some of the companies pulled out and others diversified into colonisation. But some, particularly the bigger companies, decided to carry on with cattle-rearing, at least for the time being. Developments on three big ranches – Volkswagen, Suiá–Missu and Codeara – are examined below.

Volkswagen
In 1973, the Brazilian subsidiary of the large West German car manufacturer, Volkswagen, decided to take advantage of Sudam's tax rebate scheme and move into cattle-rearing in the Amazon. With its large car plant in São Paulo, it was in a particularly good position to guarantee an adequate flow of rebates to the ranch.

Volkswagen bought 139,392 hectares of land in a remote part of the district of Santana do Araguaia in the extreme south of Pará. Much of the land was purchased from the Lunardelli group at Crs 160 (£11) a hectare. The ranch was called Vale do Rio Cristalino after the river which ran through the land.

When we visited the ranch in 1977, the team of enthusiastic young technicians running the farm was moving ahead at great speed. Forest land was being cut down and burnt, grass sown, cattle brought in – all this at a rapid pace and without adequate knowledge of the local conditions. One of the young technicians told us that he was well aware of the risk they were running. 'It could all work out well, or we could face serious ecological problems in a few years' time', he said.

Like the other ranches, Vale do Rio Cristalino used large numbers of rural labourers to cut down the forest in the early days. It also employed local inhabitants as cowhands. From all accounts, labour relations were not easy. In a booklet in English, published in 1981, Volkswagen gives a patronising account of its problems:

> The administration of personnel in a company like this, located in an extremely remote area, gives rise to problems never imagined before by those who live in the large urban centres. One of these refers to family structure. Cohabitation, the most common form of relationship in the region, in addition to causing the inevitable shocks, does not give the family stability necessary to settle men. As a result, Companhia Vale do Rio Cristalino encouraged the legislation of these de facto situations in view of the fact that, despite all the available leisure, the life of a single person is very difficult in the Amazon.

Despite the doubts of some of the technicians, the young manager, Mário Thompson, who had taken over the running of the ranch after his father's death in a plane crash, was very enthusiastic about the work which was being done and highly confident about the future. He told us that the herd of cattle, which at that time numbered 12,000, would increase to 111,000 by 1983, by when the ranch would be making a large profit.

It was clear from information I obtained from Volkswagen's office in São Paulo at the end of 1981 that the ranch was progressing, but not as quickly as Thompson had predicted. By then, the ranch had created 32,904 hectares of pasture, compared with 12,000 in 1977. It had 27,500 head of cattle, compared with 12,000 in 1977, and 267 registered employees, compared with 186.

But significantly, the company had revised its goals. Instead of the earlier plan of building up its herd to 110,000 by 1983, it told me that it intended to break even in 1985, with a herd of 86,000. Like many of the other companies, in the early days Volkswagen appears to have over-estimated the support capacity of Amazon pastures. Moreover, in a radical departure from its earlier position, the company said that it was planning to diversify into crop farming.

Volkswagen has also been the driving force behind a huge new meat-packing station, Frigorífico Atlas, situated near Campo Alegre ranch, about 70 kilometres away from Vale do Rio Cristalino. Volkswagen had earlier considered going ahead solely in association with the West German company Atlas, but had later decided that it would be more prudent politically to open the project to Brazilian groups. However, an agreement proved difficult to reach. In the first proposal, Volkswagen and Atlas suggested that they should hold a joint stake of 49 per cent in the share capital. It became clear that Sudam was unwilling to approve a project in which multinationals played such an important role. As tax rebates were to be the main source of capital, the proposal was reformulated to fit in with its requirements. Atlas pulled out as a shareholder, but agreed to supply the equipment. Volkswagen reduced its shareholding to 23 per cent. The rest of the voting capital was divided among 15 other companies, all of them with ranches in the region. They included Bradesco, Brazil's largest private banking group, which has several large ranches; Cetenco, a large construction firm from São Paulo which owns Porto Alegre ranch; Banco do Crédito Nacional, another São Paulo banking group which owns Codeara ranch; Supergasbrás, a large bottled gas distribution company; Xerox do Brasil; and Mappin, a large department store in São Paulo. After protracted discussions, this proposal was finally approved by Sudam in September 1978. Its tax rebates amounted to an enormous Crs 543.3m (£15.3m) out of a total planned investment of Crs 820.5m (£23.1m). Despite the change in share capital, the project retains a strong Germanic flavour, including a German managing director.

After successive delays, the project came on stream in late 1982. It started with a daily slaughter of 360 head of cattle, about 60 per cent of its full capacity. About a quarter of the cattle should come from the shareholders and the rest from other ranches in the neighbourhood. Many companies, which did not have a convenient outlet for their cattle, were very pleased by the opening of this packing station.

The packing station uses sophisticated equipment. As there is a chronic shortage of skilled labour in the region, intensive courses had to be carried out to train unskilled workers to do the jobs. When it is operating at full capacity, the packing station will employ about 700 people. It will produce about 53,000 tonnes of deboned meat, corned beef and meat extract each year. Full use will be made of by-products. An employee at Vale do Rio Cristalino told us that almost every part of the animal would be used to make something, from tanned leather to fertilisers. Annual turnover is expected to be about £70m.

The packing station is currently using firewood as its source of energy, but it will later switch to electricity when the region is brought on to the regional grid by Eletronorte, the state-owned electricity company. This is expected to take place in 1985 or 1986, using energy from the huge Tucuruí hydroelectric power station.

The packing station's running costs are high, partly because of the isolation of the region. As beef prices are still low, it is unlikely to make a profit in the foreseeable future. 'The short term doesn't exist for beef', said Karl Heinz Theuer, the packing station's managing director, to the São Paulo business newspaper *Gazeta Mercantil* in April 1982.[25] This will not impose a very heavy financial burden on the shareholders as much of the original investment capital came from the government through the tax rebates and the operational losses can be used for tax purposes to offset the profits made by most of the companies on their activities in São Paulo or Rio. In the long term, the packing station could turn into a highly profitable venture if beef prices rise and, as many of the shareholders hope, the area it serves in the north of Mato Grosso and the south of Pará becomes a leading beef-producing region.

Suiá–Missu

This was the most favoured of all the Sudam-backed ranches. Its four projects, presented to Sudam from 1966 to 1976, were given tax rebates worth £21.4m. It is also the largest ranch; covering 560,000 hectares. The ranch has had a chequered history. The land was once owned by Ariosto da Riva and the money he made from this deal helped him to build himself up into one of the largest landowners in the Amazon and to set up Indeco.

Da Riva did not buy the land to set up a ranch. He told us that in the mid 1950s he had become very keen to set up his own colonisation project. He had looked for an area where land was still very cheap and found it in Mato Grosso, in the wild, rough region to the north of Barra do Garças which, he said, was totally uninhabited 'except for a few Xavante Indians'. He bought up 1.8 million hectares from absentee landowners who were all too willing to sell their virtually worthless tracts of inaccessible land.

After carrying out a few tests, da Riva realised in 1961 that this land would not be rich enough for crop farming without the heavy use of fertilisers and was therefore unsuitable for a colonisation project. No cattle-rearer, da Riva was not interested in setting up a ranch, yet he was unwilling to sell up completely as he realised that the land would appreciate rapidly over the next few years. His solution was to set up a joint company in which another group, keen on setting up a ranch, should have the controlling interest. The Ometto group from São Paulo agreed to this novel scheme.

Unlike the da Riva group, which was still establishing itself in this period and was to make most of its wealth through Amazon deals, the Ometto family had already built up its fortune in the south of the country. The founder of this group, Antônio Ometto, arrived from Italy with his wife and family in the late 19th Century. After buying 12 hectares of land in Piracicaba in the interior of the state of São Paulo – which was all he could afford at first – Ometto began to learn as much as he could about sugar-cane farming. He made rapid progress and became to sugar-cane cultivation what Geremia Lunardelli was to coffee-farming. By 1979 the Ometto family was producing 30 per cent of São Paulo's sugar-cane and 50 per cent of its alcohol. In absolute terms this means about 15 million tonnes of sugar-cane and 900 million litres of alcohol, placing the family among the world's leading producers.

In the late 1950s, the Ometto family decided to branch out into beef cattle. They systematically visited various regions of Brazil, including the marshy Pantanal area in the south of Mato Grosso, where the land was not in their view suitable, and the north of Paraná, which was undergoing a severe frost at the time of their visit and had an air of desolation which was enough to deter the bravest. Finally, at da Riva's suggestion, they visited the north of Mato Grosso. They liked the land he showed them and agreed to set up a joint company to own 484,000 hectares. Over the next few years, they were to make further purchases from neighbouring landowners, many of them absentee, until the ranch covered 786,000 hectares and they owned 1.7 million hectares, an area half the size of Holland.

The partnership with da Riva was, however, uneasy from the outset: da Riva as a land developer had his eye on an easy profit, whereas the Omettos as farmers were anxious to put the land to productive use. There is a constant tension in the Amazon between these two types of landowner. Da Riva finally pulled out of the project when the Omettos decided to increase their capital outlay so that all the expensive infrastructure of an efficient and modern ranch could be set up. He accepted payment for his share of the ranch in land which he then sold to the Bordon meat-packing group as a separate ranch. Da Riva waited another decade before finally realising his dream and setting up his own colonisation project, Indeco.

One of the first measures taken by the Omettos in the early 1960s was to move the Xavante Indians, whose village with 33 huts was situated beside the Xavantino river inside the area of the ranch. The Xavantes already had some contact with non-Indians, for peasant families had reached the area in the mid 1950s. With help from both the local Salesian mission and the Brazilian air force, the Omettos took the Indians by plane to the São Marcos reserve, 63 kilometres from Barra do Garças. Some of the Xavantes died as the result of the transfer and the survivors took a long while to adapt to their new environment. Until very recently, some of the Indians used to travel back to their old lands each year, even though it meant a journey of several hundred kilometres, so that they could go hunting at the end of the rainy season.

The first few years were very difficult for the Omettos. The ranch was so isolated in those early days that they had to build an earth road, several hundred kilometres long, so that they could have a land link with Barra do Garças and thus with the rest of Brazil. But the Omettos were experienced farmers and sound businessmen. They built up the ranch in cautious fashion, testing agricultural techniques before applying them on a large scale. By the late 1960s, the ranch was making a small profit.

Largely because of a row within the family over an inheritance, the Omettos decided to sell the ranch in 1972. The buyer was the large Italian liquid gas manufacturer, Liquigás. Special authorisation for the sale had to be obtained from the National Security Council (CSN), the highest court of the land under the military regime, as it was unconstitutional for a foreign company to own such an extensive tract of land.

In grandiose fashion, Liquigás tried to rename the ranch Liquifarm. But the name did not stick, and even today people in the region still call the project by its old name, Suiá-Missu. The new owners enthusiastically drew up an impressive plan for a town (Liquilândia), an airport and a large slaughter-house, so that vast quantities of high-quality, chilled beef could be sent directly by jet to Italy. Members of the Ometto family, who stayed on for a year after the sale to sort out the legal problems, listened sceptically to these high-flown plans.

Once in sole charge, the Italian management wrought radical changes. The Ometto family had recommended that the ranch should have no more than one head of cattle grazing on each hectare of land – a very low ratio by European standards. Believing that the Omettos had foolishly under-used the pastures, the newcomers decided to expand the herd greatly, bringing it up from 30,000 to about 70,000 in a few months.

Within a year, the ranch had been almost ruined. The pastures had been stripped bare and serious problems of bush invasion and soil erosion had arisen. For some time, the new management obstinately refused to admit that it could be wrong. When we visited the ranch in 1975, the managers were still talking of bringing the herd up to 300,000 head of cattle 'by 1980, at the latest'. However, they were reluctantly forced to change their plans. The ranch was gradually brought back into shape as they unwillingly accepted low grazing ratios. By early 1979, 78,500 hectares of pasture had been formed. They were supporting a herd of 85,000 head of cattle. The ranch began to make a small profit once again. Plans for a slaughter-house, which had been shelved during the crisis, were brought out of the drawer. Probably as a means of pre-empting nationalist criticism, Liquigás arranged for a neighbouring farm, Bordon, to hold the majority stake.

However, the future of the Suiá-Missu was thrown back into the melting pot with the news in August 1981 that the Italian state-owned oil company, ENI, had bought up Liquigás. After much uncertainty – and widespread rumous that ENI had decided to divide up Suiá-Missu and sell it off as separate ranches – it was reported that ENI had decided to take over the ranch, for the time being at least. When I was in the region in November 1981, I was told that 30 ENI employees were carrying out a big study into the various options facing the company. One of the alternatives under discussion was the setting up of a large land settlement scheme, on the lines of the successful Canarana project in the same region.

In December 1982, it was reported in the São Paulo newspaper *Gazeta Mercantil*, that, after completing its £300,000 study, ENI was planning to invest £20m over the next eight years.[26] It had started to diversify into other activities and had planted cocoa, soya beans, rubber and sugar-cane on an experimental basis. The herd of cattle had been reduced to 20,000 as the company was investing heavily in the recuperation of the pastures, but it intended to built it up again to 100,000. ENI was planning to export several products, including beef and alcohol made from sugar-cane, to the head company in Italy.

Codeara

The São Paulo-based Banco de Crédito Nacional owns two large ranches, Codeara and BCN Agropastoril, which are run in close coordination. Together they cover 180,000 hectares in the extreme north-east of Mato Grosso near the hamlet of Santa Teresinha in the district of Luciara. The ranch was involved in a long conflict with peasant families in the early 1970s (see Chapter 6). We visited the ranch on three occasions, in 1976, 1979 and 1981, and were thus able to follow developments quite closely.

In 1976, the then manager, Amilcar Rodrigues Gameiro, was full of enthusiasm. He was facing some problems, mainly from toxic weeds, which were killing off cattle, and from soil leaching, but he was confident that he could defeat them. He was experimenting with legumes and was hopeful that, by creating mixed pastures of guinea grass and legumes, he would be able to maintain the fertility of the soils.

When we went back in 1979, Amilcar had left the company. Though we were able to obtain little information during our visit, we realised that the ranch was facing serious problems. It was only during my last visit, in November 1981, that I was able to get the full story. It seemed that, despite efforts to halt the process, the fertility of the soils had declined steadily in 1978 and 1979. By 1980, Codeara appeared to be faced with the bleak alternatives of either greatly increasing its investment through the massive application of fertilisers, brought up at great expense from the south, or pulling out of cattle-rearing.

The dilemma was acute. The owners in São Paulo were strongly opposed to the first costly option, yet they were equally unwilling to put the ranch up for sale, particularly in its run-down condition. They pushed for diversification into other types of farming, but the local managers said that they had not had time to test alternative activities and it would be the height of irresponsibility to take a plunge in the dark. In the end, an intelligent compromise was worked out. Though it did not solve the basic problem of what was to be done with the ranch, it gave the managers a breathing space in which to carry out experiments with other farming activities.

As a first step, the group took over Germina, a small but experienced seed manufacturer. Germina, which continued to be run as a separate company, was given a contract to produce seeds on the ranch. Despite the extremely heavy cost of bringing up fertilisers from the south, Germina was instructed to feed its seed beds well, particularly with hyperphosphates. The company produced high-quality seeds from guinea grass and legumes on 10,000 hectares of land.

In the short term, the undertaking had been extraordinarily uneconomic, for the income from the sale of the seeds had covered at best only half of the outlay. However, Antônio Carlos Negri, Codeara's agronomist, explained to me that the objective behind the whole exercise was the indirect benefit: for the land used as seed beds became fertile enough to be used as pasture for at least ten years. He said that, rather than an end in itself, the cultivation of seeds was merely a means of recouping part of the exorbitant outlay on fertilisers which was required to bring the pasture back to an acceptable standard. Though the method had been successful, Negri thought that its prohibitive cost would make it unpractical for application on a large scale to recuperate all the vast stretches of degraded pastures.

Negri said that at the same time the company had begun to diversify into crop farming so as to break the old heavy dependence on cattle. This step, he said, was a calculated financial move to give the ranch access to the heavily-subsidised lines of credit available for crop farming, but not for cattle-rearing. Negri had been experimenting with beans, rice, soya, maize and sorghum and he said that his results had been encouraging with most of these crops. During an earlier period, he had tested rubber, for which particularly cheap loans were available, and he had also recommended its cultivation on a commercial scale.

Most progress, however, had been made with sugar-cane. About 9,000 hectares had been planted and Negri said that Codeara hoped to set up its own distillery to produce alcohol fuel by the end of 1982. He said that output would be about 120,000 litres per day in 1983, rising to about 360,000 litres per day in 1986. He said that the ranch itself consumed an enormous 400,000 litres of diesel per week so that, as the first stage of the project, they would be converting all the vehicles on the ranch so that they could run on alcohol. This alone would mean a big saving.

At the end of 1981, the alcohol programme, which had been presented to the country in 1977 and 1978 as Brazil's answer to the world oil crisis, had fallen out of public favour, partly because of unexpectedly serious problems of engine corrosion. However, Negri pointed out that the criticisms made by urban inhabitants in the industrialised south were largely irrelevant for an isolated ranch like Codeara for whom it was a godsend to be able to manufacture its own fuel. He said that, even if Codeara had to put a new engine in all its vehicles each year because of the corrosive effects of the alcohol, it was cheaper than bringing up diesel from the south. Moreover, local production was much more reliable as the diesel tankers frequently got held up for days on the earth roads during the rainy season. (In mid 1982 came the news that the car manufacturers in São Paulo had solved the main technical problems. The new corrosion-proof engines would be more expensive, but this was a secondary factor for Codeara. What counted was energy self-sufficiency.)

As part of its diversification policy, Codeara had also started buffalo-farming. It hoped to increase its herd from 354 at the end of 1981 to 2,500 by 1985. Buffalo-farming apparently presented fewer problems than cattle-rearing for the buffaloes seemed to be thriving on the naturally marshy areas of the ranch. It was also setting up an irrigated rice project with the José

Augusto Leite de Medeiros group, which was providing land from its Frenova ranch, and a Rio Grande do Sul cooperative, which was supplying the technology. The businessmen, who in exultant fashion had called the venture *Vitória de Araguaia* (Victory of the Araguaia), said that they expected the undertaking to be highly profitable, thanks to the Amazonian climate which meant that they would be able to reap two harvests each year. Finally Codeara was also thinking of setting up a colonisation project. Rather than the financial return, its main objective seemed to be to set up a *cordon sanitaire* of 'safe' settlers from the south along the ranch's border with the road, which was vulnerable to 'invasion' from peasant families. This tactic had been used by other ranches we visited, and was a more subtle – and probably more effective – alternative to the gunmen employed by most ranches to keep out intruders.

Despite the successful diversification, Codeara's main activity was still cattle-rearing and it was here that the ranch was clearly facing very serious problems. After a long talk, the resident vet, Francisco Manoel Almeida dos Reis, an Angolan who had been in Brazil since 1976, admitted that he was not happy with the quality of the herd. If he could have his way, he said, he would cut the herd down from 37,000 to 4,000, keeping only cows. He would then be able to build it up slowly, in the process attaining a high standard of quality. But the vet also had a more profound criticism to make. 'I don't think that cattle-rearing makes economic sense in such a remote area,' he said. 'The costs are simply too high. Now that the tax rebates are coming to an end, the ranches will either gradually close down or switch over to some form of crop farming.'

At the end of 1981, Codeara was certainly not a profitable business. Kiyokazu Sasaki, an affable Brazilian of Japanese descent, who had taken over from Amilcar Rodrigues Gameiro as manager, was quite open about this. He said:

> This year our costs will be about Crs 300m (£1.7m) while our income will only come to about Crs 80m–100m (£440,000–550,000). And there is nothing to suggest that this ranch will balance its books in the near future. If the BCN still wants to go on with it, it is because they have other considerations in mind.

Sasaki would not elaborate, but it is not difficult to carry on with his train of thought. While it would not make economic sense to run the ranch as an isolated activity, it could be made to fit neatly into the overall operations of a large and profitable group, like BCN. For under Brazilian law, the losses registered by the ranch could be used to offset the bank's profits in other activities and in this way the 'loss' meant little more than a reduction in the income tax paid by the group as a whole. Moreover, the ranch had been largely financed by tax rebates in the past, and the future held the prospect of a very large profit as the north of Mato Grosso became more developed and the price of land increased.

This may happen more quickly than seemed likely in 1981. At the end of 1982, the government announced its decision to build the Transaraguaia, a road from Santa Teresinha across the north of Bananal island to link up with the asphalted Belém–Brasília highway. Codeara and its neighbours had been lobbying for the construction of this road for several years, for it would mean quicker and cheaper transport facilities for both the cattle they wanted to sell and the farm inputs they needed to bring in. In April 1983 came the news, published in the national press, that Codeara and the Brazilian subsidiary of the huge US tyre manufacturer Goodyear had formed a joint venture, called Araguaia Hévea SA, to set up a rubber plantation on Codeara's land. With the investment put at Crs 2.6bn (£3.7m), it is Codeara's biggest attempt so far to diversify away from cattle-rearing. A spokesman for the new company said that work would begin immediately to clear 2,500 hectares of forest land and to plant 800,000 rubber trees. If all went as planned, he said, the company would be producing 175 tonnes of rubber in 1990, increasing to 2,000 tonnes by 1997. All the rubber would be sold to Goodyear's tyre factories in Brazil.

The Giant Mining Projects

Throughout the second half of the 1970s, the government became increasingly aware that the cattle companies would continue to operate at a loss for the foreseeable future, and, worse still, irreversible ecological damage would be caused to the forest if it went on with its policy of indiscriminately approving all cattle proposals. Although it continued to provide tax rebates for existing ranches, it started to turn down most requests for funding to set up new ranches on tropical forest.

It began to look to another sector – mining – to act as the spearhead of its development thrust. From then on, cattle-raising and colonisation began to be regarded as secondary activities, to be subordinated by the big mining projects.

In this way the government began to promote directly in the Amazon region the development model it was already applying in the industrialised south. Under this model, investment was concentrated in a few big development projects, such as a huge steel mill or a big hydroelectric power station. Foreign borrowing to cover part of the cost was encouraged, as it was argued that, once the project was underway, export earnings would quickly permit the foreign loans to be repaid. On the other hand, investment in non-productive activities, such as public education and health services, was held to a minimum, so as not to divert money away from essential economic activities. It was argued that, once the region was growing rapidly, the benefits of the progress would trickle down to all inhabitants.

This development model was under increasing attack in the industrialised south, for even during the boom years in the early 1970s the trickle-down process had not worked and the disparities in income had increased. This was considered unsatisfactory, not only by left-wing politicians, but also by businessmen catering for the domestic market who were disappointed with the growth in demand for their goods. Despite these criticisms, the government pushed ahead in the Amazon, partly because it was coming under increasing pressure from its foreign debt and the new mining projects promised excellent export earnings. In this initiative, the government sought collaboration, not predominantly with leading private Brazilian companies as it had during the cattle-rearing boom, but with transnationals.

These projects were not the first mining ventures in the Amazon. ICOMI, linked to the US group Bethlehem Steel, had long been mining the huge manganese reserves in the state of Amapá, north of the Amazon river. For many decades prospectors, using very primitive mining techniques, had been extracting small quantities of cassiterite, silver and gold in many parts of the Amazon. All these earlier activities had been carried out by private enterprise, acting on its own initiative, be it mighty Bethlehem Steel or impoverished prospectors. The new burst of activity in the mid 1970s was different in that it was the first time the government adopted as an official policy the opening up of the Amazon's mineral wealth.

Not surprisingly, several of the big new projects are for bauxite mining, as the region contains the world's largest reserves. The first to get off the ground was Mineração Rio do Norte (MRN), which is controlled by Brazilian capital (46 per cent stake held by the huge state-owned mining company, Companhia Vale do Rio Doce (CVRD) and 10 per cent by Companhia Brasileira do Alumínio, a subsidiary of Votorantim, Brazil's largest private industrial group) and has minority participation from five transnational groups, including the Canadian mining giant, Alcan. This project, which came on stream in 1979, produced about 4.7 million tonnes of bauxite in 1984, of which 3.9 million were exported. It has bauxite reserves of some 600 million tonnes beside the Trombetas river, a tributary of the Amazon. Two transnationals – US Alcoa and Anglo-Dutch Shell – jointly own a 600 million tonne bauxite reserve in the same region. Half of this reserve was purchased in 1981 from Jari (discussed below). Another bauxite project, Mineração Vera Cruz, is planned as a joint venture between UK's Rio Tinto Zinc (64 per cent) and CVRD (36 per cent). It will make use of a 1.1 billion tonne reserve near Paragominas.

Two huge aluminium projects are being set up to take advantage of part of the bauxite. One, called Alumar, is a $1.3 billion joint venture between US Alcoa and Anglo-Dutch Billiton (which is linked to Shell). It is situated at São Luís on the coast of Maranhão and at present buys bauxite from MRN. It came on stream in August 1984, with an initial production of 100,000 tonnes per year of aluminium and 500,000 tonnes of alumina.

Billiton announced in mid 1984 that, because of uncertain world prospects, it was unwilling to put up further investment for the second stage of the project, which should bring production up to 245,000 tonnes of aluminium by 1986. However, Alcoa, which has a 60 per cent stake in the smelter, decided to push ahead regardless. The company was not short of funds, for earlier in 1984, as part of its strategy to 'Brazilianise' its activities, it had sold a 35 per cent stake in its countrywide operations to the large Brazilian civil construction company Camargo Corrêa, for the equivalent in cruzeiros of about £180m. The move made sense for Camargo Corrêa, which had been the main contractor for the Tucuruí dam, the huge hydroelectric dam being built on the Tocantins river. The company had grown fat on big civil construction contracts from the government in the 1970s and it knew that the days of abundant, highly-paid jobs such as these were over, probably for ever. It needed to diversify into another economic activity with a brighter long-term future and what could be better than mining, a sector highly favoured by the government.

The other project is being set up at Vila do Conde, near the mouth of the Tocantins river, by CVRD, the majority shareholder, in association with a consortium of 30 Japanese smelters. The original idea was to set up two separate projects – Alunorte, to produce alumina, which is a semi-processed form of bauxite; and Albrás, to transform the alumina into aluminium. In October 1982 the partners decided to cancel Alunorte, temporarily at least, because of shrinking world demand and the Brazilian government's shortage of funds. Albrás, however, is still going ahead, using alumina from Alumar. It should come on stream in June 1985, with an initial output of 80,000 tonnes, increasing to 320,000 tonnes by 1989.

Carajás, the biggest mining project of all, took many years to get off the ground. The rich mineral complex in the Carajás mountains, west of the Araguaia river, was discovered by chance in the late 1960s when a geologist was forced to land on a bald patch in the jungle hills. He found to his amazement that the reason why there was no vegetation was that the ground consisted of high-grade iron ore. It is now estimated that these hills hold 18 billion tonnes of iron ore, one of the largest reserves in the world. Copper, manganese, nickel and tin have also been found in commercial quantities.

The Brazilian government first tried to set up a joint venture with the US Steel Corporation, but the partnership broke up in 1977 after long wrangles over how the project was to be developed. Since then, the government has pushed ahead on its own, although with a much more modest scheme than the extraordinarily ambitious $60 billion project envisaged at one stage. Companhia Vale do Rio Doce is investing about $3.3 billion to set up a mine for the iron ore, to build a railway to the coast and to construct a giant ore terminal called Ponta de Madeira, near São Luís on the Maranhão coastline. First iron ore shipments took place in February 1985, and by the end of 1988 Carajás should be exporting 35 million tonnes of iron ore a year. If world demand proves buoyant, Carajás could readily increase its exports to 50 million tonnes, equivalent to about one seventh of world iron ore exports in recent years. Even at this high level of production, Carajás would have a mine-life of about 350 years. The Carajás project was considered extremely important by the Figueiredo government, which set up a special committee, chaired by planning minister Antônio Delfim

Neto, the government's economic supremo, to oversee its progress.

Yet Carajás will bring few benefits to the local inhabitants. Once the construction work is completed, few jobs will be created, yet the disruption will be considerable. The 890-kilometre railway to Ponta da Madeira will cross the lands of several groups of Indians, thought to total about 1,500 people, many of whom have had little contact with outsiders. The impact of the railway on two of these groups – The Parakanã and the Gavião – is discussed in Chapter 5. Under pressure from the World Bank, which is providing some finance for Carajás, the government is setting up a project to help these Indians, but anthropologists are deeply pessimistic. Many peasant families may also lose their lands, particularly if large forestation and farming projects are set up on both sides of the railway, as was proposed in an early study carried out by a Japanese consultancy. To help prevent the eruption of widespread peasant unrest, which could damage the project's foreign image, General Danilo Venturini, head of the newly-created land ministry and secretary-general of the powerful National Security Council (CSN), was brought onto the special Carajás council to take over responsibility for land.

Another huge project which includes mining among its activities is Jari, situated to the north of the Amazon river, beside the Jari river. It was set up in the late 1960s, outside the official government plans, by US shipping magnate Daniel K. Ludwig, who was attracted to the region partly because of its very remoteness. The government of that time, headed by General Arthur da Costa e Silva, gave him a warm welcome and told him that, provided he brought in his own investment capital, he would be left free to develop the region as he saw fit. Ludwig always claimed to own a vast area of 3.7 million hectares, though the government only officially recognised titles to a seventh of this area. In the early days Ludwig enjoyed excellent government contracts, for he employed a well-placed military officer, Captain Heitor de Aquino Ferreira who was to become the private secretary of the next President, General Ernesto Geisel.

Ludwig began in grand fashion. He brought in huge tractors to clear the land. He set up vast plantations with fast-growing *gmelina*, a little-known tree from Indonesia. He floated a complete pulp mill across the Atlantic from Japan. He set up a plantation of paddy rice. He began to mine the local reserves of kaolin and to draw up plans to exploit the bauxite reserves. However, in the late 1970s things began to go wrong. The *gmelina* trees did not do well on the sandy Jari soils and part of the plantation had to be replaced with eucalyptus, which everyone else grows in Brazil. Ludwig began to be increasingly criticised in the Brazilian press for the autocratic way in which he was running his estate, almost as if it were a separate country. The anti-Jari campaign began to receive support from sectors of the armed forces.

The government began to view Jari as more of a liability than an asset. Ludwig himself, by then in his late eighties, began to tire of the problems and the constant stream of criticisms. With debts of about £50 million, he decided that he had had enough. The government was anxious not to allow Jari to collapse in spectacular fashion, for fear it could damage the international credibility of the Carajás project. Too many commentators had already drawn a comparison with Henry Ford's unsuccessful attempt to set up a rubber plantation, called Fordlândia, in the Amazon region in the 1920s. It put great pressure on the top Brazilian companies to put together a rescue plan, offering them very attractive financial incentives. Although some of the participants, hard-pressed by the recession, were clearly unwilling, a consortium of 23 Brazilian banks and private companies headed by Augusto Azevedo Antunes, president of ICOMI and an old friend of Ludwig, finally took over Jari. The new owners faced many of the problems faced by Ludwig, but, after repeated injections of capital from the government, they were cautiously optimistic by early 1984 that the project could eventually be made to pay. The bail-out was strongly criticised by opposition politicians who argued that, at a time of great austerity, it was quite wrong for the government to use public funds to save a grandiose and bizarre project of doubtful long-term viability which would bring no benefit to the mass of Brazilians.

Energy for almost all of the projects discussed in this section is to come from Tucuruí, an eight million kilowatt hydroelectric power station which Eletronorte, a federal electricity body, has built on the Tocantins river about 200 kilometres north of Carajás. Shortage of government funds delayed Tucuruí, but it finally came on stream in late 1984, three years after schedule. There have already been serious problems with Tucuruí. The contract for clearing the timber off the land to be flooded for the huge reservoir, 70 kilometres across, was awarded in the late 1970s to Capemi, a military pension fund without any experience in this field. Strong evidence was produced at the end of 1982 to suggest that Capemi had been given the contract in exchange for a commitment to help fund General Octávio Aguiar de Medeiros, head of the National Intelligence Service (SNI), the intelligence forces, in his bid to take over as President from Figueiredo in 1985. Despite technical and financial assistance from Lazard Frères, a French bank, Capemi failed abysmally in its task. Lazard Frères pulled out in mid 1982 when it was clear that the undertaking was going to end in disaster. By early 1983, Capemi had completed only a fraction of the work and was bankrupt. At the end of February, the manager in charge of the project sent a telegram to General Messias de Aragão, president of Capemi, in which he warned that the labourers, who had not been paid for over two months, were in 'a desperate situation'. 'The situation is inhuman and terrifying. I do not know how long the workers will remain calm', he cautioned.

Finally, in March the federal government took over the project, but it soon became clear that the problems left by Capemi would not be readily resolved. Even if efficient managers were brought in, the isolation of the region and the disruption caused by the rainy season meant that only part of the area could be cleared before the revised date for flooding in mid 1984.

This meant that the government faced a difficult dilemma: if Tucuruí kept to its revised schedule, trees rotting under the water could produce poisonous acids which would not only kill most of the fish, but could corrode the turbines and other equipment; but, if it delayed the project for the two or three years required to clear most of the timber, the development of the Amazon would be seriously retarded because of the large number of projects – from Carajás to the meat-packing station in Campo Alegre – which depended on its energy.

But even worse news was in store. In early 1984 evidence came to light that some of the companies earlier contracted to clear the jungle had used chemicals, probably containing lethal Agent Orange. João Bastos, agricultural secretary for Pará state, said in June 1984 that empty drums of chemicals had been found in the region, some of them being used by local people to store food. Probably as a result of this contamination, women had had miscarriages and given birth to deformed children. Moreover, Bastos said that he was afraid that, if the flooding went ahead as planned, poisonous chemicals could get into the water of the Tocantins river, endangering the health of hundreds of thousands of people. The federal government body in charge of the environment (SEMA) asked Eletronorte to delay the flooding until a thorough investigation could be carried out. But the government ignored the warnings. The project went ahead and was inaugurated by President João Figueiredo in late 1984.

All these ventures together comprise the Greater Carajás project. They represent the Figueiredo government's most important development initiative. They are frequently cited by the government as evidence that, however serious the present foreign debt problem, Brazil will be one of the world's leading economic powers by the end of this century. They are a stark demonstration of the economic strategy adopted by the military governments from 1964 to 1985, which was to invest heavily in huge development projects which would boost economic output and ease balance of payments constraints by greatly increasing export earnings. It is expected that by 1990 the state of Pará alone will be exporting goods, mainly minerals, worth about $1.5bn–2.0bn.

But the whole Greater Carajás project is particularly vulnerable to the criticism raised against the military governments' whole economic model – that the huge ventures do little to raise the living standards of the mass of the population. Apart from possible short-term work during the construction phase, local inhabitants will gain little from Greater Carajás and may even finish up worse-off through the disruption and inflationary impact of the venture. Far from benefiting the local people, some actions taken in the name of development – the Tucuruí hydroelectric project is a blatant example – lead to a serious decline in living standards. Instead of promoting true development, they are a blow against the progress of the region. In the second half of 1983, the businessmen's association of Pará published a document in which they stated: 'What is the point of the government carrying out just huge economic projects in the region, if the local people get poorer and poorer, with shanty-towns swelling on the outskirts of big, medium-sized and even small towns in the Amazon region?'[27]

Notes

1. *O Estado de S. Paulo*, 31 March 1973.
2. *O Estado de S. Paulo*, 4 September 1973.
3. *O Estado de S. Paulo*, 18 August 1973.
4. Ibid.
5. *O Estado de S. Paulo*, 16 April 1974.
6. *O Estado de S. Paulo*, 15 May 1974.
7. Ibid.
8. *O Estado de S. Paulo*, 24 May 1974.
9. *Manchete*, 27 September 1975.
10. *O Estado de S. Paulo*, 4 September 1973.
11. Ibid.
12. *O Estado de S. Paulo*, 18 August 1973.
13. *O Estado de S. Paulo*, 14 September 1973.
14. *Jornal do Brasil*, 14 February 1979.
15. R. J. A. Goodland and H. S. Irwin, *Amazon Jungle: From Green Hell to Red Desert?* (Elsevier Scientific, Amsterdam, 1975), p.37.
16. *O Estado de S. Paulo*, 6 May 1979.
17. Goodland and Irwin, *Amazon Jungle*, p.37.
18. Shelton Davies, *Victims of the Miracle – Development and the Indians of Brazil* (Cambridge University Press, New York, 1977).
19. *Sunday Times*, 23 February 1969.
20. *O Estado de S. Paulo*, 9 February 1974.
21. *O Estado de S. Paulo*, 18 July 1974.
22. *O Estado de S. Paulo*, 18 February 1974.
23. *O Estado de S. Paulo*, 16 September 1974.
24. Most of the later information on Canarana and the other projects comes from an article in *O Estado de S. Paulo*, 5 June 1983.
25. *Gazeta Mercantil*, 9 April 1982.
26. *Gazeta Mercantil*, 17 December 1982.
27. Quoted in Lúcio Flávio Pinto, 'A Crise Atinge Amazònia', *Ciência Hoje*, vol.2, no.10 (Jan/Feb 1984).

4. The Escalation of the Land Conflict

So what happens? Each greedy individual preys on his native land like a malignant growth, absorbing field after field, and enclosing thousands of acres with a single fence. Result – hundreds of farmers are evicted. They're either cheated or bullied into giving up their property, or systematically ill-treated until they're finally forced to sell. Whichever way it is done, out the poor creatures have to go, men and women, husbands and wives, widows and orphans, mothers and tiny children, together with all their employees – whose great numbers are not a sign of wealth, but simply of the fact that you can't run a farm without plenty of manpower . . . Of course, they can always become tramps and beggars, but even then they're liable to be arrested as vagrants and put in prison for being idle – when nobody will give them a job, however much they want one. For farm-work is what they're used to and where there's no arable land, there's no farm-work to be done. After all, it only takes one shepherd or cowherd to graze animals over an area that would need any amount of labour to make it fit for corn production.

(Thomas More, *Utopia*, Book 1, 1516)

This leads to uncontrolled land speculation and to the emergence of large ranches which, equipped with legal and financial resources, have been evicting both peasants and Indians from their land . . . So they are turned off their plots, driven even further inland, even into neighbouring countries, transformed into nomads, condemned to wander the country's roads. Some resist and create the conflicts which are multiplying, particularly in Mato Grosso and other parts of the Amazon region. Others go to the nearest towns and create the vast migrationary flows which end up swelling the large cities.

(Document published by Brazilian bishops in November 1976)

Though the government's hostility towards the spontaneous settlement of peasant families has remained fixed throughout its many shifts in Amazon policy, it has only recently felt it necessary to intervene directly to quash the peasantry. Its new attitude stems from many varied pressures: the important change in its development strategy, with the new prominence given to big mining projects and the government's consequent reluctance to have foreign investors deterred by violent land conflict; the recent growth in militancy of peasant families, so they are now seen by the government as a threat to national security; the growing involvement of radical sectors of the Catholic Church, who are increasingly regarded by the government as dangerous opponents; and national political changes which have meant that top army officers, always keen to move in and sort out a problem in authoritarian fashion, have been able to take over from the more cautious and lethargic civilian authorities as the main power in the region. The government's new interventionist policy is a clear illustration that today, for good or for bad, the Amazon is integrated into the country and, like the other regions, is subject to the decisions of central government. In this chapter we examine all of these complex issues, except the recent emphasis on mining projects which was discussed in the previous chapter.

The Growing Resistance of the Peasant Families

The peasant families have long been reluctant to move out when a landowner from outside has arrived and claimed ownership of their land. But their disposition to fight and if necessary to die for their lands has increased dramatically over the last decade. In part, this is because of an important change in the manner of the occupation. In the 1940s, 1950s and 1960s, the peasant families at the forefront of the occupation process could expect to have to move once or twice in their lives, either because the plot of land they were occupying had become exhausted, or because they were unlucky enough to have a landowner move in and claim it. In the latter case, they usually held out for compensation, however small, for the land they had cleared and planted and for the house they had built. Though there was often conflict over the amount to be paid, the peasant families did not generally risk their lives to defend their plots for they were confident that they could find other similar ones in more remote areas of the land frontier.

However, this has now changed. As we have seen, the pace of occupation has quickened remarkably since the late 1960s, largely as the result of the government's road-building programme and its tax rebate scheme. Peasant families, which could previously expect to occupy a plot for ten or twenty years before the landowner appeared, are lucky today to be left alone for two or three years. Numerous families have been evicted four or five times and have become exhausted by the struggle to survive.

Though there are still millions of hectares of unoccupied land in remote areas of the Amazon, the peasant families realise today that almost all of this land has an owner, on paper at least, and that if they move on again, they may well be evicted yet again. As a result, even when under great pressure from a landowner or a land thief, peasant families are today extremely reluctant to leave a plot of land where they have lived for some time and have acquired some legal rights, however fragile they may in practice be.

Most of the families still show a perhaps surprising respect for the law of the land, coupled with an even stronger faith in their concept of natural justice, to which they turn for legitimisation of their claim to a holding if Brazil's legal system lets them down. For them, land in a wild and unoccupied region like the Amazon should belong to the people who have cleared it and made it bear fruit. Though often bewildered by the intricacies of the legal system, most peasant families first try, if they can, to win the right to their land through the proper legal channels, only turning to extra-legal methods if all else fails.

In strictly legal terms, the situation of the peasant family is not unfavourable. A family is entitled to settle on unoccupied land provided there is no indication that it has an owner. After a year and a day, the family automatically obtains the provisional right to occupy the land. If the land proves to be *terra devoluta* then the peasant family can obtain the legal title to its plot before the rest is sold to a private landowner. On the other hand, if the land turns out to belong to a private landowner, the peasant family's rights depend on how long it has lived on the plot.

Under the old version of the law (*lei do usucapião*), the family could keep its plot, even if the land were shown to have been privately owned on its arrival, as long as the family had lived there for at least ten years without being challenged by anyone claiming to be a landowner. In November 1981, the law was revised and the necessary period of unchallenged occupation reduced to five years. Under both the new and the old versions of the law, the landowner could apply to the courts for an eviction order if the family had not lived on the land long enough to acquire property rights. However, even if he was eventually awarded this order, the landowner would have to pay the family compensation.

In practice, however, landowners have often cheated peasant families out of their rights, using a knowledge of the ins and outs of the legal system to which the peasant families generally have no access. These malpractices are not now as common as they once were, probably because there is much less *terra devoluta* to attract landowners.

To purchase a plot of *terra devoluta*, the landowner merely had to put in a request to the local state land department which then published a notice in the little-read *Diário Oficial*, the official state government gazette, and other local newspapers, asking for any person whose interests might be affected by the sale of the plot of land to make a formal petition to the state government before a certain date. The state land department was not obliged to investigate whether there were peasant families or Indians living on the land, but merely to display the notice in a public place in the vicinity.

Very often the land department did not bother to comply with the latter requirement. Even when it did, the nearest 'public place' – which it took to mean a state government office – could be more than 50 kilometres away from the land in question. It was highly unlikely that any of the peasants living on the land would see the notice – and if by chance they did, they would probably not be able to read it.

If the peasant families did not demand their rights by the given date in the stated place, the area was considered unoccupied. In the case of a later dispute over ownership, the landowner than had 'proof' that there were no peasant families living on the land when he bought it and that any settlers on it must be recent invaders.

Some of the state land departments were so disorganised that they did not even keep a proper register of the land they sold. For example, Sagri, the land department for the state of Pará, on several occasions sold the same area to two or three different people, though each time the sale was officially registered. Jokes began to spread about the 'second and third floors' of plots of land. This lack of control has inevitably led to later conflicts, not just between peasant families and landowners, but between different landowners each brandishing a valid title.

The Catholic Church has long been critical of this system,[1] but it was not until the late 1970s that it set about helping the peasant families in a practical way to defend their property rights in law. In a document[2] published in 1981, the church's Pastoral Land Commission (CPT) gave an account of its efforts in Bico do Papagaio (parrot's beak), a region in the extreme north of Goiás. (The name comes from the shape of the region, lying as it does at the confluence of the Araguaia and Tocantins rivers.) This case illustrates vividly the difficulties faced by the families in their endeavours to legalise their occupation.

Bico do Papagaio is inhabited by some 20,000 peasants, most of them extremely poor. It became notorious for its land conflicts in the 1960s and 1970s. By then, these lands were appreciating in value, largely as a result of the government's road-building programme which had made the region much more accessible. Landowners and land thieves moved in on a large scale and set about evicting the peasant families, though some had been in the region for ten or twenty years. It is not known how many families lost their land during this period. In what it recognises are incomplete records, the CPT registered the eviction of over 400 families in 1975 and 1976 alone.

In the late 1970s, Osvaldo de Alencar Rocha, a lawyer employed by the CPT, began to work with the peasant families. He describes some of the difficulties he has encountered:

> Most of the families are illiterate. They don't have any documents either for themselves or for their land . . . As they cannot write, it is difficult for them to authorise a lawyer to act on their behalf. They have to go to the nearest town, usually 40 or 50 kilometres away, and then make a public authorisation, which they sign with a thumb print, at a legal office. This will cost them at

least 200–300 cruzeiros [£3–5]. They are so poor that most of them don't have money to pay either for the journey or the authorisation.

On the other hand the landowner, who is stealing land without any scruples, can rely on a complete machine to work in his favour. He is rich and can contract lawyers. He can make direct contact with the state's political and legal authorities. He can go to the judge's home. He can visit INCRA. He has the protection and support of those carrying out the state government's land policies. He can make the whole process work in his favour.[3]

Peasant families have reacted in many different ways to the frustration and anger they feel when powerful landowners rob them of what they believe to be their lands. Many of the families, brought up in the isolated and perhaps surprisingly peaceful *sertão* (hinterland), have been traumatised by the repression they have received from the landowners and the police and have been frightened into leaving. Other families, particularly when they have had time to form close links with their neighbours, have decided to stand up to the landowners and fight for their plots, even if this means facing up to repression on a daily basis.

The repeated evictions, almost always carried out illegally, have led to widespread discontent, not only with the landowners, but also with the authorities, who, the peasants feel, have not only failed in their basic task of law enforcement, but, worse still, have often connived at the repression. At times, this dissatisfaction has flared up into explosive anger with the authorities over a different, apparently unconnected issue.

We relate the following three tales, either because we happened to be present during an important moment of the conflict in question, or because we had access to good sources of information.[4] They illustrate the anger, the tenacity and the organised resistance increasingly shown by peasant families in the Amazon today. The tales are not typical, because they deal with communities which, in their different ways, have successfully fought back against aggression from outsiders, though many of their members earlier belonged to hamlets which were broken up. To varying degrees, these communities have become examples to others of what is possible.

The 'Confusion' at Ribeirão Bonito

Dom Pedro Casaldáliga, Bishop of São Félix, was travelling by bus towards the end of October 1976 in the company of Father João Bosco Penedo Burnier, a priest from a well-to-do São Paulo family. They stopped for the night at Ribeirão Bonito, a small village on the road running from Barra do Garças to São Félix. Local inhabitants told them that the police had tortured two women at the police station in an attempt to discover the whereabouts of a man involved in a shoot-out. Sixty-five-year-old Dona Margarida had had needles inserted under her nails and into her arms, breasts and legs. For good measure the fugitive man's wife, Santana, had also been tortured, though it must have been clear to the policemen, as it was to us when we talked to her a few days later, that she did not know where her husband was. As a gratuitous act of violence, perhaps giving vent to their frustration, the police had burnt down Santana's house while she was detained.

The bishop and the priest went at once to the police station where the two women were still imprisoned. The police reacted with great hostility to their complaints. One of them lost his temper, hitting João Bosco with the butt of his revolver, and then shooting him in the head. The priest died a few hours later.

News of the murder spread quickly among the local peasant families, who were already very resentful of the authorities' connivance in the treatment they were receiving from landowners in the region. According to the local priest, 55 of the 600 families living within a 40-kilometre radius of Ribeirão Bonito had been illegally turned off their land over the previous 18 months. On some occasions the local police force, which worked hand-in-glove with the landowners, had actually taken part in the evictions.

Lázaro Correia da Silva, one of the evicted peasants to whom we spoke, was deeply embittered.

> Now I'm living in limbo, on the edge of the world. I've lost my land, now I have to work on the ranches. I work and they don't pay me. And then there's the police here. We go to them to try and get our money from the ranches and they put us in jail. I don't know what I'm going to do. I've been studying this problem all my life and I still haven't come up with a solution. So I just wait to see what happens, to see if I can't get a little plot of land, something. Because I haven't any skills. I only know how to work the land.

A friend of his, Abraão Lourindo de Souza, a fervent member of Assembléia de Deus, an extremist protestant church, and yet – unusually for people of his faith – with a keen perception of the social reality around him, had also been evicted recently. He commented:

> The problem of the peasant farmers has reached absurd dimensions. It's not just me and few others. Nearly everyone has been evicted. You'll meet very few people here who haven't been pushed out at least once. Everyone here is trying to find work on a ranch. Everyone's doing it because there's nothing else, because they can't find a plot of land for themselves. And it's not easy to find work on a ranch. You get a job for a day or two then you spend two or three looking for another one. We all have to help those who haven't got work, tide them over. The problem is that we have to buy everything here: rice, beans, manioc flour. And everything is very expensive.

A 24-year-old woman with four children, Naide Mendes Barbosa, had had an even more difficult life. Her husband, João da Costa, had been killed six months earlier by the manager of a nearby cattle ranch. He had worked in the relatively skilled task of measuring out land and, according to Naide, had fallen out with the manager who had refused to pay him for a job. The final explosion occurred when João refused to take a fence through land already under cultivation by peasant farmers which, the manager maintained, belonged to the ranch. The manager sent in the police who shot João in the back and later alleged that 'it was all a mistake', that they had really intended to arrest his cousin.

Naide told us:

> It makes me sad not to be able to do anything against those who killed my husband. But landowners are like that. If I'm right and they're wrong, they take my right away from me and behave as if it is theirs. But I haven't money to give to the police and they do. If they want to accuse me, they can, because I haven't any money. The manager didn't care, he let everyone see that it was him who had my husband killed. The very day that my husband was killed, he invited the police for a meal at his house. That very day. None of them cared. It was the greatest injustice in the world because, if my husband had had a row with the manager and the manager had killed him, it would have been different. But my husband was working normally, out in the forest. He, the manager, filled the van with policemen and sent them there with a lie, saying that they'd come to arrest his cousin, when there wasn't even any reason to do this.

Naide had sent the two oldest children to be brought up by relatives and was earning her living by taking in washing and sewing from the few better-off families in the village, and, as this brought in very little money, by working occasionally as a prostitute.

Many of the peasants living in Ribeirão Bonito and neighbouring Cascalheira had stories like this to tell. The resentment among the local population was running very high. The murder of the priest had acted as the catalyst. It had boosted the peasants' morale to see that a priest – someone they automatically placed in a higher social class – had also become a victim of the violent and corrupt system to which they were subjected every day. For once they felt that they held the upper hand, for all of the small local police force fled south to Barra do Garças, aware that they had overstepped the mark this time.

At the customary memorial service held seven days after the priest's death, these factors fused into a spontaneous explosion of wrath. At the end of the service, the peasants erected a huge cross just outside the empty police station, very close to the spot where the priest had been shot. The cross bore this defiant inscription: 'Here Father João Bosco was murdered by a military policeman as he defended freedom.' Some 600 people took part in the procession. From our conversations with some of the participants a few days later, it appears that the idea of taking further action arose as they sang and prayed at the foot of the cross, after the service. Murmurs spread about the blatant contradiction between the cross, standing for peace and

Santana, from Ribeirão Bonito, standing among the ruins of her home.

Photo: Sarah Errington

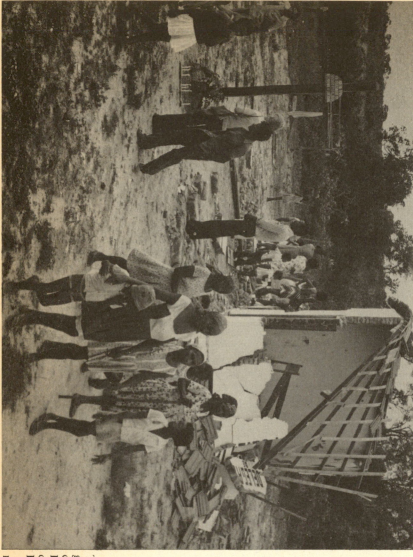

The knocked-down gaol, and the cross commemorating Fr João Bosco's death in Ribeirão Bonito

Photo: Sarah Errington

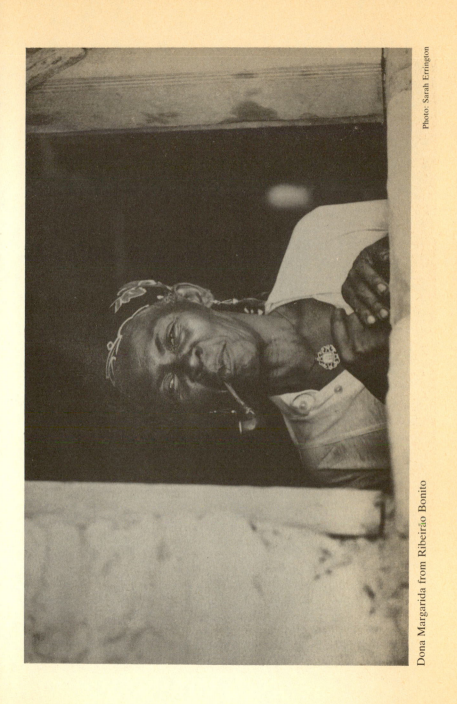

Photo: Sarah Errington

Dona Margarida from Ribeirão Bonito

Abraão Lourindo de Souza and his family in Ribeirão Bonito

Photo: Sarah Errington

freedom, and the nearby jail, symbolising repression and corruption. A lively 40-year-old woman, Carmesinha Pereira da Silva, who had been in many a tiff with the local policemen, said that she was the first to give concrete expression to their feelings. She told us that she grabbed an axe, crying out: 'I was the first to be imprisoned in this jail and I shall be the first to knock it down!'

Carmesinha's action set the anger alight. Just about everyone in the procession joined in. Dona Margarida herself commented in wonder:

> It became a real party. We were laughing and singing as we knocked it down. We used anything at hand – axes, shovels, stones. I couldn't actually help as my hands and knees were still so painful from the tortures, but I was urging them on. The jail was totally destroyed.

When news of the incident reached Brasília a couple of days later, six federal policemen were immediately sent in. Many people in the village gleefully told us that these policemen had great difficulty in identifying any instigators of the crime, for they were told on all sides: 'There were no leaders. We, the people, destroyed the jail.'

It is difficult to assess the consequences of the incident. At one level, very little changed. The policeman who killed the priest was arrested, probably as a result of the considerable repercussions of the murder. A few weeks later, however, when the furore had died down, he was able to 'escape from jail' in Barra do Garças. After a lull, the landowners carried on evicting peasant farmers in the same old way.

Yet some of the peasants to whom we spoke two years later told us that the incident had had important consequences. Although corruption and bribery were still rife, they said, the local police took care to conceal their dealings with the landowners and treated the peasants with more respect. The local priest commented on the growth of the confidence of the peasants that they could influence events and achieve what they wanted. The *confusão*, as local inhabitants refer to the incident, was not the sole reason for the change, but it certainly contributed. Moreover the event has become a landmark in peasant history. Hundreds of kilometres away, peasant farmers got to hear of the *confusão* in Ribeirão Bonito; on several occasions, peasants in very distant parts recounted to us with great glee a garbled version of the peasants' 'victory' against the police. Incidents like this have been important in helping gradually to break down the peasants' traditional belief in the invicibility of the authorities.

The Tenacious Peasants of Santo Antônio
About 15 families live just south of a little place called Santo Antônio, which lies 100 kilometres south of São Félix in the north-east of Mato Grosso. Nine of the families arrived at their present plots in 1970 or 1971, while the other six came a few years later, after they had finally decided to move on from the island of Bananal because of the terrible difficulties caused

each year by the floods. Access to Santo Antônio is difficult, linked as it is to São Félix by little more than a track which becomes impassable with rains. It is the isolation of the hamlet which explains why the families were left in peace for so many years, while peasant families in the surrounding region were being evicted.

However, this peace was finally shattered. The nearby ranch, Fazenda Marruá, owned by two farmers, Estevão Júlio Vargas and Máquines Vargas from Limeira in São Paulo, sent in gunmen in early 1981 to tell the families to leave. The peasant families refused, upon which, according to the peasants, the ranch made an agreement with the head gunman, Lindalbo Medeiros, that, if he evicted the families, he would be given half the land.

In August 1981, Medeiros returned at the head of a group of 18 gunmen. This time they did not waste time with threats. They tied up the peasants – men, women and children – and threw all 30 of them on the brushwood in the hot sun while they burnt down their huts and destroyed their stocks of food. They put into a boat the possessions which could not be burnt and let them loose in the river. The gunmen then bundled the peasants into a truck and left them by the roadside near the Canarana colonisation project. One woman was in labour by then, the birth of her child having been brought on prematurely by shock and maltreatment, but she was left by the roadside along with all the others.

The peasant families talked over their predicament and decided to go back to their plots despite everything. One of the farmers said: 'Where else could we have gone? There's no land left. If we'd settled somewhere else, we'd have been turned off. At least in Santo Antônio we have our rights.'

They rebuilt their huts as best they could and set about salvaging what they could of their crops. On 25 September, the gunmen came back. But this time the peasant families were ready. Their watch party spotted the gunmen arriving and they warned that they would shoot if the gunmen came any nearer. The gunmen, taken by surprise, went away, but came back on the following day. There was an exchange of fire, but no one was killed.

By then, the federal government had begun to get involved. INCRA officials first negotiated the offer from the ranch of compensation of Crs 40,000 (£220) for each family. But the peasants rejected the proposal with indignation. They said that they would spend this money in a few weeks if they had to live in a town, and that their plots, which occupied fertile land, were worth much more.

Then INCRA offered to resettle the families on plots on a ranch which had recently been expropriated after its owner, a São Paulo businessman, had run foul of the government. But again the families refused, pointing out that four-fifths of the land they had been offered flooded so seriously in the winter that it was virtually impossible to use it for farming.

In a much publicised speech in south Brazil in late 1981, the trusted government agent, Major Curió, cited this offer of free land to the peasant families as evidence of the government's commitment to sort out the country's land problems. But the peasants doggedly refused to budge. INCRA finally agreed to allow the families to stay and expropriated an area of land. However, the peasants did not feel secure until, in October 1983, their plots were finally marked out and they received land titles.

The 'Peasant Law' of Canabrava

Canabrava is a little community of peasant families in the north of Mato Grosso which has managed with remarkable success to defend itself from invasion by the surrounding cattle ranches. It has achieved this partly as a result of the care with which it has built up the unity and solidarity between the families. But luck has also played its role: for many years Canabrava was very isolated so it was not top of the cattle companies' list of desirable lands.

Father Miguel, a Spanish priest who has lived with the community for many years, has kept a careful record of the community's history. His records show that the first peasant families arrived from Goiás in 1956 at the vanguard of the penetration front. When they arrived, there was a village of Xavante Indians, with 33 huts, at the source of the Xavantino river not very far away.

During our visit to Canabrava in January 1979, some of the oldest inhabitants told us that they had been very scared of these Indians, who were renowned for their fierceness. They said that they had none the less managed to coexist quite happily for, whenever the Xavantes had felt that the peasant families were coming too close, they had killed one of the peasants' cattle and left it in a conspicuous place. The peasants said that they had respected the Indians' warnings and, as a result, had had no problems. The Indians were transferred in 1963 by the Suiá-Missu ranch to the São Marcos reserve several hundred kilometres away.

The early inhabitants said that the community had grown very slowly in the early days. As transport links were so difficult, they were virtually self-sufficient, buying and selling very little on the market. By 1970, they said, there were about 100 families. Many lived on their *rocqs* (cultivated plots) perhaps 20 or 30 kilometres away, only coming occasionally to the little town that was springing up.

Many more families arrived in 1974 and 1975, largely because of the construction of the BR–158, the road which was eventually to link the south of Pará with Brasília. This road made the region more accessible and ranches started to be formed in the surrounding region. The inhabitants began to get worried. There was talk that neighbouring ranches had their eye on the peasants' land and would soon be applying pressure on them to leave. They heard of the problems which other peasant families in the region were facing.

In 1977, their conflicts duly began. First, employees from the neighbouring Piraguassu ranch tried to stop them using the traditional watering-place for their cattle, saying that the stream belonged to the ranch.

The peasant families reacted furiously and drove the men away on several occasions. Then another neighbouring ranch – Santa Isabel – tried to claim some of their land. Again the peasant families successfully resisted this attempt at encroachment.

The families held several meetings and decided that they must get better organised if they were to face successfully the further conflicts that surely lay ahead. They decided that they must stop ranch employees from getting a foothold in their lands and so worked out some conditions for deciding which newcomers should be given land. We saw their document, which was eventually signed on Good Friday (24 March) 1978. It read:

> We, the peasant famers of Canabrava, have decided to reaffirm the decisions we took on 24/6/77, namely:
> (a) only to accept as fellow inhabitants people who really live from the land and do not have any other source of income except that produced by their own arms and their own hoes.
> (b) only to accept heads of family.
> (c) only to accept people who will come to live here.
> (d) only to accept people who will join us in our struggle and be united with us.

The families said that all newcomers had to accept these conditions, which they called *a lei do posseiro* (the peasant's law). If they did, they would then be given a plot of 110 hectares.

The peasants had acted not a moment too soon. Later that year they received a visit from a group of men headed by a certain Aristeu (they never discovered his full name) from São Paulo. Aristeu said that he owned the land and that they must all leave. Later officials from the IBDF visited the huts of all the peasant families telling them that they were breaking the law by cutting down the forest without authorisation. The peasant families successfully resisted these and other pressures on them.

When we went there in 1979, the hamlet was peaceful, with a warm, happy atmosphere. It was one of the most isolated places we visited and seemed to belong to another century. Nearly all the huts were made of wattle-and-daub, with roofs of palm leaves. Vans and pick-ups, which could get to the hamlet during the dry season down the rough road from Porto Alegre, were rarely seen. Nearly everyone travelled by horseback or on foot and used ox-carts to transport their crops or carried them on their backs. We saw women spinning and weaving cotton which had been cultivated on their plots or on those of their neighbours. We admired the hammocks and clothes they made.

The peasants said that there were by then about 500 families living around Canabrava and they were confident that they would be strong enough to resist any further efforts to evict them. They were pushing now for greater integration into the market economy: they wanted the road to Porto

Alegre to be improved so as to allow transport throughout the year, and they wanted the Bank of Brazil to send in a representative to buy up their surplus crops.

When I went back in November 1981, things had changed considerably. There were more vehicles in the little town. During the previous harvest the Bank of Brazil had sent in a buyer for the first time. Several farmers told me that they had been surprised how quickly they had spent the money they had received and that they would try to make it go further in the following year.

Canabrava still had no police force and few seemed to want one. The local mayor, from the pro-government Partido Democrático Social (PDS), had visited them the previous year to tell them that he would soon be building a landing strip near their village and that they would soon be seeing planes land. But the peasant families had objected. They did not want a landing strip, they had said, for they had heard all too often of ranches flying in scores of gunmen to use against peasant families. If the mayor wanted to help them, they had added, then he could use the money to improve the road. But of course he hadn't, they told us, with a twinkle in their eyes.

The peasants' land, which covered about 100,000 hectares, was by now hemmed in completely by five ranches: Manah, Tres Irmãos, São José da Liberdade, Santa Isabel and Piraguassu. The peasants were still confident, however, that they would not be evicted and that eventually INCRA would come in and give them land titles. They said that there was no land left for new arrivals.

The peasants were still united and determined. They had shown considerable solidarity with peasant families in difficulties elsewhere and they confirmed that they had sent two van-loads of men and women to help reap the crops in Ribeirão Bonito and Cascalheira in April 1981 when the peasant families there were involved in the conflict with the landowner João Evangelista. They said that they had sent in men prepared to fight when peasant families in Porto Alegre had been under serious threat from the Piraguassu ranch. However, the system of 'peasants' law' and the families' determination to govern themselves were breaking down. The peasants' attention had turned to other things, such as marketing their crops, obtaining better road links and getting bank loans.

The Radicalisation of the Catholic Church

Members of the Catholic Church have played a key role in the organisation of the peasantry in the Amazon. Their involvement has been so great that military officers have frequently claimed that radical members of the church – and left-wing activists within the church – have tried to use the peasantry to create a revolutionary force to further their own political objectives. It is evident that church members explain their present involvement from a very different perspective. They say that they were stung into action by the horror and outrage they felt at the government's gross negligence of its duties towards the peasant families and its scarcely disguised connivance with the landowners. To understand the dynamics of this complex relationship, it is necessary to look at the process by which the church changed from being a reactionary institution, linked to the ruling classes, to a progressive body, prepared to undergo considerable repression in order to defend the rights of the peasant families.

The Church's Changing Role

During the colonial epoch the Catholic Church's influence in Brazil did not stem primarily from a religious commitment to the people. There, as elsewhere in South America, the church's power was, as in Europe, largely the result of its fusion with the ruling hierarchy and its multiple involvement in education, social welfare and administration. The ruling classes supported and protected the church, giving it special privileges; and in return, the church served as an agent of colonial expansion, and as a key institution of social control.

However, after Independence in 1822, the Brazilian Church was gradually shaken out of this comfortable niche. The first jolts were the anti-clerical attacks in the 19th Century which forced the church out of some areas of public life. Later, in the 20th Century, important social changes such as the growth of large cities and the emergence of a powerful, secular, industrialised society, made further inroads on the church's position. At the same time, the church's ideological position was threatened by political groups on the left and by salvation-oriented Protestant sects. Both movements offered the population a coherent set of anti-Catholic values.

To a greater or lesser degree, these changes occurred all over Latin America. As a result, small groups of leading Catholics became concerned that the church was losing its relevance for the people and, as a result, might disappear as a powerful institution. A few people began to argue that the church must break away from its traditional association with the established ruling groups and take on a new progressive role in society. They argued that in this way the church would take on a new meaning and return to a role much closer to that played by the early church.

These endeavours gained considerable impetus from the Second Vatican Council, held in 1962, which strove to steer the church into a new phase of relevance and effectiveness. For the Latin American church in particular, the changes were given an enormous boost by the second general conference of Latin American bishops, which was held in Medellín in Colombia in 1968. For the first time, bishops from all over the continent made a 'preferential option for the poor'. The bishops committed themselves 'to awaken in men and in nations a living awareness of justice, to arouse in them a dynamic sense of responsibility and solidarity'. They stressed that this action must be given priority, with an emphasis on the need 'to define the interests of the poor and oppressed and, while favouring integration, to denounce energetically the abuses stemming from the excessive inequalities between rich and poor, powerful and weak'.

The Catholic writer Julian Filochowski puts it as follows:

It [Medellín] proved to be a watershed in the history of the Church in Latin America. The 130 bishops at Medellín, encouraged by the presence of Paul VI following his radical enyclical, *Populorum Progressio*, denounced the unjust maintenance of wealth by a privileged few at the expense of the mass of their fellow citizens – what Archbishop Hélder Câmara terms 'internal colonisalism'.

The bishops dissociated themselves from the continent's rich and powerful elites and placed themselves firmly on the side of the poor and oppressed, working for effective change and promising sustained education for liberation. With the help of expert advisers, theologians and social scientists, they examined every facet of Christian life and practice and drew up a series of documents which have been read and analysed in every corner of Latin America. According to some observers, the conclusions of Medellín have throughout the decade constituted the Magna Carta of the church in Latin America.

If events in the European Church are dated from Vatican II, in Latin America they talk of the post-Medellín Church. Certainly the conclusions of Medellín have guided and inspired many Christians during these last ten years. Over this period the theology of liberation blossomed, basic grass-roots Christian communities mushroomed, and clergy and lay people alike throughout the continent were led to a much greater commitment to social justice and to struggle for the liberation of the oppressed.[5]

The principles established at Medellín were applied in difficult political conditions much sooner in Brazil than in most other Latin American nations. Whereas in Chile and Argentina the period of harsh military rule only began in 1973 and 1976 respectively, in Brazil the regime was resorting increasingly to violent forms of repression to suppress opposition by the end of 1968. Members of the church were faced with increasingly clear alternatives: either they remained silent, and thus indirectly endorsed the government's fearful use of force; or they spoke out against the political, social and economic consequences of the government's policies, and were prepared themselves to become victims of repression.

At first, opposition to the government was restricted to isolated church groups scattered over the country. Dom Helder Câmara, Archbishop of Recife, was a highly important pioneer figure. Partly protected by his high office, he was able to voice outspoken criticisms that would have spelt imprisonment for others. Although he spread out his cloak of protection as widely as possible, several of the priests and lay workers in his team were persecuted and one was killed.

Helder Câmara and his team of workers were fairly isolated during this early period. Over the next few years, however, they began to gain much wider support, particularly in the Amazon region, as many priests and lay workers became increasingly angered by the government's refusal to curb lawlessness, and by its cynical acceptance of violence as the price of

Amazon development. These church workers began to call for a radical change in the church's role and started to organise their activities on a local and later regional scale.

In the early 1970s these members of the church grew increasingly aware that the church had become the only organisation in the country with the power and authority to stand up to the government, particularly the highly repressive security forces. To some extent the church had this new role thrust upon it, as the maimed judiciary, Congress and labour movement were clearly incapable of properly carrying out their functions. But it is also true to say that, if it had not been for the dedication and courage of many of its members, the church could have refused to take on this new challenge. With the growing awareness of the national political importance of its actions, many members began to press for national organisations to coordinate the church's activities across the country.

By then, the church had already begun to set up Basic Christian Communities (CEBs). These little groups of committed Christians met once or twice a week to discuss not only religious topics but also matters of everyday life. Because of Brazil's chronic shortage of priests, many of these CEBs were run by *agentes pastorais* (lay workers) – and the church thus helped, perhaps unintentionally, to develop local leaders. One such was Raimundo Ferreira Lima, known as Gringo, the opposition candidate in the Contag elections in Conceição do Araguaia in 1980 who was killed by a landowner. At the end of 1981, there were estimated to be 80,000 CEBs all over Brazil.

In the mid 1970s, the church began to set up national organisations to bring many of these hitherto isolated CEBs into contact with each other and to give greater force to their common demands. In 1975 it set up the Pastoral Land Commission (CPT) as the national body for the non-Indian rural poor, and the Pastoral Worker Commission (CPO) as the national body for the urban working class. At the same time, the Missionary Indian Council (Cimi) was transformed. Most of its members became passionately involved in the Indian cause and made increasingly outspoken criticisms of the policies adopted by Funai (see Chapter 5).

Soon every diocese in the country had been affected by the upsurge in political awareness. Although many individual bishops and priests were vehemently opposed to the changes, the more radical faction began to dominate. The new ideas began to filter through into official statements made by the church. Though the CPT and Cimi took the lead, the new radical stance was soon reflected in the documents issued by the bishops' conference (CNBB), the most important church forum in Brazil.

An important step was the document published by the CNBB in November 1976, just after the murder by a policeman in the north of Mato Grosso of the priest João Bosco Penido Burnier who belonged to one of Brazil's prominent Catholic families. The outrage caused by his death undoubtedly contributed to the highly critical tone of the document. For the first time, the bishops went beyond a simple denunciation of the social injustices in the country and began to develop a comprehensive theory to explain why they were occurring. They argued that the widespread poverty and social inequalities, far from being merely the result of Brazil's backwardness, were also in part the price that the country was paying for its industrial development and the opening up of the Amazon, both of which were benefiting just a tiny, extremely rich elite. The bishops called for a different form of national development in which the benefits would be distributed among the whole of society. They claimed that the present highly inegalitarian set-up was only possible because of the closed nature of the political system, based on the close alliance between the civilian elite and the armed forces, who were increasingly obsessed with the pernicious doctrine of national security.

The document states:

> The ideology of national security, placed above personal security, is spreading over Latin America, as occurred in countries under Soviet dominion. Inspired by it, regimes of force refer to the war they are waging against communism and in favour of economic development and brand as subversive all those who do not agree with their authoritarian view of the organisation of society. The training for this war against subversion leads to an increase in the brutality employed by its agents and creates a new type of fanaticism and a climate of violence and fear.

The new radical vein continued to characterise CNBB statements in following years. The important document, *Christian Demands of a Political Order*, which was approved at the CNBB's annual meeting in February 1977, contained a special analysis of the unemployed and under-employed, the so-called *marginais* (marginalised). It stated:

> The existence in vast sectors of the population of the phenomenon of marginalisation is proof that the common good has not been realised; among other causes, marginalisation tends to grow to the extent that important decisions are taken to further the interests, not of the people as a whole, but of certain classes and groups.

By now the government, the top military officers and the landowners had been angered – and scared – by the changes. Many felt that they had been betrayed by the church, which in the past had been relied upon as a conservative, traditional body. Though at first the government as such avoided public rows with the church, individuals began to express their irritation. Such was the case in March 1977 when the CPT issued a particularly virulent statement in which it said:

> We believe that the increasingly violent land conflicts which are sweeping the country from north to south cannot be resolved within a system in which money buys both justice and a man's conscience and in which the poor are neither heard nor considered.

Justice minister Armando Falcão called the statement 'unjust, improper and untrue'. The president of the Supreme Military Tribunal (STM), Brigadier Carlos Alberto Huet Sampaio, let fly: 'My church is not this Communist Church we have now. My church is the one my parents brought me up in. It is not this advanced doctrine of seizing the Host in your hand.'

None the less the radicalisation of the church continued. The CNBB stated in the document which it published after its general assembly in April 1978:

> There has been an exacerbation of the conflict between oppressors and oppressed, due to the situation of glaring social inequality.
>
> The injustice in the occupation and use of the land has grown worse, as a result of the pressure exercised by large companies on those who live on and from the land . . . The big official projects, which turn small landowners and peasant farmers off the land, paying them unjust prices after long delays, also drive unprepared and penniless peasants to live as social outcasts on the edge of the cities.
>
> This pressure is also being exercised on the Indian population, which has been progressively destroyed by the reduction in the size of its reserves, by forced migrations, by diseases contracted from the expansion fronts of rural capitalism . . .
>
> The abiding injustice has been maintained by mechanisms of institutionalised violence, by repressive. forces operating outside the law and enjoying the omission, complacency or connivance of the authorities and thus provoking desperate reactions which provide a pretext for even more violent repression . . .

The analysis was taken a step further in 1980 when the bishops approved yet another outspoken document at their general assembly held in February in Itaici near São Paulo. The document, entitled *The Church and the Land*, centred in particular on the causes of rural poverty and included what were by then habitual attacks on the country's socio-economic structure: 'The greatest responsibility lies with those who have set up and maintain a system which enriches a few at the price of impoverishing the masses.' The new element was the emphasis on worker mobilisation. The document stated:

> We reaffirm our support for workers' organisations, placing our strength and the means at our disposal at the service of this cause . . . Taking care not to be a substitute for the initiatives of the people, our pastoral action will support the conscious and critical participation of workers in trade unions, associations, commissions . . . We are in favour of the mobilisation of workers both to demand the application and/or reformulation of existing laws and to call for agrarian reform . .

Moreover, worker mobilisation was seen not only as a right but also as an obligation:

> Some responsibility [for the present situation of misery and suffering] must be attributed to the workers' failure to unite and to organise. On the other hand, the people have been barred from participation in decisions governing the destiny of the country.

In the Itaici document, the bishops moved from a position of denunciation to one of as yet cautious support for popular mobilisation. The document suggested that the bishops were beginning to look at the rural population, not only as the passive objects of exploitation, but also as subjects, who were capable of taking the initiative and helping to shape their own history. In an interview at the time, Dom Pedro Casaldáliga said that for him Itaici was a milestone. He commented, not without a touch of irony: 'We now speak of trade unions in the same tone of voice that we use for the Virgin Mary.' It is not by chance that in the Itaici document the bishops allude, if only in passing, to their concern not to preempt workers' organisations although fully supporting them. Many of the bishops were clearly beginning to examine critically the church's traditional attitudes towards the rural population in an attempt to root out the elements of paternalism which at times are expressed in the actions and observations of even the most radical bishops.

The document enraged the conservative sectors in the country. The newspaper *O Estado de S. Paulo*, which represents the traditional landed classes in the state of São Paulo, unleashed an attack on the church, publishing a series of virulently-worded editorials in mid February. It said that the 'communist' bishops had committed 'philosophical blunders which even Marx would have avoided'. Their document, it claimed, reflected 'either ignorance or bad faith, and certainly the desire to create turmoil in the country, without making any constructive proposals'.

The leading organisations of landowners followed up this offensive with their own series of attacks on the church. In March 1980, at a dinner attended by planning minister Antônio Delfim Neto, Flávio Brito, president of the national confederation of agriculture, said that the church was trying 'to impose communism on the country'. Bishop Tomás Balduino, vice-president of Cimi, retorted on the following day: 'The *latifundiários* [big landowners] are organising a witch hunt so that they can blame the church for the increasing number of land conflicts.'

Despite the waves of criticisms, the bishops pushed ahead with their efforts to redefine the role of the church. In August 1981, they published a new document, called *Christian Reflections on the Political Situation*, which stated:

> Over the last few years there has been a marked tendency in the economy to treat as priority policies which favour high-income classes, including refined

methods of bribery and corruption, in direct opposition to the people's interests. An economic model which concentrates income and promotes sophisticated consumerism, at the expense of the basic needs of the population, has made us into one of the countries with the greatest disparity between the highest and lowest income groups.

The bishops called for a radical rethink of the country's priorities.

The document then commented obliquely on the sensitive issue of the involvement of church members in politics:

> To install and maintain democracy, free elections are not enough. It is necessary to create the conditions for the people to organise . . . The church's evangelical mission does not mean it should overlook socio-political problems . . . The church does not harbour party political ambitions or pretensions . . . It does not agree with the clergy becoming party political militants, nor does it interpret party political aspirations or mediate between political factions. But this does not mean it is apolitical. Its responsibility is to remember the ethical dimensions of political decisions. The future of millions of people is at stake.

On the instructions of the National Security Council, the government launched an offensive against the church in late 1981, interrogating and harassing church workers in many regions of the country, particularly the Amazon. However, the church did not draw in its horns but kept up its verbal attacks. At its annual conference in February 1982, it surprised many observers by fiercely criticising the government for its urban policies. In a document as strongly worded as ever, the bishops placed the blame for the disorderly occupation of the cities, the mushrooming of the shanty-towns and the outrageous land speculation, on the country's economic structure, 'which forces many to work for a miserable wage, while maintaining the privileges of a few'. The bishops then called on the government to put an end to land and property speculation, to impose a capital gains tax on land transactions, and to rehouse many of the country's growing number of shanty-town dwellers.

As predicted by church members themselves, the growing radicalisation of the church brought an increase in the use of violence against them. In December 1978, the church published a little booklet[6] in which it listed the known cases of violence against church members since 1968. Five priests, one Dominican friar and one seminarist had been killed. There had been 34 reported cases of torture of priests, church workers and seminarists. No less than 273 church workers had been arrested.

The 'Red Bishop' of São Félix

The radicalisation of the church in the Amazon has occurred in some cases against the inclination of the church members themselves. The shock and horror many have felt, when confronted with the suffering of the region, have led bishops, priests, nuns and lay workers of all shades of political opinion to voice outraged protests. Some of the most impassioned defenders of the poor and oppressed today were no radicals when they first came to the region. This is even the case of Dom Pedro Casaldáliga, the member of the church who has provoked most rage among landowners.

Dom Pedro is bishop of São Félix in the north of Mato Grosso. His huge diocese covers 150,000 square kilometres, an area almost twice the size of Portugal. In order to visit with any frequency all the little villages within his diocese, Dom Pedro is constantly on the move, travelling mostly in ramshackle, dusty buses which often break down on the pot-holed roads. Dom Pedro belonged to an extremely conservative Spanish order, the Claretians, before he came to Brazil. Yet now he is one of the more radical bishops and does not believe in any form of collaboration with the government. He expresses his views in stark terms. For instance, in a little pamphlet he wrote for the peasants, he stated:

> Our Church is against the *latifúndio* and against slavery, and for this reason it is persecuted by the Masters of Money, Land and Politics. Neither sharks [landowners] nor exploiters, nor traitors to the people have a place in our church. For no one belongs to the People of God if he crushes the Sons of God. No one belongs to the Church of Christ if he does not carry out the Commandments of Christ.

Dom Pedro has expressed his political views even more explicitly in some of his poems, for which he is winning international fame. Of Catalan nationality, he has written many of his poems in Spanish or Catalan. In recent years, as he has become more immersed in the Amazon, he has started to write many more poems in Portuguese. Here is an extract from one of the most controversial, written in the early 1970s:

> Incito a la subversión
> contra el Poder y el Dinero.
> Quiero subvertir la Ley
> que pervierte al Pueblo en grey
> y el gobierno en carnicero.
> (Mi Pastor se hizo Cordero.
> Servidor se hizo mi Rey.)
>
> I encourage subversion
> against Power and Money.
> I want to subvert the Law
> that turns the people into a flock of sheep
> and the Government into a slaughterer.
> (My Shepherd became a Lamb.
> My King became a Servant.)

Dom Pedro is passionately involved with the Indians and peasant families with whom he works. He has said on several occasions that he would willingly lay down his life for them, if by doing so he could further their cause. It is perhaps ironic that the priest João Bosco Penido Burnier was probably killed by mistake, having been taken for Dom Pedro with whom he was travelling at the time. Dom Pedro once explained to the magazine *Porantim* his wish to die a martry's death:

> I don't want it to appear evangelical snobbery. Perhaps because of the life I've led, perhaps because of my temperament, which is a bit radical, I've wished ever since childhood to be a martyr and I still do. In one of my poems I say: 'By my death I shall make life come true, finally I shall have loved'.

He spoke about Rodolfo Lukembein, a priest killed by landowners attempting to take over part of the land belonging to the Bororo Indians (see Chapter 5) in northern Mato Grosso:

> By his death Father Rodolfo caused a furore, not only among his congregation, but throughout the whole country and abroad. And in this way, I think, he did far more for the Indian cause than he would have done if he had gone on working there.

Consistently with his position, Dom Pedro refuses to say mass for the landowners on their ranches. He gave us his reasons: 'In this situation of extreme exploitation and violence, there can be no half measures. Our Evangelical mission is to take up the cause of the oppressed.' Not that Dom Pedro receives many invitations from the landowners, for he arouses a startlingly intense hatred in them. It is clear that they feel threatened by his extraordinary popularity in his diocese, and the love and affection felt for him by many peasant families.

At times, spiteful and gratuitous attacks on his charismatic qualities have been made. 'Brigitte Bardot in trousers' was the irate, frustrated description made of him by one federal deputy belonging to the pro-government party after hearing Dom Pedro's impassioned speech at the parliamentary inquiry into land in 1977. And in our long interview with José Augusto Medeiros, a sharp-witted land speculator, the only occasion on which he showed any emotion was when we mentioned Dom Pedro: 'He is a dangerous fanatic. Like all Spaniards, he is hot-blooded and he hates all large landowners, on principle. A committed communist, his only goal is to overthrow the system.'

Some landowners openly admitted to us that they had been pressing for the expulsion of Dom Pedro from Brazil. A vigorous campaign was waged against the bishop in the mass media througout 1977. Edgardo Erichsen, the director of the national Globo radio and television network, violently attacked Dom Pedro in a television programme. He finished with these words:

> It seems that the bishop has exchanged his crucifix and rosary for the hammer and sickle, his prayer book for the thoughts of Mao Tse-tung, his priestly

piety for violence and that he is only waiting for the right moment to exchange his cassock for a guerrilla's uniform. Of some left-wing priests it can be said that they light one candle to God and the other to the devil. But for Bishop Dom Pedro Maria Casaldáliga, the least that can be maintained is that he lights both his candles to the devil.

The speech was reproduced as a paid announcement in a leading newspaper a few days later.

The campaign against Dom Pedro still continues in a sporadic fashion. In August 1981, Frederico Campos, governor of Mato Grosso, called for his expulsion, saying that he did not know how 'a well-known communist' was allowed to carry out freely his 'subversive activities'. He said that it was as a result of Dom Pedro's activities that the Araguaia region had become the area of his state with the most serious land conflicts, concerning both peasant families and Indians. The campaign has failed to secure the bishop's expulsion, largely because of the firm attitude taken by the CNBB, which has made it clear to the government that any action taken by the authorities against the bishop would be regarded as an act of aggression against the church itself. Indeed, the solidarity with Dom Pedro which has been shown by almost all of the country's bishops, including many with very different political views, has undoubtedly contributed to the radicalisation of the church.

The Government's Counter-offensive

Perhaps surprisingly in the face of the increasing peasant mobilisation and the growing involvement of the Catholic Church, the federal authorities have only recently begun to play an active role in the region. There is nothing remarkable about their inertia in the 1940s and 1950s, for at that time the Amazon region was of little economic or political significance. But in the late 1960s and 1970s, when the government was pouring large sums of money into the region through the Sudam tax rebate scheme and its road-building programme, it is at first sight astonishing that it did not do more to supervise the occupation of the region.

This low level of activity, however, does not mean that the authorities were unaware of what was going on in the region. When pressed, many government officials in Brasília admitted to us that they knew about the violence but believed that it played a necessary and inevitable role in the occupation. Some cited the American far west as a precedent. Others justified the expulsion of the backward peasant families in the name of development, saying that they had to make way for larger and allegedly more productive big companies. Sebastião Dante de Camargo Júnior, president of Sudeco, a body similar to Sudam which was set up for south Goiás and Mato Grosso, told us in 1972 that the eviction of the peasant families was part of the 'natural' process of occupation. Antônio Delfim Neto, finance minister during the years of the 'economic miracle', who was to become economic supremo again in August 1979, held a similar view. In 1973, he commented: 'The Amazon is still in the bandit stage. It is only later that the sheriff will be required.'

Other government officials expressed concern about the lawlessness, but claimed that the government was helpless in the face of the scale of the problem. Dom Alano Maria Pena, Bishop of Marabá, recalled that in 1971 Colonel Jarbas Passarinho, then labour minister, spoke of his despair at the situation. The colonel confided to the bishop: 'I'm beginning to think that the land situation in the south of Pará is so difficult – because of the legal anomalies, the overlapping of land titles and other irregularities – that there is no possible solution.'

This protestation of helplessness never seemed very convincing to us. When the government decided in the early 1970s that military intervention was necessary to wipe out about 70 rural guerrillas in the north of Goiás, it was able to find the resources to send in 10,000 soldiers. If the authorities had placed the same priority on ensuring a peaceful and law-abiding occupation, it could have found the money.

It seemed clear to us that the government took a deliberate decision not to supervise the occupation. In part, its behaviour may have been the result of close links between top goverment officials and landowners. Not infrequently, officials' families benefited directly from the lucrative land deals. On other occasions, government officials – both civilian and military – were given profitable jobs, usually as directors of large economic groups, on leaving office. In these circumstances it was clearly against the interests of the officials to take a principled stand over the involvement of big companies in land conflicts in the Amazon.

But it struck us repeatedly that self-interest was not a sufficient explanation. Many officials who seemed to have nothing to gain personally were firm supporters of the government's policy. What they almost all shared, however, was a view of the world in which the occupation of the Amazon was seen as part of the dynamic process of capitalist expansion and the expropriation of most of the peasantry was regarded as inevitable. Any attempt to enforce the law at an early stage would, they felt, create unnecessary barriers in the way of this process of modernisation. As a result, they were predisposed to take the side of the landowners, even if they were technically breaking the law, in their struggle against the peasant families who were widely regarded as retrogressive and anti-capitalist.

In the early 1970s the lawlessness became so extensive that it seemed that the government, despite its reservations, was becoming concerned at the possible consequences and was getting ready to take decisive action. But each time, the government's promise of tough new measures proved to be empty and, despite the publicity given to the policy shift, very little changed.

The most important of these first moves was the federal government's decision in 1971 to take away from the state governments the responsibility for the occupation of much of the region. Despite local protests, it decided to expropriate all land which lay 100 kilometres on either side of federal roads in the Amazon region. This huge area, of 230 million hectares – 27 per cent of all Brazilian territory and ten times the size of the United Kingdom – was handed over to the federal body INCRA to administer.

It was intended that INCRA should sort out the legal situation of all farmers, big and small, who had already settled on this land, and then supervise the orderly occupation of the remaining lands. This did not happen. Understaffed and poorly financed, INCRA was unable to respond to the demands of such an immense task. At times, it could not even resolve the most pressing conflicts on the land in its care and violent confrontations carried on just as in the past.

On a few occasions the change in legislation actually made the situation even worse for the peasant families. Such was the case for the 300 families which were living on land claimed by the Paraporã ranch beside the Belém–Brasília road in the south of Pará. In the late 1960s Paraporã sent in gunmen to evict these families, some of whom had been living on their plots for more than 30 years.

As frequently happened, the conflict was made worse by the negligence, or the connivance, of the local authorities. As Paraporã was receiving tax rebates under the Sudam scheme, it had earlier obtained, as part of the necessary documentation, a certificate from the local mayor which testified that there were no peasant families on the land belonging to the ranch. Paraporã then used this certificate as proof that the families were lying when they claimed to have lived on the land for decades.

The conflict flared up into open warfare late in 1971 and the state government finally decided to act. It disappropriated 17,000 hectares from the ranch and gave this land to the peasant families, some of whom had already been evicted by the ranch. But Paraporã fought a rearguard action. It sued the Pará government, claiming that it had had no right to expropriate the land as it was by then under the jurisdiction of INCRA. Paraporã won the case and the expropriated land was handed to the ranch. INCRA did nothing, as Paraporã proceeded to evict the peasant families, some of them for a second time.

By the late 1970s, it was abundantly clear that INCRA was not providing the decisive action which the government had said that it wanted. Not all of the blame can be placed on INCRA itself, for it had been instructed to carry out a large number of complex tasks: administer colonisation projects, sort out land conflicts, issue land titles, run cooperatives, carry out rural electrification programmes and others. And for all this, it was given a quite inadequate budget. Paulo Yakota, who became president of INCRA at the beginning of the Figueiredo government in March 1979, was closely linked to planning minister Antônio Delfim Neto. Though he was a skilful and efficient administrator, Yakota had to deal with the clumsy and overburdened INCRA administration. He had little chance of pulling INCRA into shape.

At the beginning of 1980, this all changed. In a momentous decision, the military-controlled National Security Council (CSN) took over responsibility for the resolution of land conflict in a key area of the Amazon, assuming despotic powers in the region. This decision was to have important consequences, not only for the Amazon but for the whole of Brazil. Although the military had been in power since the *coup* in 1964, it had not directly ruled the country. Instead, it had greatly strengthened the executive power, at the expense of the legislature, and then selected civilian technocrats to govern, while retaining the right of veto over their actions. On the whole, the largely civilian executive had operated within the limits of the law.

The main exception had been the government's handling of so-called subversives. Here the government, headed throughout the period by a retired general, had given the armed forces, particularly the army, near absolute power to deal with the problem. This had led to an enormous expansion of the repressive apparatus, with serious violations of human rights.

The decision in 1980 meant that the National Security Council had decided that land conflict in this area of the Amazon was threatening national security and should thus be handled by the armed forces, using the extra-legal methods employed against subversives. This represented a serious setback for human rights precisely at a time when the government claimed to be bringing democracy back to the country. As the alleged subversives in this case – peasant farmers in alliance with Catholic priests and lay workers – had repeatedly called for greater law enforcement in the region, there seems little justification for using extra-legal methods to deal with them.

The new development cannot thus be satisfactorily explained with reference merely to events in the Amazon. Much more important than these was the need of the powerful repressive apparatus which had emerged in the early 1970s to find a new area of activity, since the urban and rural guerrillas had been decisively defeated. After first establishing a foothold in an area of the Amazon, the armed forces were then to take on responsibility for resolving land conflict throughout the country. Indirectly, the new development illustrates one of the themes of this book – the growing integration of the Amazon into the rest of the country.

The emergence of the armed forces as the main authority over land matters was of great significance for the Amazon. Henceforth key decisions for the region would be taken by generals in Brasilia. As a result, it is worth looking in some detail at national political events which help to explain why the armed forces were able to take this decisive step.

The Changing Role of the Armed Forces

At the end of March 1964, the armed forces staged a *coup* that put an end to 20 years of uninterrupted civilian rule. They received considerable support for their *coup* from the middle classes, who had been terrified by the left-wing rhetoric of the deposed President João Goulart. As a result, the early years of military rule were not characterised by great repression. Although no political opposition was allowed and the old party system was replaced by an artificial structure of just two parties – Aliança Renovadora Nacional (Arena) the pro-government party, and Movimento Democrático Brasileiro (MDB), a ragbag of moderate opposition forces – the regime still tolerated a certain degree of criticism, particularly from the established press.

However, this began to change in the late 1960s. By then, the alliance between the military rulers and the country's technocrats had become stronger. The generals increasingly saw it as their main task to provide the technocrats with social peace so that they would have a free hand to carry out whatever policies they regarded as necessary for Brazil to achieve 'economic take-off' to use the jargon of the day imported from US political scientists. They came to believe that virtually no social sacrifice was too costly for the sake of building Brazil into one of the main economic powers in the world.

At the same time, the military rulers became increasingly influenced by the doctrine of national security which was becoming widely disseminated among Latin America's armed forces. Julian Filochowski describes this doctrine:

> According to the ideology of the National Security State, the world is divided into two opposing camps – that of evil atheistic communism and that of western Christian civilisation – which are in a state of total and permanent war. In this war against both the enemy without and the enemy within, national security overrides all other considerations and its preservation becomes the pretext for the most grotesque violations of human rights and freedom. Those who question the *status quo* and advocate reforms and a more equitable society are labelled 'subversives' and are brutally dealt with.[7]

As a result of this antagonistic, polarised view of the world, the military leaders felt the need for greater social control over the country and began to restructure and strengthen the repressive apparatus of the state. As an essential first step, they built up a new intelligence network so that they would be given early warning of any unrest or subversive activity. The backbone of the new system is the National Intelligence Service (SNI), which was set up in June 1964 by General Golbery do Couto e Silva as an organ outside the control of the ministries. It has a central agency in Brasília and state and municipal branches all over Brazil. The SNI quickly became an efficient national network and its president one of the most powerful people in the country.

Under its aegis, the military ministers established their own intelligence networks; special intelligence units were set up in non-military ministries and state companies. Federal and state police forces also set up their own services. The whole complex system has become known as the *comunidade de informações* (intelligence community). Outside the control of Congress and the cabinet, it is subordinated to the National Security Council (CSN), the most powerful body in the land. Though all civilian ministers are technically members of this council, it is dominated by top military leaders. Its official function is to advise the government on matters of national security and it tends to take charge during moments of crisis in the country.

During the same period, the government greatly increased its control over the legal system and the judiciary. From 1964 to 1974 it passed a series of Institutional Acts which created a 'revolutionary' power, outside the control of Congress, which allowed the executive to rule by itself by passing its own decrees. The most important of all the new pieces of legislation was Institutional Act no. 5. It was passed at the end of 1968, the year in which for the first time civilian opposition to the military government emerged in a big way. Thousands of students held demonstrations in Rio and São Paulo. The Catholic Church, through the bishops' conference, made its first public criticisms of the government. After several years of inactivity, workers held massive strikes in São Paulo's industrial suburbs. The lawyers began to reorganise through the Brazilian Bar Association, the OAB (Ordem de Advogados Brasileiros).

Institutional Act no. 5 gave the President power to close down Congress, which he promptly did. It also enabled him to intervene in the state governments and local district councils to remove officials and to cancel mandates. It established no time limit for its own validity, being considered permanent (unlike the other Institutional Acts). It took another Decree-Law to have it finally revoked in 1979. Institutional Act no. 5 was followed in 1969 by a modified and much tougher version of the National Security Law first established in 1964. The new law reflected the military leaders' new concept of national security by permitting repression of internal pressures and social discontent. The law defined as a crime the dissemination of any information which would 'turn the population against the constituted authorities'. It also prohibited strikes.

The hardening of the regime drove opposition underground. Left-wing groups, particularly ones set up among students, began to wage guerrilla warfare in the cities in 1969. Although they lacked the popular support to threaten the regime, they were a serious destabilising factor. Their most spectacular feat was to kidnap the US ambassador, Charles Elbrick, whom they only released after they had obtained several important concessions, including the release of political prisoners. After these guerrillas had been defeated in the early 1970s, a small group of activists moved to Xambioá in the north of Goiás. They were tracked down by the intelligence services and were forced, prematurely, to begin a rural guerrilla offensive. Though there were only 70 to 80 militants, about 10,000 soldiers were deployed to crush them. This episode was to have a profound impact on the government's Amazon policies, for it alerted the military leaders to the potential security risk in the Amazon. From then on the military leaders, channelling much of their action through the National Security Council, were to greatly increase their involvement in this region.

In turn, the outbreak of guerrilla activity gave the government a golden opportunity for pushing ahead with a further strengthening of the repressive apparatus. The armed forces, working with the SNI, set up centres for the interrogation and torture of political prisoners. The country's police forces were reorganised, something which the government had been anxious to do for some time. The military police, which had been run by the various state governments until then, were brought under the central control of the army. As we frequently saw in the Amazon, they have become a tough, well-disciplined force and are sent in to restore order at moments of great tension. But despite the reorganisation, the link with the state government – and thus with the big landowners – has remained strong. Peasant families repeatedly told us that members of the military police, known as soldiers, always took the side of the landowners.

In contrast, the army is generally respected for being tough but impartial. At moments of high tension, peasant families often ask for the army to be called in, for they are confident that it will give them a fair hearing. This happened in both the tales told later in the book. The only part of the Amazon where this is not the case is the area around Xambioá in the north of Goiás, which underwent the tough counter-insurgency operation in the early 1970s. Peasant families were forcibly moved and brutally interrogated by the army. Even today many of the families are still terrified of the army.

Though the civilian police forces in the states were also brought under a more centralised form of organisation in the late 1960s, the change was much less marked, at least in the Amazon. The civilian police have remained an underpaid and highly corrupt body which works hand-in-glove with the landowners in the region.

Because of its particularly powerful position at the centre of government, the SNI has become a highly effective political springboard. Its first president, General Golbery do Couto e Silva, was later appointed head of the President's civilian household and was, effectively, the most powerful person in the country during the government of General Ernesto Geisel (1974–9) and the first two years of the government of General João Baptista Figueiredo. Golbery's demise was largely engineered by the then president of the SNI, General Octávio Aguiar de Medeiros. Both General Médici, who took over as president of the SNI from Golbery in 1967, and General Figueiredo, who headed the SNI during the Geisel government, used their time in office to emerge as the strongest candidate for the presidency.

Within their own terms of reference, the military rulers were successful in their efforts to provide the technocrats with the social peace which was seen as essential for economic development. For many years Congress became little more than a rubber stamp for the executive's decisions, with the government using its power of *cassação* (explusion, with loss of political rights) to deal with any unruly members. The government was not as successful with the judiciary. Though it successfully undermined the independence of the judiciary, it was unable to break the resistance of OAB, the Brazilian Bar Association. As a result, OAB became the target of bomb attacks probably carried out by members of the *comunidade*. One of the bombs, which exploded in September 1980, killed the secretary to Seabra Fagundes, the president of OAB.

The military leaders believe that to a large extent they were responsible for Brazil's economic boom. From 1969 to 1972, the economy grew each year by about 10 per cent and the country's industrial base became stronger and more diversified. The military rulers saw it as right and proper that the income generated by this growth should go first of all to the top echelon of powerful economic groups which were in the best position to reinvest the money in further industrial expansion, and to a lesser extent to the expanding middle classes whose skills were required by the booming industries. It was seen as unfortunate, but inevitable, that the living standards of the mass of unskilled workers should stagnate, or even fall, during this period.

However, by the mid 1970s it was becoming clear that the military government could not continue to repress all political dissent for ever. The very dynamics of development were demanding a more sophisticated and less openly repressive form of government. In 1975 President Ernesto Geisel began a process of political liberalisation which was to be called first *distensão* (relaxation) and later *abertura* (opening). The main objective behind the liberalisation was to prevent the build up of a powerful political movement in favour of a return to civilian rule. By granting minor political reforms, the government was confident that it could win support from some of the opposition and thus play off against each other the various factions which were already deeply divided.

So the government gradually began to lift some of its strict controls. Censorship was removed from the press (but remained on television, with its much greater political impact). The authoritarian institutional acts were repealed (though the government retained the right to invoke extraordinary powers in the case of a 'national emergency'). Political exiles were allowed to return (though the government controlled the formation of new political parties).

Four new opposition parties were formed. They included the Workers' Party (Partido dos Trabalhadores – PT), founded by a group of trade unionists, headed by Luís Ignácio da Silva, known as Lula, and the Democratic Labour Party (Partido Democrático Trabalhista – PDT), set up by Leonel Brizola, who had been governor of Rio Grande do Sul state before the military *coup*. Under the new legislation, each grouping had to have the word 'party' in its official name. So the MDB became the Party of the Brazilian Democratic Movement (Partido do Movimento Democrático Brasileiro – PMDB) and Arena changed its name completely to Social Democratic Party (Partido Democrático Social – PDS).

However, while *abertura* brought back some political freedom to the country, particularly to the urban middle classes, it did not mean the end of authoritarian military government. The powers of Congress remained extremely limited, with the executive taking the major decisions, outside any kind of democratic control. The most powerful body in the country was still the National Security Council, which refused to allow any investigation into its activities.

To prevent the opposition parties from rapidly gaining control of Congress, the government resorted to ever more blatant forms of jerry-mandering and electoral manipulation. At the same time, it staunchly refused to permit any investigation into the alleged abuses committed by the intelligence services and the armed forces during the most authoritarian phase of the government.

However, it became clear that, if *abertura* was to continue defusing political discontent, the military government would have to allow further liberalisation, particularly with respect to its handling of opposition forces. To gain support for his presidential candidacy in 1978, General João Baptista Figueiredo told several top politicians in confidence that he intended, if chosen as President, to move against the *comunidade*, as he believed that it had become too powerful. As he had just left the presidency of the SNI, no one could have been in a better position to take on this difficult task.

In practice the machine proved stronger than the man (if Figueiredo was ever sincere in his commitment). The only part of the *comunidade* to be dismantled was the air force's Centre for Air Force Intelligence and Security (CISA). As a result of the personal endeavours of the air force minister, Brigadier Délio Jardim de Mattos, who is the only one of the three military ministers committed to *abertura*, albeit at a very slow pace, a new administrative unit, called Centre for Air Force Intelligence (CIA) (with, significantly, no mention of 'security' in its title), was set up outside the *comunidade*. The minister later said that dismantling CISA was the most difficult task he had faced in office.

During the early years of the Figueiredo administration, there was considerable evidence that members of the *comunidade* were still carrying out terrorist attacks against individuals and organisations whom they saw as subversive. From the end of August 1979, when Figueiredo signed an amnesty bill allowing political exiles to return to Brazil, until the end of April 1981, there were 41 bomb attacks against liberal or left-wing individuals or organisations, including the OAB and some church bodies. The police, however, refused to carry out proper investigations and only on one occasion did they make a conviction.

The growing suspicion that members of the *comunidade* were involved in these attacks became certainty in 1981. On 30 April, a bomb exploded in a police car carrying two members of the intelligence forces. One of the men was killed. The car was parked outside a festival hall where a large May Day concert had been planned by left-wing organisations. It seemed probable that the men were planning to blow up, not the hall itself, but the electricity installations to disrupt the evening's activities. The cover-up attempted by the police convinced very few. General Golbery, then head of the President's civilian household, pushed for a full investigation as the incident was proving so damaging to the government's public image. Golbery was eventually forced to resign in the face of the *comunidade*'s intractable refusal to carry out a proper inquiry. Once more, the machine proved stronger than the man, even though this time the man himself was the creator of the machine. Golbery later told the press: 'I have created a monster. Things cannot continue like this.'[8]

Though the *comunidade* received more attention for its activities in the industrialised south, it gradually became more active in the Amazon. Members of the security forces began routinely to accuse peasants involved in a land conflict of 'subversion', a convenient catch-all term which they knew would win them the immediate support of their superiors. Moreover, the officials knew that they were very unlikely to have to justify their accusation.

To cite one of many possible examples: in March 1979, Colonel Aloysio Madeira Evora, the secretary for public security in the Mato Grosso government, was told by journalists of the death of two policemen (and one peasant farmer) in a gun battle in the district of Pontes de Lacerda in the north-west of the state. Without waiting to hear details, he immediately placed responsibility for the conflict on 'agitators interested in disturbing public order and stirring up humble and well-intentioned settlers to invade land which does not belong to them'. The police investigator, Anquires Batista da Silva, who was commissioned to draw up a report on the incident, similarly blamed 'subversives', though journalists covering the case said that there were no grounds whatsoever for this allegation. One of the conclusions da Silva reached in his report revealed very clearly his preconceptions: 'We believe the recent increase in land invasions in the region to be extremely suspect and, for this reason, we consider it to be a case of subversion of order.'[9]

Abertura, with all its contradictions, continued in 1981 and 1982. The most important elections since the early 1960s were held in November 1982. The pro-government PDS obtained 42 per cent of the valid votes for Senate and 43 per cent for the Chamber of Deputies. Yet, because of the skewed way in which the government had distributed the seats between the different regions of the country, the PDS retained its absolute majority in Senate and lost by only a tiny number of seats its control of the Chamber of Deputies. Most important of all, it retained its absolute majority in the electoral college which was to select the President to take over from Figueiredo in 1985.

Though the opposition parties together won well over half of the valid votes, they were in no position after the elections to push through changes in the constitution, which is the only way in which they could wrench back a measure of real power from the executive. This was because the government, faced with the prospect of electoral defeat, had taken the precaution earlier in 1982, while it still possessed a comfortable majority in Congress, of changing the requirement for constitutional amendments from a simple majority of Congress, to one of two-thirds. In the event, this effectively blocked all significant change.

Some of the new members of Congress did what they could, given the constraints. Shortly after taking up his seat in the Senate in March 1983, Fernando Henrique Cardoso, from the PMDB opposition party, called for the setting up of a parliamentary commission of inquiry into the *comunidade de informações*. He said:

> Even the Russian KGB is less powerful than our SNI. The concentration of power and functions in the hands of the intelligence network in this country is quite unprecedented . . . If we want to take another step towards democracy, we must discuss clearly the role of the armed forces. Our aim must be to decide what role it is legitimate for the armed forces to have in a democracy and work towards that. We must dismantle the police functions carried out by the armed forces.[10]

The most important gain for the opposition parties was the winning of 10 of the 22 state governments. Though the capacity for effective action of these governments was greatly limited by severe financial restraints, the very fact of having opposition governments in power lifted the climate of repression. This was particularly important in early 1984 when millions took to the streets in the biggest campaign in the country's history to protest against the severe recession imposed by the International Monetary Fund and to demand a return to full democracy with a popularly-elected President. By putting great pressure on PDS deputies, the government just prevented the opposition parties obtaining the required two-thirds majority to push through the Chamber of Deputies a constitutional amendment to bring back direct elections for President. But, such was the pressure for change, this setback was not decisive. In mid 1984 a faction of the PDS broke with the government, forming an alliance with the PMDB. The military lost control of the process and this coalition's candidate, Tancredo Neves, was elected president by the college in early 1985. As this book went to press, Brazil was in crisis, as Neves had died, after falling ill on the eve of his inauguration.

During this period, the *comunidade* wisely kept a low profile. Though conclusive proof is difficult to obtain, many opposition politicians believe that it undertook several acts of sabotage in 1983 and 1984 in an attempt to destabilise the process of political liberalisation. For instance, it was widely believed to have been responsible for a six-hour black-out which unexpectedly hit the south-east of Brazil in April 1984, a few days before voting on the constitutional amendment. The *comunidade*'s objective, the politicians claim, was to provoke rioting and plundering in the cities and thus, in the already tense political climate, create conditions for the declaration of a national state of emergency. In the event, the urban inhabitants, well accustomed to poor public services, stoically accepted the additional inconvenience and handled the disruption far more smoothly than anyone could have anticipated.

It is clear, however, that the *comunidade* has made a tactical retreat but has not been defeated. Yet without the dismantling of the *comunidade* Brazil will not have a fully democratic government. One of the areas where it is most firmly entrenched is the countryside, particularly in the Amazon, where it has become the main political power. Land use is a vital issue which will have to be confronted by the civilian government if any real progress is to be made with the country's pressing problem of social inequality. We now turn for a closer look at the process of militarisation of the Amazon.

The Militarisation of Amazon Policy-making

Though there were clear indications of growing military interest in the region in the years following the crushing of the rural guerrilla movement, the first important move was only made in 1980. In January of that year, the National Security Council set up a new body, the Executive Group for the Araguaia–Tocantins Region (GETAT), to take over from INCRA in a particularly turbulent area of 45 million hectares which overlapped three states: the south of Pará, the northern tip of Goiás and the south-west of Maranhão. It was able to take this decision without consulting Congress because, despite all the advances of *abertura*, it was still the strongest body in the land.

But GETAT was no simple replacement for INCRA. It was given a far more ambitious brief and endowed with far greater powers which in many ways placed it above the law. Paulo Yakota said in an interview soon after the creation of GETAT: 'The big innovation with GETAT is that it will have the power to overcome the bureaucratic limitations imposed on INCRA when it is dealing with land conflicts and issuing land titles.'[11] Many of these 'bureaucratic limitations' stemmed from the need for INCRA, as a civilian body, to operate within the limits of the law. Though many of the top positions were filled by military officers, GETAT took over INCRA's administrative staff in the region and retained most of its employees. The National Security Council (CSN) directly appointed its president, Iris Pedro de Oliveira, formerly director of Iterpa (the Pará land institute) and an old friend of many of the country's top generals. INCRA's functions in the rest of the country were also quietly streamlined after the creation of GETAT. Some of its tasks, such as rural electrification and the running of cooperatives, were gradually handed over to other government departments and it began to concentrate on two main tasks: the issuing of land titles to families who already occupied the land in areas outside the influence of GETAT, and the administration of its colonisation projects.

It is believed that the creation of GETAT was suggested to the Security Council by Lieutenant-Colonel Sebastião Rodrigues de Moura, an extraordinarily skilful agent of the SNI. Though he was acting under a different name at the time, this SNI agent became well known in the Amazon region in the early 1970s when the government was combating the rural guerrillas. Though no conclusive evidence of his involvement has been produced, many people told us that he masterminded the most effective anti-guerrilla operations and helped torture the captured guerrillas. At that time, he earned the nickname of Major Curió (Major Finch), because of his skill in extracting information from arrested guerrillas. 'Just like a finch, his song enthralls you', an inhabitant of Marabá told *Veja* magazine.[12] Major Curió also set up an efficient network of informers among the peasant families, which undoubtedly contributed to the defeat of the guerrillas.

If, as our earlier analysis suggests, the armed forces were keen to expand their activities, there were good reasons why they should welcome Curió's suggestion that they move first into the Araguaia–Tocantins region, for this area included Xambioá, the base of the rural guerrilla movement in the Bico do Papagaio, and the south of Pará, both of which regions had been shaken by particularly serious land conflicts. It was also close to the multi-billion dollar Carajás mining project, which had become by then the government's leading flagship abroad, and to which the government hoped to attract heavy investment from transnational companies. Perhaps most important of all, however, it was a region where left-wing priests and lay workers had been very active and were building up considerable political support. The armed forces were clearly worried that, unless decisive action was taken, the dissatisfied peasantry, encouraged by a powerful sector of the church, would become an important revolutionary force.

GETAT officials have never given a very clear account of the task they were instructed to carry out with their extraordinary powers. But it is possible to draw some conclusions from their actions and from occasional remarks made by leading officers. It appears that GETAT's main task was to combat the influence of the Catholic Church which was considered to be mobilising the local population against the government. To do this, GETAT was told, not only to move directly against church workers and to intimidate its supporters among the peasantry, but also to build up a local power base for the government. As a secondary and complementary task, GETAT was instructed to pave the way for the profound economic and social upheaval that lay ahead for the area under its control, with the setting up of the Carajás mining complex. The government had allocated this region a key role in its national development plans and GETAT was told to make sure that nothing went wrong.

As a result, despite its hostility to peasant families, GETAT was no automatic ally of the traditional reactionary landowners. On the contrary, it was instructed to foster modern capitalist attitudes so that the area would be receptive to foreign investments and welcome rapid economic development. It was told to ensure that this new phase was not jeopardised by social unrest.

GETAT's Achievements

By the end of 1982, GETAT had achieved mixed results with respect to its complex objectives. Because of the importance attached to the creation of a local power base, businessmen from the south, who had played such an important role in the formulation of Amazon policy in previous governments, were excluded from the executive council of GETAT. José Carlos de Souza Meirelles, then president of the Association of Amazon Businessmen (AEA), immediately protested about the omission in a telex he sent to the government on 1 February 1980. In it, he suggested that representatives of both his association and – perhaps surprisingly – the rural unions should be on the council. 'It is essential that GETAT should have the assistance of bodies with years of experience in the Amazon', he wrote. But his advice was not taken.

The National Security Council has had a two-pronged strategy, attempting both to ally itself with one of the existing political factions in the area and to build up an entirely new political base. The pro-government PDS was divided in the state of Pará and GETAT was instructed to ally itself with the faction headed by Jarbas Passarinho, minister of state in two federal administrations since 1964 and at that time senator for the state of Pará. As a result, it earned the hostility of Alacid Nunes, the state governor of Pará who was from the other faction of the PDS, but, as he had been involved earlier in a serious conflict with the federal government, this had seemed likely in any case. In the event, this strategy was not very successful. After further bitter wrangling with the federal government, Alacid Nunes and his supporters defected to the main opposition party, PMDB, and, to the consternation of the federal government, they won the election for state governorship in November 1982. The National Security Council made it clear that, if Nunes made difficulties, it was prepared to create a new administrative region – the territory of Tocantins – to take over responsibility for the area of GETAT, and to ensure the smooth implementation of the Carajás project. It was reported that, if this were to happen, Major Curió would be made the first governor of the new territory. In the event, Nunes has played it safe. Though there have been minor clashes, his government has not been involved in a serious confrontation with GETAT.

The National Security Council has been fairly successful in its second objective – the creation of a new political base. Its most spectacular achievement has been at the *garimpo* (gold mine) of Serra Pelada in the south of Pará. It is worth looking at the story of this mine in some detail.

In January 1980 a landowner called in a geologist to examine the traces of gold which had been discovered on his land. Even before the survey had been completed, news of the find had spread very rapidly across the region. By the end of the month, about 5,000 *garimpeiros* had swarmed to the site. The men marked out their individual stakes across the rough inhospitable terrain of small ravines and rough ledges. The place was christened Serra Pelada (bare mountain ridge) because, unusually, it had no vegetation to provide protection from the hot sun. The men then dug pits and started to extract the gravel, in which they hoped to find gold. They worked all day on

The Greater Carajás project

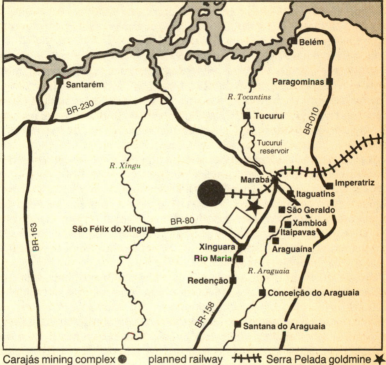

Santarém

BR-230

Belém

Paragominas

R. Tocantins

Tucuruí

BR-010

Tucuruí
reservoir

R. Xingu

Marabá

Imperatriz

Itaguatins

São Geraldo

Xambioá

Itaipavas

BR-163

São Félix do Xingu

BR-80

Araguaína

Xinguara

Rio Maria

R. Araguaia

Redenção

Conceição do Araguaia

BR-158

Santana do Araguaia

Carajás mining complex ●   planned railway ╫╫╫╫ Serra Pelada goldmine ✶
Tupã-Ciretã ranch ☐

the bare mountainside in the hot tropical sun. In the evenings they carried the gravel in sacks to the shed where it was sorted, washed and panned. The men were paid in cash for any gold found.

The men set up rough shacks with roofs made from plastic sheeting or palm leaves. As so many were crowded together without running water or sanitation, illness was rife. It was a typically wild, isolated mine, with much drinking of *cachaça* (cheap rum) and evening brawls, particularly over prostitutes.

By May there were about 25,000 *garimpeiros* at Serra Pelada. As the finds were not properly registered during these early months, no one knows how much gold was found. But, by all accounts, it was a lot, possibly as much as one tonne. After receiving reports of the feverish activity, the federal government decided that it must take over control of what could be the country's largest gold mine.

As a first step, the government formally transferred ownership to Docegeo, the prospecting subsidiary of the huge, state-owned mining company, Companhia Vale do Rio Doce (CVRD). But there was no consensus within the government as to the best method of mining the ore. Mines and energy minister César Cals believed that the mine should immediately be mechanised so that the reserves could be mined as rationally as possible. But Major Curió disagreed. With the discreet backing of GETAT, within whose jurisdiction the mine lay, he argued that the mechanisation of the mine would deprive 40,000 people (the *garimpeiros* and their assistants) of their livelihood and would thus create considerable social unrest. He believed that the government had been given an excellent chance to create a political basis outside the influence of the church and that this opportunity should not be wasted. He reminded the government that the *garimpeiros*' votes would be very useful in the important elections in November 1982.

Major Curió won the day and took over the running of Serra Pelada. In his first day in office, he called together all the *garimpeiros* and told them: 'You can keep your guns for the meantime, but don't forget: the revolver with the surest shot is mine.' With that, he pulled out his gun and shot into the air. Within a month, the *garimpeiros* had agreed to give up their guns.

Other equally impressive changes were achieved. Along with the guns, Major Curió got rid of prostitutes and alcohol and the mine became extraordinarily quiet and peaceful at nights. At the same time, he brought down the price of all goods, particularly foodstuffs, sold in the mine. Thanks in part to his charismatic appeal, he was able to achieve all this and win the support of almost all the *garimpeiros*.

Manoel Alves de Santos, one of the first to arrive in Serra Pelada, told a reporter from the *Folha de S. Paulo*:

> What is important to understand is that he brought law and order to Serra
> Pelada. Before, we used to feel insecure the whole time, afraid of what could

happen. People were killed by thieves. There were a lot of fights over women and drink. And in the end the gold went into the pockets of the people who sold us food.[13]

José Pereira Neto, a prospector from São Paulo, went on: 'I've been to mines all over the place, even in Venezuela. And I can tell you – Serra Pelada is the best place in the world to earn money.' The barber at Serra Pelada told a journalist from the magazine, *Veja*: 'For us, Major Curió on earth is like God in heaven'.[14] The small town which sprang up on the main road (PA–150), where a rough track led off to the mine, was called Curionópolis.

Now and again Major Curió gave the *garimpeiros* a glimpse of his great influence with the federal government. On one occasion, the head administrator at the post office in Belém turned down Major Curió's request that a branch office should be opened in Serra Pelada. Just a few days later the administrator was ignominiously transferred to an obscure branch in the distant state of Minas Gerais and the new appointee rapidly carried out Major Curió's request.

Major Curió put an end to smuggling and made sure that all the gold output from the mine was sold to the state company Docegeo. In 1980 Serra Pelada produced 6.5 tonnes of gold, almost half of Brazil's total output of 13.8 tonnes. Though production fell to a disappointing 3.2 tonnes in 1981, the government was confident that it would increase once more in the following years.

Major Curió took advantage of his support among the *garimpeiros* to build up an electoral base. In 1981 he announced that he would be standing as federal deputy in the elections in November 1982. From then on all new *garimpeiros* had to express support for the pro-government PDS party before they were admitted to the mine. In his electoral speeches, Major Curió closely aligned himself with the Passarinho faction of the PDS.

Major Curió frequently told the *garimpeiros* that he had the personal backing of President Figueiredo, a claim that seemed to be justified when in October 1982 the President paid a visit to the mine. In sharp contrast with the cool reception he was given in Santarém, an opposition stronghold, Figueiredo was given a hero's welcome in Serra Pelada. Numerous rockets were let off when he arrived and, after a speech which was enthusiastically applauded, he was carried off on the shoulders of some of the *garimpeiros*. In the election in the following month, Major Curió was elected deputy with a large majority, though the PDS lost the election overall in the state of Pará.

In Congress Major Curió provoked a dramatic confrontation. José Genuíno Neto, one of the few to have fought with the guerrillas in Xambioá in the early 1970s and to have survived, served a prison sentence and was then elected federal deputy for the Workers Party (PT) in the elections in November 1982. In one of his first speeches in Congress in April 1983, Genuíno bitterly attacked the government's economic policies, dedicating his speech to 'those comrades who died in the guerrilla war in the Araguaia'. Major Curió leapt to his feet. 'Which dead are you referring to?', he demanded. 'Ours or yours?' 'Those your Excellency killed', retorted another opposition deputy.

In early 1983 it was announced that Serra Pelada was to be mechanised and the whole operation handed over to Docegeo. It seemed that, having served their purpose in providing Major Curió with a political springboard, the *garimpeiros* were to be disbanded. Local people were angry. A PDS politician from Imperatriz, one of the towns near Serra Pelada, gave an angry speech in June 1984 after visiting the mine. He warned the government:

> Serra Pelada is today a powder keg, ready to explode. The 50,000
> *garimpeiros* don't want to leave and, to get rid of them, the government will
> have to send in the whole of the Eighth Battalion of Jungle Infantry . . . It will
> be a terrible social problem to have 30,000 unemployed and impoverished
> men suddenly loose on the streets of Imperatriz.

The *garimpeiros* fought back. In October 1983, about 3,000 of them, in about 80 coaches, descended upon Brasília. They said that they would only leave after the government had revoked its decision to mechanise the mine. The climate was tense for the *garimpeiros* were convinced that their mining activities at Serra Pelada were being sabotaged by employees from Docegeo and the government body in charge of prospecting, Departamento Nacional de Pesquisa Mineral (DNPM), who, they claimed, were anxious to mechanise the mine. Some *garimpeiros* even claimed that a landslide in March 1983, which had killed 21 people, had been deliberately engineered by the employees to provide evidence that primitive mining methods used by the *garimpeiros* were extremely dangerous.

Though the discontent among the *garimpeiros* was undoubtedly genuine, it is likely that their successful lobbying was organised by Major Curió, who was unwilling to lose his political base so quickly. Major Curió presented a bill to Congress to allow the *garimpeiros* to work at Serra Pelada for a further five years. After Figueiredo had expressed his opposition to this bill, it was withdrawn, but the government agreed to review its policy. In May 1984, the government presented its own bill in which mining activities at Serra Pelada were divided between Docegeo and the *garimpeiros*. The bill allowed the *garimpeiros* to go on working for three years or until an excavation 20 metres deep had been dug, whichever proved the shorter period of time. It allowed for the administration of the work done by the *garimpeiros* to be carried out by a cooperative of *garimpeiros* to be set up by INCRA.

In May 1984, about 2,000 *garimpeiros* travelled to Brasília to put pressure on the deputies. Major Curió warned in a speech in Congress: 'The *garimpeiros* have been unable to work for six months. In a state of desperation because of hunger and other privations, these men, who today number about 110,000, could at any moment resort to violent acts of unpredictable consequences.' The bill was passed and CVRD was paid hefty compensation for the gold it lost. An uneasy peace returned to Serra Pelada as the *garimpeiros* were finally able to work once again. Mining businessmen were unhappy with the compromise solution. Iguatemy Mendonça Filho a director of the Brazilian Association of Gold Mining Companies (Associação Brasileira de Mineradores de Ouro – Abramo), said in July 1984 that he believed that the bill had established 'a very serious precedent' by handing over the administration of part of the mine to a cooperative of *garimpeiros*. 'This could encourage others elsewhere in the country to push for a similar scheme', he warned.

GETAT has faced serious problems in its second objective: to modernise the region. It has proved difficult to reconcile this objective with its alliance with the Passarinho faction of the PDS which contains some of the most backward and traditional of the landowners. Many of the landowners in the region are old-fashioned cattle-rearers or *castanheiros*, that is, landowners who pay local peasant families to collect the Brazil nuts from the trees which by chance grow on their land. They belong to a dying class of reactionary landowners which has often acted as a barrier to the type of modern dynamic capitalism, with efficient cash-crop farming, which the government wishes to bring to the region.

In the short term at least, GETAT has been fairly successful in its third and most important objective: to undermine the influence of the church. GETAT did not seek merely to reduce the church's influence in land conflicts, but to break its power in other areas, particularly the rural union movement.

One of the main confrontations concerned the elections for the presidency of the Conceição do Araguaia branch of Contag, the agricultural workers' union. The church supported the opposition candidate Raimundo Ferreira Lima (Gringo), who was an *agente pastoral*. GETAT, on the other hand, threw its weight behind the incumbent president, Bertoldo Siqueira de Lima, who had been appointed to the position during a period when the union was under direct government control. The elections were due to be held in May 1980. The campaign was marked by considerable violence, largely because the contest came to represent the struggle for power in the region between the peasant families and the Catholic Church on the one hand and the landowners and GETAT on the other. Each of the candidates became clearly identified with one or other of the opposing factions.

On 13 May a group of 42 peasant families killed Fernando Leitão Diniz, a local landowner. The peasants had been involved in a long conflict with him over land in Itaipavas in the south of Pará. After his death, the peasants fled into the forest leaving a message by the corpse: 'We will not give ourselves up to the military police, only to the army. We don't advise the military police to come in after us.' The local landowners made political use of the incident. Taking advantage of the fact that Itaipavas is situated on the other side of the Araguaia river from Xamboiá (the base of the earlier guerrilla movement), they sent a telex message to justice minister Ibrahim Abi-Ackel saying that the 'guerrilla movement has reemerged in Xamboiá'. They also claimed that the church was encouraging the peasant families to stay on their land and had given arms, including machine guns, to a group of about 300. The minister quickly contacted General Otávio Medeiros, head of the SNI. Members of the government, including generals, later accused the landowners of exaggeration and misrepresentation.

On the advice of a French priest, Aristides Camio, the peasants came out of hiding of their own accord and went to Conceição do Araguaia to give the police their version of what had happened. A day later, Gringo, who also came from Itaipavas, was shot dead by a gunman in Araguaína. Though the authorities have never carried out a full investigation into his death, members of the church have repeatedly claimed that he was killed in revenge by José Antônio, an adopted son of Fernando Leitão Diniz. A public meeting in Conceição do Araguaia to protest over Gringo's death was attended by about 4,000 peasant farmers.

The situation continued very tense. It was rumoured that Impar – a local association of timber merchants and landowners – had drawn up a blacklist of seven people – Gringo, Aristides Camio, a woman lay worker, two union leaders and two peasant farmers – whom they had condemned to death. A new opposition candidate was chosen to replace Gringo. He obtained more votes than Bertoldo Siqueira de Lima but, as there were other candidates, he failed to obtain an absolute majority. Finally, after many delays, it was decided to postpone the elections until the following May.

The tension increased throughout 1981. Oneide, Gringo's wife, continued to criticise the government, with the full support of the church. In April, a gunman employed by a local landowner, Neif Mourad, was killed by peasant farmers. Two of his other employees had been killed the previous August. The church was repeatedly accused of being behind these murders. Three peasant farmers were arrested by the police and accused of the latest murder, but instead of being taken to Conceição do Araguaia, they were driven to the landowner's ranch where they were tortured.

Major Curió was very active in the campaign for the union elections and his activities were bitterly criticised by opposition politicians. Ademir Andrade, an opposition deputy, said in the state assembly in May 1981:

> It is absurd to see a Lieutenant-Colonel from the army, who is also, as far as we know, active in the area of national security, use one of our armed forces' helicopters to support the campaign of the incumbent president, when we all know that the armed forces should not take part in party politics, much less in trade union affairs. Moreover, though he is a member of the armed forces, Curió has been speaking in the name of the President of the country, saying that he will provide the region with all sorts of assistance if Bertoldo Siqueira de Lima wins, but withdraw all help if he loses.

Bertoldo Siqueira de Lima was finally re-elected, though the church has alleged fraud, for GETAT counted the votes without any outside supervision.

Building on this success, the government decided that it was time to take direct action against left-wing members of the church. It appears to have been particularly anxious to stop the work of the priest Aristides Camio. Camio realised that he was under surveillance, and in a letter he wrote in September 1980 to Dom Albano Cavalin, assistant bishop of Curitiba, Paraná, he said:

> My situation is increasingly difficult. They are trying to involve me in everything that happens in the region. At the end of August, two employees at Neif Mourad's ranch were killed. Once again, it was my fault. I think I have become a kind of scapegoat.

The incident which finally provoked his arrest took place in mid August 1981. A group of peasant families had been under pressure from a nearby landowner to leave their land. The usual tactics had been used: gunmen had been sent in, houses burnt down and families threatened. Major Curió played an obviously important, but not fully clarified, role. He had won the confidence of many of the peasant families and had encouraged them to take a firm stand against the landowner, whose claim to the land, he said, was not valid. He told them that he would use his considerable influence with the government to help them win the rights to their land. Some church workers now believe that he may have played the role of an *agent provocateur*, deliberately encouraging the peasants to resort to violence so that he could use the incident to unleash a virulent campaign against the church.

Early in August, gunmen sent in by the landowner boasted to the peasant families that Major Curió had fallen from power and that the landowner was now going to send in a large group of gunmen to evict them. The families were greatly upset at the news and, in near desperation, decided to barricade themselves in and take on the gunmen. On 13 August two cars drove towards the peasant families' plots. The farmers, who had mounted an ambush, believed that the gunmen were arriving and opened fire. One of the passengers was killed and several wounded. The peasants were then told that they had jumped to a false conclusion and that the man they had killed was a ranch manager and several of the wounded passengers were GETAT officials. The peasants were appalled. (During the trial, however, it became clear that the peasants had been somewhat misled: Luiz Antônio dos Santos, the man they had killed, was on the run from the police and had probably been employed by the ranch as a gunman, not a manager.)

The 13 peasants involved in the ambush fled into the forest but gave themselves up a few days later. Camio had had little contact with these families, but had said mass in one of their huts at the beginning of the month. By chance he had been accompanied by another French priest, Francisco Gouriou. The evidence against them was extremely flimsy, but it was enough for the authorities.

The government moved carefully. The CNBB, the bishops' conference, had published a new hard-hitting document that month. In what with hindsight was clearly a carefully planned move, the government broke its tradition of refusing to become involved in verbal battles with the church and responded to this document. Jarbas Passarinho, at the time president of Senate, gave a press interview in which he strongly criticised the document and said that the progressive wing of the church was the most serious challenge faced by the PDS. Using language of unprecedented virulence, he accused the church of opting for socialism, of organising land invasions, particularly in the Amazon, and of creating a climate of social unrest which could result in a bloodbath. In the following week, the two French priests were arrested. They were accused under the national security law of inciting both 'collective disobedience of the law' and 'violent struggle between social classes'.

Many of the peasant farmers in the region blamed GETAT for the conflict. Feliz Resplande Coelho, the brother of one of the arrested farmers, told the press: 'It is all the fault of Carlos Chaves, GETAT's coordinator in São Geraldo. If he had found us alternative plots of land as he promised, none of this would have happened.' Ironically, Camio appears to have believed that Major Curió, whom he knew quite well, approved of his work in the region. In an interview in January 1981, he had called Major Curió a 'true leader for the region', and after his arrest he asked for him to be called as a witness in his defence. There could perhaps be no more eloquent illustration of Major Curió's charisma.

In the event, Major Curió's evidence was damning. In a press interview shortly after the priests' arrest, he said that he was convinced that Camio had been trying to get the local population to rise up against the government. He explained: 'The aim behind Father Camio's activities was to upset the established order and to create a negative climate.' He said that before the priests' arrest he had sent a secret report to the government asking for Camio's expulsion from the region because of his 'subversive activities'.

The government kept up its offensive against the church even after the priests had been arrested. Priests and lay workers in the south of Pará were detained for short periods or brought in for questioning. Passarinho continued to play a key role in this campaign. On 9 September, he broke a 15-year tradition, by which no president of Senate had made a political speech in Congress, to launch an attack on the church. It was clear that for this he must have received the go-ahead from the highest echelon of government which in itself is an indication of the importance that the government attached to this issue. He accused sectors of the church of being 'Marxists and Socialists' and of unscrupulously using their power and influence as religious leaders to persuade voters to support the PT, the socialist party set up by Luis Ignácio da Silva, 'Lula', the metalworkers' leader in São Paulo. He said:

> Some church groups [CEBs] are encouraging the invasion of private property, although this was firmly condemned by the Pope. They are waiting

for a good moment to unleash a bloody conflict of such seriousness that I am fearful of the future.

Over the next few months, the government kept up the pressure on the church. Though the church carried on with its fierce criticisms of the government's actions, its workers in the GETAT area were forced to act with great caution. In April 1982, Iris Pedro de Oliveira noted with satisfaction that the church was playing a less significant role in land conflicts in the region. He said that he would be attempting to talk to leading members of the church in the region to see whether, given their common concern with the region's development, some form of collaboration was possible. His proposal was not warmly received, for nearly all sectors of the church had been infuriated by the arrest of the priests, particularly on such flimsy evidence.

Both the peasant farmers and the French priests were refused bail. Though the peasant farmers were understandably reluctant to accuse the authorities while still in jail, there was considerable indirect evidence that they had been tortured during the early days of their detention. The daughter of João Matias, who was generally considered the leader of the peasants, said that her father had been kept handcuffed inside a jeep for eight days after his arrest. One of the prisoners had told her that they had all been subjected to torture by electric shock.

The peasant farmers were held in the São José prison in Brasília. Major Curió paid secret visits to the prisoners late at night without obtaining proper authorisation from the prison governor, Colonel Azevedo Bahia Filho. The governor made a statement in which he complained about this infringement, but, in violation of the code of military penal procedure, the court later refused to accept it as evidence. The governor was soon transferred to another prison.

At the end of August, all but two of the 13 peasants changed their original statements to place responsibility for the crime on the French priests. They also refused to accept the services of the lawyers contracted by the church on their behalf, preferring those of Djalma Farias, a former agent of the federal police.

The trial was finally held in Belém in June 1982. According to the report prepared by an observer sent by Amnesty International, the trial took place in a 'climate of hostility and intimidation'.[15] Between 1,500 and 2,000 soldiers were brought into the town. Armoured cars, mounted soldiers, machine guns, tear-gas canisters and dogs were in evidence. Ten military policemen, two armed with sub-machine guns, were placed inside the courtroom.

In its report, Amnesty International pointed to 'manifest weaknesses and contradictions in the prosecution's case and irregularities in the police investigations'. Particularly glaring was the failure of the peasant farmers' lawyer to present a defence. All the accused were found guilty by the military court. Aristides Camio was sentenced to 15 years' imprisonment and François Gouriou to ten. The peasant farmers were given terms of imprisonment which ranged from eight to nine years. Amnesty International concluded that the priests had been imprisoned for 'nothing other than expressing their conscientiously held beliefs and for practising, in the course of their normal pastoral duties, the official policy of the Roman Catholic Church in Brazil'. They were consequently adopted as 'prisoners of conscience' by the organisation.

The priests' lawyers appealed against the heavy sentences to the Supreme Military Tribunal. The appeal was heard in early December 1982 and the priests' sentences were reduced, from 15 to ten years for Aristides Camio, and from ten to eight years for François Gouriou. The peasants' sentences were retained. As the court's decision was not unanimous (9–4), the defence lawyers were able to make another appeal. As they waited, the priests were held in fairly comfortable cells at the federal police headquarters in Brasília, while the peasants were still detained in tough conditions at the army barracks in Belém. At the end of 1982, several were reported to be very depressed, partly because they felt betrayed by Djalma Freitas who had promised them acquittal if they gave evidence against the priests. One was reported to have required hospital treatment after banging his head against his cell wall on hearing the decision of the STM. After repeated requests, the OAB was allowed to speak to eight of the 13 peasants in April 1983. Several of them asked to change their lawyer and several complained that they had been beaten up and tortured with electric shocks. One of them said: 'They told us to speak badly of the priests so that we would be acquitted.'

The second appeal was heard in October 1983, but the sentences were upheld with a smaller majority of the judges than before. This allowed the prisoners to appeal to the Supreme Federal Tribunal (STF). However, a new, milder version of the security law came into force in December 1983. Both the priests and the peasants were released, as they had already served the maximum sentences to which they could be condemned under the new law.

Over the following few years, the government avoided another direct confrontation with the church, probably because it had seen how quickly the church united when its members were under attack. But it continued to harass left-wing priests and lay workers, letting them know that they were under constant surveillance. The waning of the church's influence may have been partly responsible for the increase in wild and desperate acts of violence carried out by some groups of peasants in the GETAT area. The church has always encouraged the families to use other methods, such as pressure on the government through the rural unions or through publicity in the press. It has cautioned against the use of violence, except possibly as a very last resort. Though is it difficult to obtain full information, the following tales give some indication of the impact of GETAT on the lives of some of the peasant families.

Bico do Papagaio Revisited: Despite the problems outlined at the beginning of this chapter, the church's Pastoral Land Commission decided in the late 1970s (before the creation of GETAT) to try to help some of the families in Bico do Papagaio obtain legal rights to their land. In December 1979, INCRA published one of its routine, discreet notices in *Diário Oficial* and other newspapers in the state capital, Goiânia, in which it said that it would be selling a large area of *terras devolutas* in the north of Goiás and requesting any persons whose interest would be affected by this sale to appear with their lawyers at a hearing in Goiânia on 11 March 1980. As usual, the procedure was a grotesque mockery of any form of justice, for the notices were published in a town about 1,500 kilometres away from the area in question and no attempt was made by either the state authorities or INCRA to alert the peasant families concerned. It looked as if the area was going to be sold as 'unoccupied', and that the new landowners would be given some legal grounds for evicting the families.

However, for the first time in the history of the Amazon, hundreds of families were told what was going on and decided to do something about it. After church workers had informed them of the imminent sale, most of the little communities held meetings and decided to send representatives to Goiânia, dividing the cost of the fare between them. However, the mobilisation appears to have gone unnoticed. On 11 March, the well-dressed government officials, landowners and lawyers were visibly shaken when in walked about 50 peasant farmers, wearing shabby, faded clothes and peasant hats, as different from the rest of the people in the room as chalk from cheese.

The judge decided immediately to postpone the hearing until 12 May, saying that the recently created GETAT had not yet had time to take over INCRA's role in the proceedings, as it was now by law required to do. The peasant farmers' lawyer, from the church, then requested that the new hearings should be held at Itaguatins, a small town much closer to the area in question. The judge agreed, on condition that GETAT covered the cost of taking the court to the other town. GETAT refused, but several weeks later, after receiving a petition from dozens of peasant families, the judge agreed to the transfer none the less.

The mayor of Itaguatins agreed to help publicise the hearings, no doubt aware of the political support to be obtained from the peasants. Numerous announcements were made on the local radio and at May Day gatherings. However, on 4 May, the judge once again announced that the hearing had been postponed. It was too late to tell all the peasant farmers and about 1,000 turned up. Despite heavy policing in the town, a large protest demonstration was held.

After this, the level of violence used against the families increased dramatically. No doubt at the behest of GETAT, the Goiás public security department began a large military operation, allegedly to put an end to the 'agitation' in the area. The participation of the local landowners was particularly marked, for their farms were used as prisons and their cars and pick-ups were used to transport the members of the military police who carried out the operation. By the end of September, the CPT reported that about 250 families had been evicted.

The pressure on church workers also increased greatly. Early in 1981, Osvaldo de Alencar Rocha, a church lawyer working in this region, described the climate of fear which had been created:

> As well as the practical difficulties, lawyers working for the church's land commission are also frequently threatened. I've received threatening telephone calls, anonymous letters, direct threats from landowners and their gunmen. They are trying to stop us working, to stop us helping the peasants. Well, all this creates a climate of insecurity. The peasant families start thinking that all is lost, that we can't do anything to stop it. The peasants are very poor and disorganised and they are in a desperate situation. They panic. They don't know what to do. It just takes a strange car to arrive and the children run off into the forest, the women run out of their huts. They panic so easily because the land thieves, who have been particularly active since the end of last year, have behaved in a brutal and indiscriminate fashion. They bring in the police, who force the peasants to kneel down, or pull their clothes off them, or take them away under arrest. It is real pandemonium. The peasants are humble, respectful people. Regular contact with this type of violence completely unnerves them.[16]

The repression worked, in the short term. An uneasy peace returned to the region in 1982.

However, more violent conflicts broke out at the beginning of 1983. On 26 February, after a clash between peasant families and a landowner, local policemen without arrest warrants detained two peasant farmers. According to the CPT, they were both brutally beaten up at the police station. As their arrest was illegal, Osvaldo de Alencar Rocha tried to get the courts to order their release, but in vain. Dom Pedro Casaldáliga said that the CPT believed that the incident might form part of a destabilisation campaign. In the direct elections in November 1982, Iris Resende, the candidate for the opposition party PMDB, had been elected state governor. He was due to take office in mid March and many powerful people in the state were keen to create problems for him.

Resende took office and the violence in the countryside continued at a high level. On 20 March, the CPT took the first steps in the courts to sue Iris Pedro de Oliveira, the president of GETAT, for slander, as in an earlier press interview he had blamed the CPT for the upsurge in land conflicts in the Bico do Papagaio. Mário Aldighieri, a priest working for the CPT, told the *Folha de S. Paulo* newspaper in late March: 'There is a national campaign against *agentes pastorais* and now we are going to make them prove their accusations.'

Over the months, a basic pattern has emerged in GETAT's actions. Where serious conflicts have arisen, GETAT has moved in, imposed some kind of solution in authoritarian fashion and then treated all those who have refused to accept its ruling as criminals. Apparently envisaging its operation in military terms, it has used classic divisive tactics. It has often supported the land claims of those it considers the key families, who have a leadership role, and whose eviction could cause considerable unrest in the region, and then firmly rejected the claims of the remaining families. If GETAT has believed it to be politically convenient to give land to certain families, it has done so, whether or not their legal case for owning the land is sound. In the same way, it has had no scruples in evicting families with valid legal titles to their plots. GETAT has been fairly active in sorting out land conflicts in this way. According to its own statistics, which may not be entirely reliable, it had issued 31,367 land titles by the end of September 1983. Of these, 72 per cent were for plots of up to 100 hectares. It had sorted out the legal situation of about a fifth of the 45 million hectares under its control.

GETAT's Strategy in Xinguara: At the time of our first visit in mid 1976, Xinguara such did not exist. There was just a tiny, unnamed hamlet of about three or four houses, situated some 250 kilometres south of Marabá on the road to Conceição do Araguaia. Eighteen months later, when we visited the region again, Xinguara had 1,800 houses with about 15,000 inhabitants. One reason for the spectacular growth was Xinguara's location, at the junction with the branch-road, still not properly completed in 1978 but already carrying traffic, which runs west to the rich mineral deposits and farming land beside the Xingu river.

However, this was not the main factor behind the population explosion, which was startling even by Amazonian standards. As a vote-catching gambit before the elections in November 1976, the Pará government announced that farming land was to be distributed free around a little hamlet called Xinguara (but to be rechristened Aloysio Chaves after the then state governor). The measure received considerable coverage on radio and television. The new name did not stick but the response was overwhelming. The great attraction was the promise of secure land tenure with the provision of titles to the land. Peasants moved in from all over Brazil, even travelling up from Rio Grande do Sul, the southermost state, which is 3,000 kilometres away. The inhabitants joked that their town literally grew overnight, as at least one new shack was erected each day.

With fascinating speed, Brazil's class society was recreated in microcosm. Some of the settlers from Paraná, Rio Grande do Sul and Minas Gerais arrived with capital and set themselves up as the local bourgeoisie. Many from this stratum were involved in the lucrative timber business, setting up sawmills for the local mahogany and other valuable Amazon timbers. Some of the relatively well-off timber merchants felt greatly superior to the hundreds of penniless families that were arriving. Sadi Grassi, who is one of the most successful, confided to us: 'The people here are like animals. You can only get them to work if you drive them with spurs or with fire.'

The mass of settlers, however, arrived with very little money. They clustered in precariously constructed shacks on the outskirts of the village, hopefully waiting for the promised plot of land. Although these huts were very simple, with beaten earth floors, some were built, bizarrely enough, out of rough planks of mahogany simply because this was the most readily available type of timber.

However, after the elections, the politicians lost interest in Xinguara. In April 1977, the state authorities discovered that the hamlet lay within 100 kilometres of a federal road and thus, according to the law passed in July 1976, the area should be administered by INCRA. The unfinished business of Xinguara was thus handed lock, stock and barrel to the federal government. While the authorities slowly chewed over the problem, the peasant families had to find some means of survival. Some of the men travelled down the road to São Félix do Xingu to look for work in the tin mines. Others went prospecting, as gold deposits had recently been found in the region. Other families sought out a plot of unoccupied land on their own initiative.

When we were there in November 1977, INCRA finally settled the first 50 families on plots of land in nearby Rio Maria, providing them with provisional land titles. In marked contrast with the way in which the project was originally announced, the INCRA officials sternly warned the settlers not to spread the good news among relatives in other parts of Brazil.

Eventually, INCRA settled about 1,000 families on plots in Rio Maria. But the problems were not over for these families. In 1979 INCRA was defeated in court by six big companies which claimed to be the owners of the land where the families had been settled. The families were eventually evicted. Rio Maria was not the only case of administrative bungling in the Xinguara area. It was estimated in mid 1980 that no less than 10,000 peasants were involved in land conflicts in the Xinguara area, many of which had been created by the incompetence of the authorities.[17]

The level of discontent was running exceptionally high and it is not by chance that the first administrative act taken by GETAT in mid 1980 was to issue 600 land titles to families in Xinguara and Redenção, another little town renowned for its violence in south Pará. However, GETAT did not follow up this initial move with the decisive action needed to sort out the mess. Serious conflicts were allowed to drag on and were only tackled, after long delays, if they erupted into particularly unpleasant violence.

One of the fiercest conflicts in the Xinguara area concerned a plot of land beside the PA–150, the road leading to Marabá. In desperation, because INCRA was taking so long to find them land, about 400 families had settled here in 1978. At the time, the land was completely unoccupied and there was no indication that it had an owner. In 1979, however, a São Paulo banker, Flávio Pinho de Almedia, employed by the large banking group Comind, appeared and claimed to be the owner. He called his ranch Tupã-Ciretã, meaning 'God has been here' in the language of the Gorotire Indians. He laid claim to 40,500 hectares, including most of the land occupied by the peasant families, and began to put pressure on them to leave. As the families resisted, the pressure was increased. Local policemen were brought in to impose a road block, making it difficult for the families to carry out their normal farming activities. Though no eviction orders were issued, gunmen constantly harassed the families, finally forcing 60 of them to leave.

Pinho de Almeida then pulled the gunmen out, confident that he had defeated the peasants. But he was proved wrong: no sooner had the gunmen left than many of the families returned to their old plots. Pinho de Almeida sent the gunmen back in, instructing them to use tougher tactics. He also called on the military police for help. On 6 October 1979, 14 peasant farmers were illegally arrested by 15 soldiers from the state of Pará's military police force who came to the peasants' huts in the company of ranch employees. Franscisco Lobo Filho, one of the arrested peasants, said afterwards:

> The police took away all our guns, even the ones we use for hunting. They started to hit us, kicking our legs, beating us on the head, the ears. I was arrested with 13 others. We were forced to run in front of a car. I was hit with a gun. One of us tripped over and was knifed in the back.

Lobo Filho spent a night in hospital and was then freed, after he had been forced to sign a statement saying that he had not been maltreated.

The military policemen also called on one of the other peasant farmers, 59-year-old Antônio Costa. They beat him up, breaking his collar bone, and then threatened his family with a machine gun. Though Costa and a fellow peasant farmer had not attempted to fight back, they were told to take their clothes off and were forced at gun point to carry out homosexual intercourse in front of their families. Antônio Costa came out of the experience a broken man. He said later:

> I spent days after this unable to eat anything except cress soup [a traditional herbal medicine]. But I'm a finished man. I could have put up with the beatings. But what they did was to break down my morale. If we don't win our cause here, I shall just disappear into the world and live as a beggar a long way off from here.

The atrocities committed against these families were remarkable even by the standards of the Amazon. The local branch of Contag called for a 'public act of protest' on 21 October 1979. An unexpectedly large number of peasants – about 10,000 – and some well-known public figures, including Dom Pedro Casaldáliga, Bishop of São Félix, and some Catholic lawyers from São Paulo, attended the demonstration.

Paulo Fonteles, a lawyer linked to the CPT, commented to a journalist:

> According to Contag, it was the largest peasant gathering in Brazil for the last 15 years. And it was virtually spontaneous, for we had only five days in which

to organise it. We couldn't put the protest off any longer. For the violence of the police and the gunmen is assuming totally unacceptable proportions. And the consequences have become quite unpredictable. Or rather, they *are* predictable: we are heading towards a confrontation in which many people will be killed. The public act was above all a demonstration of the despair of the people in the face of this violence.

In the previous few months there had been a significant change, the lawyer said, in the peasants' response to the harassment from the ranch-owners:

Before, it was violence on one side and the peasants on the other. In nearly all cases the peasants left peacefully. But now the peasants do not seem prepared to accept eviction peacefully as in the past. And the cattle-rearers in their turn are sending in larger and larger numbers of gunmen.

In spite of the demonstration, the authorities took no action to resolve the conflict. Most of the peasant families were evicted during 1979, but they gradually returned to their plots in 1980. As the area was still very remote, it was impossible for Flávio Pinho de Almeida to prevent this without going to great expense. In 1981, however, he began another big offensive, taking care this time to prepare legal backing for his actions. He obtained eviction orders from Juraci Marques Tavares, the judge in Conceição do Araguaia, who had been nicknamed *despegeiro* (evictor) by the local population because of his readiness to provide landowners with eviction orders against peasant families.

In June 1981, about 60 soldiers of the military police were sent in. The families did not attempt to take them on in a shoot-out, but slipped away into the forest before they arrived, knowing that it was virtually impossible for them to be found. After the police had left, the families once again reoccupied their plots. On 14 September, 200 soldiers of the military police came back with a large number of gunmen. On 17 September, they shot 70-year-old Angelo Ribeiro da Silva in the back and beat up several peasants who had not managed to flee into the forest in time. Some of the gunmen remained, waiting for the peasants' return.

A few of the evicted families decided to make another appeal to the authorities. Five families went to Xinguara and camped outside the GETAT office. As this got them nowhere, two women – 19-year-old Maria Rocha Alves and 26-year-old Marli dos Santos Macedo – went to Brasília at the beginning of October to ask for help from the federal government. Marli told journalists what they were trying to do:

We are here to see if we can find the law. But if we don't find it we shall go on struggling all the same. We are frightened of being killed, but even so it is better to stay in the forest where we can feed ourselves than to roam around the country, starving.

Maria spoke of the violence used against them: 'They are making some of our men behave like women for them. They make them swallow lighted cigarette butts. They drag our children by the ear and ask us which one they should cut up first.'

The women managed to reach the top of the government, and spoke to justice minister Ibrahim Abi-Ackel who promised to take measures to put an end to the violence. They were told at GETAT's headquarters that, although Flávio Pinho de Almeida's land titles were valid, something would be done to help them. Despite their promises, the authorities took no action. By mid October, the families camped outside GETAT's office in Xinguara were desperate. According to a newspaper report, they appealed to Zozomilton de Oliveira, the GETAT coordinator in Xinguara: 'The gunmen are planting grass seed on our land. We must get back on our lands, for we need to plant our crops. We will go back!' De Oliveira remonstrated: 'I didn't tell you to settle on the land in the first place and leave it now. But how can you go back? How can you get the gunment out?' The peasants replied: 'We don't know if we can, but it's worth a try.'

On 14 October the peasant farmers made their desperate attempt, though they knew there was a large gang of gunmen, headed by two well-known thugs, nicknamed Chapéu de Aço (steel hat) and Joaquinzão, waiting from them. Throughout the following week there was a series of ambushes and shoot-outs. On one occasion different groups of gunmen starting firing on each other by mistake. By the end of the week the peasant families had managed to win a surprising victory and had driven the gunmen out. There were at least four dead, all gunmen, and a total of ten wounded from both sides.

At this late stage the authorities decided to act. No sooner had the peasant families recovered their plots than the military police arrived and they had to hide in the forest once more. After the police had left, the families moved back.

The situation dragged on for months without a solution. Finally, in April 1982, Zozomilton de Oliveira, accompanied by Bertoldo de Siqueira, the president of the rural union in Conceição do Araguaia, visited the plots. On the basis of the report sent by de Oliveira, GETAT decided that only 124 of the 500 plots were occupied by genuine peasant families; the rest, it said, were occupied by employees from local sawmills who did not intend to farm the land but merely to extract the mahogany. GETAT suggested that 18 of the 'genuine' peasant families – the most needy – should be immediately settled on their land and issued with valid land titles, while a compromise solution was worked out with the landowner for the other 'genuine' peasant families. Later GETAT asked Flávio Pinho de Almeida to allow the 106 'genuine' peasant families to stay on their plots, and proposed that in compensation for the area he would lose he should receive another piece of land of comparable size adjoining the far side of his ranch. GETAT told the other 376 families that they must leave and would be dealt with harshly if they refused to comply. Though the families denied GETAT's assertion that they were not genuine peasant families, most of them saw no alternative but reluctantly to leave their plots.

GETAT took a similarly tough position in another conflict at Rio Maria near Xinguara. A group of peasant families were involved in a conflict with a landowner called Alípio Cardoso over land which they had occupied but which he said formed part of his ranch, Santa Cruz. Though the land had not formed part of the official colonisation project, some of the families had settled there in 1978 on the advice of INCRA, which had told them that the area was *terras devolutas* and thus available for them. These plots formed part of the area over which INCRA fought an unsuccessful legal battle. Even though INCRA lost, the families had refused to move out.

GETAT backed up the court's decision and tried to resettle some of the families. Anibal Patrocínio Morais, 65, who was later arrested, described his experience: 'I tried to make it work out with the plot I got from GETAT. But it was no good. The land was on a mountain in Araguaxirim and it was very difficult to survive there. So I came back.' On 16 April 1982 a group of peasants killed João José Ferreira, a ranch employee, who had been sent in with a group of gunmen from the ranch to evict them. Except for Anibal, who had not been involved in the killing, all the peasant farmers fled into the forest before the police arrived.

Iris Pedro de Oliveira, president of GETAT, said later that the peasants from Santa Cruz had received help from the families in Tupã Ciretrã, who, he claimed, had been hoping to spark off generalised peasant warfare in the region. He said that the government would take very firm action against this type of subversive activity. The peasant families in Santa Cruz had lost their case, he stressed, and they must leave. If they refused to go, the police would be sent in to deal with them as criminals. Though full information is difficult to obtain, these families too are reported to have reluctantly left.

The Government Wages 'War'

The creation of GETAT did not bring greater tranquility to the region. The CPT published a report in September 1981 which showed that 151 conflicts had been reported in Pará over the previous year and a half. Many had occurred within GETAT's area of influence. In another report, published in June 1982, the CPT said that there had been a marked increase in the violence of the conflicts in Pará over the previous nine months. Twelve peasants had died as a result of land conflicts during this period.

In a report on land conflicts published in January 1983, the CNBB said that no less than 49 out of the 80 conflicts reported in the last four months of 1982 had occurred in the states of Pará and Goiás. According to this report, the GETAT area had become the most violent region of Brazil and members of both the federal and military police forces were known to be taking part in some of the conflicts.

In another report, published in February 1983, the CPT said that there had been an increase in violence in six dioceses in Pará, Mato Grosso and Goiás in 1982. It had recorded ten deaths, 26 cases of people being wounded or beaten up and eviction threats against 13,860 families in these areas during the year. It commented: 'These numbers are an indication of the level of violence in the countryside where the authorities back land thieves and gunmen, with total disrespect for the law.' The CPT claimed that these problems were 'a natural consequence of the government's economic policy, which is forcing land concentration at any price, so that it can carry out its megalithic projects, such as Carajás'.

Contag has also reported an increase in the violence generated by land conflicts, particularly in the Amazon region. In a document published in July 1982, it expressed its concern at the 'escalation of violence and terror' which had resulted over the previous two years

> in the deaths of dozens of comrades, including workers, union leaders, lawyers and collaborators... Just yesterday, a peasant farmer called Marcos was killed by an unidentified soldier in the military police in Cachoeirinha near São Geraldo do Araguia in Pará.

However, despite this, the federal government seemed satisfied with GETAT's achievements, largely no doubt because it had effectively blocked the work of the church in the region. In July 1982 Iris Pedro de Oliveira said that all the 'critical' problems in the GETAT region would have been resolved by early 1985.

In August 1982 the government decided to build on GETAT's success and apply a similar policy on a national level. It said that it would be setting up an 'extraordinary ministry for land affairs', to be headed by General Danilo Venturini who had previously been in charge of the President's military household. Venturini would also be taking over as secretary-general of the National Security Council, an extremely powerful position.

INCRA, the civilian institute for agrarian reform and land colonisation, which formed part of the agriculture ministry, was not abolished but became responsible only for the government's rural cooperatives. All its key tasks – the formulation of land policy, the distribution of land, the sorting out of titles on *terras devolutas* and on the vast areas beside federal roads, and even the collection of rural taxes – were taken over by the new ministry. The change was a political development of great importance; it took responsibility for land away from the agriculture ministry, over which Congress had some influence, and placed it in the hands of the closed military establishment. In this way, it hit at the heart of the process of political liberalisation for it was a blow against the accountability which, more than anything else, is essential for democratic rule.

The opposition parties seemed to fail to grasp the importance of the new development. Once again, the Catholic Church and the rural unions were the only bodies to speak out firmly and repeatedly against the new measure.

In a statement published in mid August 1982, the CPT said:

> From now on, agrarian reform, if it is permissible to abuse the term in this way, will become a military question. Land throughout the country is going to be administered by one enormous GETAT which has swallowed up INCRA and other small bodies.

It said that the announcement of the new ministry had been made at a time when rural violence was increasing throughout the country. The measure suggested that, from then on,

> land problems will be seen as a question of national security. But it is precisely GETAT, which is already linked to the National Security Council, the federal police and the army, which has committed most crimes of violence against the peasants . . . What treatment can peasants expect from a body which is repressive in its very nature? . . . Land conflicts will be treated like a war. One of the fundamental objectives of the new ministry will be to suppress, systematically, land conflicts and to stop peasant families from forming organisations to defend their right to occupy a plot of land.

The leaders of Contag also fiercely attacked the creation of the new ministry. They too felt themselves victims of discrimination: 'Why has only land policy become an issue of national security? Why haven't exchange policy and wage policy also come under the control of the National Security Council?'

One of the reasons for setting up the new ministry was to strengthen the hand of President João Baptista Figueiredo in the behind-the-scenes power struggle over the presidential succession. General Danilo Venturini would have had to leave the President's cabinet at the end of 1982, if he had remained head of the President's military household and secretary-general of the National Security Council. This is because Venturini reached retirement age then and both these posts can only be held by active members of the armed forces. By making Venturini a minister, Figueiredo was able to keep him in the cabinet and also appoint another close ally – General Rubem Ludwig – to take over as head of the military household. Figueiredo kept Venturini as secretary-general of the National Security Council by passing a special degree which temporarily allowed a retired officer to hold this position.

However, these tactical manoeuvres do not explain why Figueiredo chose to set up a land ministry, as opposed to any other additional ministry. It seems clear that the military leaders wished to increase their involvement in some aspect of government, partly to make up for the less active role they were playing in anti-terrorist operations in the cities and partly because land conflict, with its potential for violent clashes, seemed the ideal issue. It is no coincidence that the National Security Council also began to play a much more active role in Indian affairs during this period.

Venturini kept a low profile as land minister over the next couple of years. He set up an efficient intelligence network and expropriated some particularly tense areas, but he made no important policy changes. He proved fairly effective in stemming the influence of the left-wing faction of the church, partly by skilfully cultivating the more conservative members of the church and impressing them with his grasp of the issues and his willingness to work with the so-called 'responsible' members of the church.

Though reasonably successful in the short term, Venturini's strategy is no more than a holding operation, which does not resolve the underlying problems. Most peasant families in the Amazon are undoubtedly eager to enter the modern world and be successful in it. They want, first of all, to become owners of their plots of land, and then to become fully integrated into the market. They want cheap bank loans so that they can purchase tractors and fertilisers and thus increase their harvests. They want the Bank of Brazil to send in buyers so that they can get better prices for their crops and break the present hold exercised by a small network of private middle men. They want better roads, which do not become impassable during the rainy season. If they are given half a chance, the peasant families in the Amazon will become a productive, stable and fairly conservative force.

However, partly because of the tremendous political leverage of the big landowners and business groups from the south, the military government has never been prepared to give the families this half chance. For decades, the government gave the landowners and land thieves free rein, so that hundreds of thousands of families were evicted and forced to push on westwards in search of another plot of land. The government deliberately kept out of the region so as not to hinder the 'natural' process of occupation.

The government only changed this policy because of the growing resistance offered by the peasant families. More and more families refused to move out, even if they were repeatedly threatened by gunmen, and began to reoccupy their plots if forcibly evicted. Peasant families, with their deserved reputation for humility and respect for the law, began to show an unsuspected capacity for armed resistance. In some cases, the very experience of the conflict began to have a profound effect on the peasants' political beliefs. The possibility of peasant warfare – or even peasant revolution – became real, if still remote. The government immediately blamed left-wing priests and *agentes pastorais* for the changes, but, as far as we can tell, the influence of the church, though important, was not decisive. The creation of GETAT, and later the ministry for land affairs, was an attempt, first, to neutralise the 'harmful' effect of the church and, secondly, to suppress the peasants' attempts at organised resistance. It did not tackle the heart of the problem: the failure to provide a large sector of the peasantry with land.

Unless the new civilian government takes decisive action in the countryside, the level of violence is likely to increase over the next few years. Despite impossible odds, desperate families will cling to their plots and, after eviction, organise attempts to reoccupy them. Both the isolation of the families, and their vulnerability to repression, make it unlikely – but perhaps not impossible – for the region to be engulfed in generalised peasant warfare. The main impact will be felt in the towns, both in the region and further south. Cuiabá, the capital of Mato Grosso, has been growing at about 16 per cent a year, largely as the result of the influx of peasant families who have either been evicted from their plots or have returned south after an unsuccessful search for an available plot of land. Gustavo Arruda, mayor of Cuiabá, complained in 1982 that about 50 per cent of the city's population of about a quarter of a million was made up of migrant families or shanty-town dwellers. 'We simply do not have the resources to deal with the social problem', he complained. He said that the problem was largely caused by the migrants' utopian dream of finding a plot to farm. 'But it doesn't happen, so the migrants end up in the cities.'[18]

After stopping off at Cuiabá or another of the towns in the north, many of the families will move further south, to the medium-sized towns or to the very big metropolitan centres. At the end of 1983 Greater São Paulo had a population of 14.2 million, which is 1.6 million more than at the end of 1980. The city's population had grown 4 per cent a year, compared with the national average of 2.4 per cent. In other words, the city was still attracting migrants, despite the severe recession. The vast majority of the new inhabitants were unable to find jobs; the industrial sector in Greater São Paulo employed 1.8 million people at the end of 1983, just 10,000 more than in 1977. The government's failure to fix people in the countryside is putting intolerable pressure on the cities. According to a World Bank report published in July 1984, São Paulo will have 25.8 million inhabitants by the year 2000, if it continues to grow at its present rate. It will be second only to Mexico City, which is predicted to have 31 million people by then. The complex syndrome of problems arising from urban hypertrophy will undoubtedly be one of the key questions to be faced over the next few decades by successive Brazilian administrations, whatever their political composition.

Notes

1. *O Estado de S. Paulo*, 28 January 1972.
2. Commissão Pastoral da Terra, *Denúncia – Caso Araguaia–Tocantins* (1981).
3. Ibid., p.16.
4. We relied at times on the press, particularly to update stories after we left. We used heavily *Aconteceu*, the weekly publication brought out by the CEDI, which brings together news about rural and urban workers, Indians and the Catholic Church from a wide variety of Brazilian publications. Not infrequently, however, the areas we visited were too remote to be covered by the press. In these cases I

often have no further information since the time of my last visit, which took place in late 1981 for some areas and early 1984 for others.

5. Julian Filochowski, 'Medellín to *Puebla', in Reflections on Puebla* (Catholic Institute for International Relations, London, 1980).

6. *Repressão na Ingreja no Brasil: reflexo de uma situação de opressão (1968/1978)* (Comissão Arquidiocesana de Pastoral dos Direitos Humanos e Marginalizados da Arquidiocese de São Paulo, December 1978).

7. Filochowski, 'Medellín to Puebla'.

8. *Latin America Regional Report, Brazil,* 16 October 1981.

9. *O Estado de S. Paulo*, 14 March 1979.

10. *A Folha de S. Paulo*, 14 March 1983.

11. *Jornal do Brasil*, 2 February 1980.

12. *Veja*, 12 November 1980.

13. *A Folha de S. Paulo*, 3 May 1982.

14. *Veja*, 12 November 1982.

15. *A Report of the Trial of Father Aristides Camio and Father François Gouriou, Belém, 21–22 June 1982* (Amnesty International, AMR, 19 July 1982).

16. Comissão Pastoral da Terra, *Denúncia – Caso Araguaia-Tocantins*.

17. *Jornal do Brasil*, 18 June 1980.

18. *O Estado de S. Paulo*, 23 April 1982.

5. The Indians and the Encroaching Society

If today we were to compare the two civilisations, the two humanities in the words of Lévi-Strauss, we could say that the 'civilised' are an advanced but suffering society. In contrast, the Indians have in one sense stood still in time and space: they are still making the same kind of bow as their ancestors made a thousand years ago.

But, though they have stood still in this sense, they have evolved in their social behaviour. The Indian has a stable and tranquil place in his tribe. He is totally free, and doesn't have to account to anyone for his actions. All the tribal stability, all the cohesion, is based on a mythic world.

What an enormous difference between the two worlds: one, peaceful, where man is in charge of his own actions; the other, a society which is exploding, where a state apparatus, a repressive system, is required to maintain order and peace in the society.

If an individual shouts out in the centre of São Paulo, a police car may carry him off under arrest. If an Indian lets out an enormous yell in the middle of his village, no one will look at him, no one will ask him why he shouted. The Indian is a free man.

(Orlando Villas-Boas)

Our main focus during our trips to the Amazon was not the Indians, but they repeatedly forced themselves on our attention. We saw thousands of detribalised Indians living in pitiful conditions in shanty-towns outside Manaus. We heard talk in peasant communities of attacks carried out by the Txukurramãe Indians on lorry drivers. We saw emaciated, silent women, from the Kreen-Akarore, the so-called 'Giant Indians', working as prostitutes along the Cuiabá–Santarém road. We were taken by motor-boat by one of the ranch managers to see a small group of sick Avá-Canoeiro Indians, all of whom were later to die, who had been contacted against their will a few months earlier.

We also encountered a great deal of resentment about the large tracts of land occupied by the Indians. While the transnationals, big Brazilian companies and members of the federal government are generally more sympathetic to the Indians' cause – or, at least, are more careful not to make anti-Indian remarks to outsiders – the local politicians and the local landowners feel far fewer restraints. Many of them have become famous for their virulently anti-Indian remarks. At a congress on the occupation of the Amazon in April 1982, many officials from state governments and leading local businessmen criticised the Indians. Jorge Teixeira, governor of Rondônia, said that it was 'absurd' that the Indians should occupy 200,000 hectares of land in his state. He called on Funai to cut back drastically the size of the Indians' reserves, saying that it would be sufficient for each Indian to have five hectares of land. In his turn, Frederico Campos, governor of Mato Grosso, complained about the Indians' idleness, saying that 'they must become productive, just as we are'. Similar sentiments were expressed by other speakers.

We could understand that politicians, with ambitious development plans for their states, and landowners, eager to expand the size of their estates, should feel some resentment towards the Indians. But by the end of our trips we were convinced that the widespread hatred of the Indians among the local ruling classes was not fundamentally rational. It was quite different in intensity to the scorn and dislike that many landowners felt towards peasant families who were also occupying land that they might feel should be theirs. It seemed to us that many of the landowners hated the Indians, not just for the economic threat they represented, but also because they belonged to a different culture that the landowners did not understand and, perhaps subconsciously, feared.

The Indians attach a religious significance to their lands, which means that normally they are not willing to sell them even if they are offered a fairly large sum of money. A Taxáua Indian expressed his feelings towards his land as follows: 'No one sells his own son or his mother, because he loves them. In the same way, it is an absurd idea for an Indian to sell his land.' He continued later: 'An Indian is an Indian and can't change himself any more than he can change the blood that runs in his veins. In the same way, we can't change our feelings for our land, which is where our ancestors are buried.' The Indians organise their tribal life on non-hierarchical and non-authoritarian lines. Even children are treated with great personal respect. An Indian will never take away a necklace given to a child, however high a price he or she is offered for it.

We experienced anti-Indian feeling in a particularly virulent form in mid 1976. By chance, we were travelling through Barra do Garças, a hot and unpleasant little town on the Araguaia river which is a well-known meeting place for local landowners. The atmosphere in this town was tense because of a conflict with the nearby Bororo Indians. This group had been in contact with national society for many years and had been cared for by conservative Salesian missionaries. In the 1940s their morale had reached such a low ebb that, like the Parakanã Indians, they decided not to have any more children. Many of the women made themselves infertile by using forest herbs.

In 1974 a West German missionary, Rodolfo Lukembein, took over the running of the mission. He was distressed by what he saw and made a great effort to restore the Bororo's pride in their ethnic identity. His endeavours were largely successful and the tribe began to recover. In 1976, at Lukembein's request, Funai sent in a team to demarcate the Indians' reserve and to evict the landowners who had settled on their land. The local landowners were outraged and a large group, headed by a man known as João Mineiro, invaded the mission and killed a Bororo Indian and Lukembein in cold blood.

We witnessed the celebrations which stretched far into the night in Barra do Garças after the group of landowners returned. Violent anti-Indian sentiments, of the type which are generally suppressed, were being freely voiced. We heard one landowner sneer: 'Indians are worse than animals. They are not even good to eat.' We were told that there was even more rejoicing in February of the following year when, despite the overwhelming evidence, a local jury cleared João Mineiro of the charge of murder and justified his action, saying that he had acted in 'legitimate self-defence'.

Our interest was aroused by these tantalisingly brief encounters with Indians and Indian haters. We decided to look in greater detail at the rapidly-changing interaction between Indians and non-Indians.

The History of the Indians

When Brazil was discovered by the Portuguese in 1500, there are estimated to have been between three million and five million Indians scattered all over the country. As the penetration front progressed, the Indians were constantly driven further and further inland, and they suffered a terrible toll, not only from massacres and enslavement, but also from disease. By 1900, there are estimated to have been only about one million Indians left. By 1960, their numbers had dropped to about 200,000. The Indians seemed doomed to extinction.

Throughout the Empire (1500–1889), the Indian was viewed as a kind of natural resource, whose lands could be stolen and whose labour could be exploited for the benefit of the dominant economy. Very little attention was paid to the Indians' own rights. This view began to be challenged in the early 20th Century. At that time, large areas in southern Brazil were engulfed in racial conflicts.[1] The Botocudo Indians in the states of Minas Gerais and Espírito Santo resisted the invasion of their tribal lands, and almost forced the colony of settlers at São Mateus to leave. In the state of São Paulo, the Kaingang Indians halted the construction of the north-west railway and controlled an area of 500 square kilometres. News of these and other conflicts filled the newspapers. Several European missions called for immediate measures from the federal government to protect the lives of European settlers in Brazil. These demands were reinforced by the racist social doctrines which were being propagated by teachers of European origin at some of São Paulo's universities. The lobby was so strong that on several occasions the President called a meeting of his cabinet to consider the use of the army to put an end to the conflicts, though he never actually took this step. Some members of Congress went even further, arguing that, in the interests of national development, Brazil should use the same extermination tactics which had been used against the Indians in the United States.

At the same time, another current of opinion emerged. It came almost entirely from upper-class scientists and philanthropists. Heavily influenced by French positivism, they attacked the racist theories being taught at some of the universities and were strongly critical of the proposal that the Indians should be systematically exterminated. Arguing that in time the Indians would become responsible citizens, they claimed that it was the duty of the government to protect them.

The main spokesman for this faction was a young army officer, Cándido Mariano da Silva Rondon, born in 1865 in Cuiabá, at that time a small town in the interior of Mato Grosso. In 1880, Rondon was instructed by the government to carry out a series of military and scientific expeditions into the interior of the country. Over the next 25 years, Rondon mapped over 50,000 square kilometres of unknown territory, discovered about a dozen new rivers in Mato Grosso and other parts of the Amazon and established telegraphic links across 2,270 kilometres of Brazilian territory. In 1913, he took Theodore Roosevelt, the former president of the USA, on a geographical expedition into a wild region of Brazil. His work became famous in Brazil and abroad, and in 1956 the territory on Guaporé was rechristened Rondônia in his memory.

Rondon established contact with hitherto isolated groups of Bororo, Nambikwara and Paresi Indians. Over time, he grew to feel a warm affection for these people, whom he considered to be neither wild nor barbarous but simply at a different level of development. He began to lobby the government to set up a body which would provide these and other Indians with the necessary conditions for survival. Finally in 1910 the government created the Service for the Protection of the Indians (SPI), the first national body ever set up to defend the rights of the Indians. Rondon was made its first president.

In the early years the SPI made a real effort. It sent in groups of *sertanistas*, or Indian specialists acquainted with the hinterland, to establish contact with isolated tribes. These dedicated men respected SPI's motto: 'Die if necessary, but never kill.' For the first 20 years no Indians were killed or wounded, while many *sertanistas* died. At times, the *sertanistas* waited patiently for months on end to establish pacific contact. During the first few decades, it set up 67 Indian posts in various pioneer regions and made peaceful contact with dozens of tribes.

Yet, despite the idealism and dedication of these early *sertanistas*, the Indians fared badly. After the initial contact had been made, the SPI was not powerful enough to hold back the encroaching society. Big farmers, mining companies, timber merchants, peasant families and others invaded the Indians' lands, driving them out altogether or leaving them with just tiny reserves. The anthropologist Darcy Ribeiro has examined the fate of many of the groups contacted during this period.[2] His list of groups which lost their lands includes the Kaingang in São Paulo and Paraná, contacted in 1912, whose lands were soon converted into fertile coffee plantations, and the Botocudos in Santa Catarina, contacted in 1914, whose lands became one of the richest farming areas in the state. Moreover, Rondon lost his job in 1930, after the *coup* which eventually brought Getúlio Vargas to power. Without his firm leadership, the SPI rapidly declined. Its officials became notorious for their corruption and for their collaboration with landowners.

Over the next 30 years, there were sporadic attempts to wipe out corruption and to revitalise the SPI. The most vigorous of these endeavours was undertaken by José Maria da Gama Malcher, who was president of SPI from 1950 to 1954. It was during his presidency that the Xingu National Park was set up. This park was the brainchild of the three Villas-Boas brothers. In 1943, they had taken part in the Roncador–Xingu expedition into the little-known interior of the country. The expedition was organised by the Getúlio Vargas government in response to fears from some nationalist sectors that, as a result of World War II, large numbers of Europeans would emigrate to the Brazilian hinterland. The government was thus anxious to create a series of emergency landing strips from Manaus to southern Brazil so that it would be in a position to control any wave of immigration.

The expedition lasted several years and made contact with various Indian groups, including the Xavantes and, later, the groups which inhabited the upper reaches of the Xingu river. The brothers were fascinated to discover that, apart from a marked reduction in number and the introduction of a few metal tools, these latter Indians were living in practically the same conditions as those described by the German ethnologist, Karl von den Steinen, in 1884.

As the result of these early experiences, the Villas-Boas brothers decided to stay in the region to do what they could to help the Xingu Indians, They looked back critically at what had been achieved by the SPI and realised that, even when it had been run by dedicated officials, it had done very little of lasting value through its peaceful contacts. The brothers decided that the Indians would only be saved if, before the occupation front reached them, the government created a large reserve, closed to outsiders, which would protect them from disease and guarantee them the right to their lands. The brothers thus began a national campaign for the creation of a park to save the Indians in the upper Xingu. The park was created in 1952 and its legal frontiers were finally approved by Congress in 1961.

In the meantime, however, the SPI declined even further. The situation became worse after the military *coup* in 1964, when military officers without any previous experience with Indians were appointed as SPI directors. Criticisms were voiced at home and abroad and the government began to be accused of genocide. Detractors dubbed the SPI the Service for the Prostitution of the Indians. In 1967, General Afonso Augusto de Albuquerque Lima, the new interior minister under President Arthur da Costa e Silva, instructed Jader Figueiredo, the prosecutor-general, to investigate the charges of corruption which had been made against SPI officials. Figueiredo took the job seriously, travelling 16,000 kilometres and visiting 130 posts, and at the end presented a 5,115-page report.

In March 1968, Albuquerque Lima gave a press interview in which he announced some of the conclusions reached in the report. He said that 'widespread corruption and sadism have been discovered, extending from the massace of whole tribes with dynamite, machine guns and poisoned sugar, to the removal of an 11-year old girl to work as a maid for an SPI official.'³ In view of these findings, Albuquerque Lima said that he had decided to abolish the SPI and to replace it with a new body, to be called the National Foundation of the Indian (Funai). He also promised to punish the guilty SPI officials and to hand back to the Indians the land which had been stolen from them. However, Albuquerque Lima was soon replaced at the interior ministry by General José Costa Cavalcanti, known for his developmentalist fervour. Though it appeared that no fewer than 500 of the 700 employees at SPI had been involved in the accusations of corruption, very few were punished. It seemed that the government carried out a big cover-up operation.

But the important change was the creation of Funai. The new body was given much broader responsibilities than the SPI. It was instructed not only to protect the Indians from the encroaching society, as the SPI had been supposed to do, but also to help the Indians to adapt to their new situation. For a while it seemed that Funai represented a real advance, though in retrospect it is clear that it suffered from a serious defect from the outset. For, like the SPI, Funai was created as part of the interior ministry, which contained all the development agencies including Sudam. However dedicated Funai's top officials might be, this small body was in a very weak institutional position, for within its own ministry it faced the power and leverage of Sudam, which had the backing of the big cattle companies from São Paulo, and other similar bodies. Funai could only have been truly effective as a body directly subordinated to the President of the country.

Moreover, old habits die hard. Though the personnel appointed by Funai were a great improvement on the old SPI officials, corruption was not wiped out even among the top people. In 1970 José de Queiroz Campos, Funai's first president, was forced to resign because his sister had been caught stealing equipment from Indian hospitals. His replacement – General Jerônimo Bandeira de Mello – soon established himself as one of the worst presidents imaginable. As well as being corrupt, Bandeiro de Mello was an enthusiastic exponent of the new developmentalist ideology which dominated the government of General Emílio Garrastazu Médici. On several occasions, he stated publicly that he did not believe that the Indians should be allowed to hold back the progress of the country and that his main goal as president of Funai was to integrate the Indians into modern Brazil, a process which he thought could be undertaken very rapidly. He is reported to have shouted at the British anthropologist Robin Hanbury-Tenison in 1971: 'It is no longer necessary to use the old slow process of integration. Now we have new psychological methods for doing it in six months.'[4] When Hanbury-Tenison asked what these methods were, he replied:

> We have applied psychology to the subject and we resettle them as quickly as possible in new villages and then remove the children and begin to educate them. We give them the benefit of our medicine and our education, and, once they are completely integrated citizens like you and me and the minister here, we let them go out into the world.

The minister in question was the interior minister, José Costa Cavalcanti, who, despite his well-known developmentalist ideas, could not go as far as supporting Bandeira de Mello's plans. He said that integration could take three generations in some cases.

Bandeira de Mello worked closely with Sudam. As part of the government's official endeavours to protect the Indians, the companies needed a certificate, attesting the absence of Indians from the area where they planned to set up their ranch, before they were entitled to tax rebates. In practice, the procedure offered little protection to the Indians. The cattle companies often obtained the necessary certificate without Funai carrying out even a superficial survey of the land in question. One of the many companies to benefit was the mining company Sanchez-Galdeano, which was authorised to mine cassiterite in an area in Rondônia though this land had long been inhabited by the Suruí Indians. Coincidence or not, Bandeira de Mello became a director in this company after he left Funai in 1974.

It was during the presidency of Bandeira de Mello that Funai systematised the Indians' rights for the first time, drawing up the Indian Statute which became law in December 1973. The statute recognised in principle the Indians' right to remain on their land and to be exclusive beneficiaries of any wealth derived from these lands. However, it also authorised the government to intervene in the Indians' territories 'in the interests of national security', 'in order to carry out public works in the interests of national development' and 'to explore the riches of the subsoil if they are of outstanding interest for national security and development'. Given the government's broad definition of national security, this qualification in practice gave it *carte blanche* to overrule the Indians' right to their lands whenever it wished.

Though Bandeira de Mello's administration was harmful to the Indians in many ways, two of its actions raised particularly forceful criticisms. In 1970 Funai acquiesced without protest in the plan to build the Trans-amazônica highway with extraordinary haste across the heart of the Amazon jungle. The road crossed the lands of five Indian groups – the Juruna, Arara, Parakanã, Asurini and Kararão. It was the biggest thrust into the Amazon ever made by the federal government. As such, it required at the very least a comparable effort by Funai to protect the affected Indians.

In the very early days, it looked as if the government, in consultation with Funai, would for once be taking elementary precautions to soften the impact. Eduardo Galvão, director of the Emílio Goeldi Museum in Belém, said that the first government work group, in charge of planning the exact route for the road, had agreed to keep at least 50 kilometres away from any Indian village. However, it was not long before the government had second thoughts about this concession which would undoubtedly have increased the cost of construction. The engineers were soon instructed to plan the road according to strictly technical criteria, without taking into consideration the villages and hunting grounds of the Indians.

So in the end, Funai was given a merely functional task: to clear the Indians out of the way in order to minimise the possibility of conflict. Yet even this limited task was not carried out efficiently. Funai originally planned to fly over a corridor of 100 kilometres on either side of the planned route so that the location of all the villages could be accurately plotted, and then to send in 'attraction fronts' to establish contact with the Indians. It intended to use the *namoro* (courtship) technique by which contacts are built up gradually, after the Indians' trust and confidence have been won.

However, partly because of the haste with which the road was constructed, little of this was done. For reasons which have never been properly established, Funai decided not to carry out a thorough survey of the region, but to send in groups ahead of the tractors to establish 'dynamic' contact with any Indians they might encounter. On several occasions, groups of Indians came to the road and, in what was probably their first contact with non-Indians, met construction workers who had not been prepared psychologically or medically for these encounters. In one of the unexpected meetings, a group of Arara Indians appeared on the road 123 kilometres from Altamira, the most important town on the highway, and killed three construction workers. None the less, the road was built with surprisingly few violent clashes, probably because most of the Indian groups retreated further into the jungle, frightened by the noise of the construction work. Though Funai immediately claimed that it had carried out its work with great success, it was clear that it would take several years to assess the full impact of the road on the Indians' lives.

The other widely criticised measure taken by Bandeira de Mello concerned the Xingu Park. In 1971 he agreed to the cattle companies' proposal that a road (BR–80) should cross the park and that the area which lay to the north of the road, about a fifth of the total, should cease to be part of the park and be sold to cattle companies, while another area, of comparable size, should be added to the southern frontier of the park (see Chapter 2). The Villas-Boas brothers vigorously opposed the construction of the road, for they did not want to transfer the Indians out of their original habitat and they were afraid that the Indians' lands would gradually be invaded and contaminated by the cattle companies if the northern frontier of the park became a road. They also pointed out that the new area to be given to the Indians was much less fertile than the stretch of land they were to lose.

In their turn, top Funai officials attacked the Villas-Boas brothers for their retrograde views. In an official note issued in March 1971,[5] Funai called the Xingu Park 'a typical example of isolationism' and described the new road as 'a land link of vital importance for the development and security of the country', which would 'encourage the Indians to play a greater role in the national economy'. Bandeira de Mello told the press: 'The Indian is not a guinea pig, nor the property of half a dozen opportunists. The development of Brazil cannot be held back because of the Xingu Park.'

Some anthropologists have criticised the way the park has been run. They claim that the Villas-Boas brothers tried in paternalist fashion to protect the Indians rather than preparing them for the inevitable contact with the surrounding cattle ranches. At the same time, the brothers are accused of having encouraged visitors to make gifts to the Indians, with the result that the sudden influx of modern consumer goods played havoc with their traditional values and life-style and created a harmful dependence on a supply of products from outside. Yet all anthropologists agree that the park, despite its flaws, has been a boon for the Indians, and, indeed, represents the last hope of survival for several tribes. It was a sobering experience for many of them to discover that for the authorities the park was just a showplace, useful in that it projected an image of a caring, humanitarian government, but not important in itself.

As the anthropologists and the Villas-Boas brothers predicted, the road created serious problems for several Indian groups. In 1979, Orlando Villas-Boas commented bitterly: 'The BR–80 has brought nothing but trouble to the region – *cachaça*, prostitution, forest cutters, adventurers and so on'. In 1982 the then interior minister, Mário Andreazza, who had been minister of transport in 1971, said that he would not have given the go-ahead for the road if he had known at that time the problems it was to cause. Its impact on the Txukurramãe Indians is examined later.

When General Ernesto Geisel became President of the country in March 1974, Bandeira de Mello was replaced by General Ismarth de Araújo Oliveira. Though the latter showed greater respect for the Indians' way of life, he was also committed to the development of the Amazon and to the integration of the Indians into national society. Under his presidency, Funai drew up a controversial 'emancipation project' under which it proposed to abolish the special status as minors of all those Indians considered to have had sufficient contact with national society. The proposal was presented as a progressive move which would put Indians on a par with other Brazilians.

However, the project had a sting in its tail, for it would have abolished the special protection afforded by Funai to the Indians' land which made it impossible for the Indians to sell off, either individually or collectively, any part of their lands. Ignoring the Indians' collective form of land ownership, Funai intended, after emancipating a group, to divide its land up into family plots. It would have thus become much easier for cattle companies to take over the land by buying up individual plots one by one.

A vigorous campaign against the project was organised by Cimi, and by groups of anthropologists. Bishop Tomás Balduíno, then president of Cimi, accused the government of genocide. He said that, for the first time in Brazilian history the government was proposing to act as an institution against the Indians and deliberately to put into effect a measure which it knew would lead to the cultural extermination of many tribes. In the past, he added, the heavy toll on Indian lives had resulted from government omission and had not been the result of a conscious policy.

The counter-offensive was successful and the government dropped the project in early 1979. In March 1979 General João Baptista Figueiredo took over as President from General Ernesto Geisel. Breaking a tradition of over a decade, a civilian – Ademar Ribeiro da Silva – was appointed as head of Funai. None the less, the appointment was initially greeted with a spate of criticisms, for Ribeiro da Silva had previously been a director of DNER, the national road-building department; his appointment seemed like a joke in bad taste to many anthropologists. However, unlike his predecessors, Ribeiro da Silva showed a refreshing willingness to learn and an eagerness to maintain close contact with anthropologists and Cimi. But the new climate of freedom was short-lived. Probably as a result of pressure from the cattle companies, Ribeiro da Silva lost his job after just six months. President Figueiredo clearly regretted having strayed outside the armed forces for his first appointment and made a safe choice second time round – Colonel João Carlos Nobre da Veiga.

The colonel brought in as advisers a group of about a dozen colonels, many of them drawn from the security forces. Whereas in earlier years Funai had been regarded as a backwater for military officers who had failed to make the grade elsewhere, this virtual takeover by younger and more energetic officers reflected the new importance that the Indian question was assuming. For the first time, the powerful National Security Council was involved in the formulation of Funai's policies.

One of Nobre da Veiga's first moves was to weed out members of Funai whom he regarded as undesirable. No less than 39 employees, including some of the most experienced *sertanistas*, were sacked during the first half of 1980. Some of them were replaced by more military officers. 'Discipline' became the new catch phrase. Nobre da Veiga remained faithful to the developmentalist ideas of his predecessors, but he worked out a new strategy for speeding up the integration of the Indians. He established two new objectives: to decentralise Funai's administrative structure, giving much greater autonomy to the branches in each of the states; and to set up so-called economic projects so that Funai could become self-sufficient in financial terms.

The Indians were unhappy with both of these aims. They knew from their own experience that the local branches of Funai were more vulnerable to pressure from the landowners, who were often powerful political figures in state politics. They were also concerned that the new interregional links that some of the Indian groups were forging, often to oppose policies adopted by Funai, could be damaged by the fragmentation of Funai into largely independent state bodies. Some Indian leaders even suspected that the whole project was one of Funai's tactics to prevent the emergence of a strong, articulate national Indian movement.

Though the economic projects brought money into the villages, many Indians were critical of them, largely because of the authoritarian way in which Funai set them up. Often the Indians were not allowed to participate in the choice of project, nor even to carry out the initial phases of the work, as Funai preferred to bring in outside labour to do such jobs as land clearance. As a result, many of the projects had a harmful impact on the Indians' self-esteem and, indirectly, on their culture.

Some anthropologists and members of the Catholic Church believe that these pernicious effects were deliberately planned by Funai. Archbishop Quirino Adolfo Schmitz spoke to the press in July 1981 to summarise the conclusions reached at Cimi's fourth national assembly. He said:

> After the failure of its emancipation project, Funai adopted another tactic – the economic projects. These have been used to corrupt the Indian leaders, through presents such as tractors and other modern farm inputs and through funding. Never before have the Indians received so much money. By combining these economic projects with the repression of the most militant Indian leaders, Funai has found a very clever and ingenious way of wearing down the Indians' resistance. It is also one which is much more acceptable to public opinion, at home and abroad, because it gives the impression that Funai is really doing something to promote the well-being of the Indian communities.

At the same time, Funai began to take the initiative on the vexed question of the Indians' lands, an area where it had been highly negligent in previous administrations. After years of delay, it had been established in 1973 in the Indian Statute that all the Indians' reserves would be demarcated 'within five years'. Yet by December 1978, only a third of them had been marked out, and even then only imperfectly. Nobre da Veiga told the chamber of deputies in Brasília in September 1980:

> The most serious problem facing the Indians is possession of their lands, as Funai has not yet managed to sort out completely the legal problems in a single one of the country's 250 reserves. As a result, there are conflicts in nearly all of them.

He said that he was trying to make up for earlier negligence and in 1980 had increased the funds going to land demarcation to Crs 252m (£2m), a 500 per cent rise on the amount allocated in 1979.

Once again, Cimi and many anthropologists were sceptical. They said that as yet Nobre da Veiga's promises had led to only a small improvement in the rate of demarcation. But the initiative was enough to win the cautious support of some *sertanistas*, including the Villas-Boas brothers. 'Never before has Funai been so concerned to demarcate the Indians' lands', Orlando Villas-Boas commented with approval in July 1981.

After the influx of military officers, Funai also revived an old project for establishing criteria for distinguishing Indians from non-Indians. After examining all the alternatives, Colonel Ivan Zanoni Hausen, who was in charge of this project, proposed the allegedly scientific method of identification by blood group. The colonel said that, as all pure-bred aboriginal Amercians had O/rhesus positive blood, a simple blood test could establish who were real Indians. The project was violently criticised by anthropologists, Indians and Cimi. They claimed that it was far too mechanistic, for several groups had occasionally intermarried with outsiders without becoming any less Indian. Eunice Durham, an anthropologist, said: 'The only way of knowing whether a person is an Indian or not is through the attitude of the Indian community towards him or her.' She claimed that Funai's proposal, as well as being irrational, was 'dangerous, fascist and racist'. Such was the barrage of protest that Funai was eventually forced to shelve its project.

Despite the changes, Funai retained some of its old defects, including corruption. Nobre da Veiga was finally sacked in December 1981 for using Funai funds to buy up property in Rio. He was replaced by another military officer, Colonel Paulo Moreira Leal, who had previously been working for the National Security Council. For weeks it was rumoured that Funai might be taken away from the interior ministry and, like GETAT, be subordinated directly to the National Security Council. But this move was never formally taken.

The new appointment led to an immediate change in managerial style, for Colonel Leal went to great pains to improve Funai's public image. Shortly after he took office, Colonel Leal explained to the press that he had had considerable experience with Indian affairs for he had worked previously with the National Security Council's 'psycho-social department' which dealt with 'tensions, conflicts, things of this kind'. He said that in his work he had become concerned about the fate of the Indians. He adopted a much more conciliatory attitude towards both the Cathlolic Church and the Indians themselves. One of his first moves was to talk to Paulo Suess, secretary-general of Cimi, and to tell him that Funai would be lifting the ban on Catholic missionaries which existed in some reserves. Unlike his predecessors, he also encouraged the Indians to set up their own national organisation and listened with much greater attention to their own views. Over the following few months, Colonel Leal took some important measures to help the Indians, including the first steps towards setting up reserves for both the Nambikwara and the Yanomami.

Yet several factors raised doubts as to Colonel Leal's overall intentions. He kept as his close advisers the group of military officers headed by

Colonel Zanoni, even though they were much hated by the Indians for their callousness and their ignorance of Indian culture. Even more significantly, he retained Nobre da Veiga's two most important objectives: the decentralisation of Funai and the setting up of the economic projects. He never publicly criticised the government's developmentalist goals. No fundamental change in Funai's basic orientation occurred under Leal. Two examples will suffice.

In the first half of 1982, Funai made a study of the possible impact on Indian groups of the construction of the 900-kilometre railway which was to be built from the Carajás mining complex to the coastal port of Itaquí in the state of Maranhão. The railway would cut across the territory of nine Indian groups, including the Parakanã and the Gavião, and would affect the lives of 4,000–5,000 Indians. The report, which Funai claimed to have drawn up on 'an absolutely scientific basis', gave a short historical summary of each of the groups, made an estimate of their numbers and predicted the outlay required for the measures it proposed. The document showed that Funai was drawing up its plans with more care than in the past, but it reflected the same basic developmentalist attitude. Far from suggesting any rerouting of the railway to reduce the harm done to the Indian communities, the document did not even acknowledge that the Indians would be adversely affected.

Similarly Leal did little to root out incompetence and corruption. The Villas-Boas brothers retired in the mid 1970s. After a brief period under the progressive management of Olímpio Serra, the Xingu Park was taken over by Francisco de Assis da Silva. By early 1983, the Indians in the park were very discontented. Raoni, a Txukurramãe Indian, said that medical assistance had become very poor. 'In just January of this year', he said, 'five children and five adults died unnecessarily, from what seems to have been malaria or flu.' The Cimi-backed Indian magazine, *Porantim*, accused Assis da Silva of corruption, claiming to have evidence that he had fiddled the accounts for his own benefit. In February, Assis da Silva was finally removed from the park, but, instead of ordering an enquiry, Leal reappointed him to another prestigious job, as director of the Aripuanã Indian Park. Asked whether the new director, Cláudio Romero, would be any better than Assis da Silva, Olímpio Serra replied: 'The situation in Xingu is so bad at the moment that any change has to be an improvement.'

The most significant alteration to have occurred under Leal's presidency is believed to have occurred at the suggestion of the National Security Council. In February 1983 the government issued Decree-law no. 88,118 which took final authority for the demarcation of Indian lands away from Funai and handed it to a work-group made up of representatives from the interior ministry, the land ministry, Funai and 'other federal and state bodies considered appropriate'. Funai would make proposals to this group, but it would only have a minority say in the final decision. As land demarcation is the most important problem facing the Indian groups, this new legislation meant, effectively, that Funai's authority suffered a very serious blow.

The Indians Fight Back

Leal's overthrow and subsequent developments in Funai are closely linked to the emergence of a strong Indian movement. Over the previous decade, Indians had become much more aware of the nature of the problems they faced and increasingly more determined to defend their lands and their culture. The sacking of Leal was the first time that this new Indian movement revealed its political strength at a national level but it had been quietly gathering force in earlier years. To understand the growing momentum of this movement, we need to look at the changes that Indian groups have undergone on contact with outsiders.

The most dangerous period for Indians is the initial contact when they are under serious threat of physical extermination from disease and of cultural annihilation through the collapse of their tribal way of life. If they can survive this period, many groups show a surprising capacity both to organise the militant defence of their lands and their culture and to adapt to the inevitable changes in their way of life which result from the arrival of the occupation frontier.

The Catholic Church has played a key role in this process. In the early 1970s it became increasingly outspoken in its criticisms of the government's policies. A milestone was the publication in 1973 of a document entitled *The Indians – A People Sentenced to Death*, the signatories of which included six bishops. It called for a fundamental change in the government's policies:

> If we are denouncing the government's present Indian policy as the most immediate cause of the situation in which our Indians are living (and dying) today, we are fully aware that the real, underlying cause is the over-all strategy behind the 'Brazilian miracle'. And, if we say that it is necessary to alter radically Funai's policies, we know that this will only be possible if profound changes take place in the whole of Brazilian politics. Without these changes, neither Funai nor any other body will be able to do more than provide cheap and pharisaic assistance to a people which has been sentenced to death, to camouflage the unconfessed support given to large landowners and to exploiters of national wealth. In this context, the much-acclaimed Indian Statute will be no more than an opportunistic piece of publicity or a posthumous homage.
>
> Nothing will be achieved through the reorganisation of Funai, if the developmental psychosis, motivated exclusively by economic interests and by a false sense of national prestige, continues to dominate the country's over-all policies.

Cimi, until then a conservative body for missionary affairs, was radically changed by the upsurge in political awareness. Dom Pedro Casaldáliga, Bishop of São Félix, believes that the radicalisation of Cimi was 'the greatest ecclesiastic event in the history of the country'. In 1974 Cimi decided that it was not enough for the church to criticise the government's policies, however violently. It was more important, it believed, to help the Indians understand the common nature of many of their problems so that they could start organising their own fight for survival. It was no easy task, as the Indians were scattered over a large area of the country, spoke different languages and were not infrequently divided by traditional hostilities. As a first step, Cimi decided to organise an assembly of Indian leaders so that Indians from different tribes could get to know each other. It was a success, and it was followed by others. By the end of the decade, there had been about a dozen of these assemblies.

Most of these inter-tribal meetings were closed to outsiders. From the accounts of these meetings, first given by participants themselves and later published in Cimi bulletins, the Indians seem to have shown both an insatiable curiosity about the lives of other tribes and a constant desire to discover to what extent other tribes shared their problems. Various common themes emerged: the danger that the white man's cattle ranches represented for their lands; the sicknesses brought by the white man; the upheavals caused by road construction; the inadequacy of the help provided by Funai; the general characteristics of the process of eviction that they were suffering all over Brazil; and the nature of white man's values.

The second assembly of Indian chiefs took place in May 1975. An Indian spokesman gave an account of one of the long sessions:

> The Xerente said that we are all suffering from the same massacre. The civilised people invade, kill our children. We have no support. Funai doesn't defend us. People let cattle loose all over the land of the Indians. The oldest shamams are dying off. The young ones don't have the knowledge that the old ones had . . . The Xerentes have feasts and dances – the feasts of yam, of honey, of the cutting of hair. They have their own language. When they return from hunting, they don't rest immediately, but wait for the old shaman. Then they relax slowly, while the shaman sings and prays to god.
>
> When a son is born, they go on a diet. The father doesn't eat manioc flour. He doesn't kill snakes. He doesn't collect feathers. Only after spreading honey on his face does he eat honey. When someone dies, he weeps.
>
> When the Indian is about to travel, people join with him and sing and cry with him. When he returns, there is another feast of joy – because he went and he returned. When the moon is beautiful, everyone sings. They sing with bowed heads. Only the chief looks at the moon.
>
> Every full moon they sing and celebrate. But ever since civilisation came, they have suffered tremendously. Flu, which they never had in the past, has appeared. The shamans are no longer able to carry out cures. Tuberculosis is what most affects the Xerente today.
>
> The Nambikwara Indian spoke and said that they also hunt at night, kill animals and go back to the village. The women prepare *chicha* [a fermented drink made from maize, nuts and honey]. The meat dries. Everyone sits in a line, with little gourds. They take some *chicha* and drink. They eat tapioca

cake and celebrate . . . They used to take medicines from the forest, but there is nothing to deal with the sicknesses of the civilised people. They tried medicines from the forest, but they don't help. They asked the priest to get them some medicine for the sicknesses of the civilised people. And now they are a bit better. There is a cooperative. This year there was no big sickness. That's good.

Another Indian gave an account of the discussions at one of the other closed sessions at the same assembly:

The Xavante said that they didn't want a road cutting through their reserve. Though the road had been started, they managed to stop the construction. The road would divide the land and the group. The people who use the road would bring sickness. They would upset and exploit the Indians because they would want to buy things too cheaply. And those whites who are up to no good would bother the Indian women. 'So we turned the whites off our reserve as soon as we could', said the Xavante. 'We stopped the construction of the road, fighting it by all possible means.'

The Indians at this assembly all expressed dissatisfaction with Funai. A Munduruku said:

We are doing fine. We have planted fields with rice, sugar and bananas. We wouldn't have anything to do with the SPI and we also got rid of the people from Funai who were wanting to set up another post. When they told us that they would be sending in a Funai official, we said: 'All right, let him come but we shall kick him out.' The land is ours, but it hasn't been marked out and we haven't got land titles. And we know that Funai won't do anything to help us with this.

A Kayabí said: 'The civilised man has come to our countryside. We are defending our lands from him. Because of this, Funai gives us little help.' A Tapirapé said:

We used to have help from a priest. He brought salt, brown sugar and clothes to the village. We threw out the clothes, but kept the rest. But now we have no help, only a sister, who is as poor as us. But she gives us medicines. Funai do very little to help us.

A Bororo said: 'Funai should be there to proect our health. The missionaries are defending the Indians, but Funai should be doing it. The priests were not supposed to help the Indians, but they do more than Funai.' A Xerente concluded: 'I was pleased to see that our brothers also do not approve of Funai. They do not give us the help that the priests do.'

An Indian from the Xavante, a tribe with great experience in dealing with landowners, offered advice to the others:

Whatever they say, the whites have nothing to accuse us of. We are in the right. We must not let them interfere with our culture. If the white man offers us alcohol, he should go to jail because this causes us harm. It is bad for the Indians. If he makes use of our women, he should go to jail. What is important is our life, our customs. We cannot give up these things to take on the ways of the white man. We have everything. We must not lose it.

If we lose our customs, ruin and destruction will put an end to the Indian. Because the way we live is what we are. Because we cannot live among the whites. We do not live only for the present. We need the ground under our feet, a piece of land, not all the land, only a piece of it. We have asked the president of Funai for help in getting this land. He said that he would help and now we are waiting for him to keep his promise.

The Indians took another step forward at the third assembly of Indian chiefs, held at Meruri in September 1975. Several of the Indians showed that they were able to put forward their case in terms understandable to non-Indians. Dotoris, a Xavante, showed a particularly clear grasp of white man's logic:

This land – the civilised always say that it does not belong to the Indians. Now, what proof have we that it belongs to the Bororos, the Xavantes? What's the proof? Look at the old villages which already existed in our grandparents' times, look at the broken bits of pottery. That's the proof. Our grandparents were around everywhere here. There, by the river of the dead, beyond the river of the dead, there were no civilised. How is it then that the landowners are invading our land, more and more, making this huge invasion?

The Indians were evicted from São Paulo, from Goiás. They were driven further inland, further and further. Up to here, where there were only Indians. Poxoreu had civilised people and Barra do Garças had a few. That's all. Then the SPI sold the Indians' lands. If the Indian hadn't been asleep, this wouldn't have happened.

We can't despair. I'm going to die. Everyone is going to die. And later? Are our children, our grandchildren, going to suffer as we have? We need to think of the future. So that our children can live well, growing, increasing.

We are going to work, just like the Xavantes in São Marcos are working. Every day to their plots, carrying hoes on their backs, their hands aching. Our work is hard. We can't rest. I admire the plots you are farming here. It's good to do this. In this way, the children grow, increase.

At the later assemblies, the Indians began to draw up documents and to acknowledge publicly their commitment to the values of their own societies. For instance, representatives from nine Indian tribes stated in April 1977:

To end our message of the Day of the Indian, we wish to offer a little of our values to white society which is stripped of spiritual and human values. These values you will find in the simple way we live our lives.

196

They began to assert their independence even from Cimi. The representatives at the eleventh assembly of Indian chiefs, held at São Marcos in Mato Grosso in May 1978, stated proudly:

> Above all, we want to make clear that the initiative for this meeting and for these declarations comes purely and solely from the Indians. It is the opposite of what many think, mainly those interested in exterminating the Indian societies, who say 'the priests are behind the Indians'. This is a very serious mistake, because they do not want to recognise that we are also capable of seeking each other out, of discussing and solving our problems. And, if we have not been capable of this until recently, it really shows how we have been massacred, oppressed, mainly by government bodies – firstly the SPI and now Funai – which did not take the initiative of explaining our rights to us. On the contrary, they have helped those who see the Indian as an obstacle to development. To make our point, it is enough to take a glance at the present situation of Indians in the whole of this country.

The Indians moved on later in their declaration to the heart of their demand:

> Our cries go out to the four corners of the country, not to demand health and community development projects. This is secondary in the present drama being lived out by the Indian people of Brazil. What is more important at the moment is the guarantee of our lands, our heritage and the cradle of our cultural traditions.

As the Indians became increasingly dissatisfied with the assistance given to them by Funai, they began to resort to collective violent action to achieve their goals. The Xavante Indians in Mato Grosso were the precursors in this deliberate use of violence to achieve specific goals, which was very different from the earlier clashes between Indians and non-Indians. The Xavante Indians drove cattle companies off their lands as early as 1975 and since then have taken a tough, and largely successful, stance with outsiders. In 1979 they attracted the attention of the world's press when about 100 warriors, their bodies decorated with charcoal and *annatto* dye in traditional black and white war designs, attacked several cattle ranches. Their message was the same as in earlier raids: 'Move off our lands.' The Xavante have also resorted to direct action to press home their point to Funai. In May 1980, 40 warriors, all armed with modern weapons, occupied Funai's headquarters in Brasília and left only after they had been given a guarantee from Nobre da Veiga that an extra 60,000 hectares would be added to their reserve at Pimental Barbosa.

Other groups believe that the Xavante have shown that both Funai and the landowners only listen to demands backed up by force. The Kaingang

Indians in Rio das Cobras and the Nonoai in Rio Grande do Sul were consciously following the example of the Xavante when they forcibly evicted settlers from their land in 1978. The Tapirapé, who decided in 1980 to demarcate their own lands, were also influenced by the Xavante.

In early 1980 the Indians began to feel that the holding of occasional assemblies was not enough and that they needed a permanent national organisation. At a meeting in Brasília in April, various Indian chiefs proposed the formation of the Union of Indian Nations (UNI) 'to bring together all Indians who are fighting for an Indian policy which will benefit the Indians themselves', to quote from the statement they issued. Their proposal was immediately turned down by Nobre da Veiga. He was supported by the Villas-Boas brothers. Alvaro Villas-Boas told the press in July:

> Brazil is divided into states, territories and the federal district of Brasília. If everyone wanted to found his own confederation, we should have confederations of Italians, Japanese and so on. It would become impossible. If an Indian is unhappy with the extent of his present rights, he should ask to be emancipated and then go and live in a town.

The Indians were beginning to assert their collective rights in other ways too. Pope John Paul II visited Brazil in mid 1980. Dom Milton Corrêa, the conservative Archbishop of Manaus, arranged for a group of Indians to perform their traditional dances on the one occasion that the Indians were to meet the Pope. However, about 60 Indians from 25 tribes met in Brasília shortly before the Pope's visit and turned down the idea of putting on a 'tourist spectacle'. Instead, they wrote an impassioned letter in which they listed the names of nine Indians who had been recently murdered, apparently at the hands of landowners, and asked the Pope if he was 'not sad, even to the point of crying, to know that a people can no longer sing and dance, because their lands are being stolen, their leaders murdered and thousands of their numbers forced to work like slaves.' The letter was handed over to the Pope by Dom Tomás Balduíno, vice-president of Cimi. Dom José Gomes, president of Cimi, commented at the time:

> But the Indians will not be saved by the Pope, or much less by us, the missionaries. It is only the Indians themselves who can do this. And one important step to this end is exactly what they are planning to do – set up a national organisation.

Not everyone was happy with the independence that the Indians were showing. Nobre da Veiga said that the letter handed to the Pope had been drawn up not by the Indians, but by people wishing to take advantage of them: 'It was pure demagogy, sensationalism, which is not in the Indians' long-term interest.' And Father João Vincente César, who had been president of Cimi before it was radicalised, complained that Cimi was taking on a political role which was destroying the moral authority that the Catholic Church had always enjoyed among the Brazilian people.

Despite Funai's unwillingness to listen to them, the Indians pushed ahead. In June 1980, a group of 40 Indians, from 12 different tribes, occupied Funai's headquarters in Brasília to call for the sacking of the group of military officers headed by Colonel Ivan Zanoni and to demand a radical reorganisation of Funai. Unlike the Xavantes who had occupied the building a few weeks earlier, these Indians were not successful. At the end of the month, 54 leaders from 25 different tribes held the 24th assembly of Indian chiefs. Despite Funai's continued opposition, the Indians reiterated their determination to set up a national organisation. Finally, despite the threat of reprisals from Funai, 73 leaders from 32 tribes founded UNI at a meeting in São Paulo in May 1981.

A head-on confrontation with Funai was averted by the sacking of Nobre da Veiga in October 1981. The new president, Colonel Paulo Leal, raised no objections to UNI and, in return, the Indians agreed to collaborate with Funai. Some anthropologists were very critical of this truce; they believed that by allowing Funai to have some influence over their new organisation, the Indians had compromised its independence. Marcos Terena, who had been elected the first president of UNI, explained why they had done so: 'We may be able to reduce the number of mistakes made in official policy. And this is very worthwhile. For one mistake, however small, can have disastrous consequences for Indians, even resulting in deaths.' In June 1982 the Indians held the first national congress of Indian people in Brasília. The Indians welcomed the achievements of Leal during his first seven months in office, but continued to call for the resignation of Zanoni and the other military officers in top positions at Funai. They also expressed firm opposition to Zanoni's proposal to identify real Indians by a blood test. As always, much of the meeting was taken up with discussions over problems with Indian lands.

Over the following year Leal failed to push ahead with the demarcation of reserves, as he had promised, and the Indians became increasingly discontented. In the congressional elections in November 1982, an Indian was elected into office for the first time. Mário Juruna, a Xavante Indian, who was elected federal deputy for Rio, has been criticised for giving up his Indian way of life, but his election was politically important, particularly as he became an outspoken critic of the government, both for its Indian policies and its corruption.

Juruna's first act in Congress was to call for a parliamentary inquiry into the state of the Indians in Brazil. Juruna, who has become one of the most popular federal deputies in the country, is greatly disliked by the top military officers. After the air force minister, Brigadier Délio Jardim de Mattos, referred disparagingly to his 'exotic' appeal among the electorate, Juruna wrote a much-publicised letter in reply in which he said: 'To become deputy, I won popular support, with 80,000 votes. Now I ask you: how many votes did you get when you were elected minister?'

In May 1983, Juruna had an interview with General Danilo Venturini, secretary-general of the National Security Council. Juruna pointed out that, in the ten years in which it had been in existence, Funai had managed to demarcate less than 5 per cent of the Indians' lands. He said that he feared that the new decree, by involving more government officials in the process, would merely lead to further delays. He was also bitterly critical of the group of military officers in key positions in Funai. Venturini listened carefully and promised to take into consideration his remarks.

On 26 June, 14 Xavante Indians occupied the Funai building in Brasília to demand the sacking of the hated colonels. Colonel Leal reacted angrily, telling them: 'I don't agree to sack anyone. I'm the one who takes decisions in Funai and I don't act under pressure. So you're not going to get anywhere with these tactics.'

But ten days later, not only the officers, including the detested Colonel Ivan Zanoni Hausen, but also Colonel Leal himself, were dismissed. A civilian, Otávio Ferreira Lima, was selected as the new president. The main reason for these unexpected changes does not seem to have been any great desire to placate the Indians, but the wish by the interior minister, Colonel Mário Andreazza, to put an end to the Indians' mobilisation, which was giving Funai a bad name in the press. Andreazza had become one of the main contenders to take over as President from Figueiredo in 1985 and he did not want his campaign damaged by reports in the press of embarrassing events in any part of his ministry.

But Otávio Ferreira Lima was to prove little improvement on Colonel Leal. New threats to the Indians emerged in the second half of 1983. Two were particularly serious. The PDS deputy Mozarildo Cavalcanti, from Roraima, presented a project (no. 1,179/83) to authorise cassiterite mining in the Serra dos Surucurus, in the heart of the land occupied by the Yanomamis, Brazil's largest group of largely-isolated Indians. Before voting took place on this project, President João Figueiredo signed a decree, on 10 November 1983, permitting private companies to request authorisation from Funai and the DNPM to prospect for minerals on Indian lands. Until then only state companies, under exceptional circumstances, had been allowed to enter Indian lands. On 14 July, the day on which the project should have been voted in the Chamber of Deputies' Indian Commission, Cavalcanti realised that it would be defeated so he withdrew it for revision. The danger had not completely passed, however, because Cavalcanti could re-present the project later.

The second threat came from a proposed alteration in the civil code to change the status of the Indian from 'relatively incapable' to 'absolutely incapable'. It amounted to a new indirect endeavour to push through the emancipation project, for it would have forced many Indians to opt for emancipation rather than be treated like people suffering from severe mental retardation. This amendment, which was put forward by the PDS deputy João Batista Fagundes, a landowner from Roraima, gained little support. In April 1984, President Figueiredo bowed to popular opinion and in the constitutional amendment he sent Congress he retained the expression 'relatively incapable'.

Ferreira Lima's failure to stand up for the Indian cause increasingly irritated the Indians. Their discontent was to erupt spectacularly in April 1984. On 21 March, a *despacho*, a voodoo work of sorcery, was left outside Funai's headquarters in Brasília. Apart from the traditional candles, dead black hen and white rum, it contained pigeons with the names of Funai's directors around their necks. Funai employees let the pigeons free, but the one bearing the name of Otávio Ferreira Lima died mysteriously. Coincidence or not, nothing went right for Ferreira Lima after that.

On 24 March, 80 Txukurramãe Indians in the Xingu Park, exasperated by Funai's failure to attend to their land demands (see below), hi-jacked the ferry that took traffic on the BR–80 road across the Xingu river. They told Funai that they would only allow traffic to travel on the ferry again if Ferreira Lima came to the Xingu Park and sorted out their land problem. Apparently at the express order of the National Security Council, which had been informed of rumours that the Txukurramãe were planning to kidnap him, Ferreira Lima refused to go.

The Txukurramãe were extremely irritated. A large delegation went to Brasília to take part in the second national meeting of UNI, from 2 to 4 April. They received considerable support in their demands from the other 300 Indian delegates. The atmosphere at the gathering was very different from the conciliatory mood of the UNI meeting in the previous year. The Indians refused to allow Funai or interior ministry officials to attend. 'We don't trust them any more', explained the Xavante chief Aniceto.

The Indians called for a new president of Funai and sent a petition to the Supreme Federal Tribunal (STF), asking it to declare as unconstitutional Decree-law 88,118, which was the measure decreed in February 1983 which had taken away from Funai the authority to demarcate reserves. The Indians pointed out that since then not a single reserve had been demarcated. Fearful that the deeply-discontented Indians might organise an occupation, the government sent armed guards to protect the Funai and interior ministry buildings during the meeting.

On Friday, 13 April, the Txukurramãe, back in the Xingu Park, decided to take further action. They kidnapped three Funai employees, threatening to kill them unless Funai accepted their demands for a larger area of land and for a new president of Funai. Ferreira Lima reacted angrily to this new development. He refused to talk to the Txukurramãe and blamed Cláudio Romero, the director of the Xingu Park, for putting them up to it.

Mário Juruna flew to the park. He suggested that the Indians should free one of the hostages and send two delegates with him to talk, not to Ferreira Lima, but to ministers. Raoni, the leader of the Txukurramãe, initially agreed, but was forced to change his mind in view of the uncompromising attitude adopted by most of his group. Reports suggested that the most militant of all were the women, who, not allowed by the customs of the group to enter the men's hut where the talks with Juruna were taking place, were marching around outside, painted in war colours and smoking pipes. As they were able to hear most of what was being said through the walls of the hut, they repeatedly uttered war cries and urged their sons and husbands not to back down. By now, the Txukurramãe kidnapping was a leading news story in all the national newspapers. Though the kidnapped officials were sympathetic to the Txukurramãe's cause, it was clear that the Indians would kill them, if they felt it was essential to their cause.

After several tense days, the Txukurramãe were granted most of their demands. Ferreira Lima was sacked and the Indians were given a new tract of land, a sizeable proportion of what they had demanded. On 3 May, the hostages were freed and they flew back to Brasília. One of them, Sidney Possuelo, said at the airport, with tears in his eyes, that, despite the fear he had felt, he was 'happy to have taken part in the first big political victory won by the Indians in Brazil'.

The Indians made some important advances in the wake of this victory. The new president of Funai, Jurandy Marcos de Fonseca, was an experienced Funai official, who had spent most of his life with Indians and was generally respected by them. In an important break with established practice, Fonseca appointed Indians to top administrative posts. Megaron Mentuktire, Raoni's nephew who is being prepared as the next leader of the Txukurramãe, became director of the Xingu Park. The Carajá leader, Daniel Koxini, became director of the Araguaia Park. Many experienced *sertanistas*, sacked during Nobre de Veiga's administration, were brought back. For the first time the Indians felt at ease at Funai's headquarters in Brasília.

The shake-up created problems. Some of the established Funai officials, including Alvara Villas-Boas, the only one of the brothers not to have retired, and Apoena Meirelles, resented the changes. For several months Fonseca faced disturbances, but skilfully outmanoeuvred most of his opponents. But many Indians and anthropologists were sceptical whether Funai would achieve much, even under much more responsible leadership. With decree 88,118 and other measures, Funai had become a consultative, rather than an executive, body.

Porantim, the monthly magazine on Indian affairs, suggested that the shake-up at Funai formed part of a new strategy worked out by the National Security Council for dealing with Indian unrest. Under this, Funai would become a buffer between the Indians and the government, for it would be very difficult for Indian groups to put heavy pressure on Funai to speed up demarcations if the latter was staffed by Indians. At the same time, Funai's capacity for effective action could be severely limited by strict controls over its sphere of influence and by tight financial constraints.

Fonseca's administration was short-lived. In September 1984, he was unexpectedly removed. Fonseca claimed that he had been sacked by the interior minister for failing to sign the decree authorising mining companies to prospect for minerals on Indian lands. By then many Indian groups had begun to lose faith in Fonseca. Rightly or wrongly, they believed that he had been ·sucked up in the general corruption in Funai and was making no serious attempt to defend their interests. As a result, they did little to defend him. He was replaced by Nelson Marabuto, a former federal police chief in São Paulo.

The Fate of Individual Groups

There seems no better way of looking at the diversity of situations in which Amazonian Indians are found than to look in comparative detail at some groups. Although we did not select them by this criterion, all the groups have been affected to a lesser or greater degree by the government's recent development projects.

The Nambikwara

Though the Nambikwara were first contacted by the Portuguese in the late 18th Century, they remained largely isolated until the 1920s. It was then that rubber-tappers and collectors of ipecacuanha root began to move into the region. Though the SPI sent in a group to establish regular contact with them, it could do little to mitigate the terrible toll that disease imposed on them. Their numbers fell from an estimated 10,000 at the turn of the century to 2,000–3,000 at the time of Lévi-Strauss's visit in the mid 1930s.

The various groups were not all affected to the same extent. Those which lived to the north of the Chapada dos Parecis, a high ridge of land in the north-west of the state of Mato Grosso, were worst hit by this first wave of decimation. Rondon established permanent contact with these groups in 1909 when he was setting up the telegraph line to link Porto Velho with Cuiabá.

Other groups, which lived further south, in the valley of the river Guaporé, only emerged from their isolation in the early 1960s when the first road from Cuiabá to Porto Velho was constructed. Though the road itself did not pass through their lands, smaller feeder roads were built to permit access to the Guaporé valley. Cattle companies moved into the Indians' lands and cleared much of the area of forest, which they replaced with grass for pasture.

By the early 1970s, the Nambikwara in this region seemed to be heading towards rapid extinction. They had been left with just a few strips of untouched forest and even became dependent on the cattle ranches for their food. Their numbers fell rapidly as they succumbed to measles, flu, tuberculosis, pneumonia and malaria, which spread to the area after the forest clearances. They suffered from chronic dysentery because the water they drank was polluted by cattle dung. Their lands were occasionally sprayed with the defoliant Tordon 155, a form of Agent Orange. After visiting the area in March 1973, Bo Akerren, a Swedish doctor attached to the international commission of the Red Cross, said: 'The condition of these Indians is a disgrace not only for Brazil, but for mankind as a whole.'

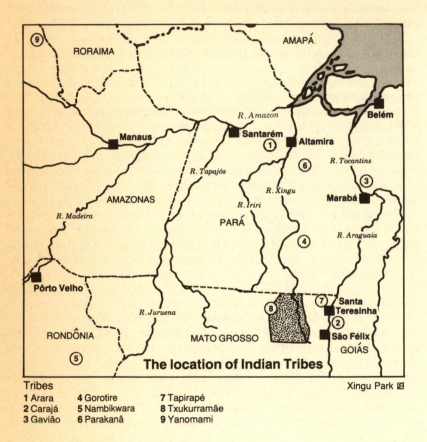

The location of Indian Tribes

Xingu Park

Tribes

1 Arara	**4** Gorotire	**7** Tapirapé
2 Carajá	**5** Nambikwara	**8** Txukurramãe
3 Gavião	**6** Parakanã	**9** Yanomami

Funai's record has been particularly poor. In 1968 it created the first Nambikwara reserve in an area composed largely of barren scrubland to the east of the Chapada dos Parecis, outside the Guaporé valley. The reserve contained only two Nambikwara villages, with just a tenth of the total population. Just a few days after establishing this reserve, Funai began to issue cattle ranches with certificates which stated that there were no Indians in the Guaporé valley. One of the first ranches to obtain such a certificate, which permitted it to obtain tax rebates under the Sudam scheme, was Sapé Agropecuária, partly owned by the son of the then interior minister, José Costa Cavalcanti.

In the early 1970s, Funai tried to move the various groups inside the reserve. But, largely because of the hostile nature of the terrain, they nearly all refused. As the scheme was working out so badly, Funai came under considerable pressure to find another solution. In 1974 General Ismarth de Araújo Oliveira, then president of Funai, created a new reserve, 300,000 hectares in size, between the Galera and Sarará rivers which were the only tributaries of the Guaporé river which had remained relatively free of cattle companies. A US anthropologist, David Price, was contracted to set up the new reserve and to persuade the groups which lived outside the area to move in.

Many of the groups agreed, partly because the new reserve provided better conditions than the first. Unfortunately, however, they did not adapt to their new environment. They were decimated by disease, particularly malaria, and they found it very difficult to become accustomed to the loss of their traditional sacred sites – the springs and caves where their ancestors are buried. By 1975 there were only 750 Nambikwara survivors. These decided to return to their traditional lands, despite all the problems they would encounter there.

Many of the cattle companies reacted angrily and treated the Indians as intruders. Some of the cattle managers sprayed with grass seed the patches of ground that the Indians had planted with food crops. Others denied the Indians medical attention at the ranches. Reports of the terrible problems faced by the Nambikware were published in the press and once again Funai came under pressure to take action.

Against the advice of most anthropologists, Funai decided to abandon most of the large reserve and to replace it with a series of small reserves to be created around each of the traditional areas. The new reserves varied in size from 12,000 hectares to 22,000. The landowners were not happy with the scheme and, by exerting heavy political pressure, managed to delay the demarcation of the reserves. Neither was the scheme satisfactory for the Indians. Hemmed into the small reserves in the midst of huge ranches, the Nambikwara were unable either to hunt and fish as in the past, or to carry out their traditional practice of intermarrying between groups.

In July 1979, during the relatively free atmosphere prevailing in Funai under Ademar Ribeiro da Silva, Noraldino Viera Cruvinel, an anthropologist sent in by Funai, suggested the creation of a single large reserve as the only way of saving the Nambikwara from physical or cultural extermination.

Though originally well received, this proposal was shelved by the new president, Colonel Nobre da Veiga, when he took over in September 1979.

It was then that the government announced an ambitious new project, called the Integrated Programme for the Development of the Northwest of Brazil (Polonoroeste), which involved investments of about £1 billion, of which the World Bank was to provide a fifth. The objective of the programme was to bring into productive use about 25 million hectares of fertile land along Brazil's frontier with Bolivia. It would entail the asphalting of the road from Cuiabá to Porto Velho and the construction of a further 3,500 kilometres of feeder roads to break the isolation of the region. At the end of December 1981, interior minister Mário Andreazza said:

> Today the northwest of Brazil produces about 30,000 tonnes of perennial crops (coffee and cocoa), about 160,000 tonnes of annual crops (mainly rice, maize, beans, manioc, groundnuts and cotton), about 120,000 tonnes of timber and about 25,000 tonnes of beef. By the time the new programme is properly under way, which will be by about the end of the decade, the farm output of the region should have increased fivefold.

The Indians were only mentioned in the programme in the context of their becoming a possible impediment. It seemed that this new developmental thrust would be the final lethal blow for the beleaguered Nambikwara. Anthropologists and Cimi began a last desperate campaign to persuade the government to create a large reserve for them so as to give them a chance of survival. The campaign was given considerable attention abroad and pressure was put on the World Bank not to participate in a project which seemed likely to wipe out an entire tribe.

The lobby had some success. Apparently under pressure from the World Bank, for the first time Funai took firm action to protect the Nambikwara. In December 1981 it created three reserves for them – two small ones, of 30,000 hectares and 68,000, along tributaries of the Guaporé river; and one big one, of 243,000 hectares, in the Guaporé valley itself. The measure caused a furore. The local mayor immediately dispatched a protest telegram to the interior minister. Domingos Sávio Brandão, a top Mato Grosso judge, protested to the federal government in the name of the state authorities. He said:

> Mato Grosso is not the fiefdom of Funai . . . I am going to mobilise national opinion against this insult to our state and this impediment to our progress, in favour of just 125 natives who possess an area of almost two million hectares.

In January 1982, Frederico Campos, the governor of the state, joined in the chorus of complaints. He sent another message to the federal government in which he claimed that the state authorities had not been properly consulted, as the law demanded, and that the Guaporé valley contained 250 ranches whose lands were not occupied on either a permanent or temporary basis by the Indians.

It seemed that Funai would be unable to withstand the pressure. On 22 January, Colonel Darcy Alvares da Cunha, the Funai representative in Cuiabá, said that the decrees which had created the reserves would be revoked. But on the following day Colonel Paulo Leal, the president of Funai, energetically denied this report. Over the next few months he repeatedly claimed that these reserves would be set up. Possibly as part of a new strategy to improve its public image at home and abroad Funai was taking an unexpectedly strong stand. But the battle was not yet won for the Indians. On 20 June 1982 Antônio Iasi Junior, a Catholic priest who has worked with the Nambikwara for several years, complained to the press that Funai had as yet made no move to demarcate the new reserves. He said that several ranches were still installed within the new reserves and that Funai had done nothing to evict them. If Funai continued to drag its heels in this way, he warned, the creation of the reserves would become meaningless, for the Indians would all have been wiped out by disease.

By the end of 1982, Funai had still taken no action. Its officials blamed the federal government, claiming that Funai had asked for authorisation to contract further personnel to set up the Nambikwara reserve, but as yet it had not been given the go-ahead. The officials expressed perplexity at the delays, as the cost was to be covered by the World Bank which had promised US$1.7 million for this work. In late March 1983, the World Bank sent a telex to Funai, asking for clarification as to why the reserves had not been marked out. Colonal Paulo Leal once again blamed the federal government, claiming that the planning ministry had not given him the money to make the necessary compensation payments to the cattle-rearers. He said that, according to the survey carried out by Funai in May 1982, about Crs 250m (£830,000) was required, but, as yet, Funai had only received Crs 34m (£110,000). The World Bank is reported to have warned the Brazilian government that, unless the demarcation was carried out, it would have to reconsider its decision to provide further financing for the Polonoroeste programme.

The pressure seems to have worked. Funai received the funds from the planning ministry and at last, in June 1983, the army began to mark out part of the reserves. Landowners, however, continued to dispute ownership of part of the land claimed by the Indians. Finally, at the end of May 1984, the Supreme Federal Tribunal (STF) judged unanimously in favour of the Nambikwara. Anthropologists became cautiously optimistic that some of the ranches installed within the reserves might finally be expropriated.

The Parakanã

The Parakanã is another tribe which has suffered greatly from its contact with the encroaching society. One group of about 190 Indians met pelt-hunters and prospectors in 1953. After 50 Indians had died from flu within a year, the rest fled back into the forest. The next contact did not occur until the end of 1970, when work began on the Transamazônica highway, which was to pass just 28 kilometres from one of their villages.[7] The Indians in this village were contacted by a Funai group in April 1971 after an eight-month period of attraction. The group suffered severely. Several of the women caught venereal diseases from construction workers or, allegedly, from one of the Funai employees. After an outbreak of gonorrhoea two children were born blind. The cultural life of the group was also severely shaken. The number of Indians fell drastically, from 150 in 1970 to 82 at the lowest point in 1972. The decline was largely caused by deaths from illness, particularly malaria, but also by a refusal of the Indian women to have children.

Antônio Cotrim Soares, one of Funai's most respected *sertanistas*, resigned in May 1972 because of Funai's negligence with respect to the Parakanã. He said that unfortunately the Parakanã could not be seen as an isolated case, for, to Funai's shame, nearly all newly-contacted tribes were suffering from veneral diseases and other illnesses. He concluded: 'I am tired of being a grave-digger. I don't intend to go on helping powerful groups become even richer at the expense of the extermination of primitive societies.'

Despite the enormous problems, the group was beginning to recover slowly when it was delivered yet another blow. It was announced in the mid 1970s that the Parakanã were to lose about 5 to 10 per cent of their reserve, which had still not been demarcated, as the land was required for the reservoir for the Tucuruí hydroelectric power station. The ecologist Robert Goodland, who was contracted by the state-owned electricity company Eletrobrás to carry out a study of the environmental impact of the Tucuruí project, said that, apart from the group already in contact with Funai, this measure would affect two other hitherto isolated groups of Parakanã, estimated to contain about 100 and 400 Indians.[8] He said that Funai believed that there could well be further groups, whose existence had not been discovered. Though the area to be lost was relatively small, two groups of Parakanã had to be transferred. They reacted badly when Funai told them of its plans and, during the last year in their old habitat, suffered serious problems of malnutrition because in their depressed state they did not bother to plant enough crops. The transfer was finally carried out in 1981.

Earlier that year the Indians suffered another setback when about 100 *garimpeiros* invaded their reserve to pan for gold. After considerable delays, the *garimpeiros* were finally evicted by the federal police. Around the same time, the Parakanã learnt that they were to lose yet another part of their reserve for the railway which is to be built to connect the huge Carajás mining complex with the port of Itaquí in the state of Maranhão. After this quick succession of traumatic shocks, their chances of survival cannot be rated very highly, even though in early March 1985, President Figueiredo signed a decree creating a 317,000 hectare reserve for these Indians.

Contact is also being made with the remaining isolated groups. In January 1983, a Funai attraction team discovered an abandoned village and 13 hunting camps belonging to a Parakanã group near São Félix do Xingu. It is believed that these Indians originally lived with the main group, but fled after the first disastrous contact with Funai in 1971. In early February 1983, the Funai team made contact with the group, which was found to consist of 43 Indians.

Later in February, another isolated group, also living near São Félix do Xingu, attacked their traditional enemies, the Araweté Indians, who were already in contact with Funai. The head of the Funai post in the Araweté reserve was killed during the attack. At the beginning of March, a group of 45 Araweté warriors killed in revenge two Parakanã Indians whom they had tracked down in the forest. On 24 April the Parakanã retaliated, killing two adult Araweté and one child. The Araweté captured one of the Parakanã warriors, decapitated him, and began preparations for a further punitive expedition. Though by then Funai had sent in a team to try to make peaceful contact with this group of Parakanã, it seemed that this tragic and senseless war between the two tribes would continue for the foreseeable future.

The Txukurramãe[9]

The Txukurramãe are Kayapó Indians, who traditionally lived in the upper reaches of the Xingu river. They were 'pacified' by the Villas-Boas brothers in 1952 and then, after the creation of the Xingu Park in 1961, brought to live within its frontiers. When the anthropologist Terence Turner visited their village in 1966, he found them extremely dissatisfied, partly because a series of Asian flu epidemics was sweeping the entire Xingu area and, during his visit, killed off five of their population of 168. But they were also very unhappy with the way the park was being administered by the Villas-Boas brothers and about a third of the village was actively considering leaving the park and returning to the area to the north, Jarina, which had been their original territory.

The decision by the federal government in 1971 to divert the BR–80 road from its planned course so as to amputate the northern fifth of the park greatly exacerbated the discontent among the group. The Villas-Boas brothers proposed to move them about 40 kilometres further south, as the new road was to run just four kilometres away from their village. One group, of about 60 to 70 people, refused to be moved deeper into the park and, instead, decided to return to their original lands at Jarina. Raoni, the leader of this group, explained their stubborn refusal in the following way:

> Every Indian who has let the white man come into his territory has ended up losing almost all his land, as has happened with the Tapirapé and the Carajás. The lands of the Xingu belong to us, the Indians, the Txukurramãe, the Suiá, the Juruna, the Kamaiura, the Trunai and others.

Even the somewhat larger group which agreed to the move was divided between a 'peace' faction, which believed that the group should obey the

Villas-Boas's instructions and move peacefully, and a 'war' faction, which believed that the group should wage war on the construction workers. This latter faction, which was eventually outnumbered, managed first to organise a successful raid on a construction site for a big new port which was to be built on the banks of the Xingu river. A group of Indians swam out under cover of darkness to a large sea-going tug brought up the river to assist in the construction works. They sank the boat by chopping a hole in the hull with axes. Others made off with a large launch complete with outboard motor. Though no one was hurt, the construction workers were greatly alarmed by the incident and the company eventually abandoned its plans for a river port. The hulk of the ruined tug was pulled out of the river and still stands beside the road as a monument to the effectiveness of the Txukurramãe's opposition.

After vain efforts to persuade the group at Jarina to move south, Funai had little option but to create a new reserve to the north of the BR–80, on the western bank of the Xingu river. Though the Indians claimed that the land to the east of the river also belonged to them, Funai ignored these demands and, over the next few months, issued 22 certificates attesting that this land was not occupied by Indians, thus paving the way for the setting up of cattle ranches. The area was soon opened up. A ferry boat service was installed to take traffic across the Xingu river. A small hamlet, São José do Xingu, was founded near the ranches on the eastern side of the river. In time, this village was nicknamed São José do Bang-Bang by the local inhabitants because of the almost daily occurrence of gun fights, which made it renowned for its violence and its lawlessness even on the wild Amazon frontier.

The Txukurramãe, however, continued to view the road as a violation of their traditional rights. They repeatedly harassed travellers, particularly those waiting for the ferry. They also disrupted the ferry service and frightened off the operator, who refused to go on living by the river and moved to the relative safety of São José do Bang-Bang, 41 kilometres away. This caused tremendous delays when, as frequently happened, a lorry arrived without its driver having made a prior arrangement with the operator.

The Txukurramãe themselves suffered heavily in the beginning from the close contact with non-Indians. They caught flu, venereal diseases and other illnesses which weakened the group and caused some deaths. The Xingu river, from which earlier they had obtained much of their food, was over-fished and polluted by the cattle-rearers. The Indians called for the creation of a 40-kilometre buffer zone along the eastern bank of the river, but Funai prevaricated.

However, when Terence Turner returned to the Xingu in 1976 after an absence of ten years, he was pleasantly surprised by the state of the Indians. Though he only visited the Indians inside the park, he was told that both groups were in good health and that the population of both was rising. The Txukurramãe inside the park were in the process of clearing large new plots of land on which to cultivate rice and beans (the staple diet of most

Brazilians) which they intended to sell to the local non-Indian population. Armed groups of Txukurramãe warriors periodically patrolled the Xingu river and its tributaries in the motor launch that they had taken from the construction company a few years earlier, or its twin, supplied by the park management for that purpose a few months before Turner's visit. One of the Indians had learnt how to repair the engines and was keeping both launches in perfect running order. The medical care supplied by Funai was very good.

Despite these improvements, some of the Indians greatly missed their earlier life. Puyũ, a Txukurramãe leader, said at a meeting of Indian leaders in the mid 1970s:

> Outside the park our lives were more carefree. There were no diseases like measles, influenza, malaria and those sicknesses white men give Indian women. In the time we lived further to the north, outside the reserve and without white men, our people were stronger. Indians only died when they were very old.

Moreover, clashes continued between the Indians, particularly the group living in the Jarina reserve, and the cattle companies. In June 1979, about 200 Indian warriors attacked a nearby ranch, called Agropexim, owned by a São Paulo farmer. About 100 people were driven off the ranch. The cattle company had been repeatedly warned by the Indians not to send its labourers into the Indians' lands. After many delays, Funai finally agreed to the creation of a buffer zone. However, it reduced the width of the zone to 15 kilometres and gave the land, not to the Indians, but to the forestry commission (IBDF) to administer as a nature reserve. The solution was not satisfactory for the Indians for it meant that they would not be allowed to hunt and fish within this new area. Moreover, for months after agreement had been reached, neither Funai nor the IBDF made any move to measure out the new zone.

The most violent clash occurred on 8 August 1980 when several dozen warriors from Jarina murdered 11 hired labourers who were clearing the forest within their reserve. The area was close to the headquarters of the Agropexim ranch which had been closed down after the earlier Indian attack. The Txukurramãe closed the BR–80 road after the incident but reopened it several days later after they had been given assurances by Funai that all cattle companies would be removed from their lands within two months. The Txukurramãe first demanded that the BR–80 be rerouted but withdrew this demand after Funai had convinced them that the only other possible route for the road would be through land belonging to the Menkranontire Indians, also of the Kayapó tribe, and regarded as relatives by the Txukurramãe.

The Catholic Church as a whole gave qualified support to the action taken by the Txukurramãe. Bishop Tomás Balduíno, vice-president of Cimi, said:

The solution to the Indians' problems must come from the Indians themselves. They must unite and turn the invaders off their lands. It was unfortunate that in the massacre that occurred last week in the Xingu the wrong people died. Instead of the 11 labourers, the landowner himself should have been killed.

The Txukurramãe leader Raoni was despondent about the future of his group unless urgent measures were taken against the cattle companies. He went to Brasília after the conflict to talk to Funai officials and told journalists:

They are cutting down everything. You don't see any more *jaboti, paca, tatu* [all wild animals]. Even the fish are coming to an end. I told the president of Funai at one stage during the meeting that it was better to put an end to the Indians straightaway rather than have the situation go on as it is.

In February 1982, Raoni called for the creation of one large reserve, taking in the north of Mato Grosso and the south of Pará, in which all the Kayapó Indians could live 'without landowners in the middle, who wipe out parrots, fish, animals'. Raoni said he would be holding a meeting with other Kayapó Indians – Gorotire, Menkranontire, Xicrin and Kuben-Kran-Kren – to discuss this proposal.

The Txukurramãe gave Funai until the end of June 1982 to mark out the buffer zone. At the end of June – and then again at the end of the year – anthropologists warned Funai that, as it had failed to respect this deadline, the situation had become extremely tense. On leaving office as director of Xingu Park in February 1983, Francisco de Assis da Silva also cautioned Funai that at any moment the Txukurramãe could attack a ranch, as they had done in August 1980, for they were 'tired of waiting for the demarcation of the zone'.

Finally, in April 1984, the Txukurramãe resorted to violence again, as had long been feared. In an incident which has been described earlier because of its impact on national policy, they held three Funai officials hostage. In exchange for their release they demanded an area 60 kilometres long and 40 kilometres wide to the east of the Xingu river, as well as an area of sacred land, known as Capoto, 70 kilometres by 15 kilometres, which also lay outside the limits of the park. The Txukurramãe finally settled for a band 70 kilometres by 15 kilometres by the river, together with the Capoto area. At the same time, a leading Txukurramãe, Megaron, was appointed director of the Xingu Park, a development regarded with apprehension by some anthropologists, fearful that it could aggravate the hostility between the groups. In all, it was regarded as a big triumph for the Txukurramãe.

The Gorotire

The Gorotire, a subgroup of Kayapó, live in a reserve in the south of Pará. They were 'pacified' in 1952 and given their reserve by President Jânio

Quadros as long ago as 1961. However, Funai only began to demarcate the reserve in 1978 and the work is still far from finished. In April 1982, Paulo César Abreu, the regional Funai delegate, gave the familiar explanation for the long delays: lack of funds. He said that it cost Crs 80,000 (£300) to demarcate one kilometre along the reserve's boundary. However, while Funai has been prevaricating, the occupation frontier has reached the Gorotire and their reserve has been invaded on many sides.

These invasions, which began on a large scale in the late 1970s, intensified in 1980 after gold was discovered in the Fresco river on the Indians' land. A gold mine was opened at Camaru and thousands of *garimpeiros* poured into the reserve. After several warnings, the Indians turned 300 of these prospectors off their land in early June 1980. On 25 July, Nobre da Veiga visited the reserve and tried unsuccessfully to persuade the Gorotire to learn mining techniques from their traditional enemies – the Munduruku Indians, who live further to the east, near the long-established gold rush town of Itaituba.

In early September, a cattle-rancher sent 600 men into their reserve to start clearing a plot of land which he claimed belonged to him. There were rumours that a further 1,800 men were on their way. The Gorotire began to fear the systematic invasion of their lands all along the eastern boundaries. They resorted to desperate action. They painted red and black designs on their bodies, which is their traditional way of preparing for an attack, and went in a large group to a nearby farm. They clubbed to death 20 people, including children and two pregnant women. They left their clubs and red parrot feathers beside the corpses.

The Gorotire chief, Kanhok, said later that they had not gone to the farm with the intention of killing the settlers. He said that a row had broken out when the settlers refused to move out and that a woman, later to be killed, had stabbed one of the Indians with a knife. This may explain the uncharacteristic killing of women and children. Anti-Indian feelings were running very high among the settlers and ranch hands. Luis Carlos Silva, the rancher who employed most of the people on the farm, told a US journalist shortly after the massacre: 'The USA solved the problem with its army. They killed a lot of Indians. Today everything is quiet there and the country is respected throughout the world.'

Major Curió, a special envoy of the National Security Council, went into the region with half a dozen federal police officers shortly after the massacre. While he attempted to quieten down the Indians, he sent the police officers to the nearby non-Indian settlements to prevent the formation of unofficial vigilante groups bent on revenge. Major Curió showed surprising sympathy for the Indians' case. He indignantly denied press reports that the dead women had been raped: 'Anyone who knows anything at all about Indians knows how much they respect the dead. There can be no doubt about this.' He also firmly dissociated himself from the attempt made by Nobre da Veiga to place the blame on Alceu Cotia, an anthropologist who had visited the Gorotire shortly before the incident. He said: 'Alceu Cotia is a competent professional and cannot be held responsible for the recent events.' Major Curió admitted indirectly that much of the responsibility for the tragedy lay with Funai which had not marked out the Indians' lands.

However, despite Major Curió's remarks, the government did not take immediate action to evict the *garimpeiros* from the Indians' land though their presence was clearly a provocation. In November, it was reported that there were 5,000 *garimpeiros* panning for gold in the Indians' reserve. At the end of the month, the Gorotire went back on their earlier decision not to have anything to do with gold-mining and Kanhok asked Funai to send in technicians to teach them so that they could take over from the non-Indians and in this way expel them from their lands.

To the Indians' delight, federal policemen were finally sent in to evict the *garimpeiros* in December 1980. However, their satisfaction was short-lived. In January 1981, the operation was unexpectedly suspended. From press reports at the time, it seems that Docegeo, the state-owned prospecting company, was greatly opposed to the closing down of the gold mine and had insisted that Funai work with its officials to reach a compromise solution by which the mine would remain open, but the damage to the Indians would be kept to a minimum. The ending of the evictions amounted in practice to an invitation to the *garimpeiros* to return. By February 1981, there were 10,000 of them panning for gold once more. Some of them had come from Serra Pelada, where the vein of gold was thought to be running out. In July 1981, officials from the mining research body DNPM said that Camaru had become 'the greatest hope of Brazilian gold-mining'. The mine was producing about 10 kilos of gold a day, about a sixth of Brazil's total output.

By then, the plight of the Gorotire was becoming well known among other Indians. In the middle of the year, Raoni, the leader of the Txukurramãe, said at an official ceremony in Brasília that he would do all he could to 'solve the problems of the Gorotire, who are Kayapó like us and thus our brothers and sisters'. However, the situation went from bad to worse. By August there were estimated to be 24,000 *garimpeiros* working at Camaru. They used a solution containing mercury to help identify the gold and then threw the residue in the river. As a result some of the 561 Indians who lived downstream were suffering from dysentery.

The Gorotire became increasingly concerned and applied greater pressure on Funai. In September 1981, Kanhok repeated his proposal that, if the government was determined that the gold should be mined, then it should be the Indians who did the job. Once again, the Indians received no reply. In late 1981, one village of Gorotire Indians decided that, if they could not get rid of the *garimpeiros*, they might as well make some money out of the situation. So they signed an agreement with a mining company, Shellita, giving it permission to mine for gold on their lands. Funai was extremely angry and began legal action to annul the contract. By the end of 1984 the situation had not been resolved.

The Arara

The Arara are Karib Indians, who were given the nickname of *arara* (parrots) by the non-Indian inhabitants in the region. The Arara have a tragic history of contact with non-Indians. As early as 1943, frontiersmen, who had come to the region to extract oil from *copaiba* trees, killed two of them. No more was heard of them for many years and in 1957, when Darcy Ribeiro wrote a book called *Os Indios e A Civilização*, he classified them as an extinct tribe. However, news in the early 1960s of further conflicts showed that he had been wrong. The Indians began to fight back, occasionally killing outsiders found on their land. The Arara were pursued by leopard hunters and, on at least one occasion, given poisoned sweets.[10] In 1969, a group of frontiersmen killed a further 12 Arara.

The construction of the Transamazônica highway was a further serious blow. The road passed between two of their villages just three kilometres from one of them.[11] Despite early plans by anthropologists for an orderly and harmonious contact with all the Indians, the very haste with which the road was built made this impossible. On one occasion, a group of hitherto isolated Arara appeared on the road near Altamira and killed three construction workers.

Between 1970 and 1974, a Funai *sertanista*, Afonso da Cruz, tried to make contact with them. Though he saw them on several occasions, they made it clear that they wanted nothing to do with him. They continued to attack outsiders on their land. In 1976, they killed three surveyors from the government's prospecting company CPRM. In June 1977, they killed a settler who had moved on to their lands. Three months later, they wounded one of the members of a group sent in by Funai to establish contact with them.

Meanwhile, at the national level, Funai showed itself worse than incompetent in defending the rights of the Arara to their lands. In 1971 and 1972, it made no protest when settlers from the state colonisation institute INCRA moved on to part of their lands. Then, in 1974, it actually provided Cotrijuí, a large cooperative from Rio Grande do Sul, with a certificate stating that an area traditionally inhabited by the Arara had no Indians on it and that the cooperative could go ahead with its 400,000 hectare colonisation project. But the continuing violence was a source of embarrassment to Funai. In February 1980, it sent in the *sertanista* Sydney Possuelo at the head of a large expedition to make contact with the Arara. Then, in July, after consulting the powerful National Security Council, Funai went back on its earlier decision and withdrew its authorisation of the large Cotrijuí project. At the same time, it set aside a provisional area of 257,000 hectares to turn into a reserve for the group.

The attraction group headed by Possuelo was attacked by the Arara on several occasions, but finally established peaceful contact in February 1981. Possuelo began to campaign for an extension of the Arara's reserve to 800,000 hectares, partly because it was already becoming clear that the Arara would lose some of their original reserve when a planned hydroelectric complex, composed of three interlinked power stations, was built on the Xingu river. Even while these early contacts were being made, the Arara's lands were being invaded by two groups of peasant families and by gold and diamond prospectors.

At the beginning of 1982, the Arara invited Possuelo to visit their village; this was seen as an indication that he had finally won their confidence. However, tragedy soon hit the group in a sadly predictable fashion – through disease. Despite Possuelo's attempts to dissuade them, a group of Arara insisted on visiting the nearby town of Altamira. It was clear that the trip would be particularly dangerous for the Indians as they had refused preventive medical treatment.

In March, they flagged down a bus on the Transamazônica. As they were naked, some passengers gave them some clothes. The group spent two days in Altamira and then returned to their village. A few days later, they went down with influenza and spread the disease to other members of the group. After a considerable delay, Funai sent in a medical team. They contracted a film-maker, Luis Carlos Saldanha and a young photographer, Marcos Pereira, to make a film of the Funai team carrying out medical assistance.

However, Funai's publicity stunt backfired. The medical team consisted of a colonel (who left the village after a day and a half, having been filmed embracing the Indians), a sergeant and four soldiers. No one appeared to be properly qualified. Possuelo, who readily admitted that he knew little about medicine, was left to manage as best he could. Seven Indians died before the epidemic abated. By threatening the film-makers and others who knew of the tragedy, Colonel Zanoni, from Funai's head office, kept the story out of the press for over two months. It was finally broken by a journalist from the *O Estado de S. Paulo* newspaper who visited the village and saw for himself what had happened.[12] Marcos Pereira then spoke to the press, though he realised that the interview would cost him his job with Funai. His visit had clearly made a deep impression. He said that he had been deeply shocked by Funai's passivity and the indifference with which it treated the deaths, and had been moved by the innocence of the group in the face of the dangers which surrounded it. He said:

> They are very sad because of the illness and the deaths, but they have still retained their emotional warmth. The importance of touch and caresses in the community is incredible. They want to hold your hand the whole time. They smile at you, they caress you. You have to discard all your prejudices to live with people like them. But it is a journey of self-discovery and you have a shock when you get back to the cities.[13]

There are estimated to have been about 1,200 Arara in the various groups in 1970. Many lives have been lost since then. The group contacted by Possuelo had 56 members, now reduced to 49. It is not known how many Indians there are in the other groups.

In January 1983 the *sertanista* Wellington Figueiredo made contact with another group of hitherto isolated Arara, also living near the Transamazônica. He met 13 Indians and was told, through an Indian interpreter, that there were another 11 in their village.

The Gavião[14]

The Gavião have been severely harmed by developmental schemes set up by the government for the Amazon. One group, called the Gavião da Montanha, was first decimated by disease after the initial contact, and then forcibly moved by Funai in June 1977, after it had agreed on a compensation payment of Crs 77,000 (£2,960) with the state electricity board, Eletronorte. The area originally occupied by this group was flooded in mid 1984 to form part of the huge reservoir for the Tucuruí hydroelectric power station.

In 1981 most of its members joined another group of Gavião, which lives in the Mãe Maria reserve in south Pará. This was one of the fiercer groups and it had resisted permanent contact with the regional population for more than 50 years. These Indians were finally 'pacified' by an SPI team in the 1950s, an experience which cost them more than two-thirds of their population. When they were visited by a Brazilian anthropologist in 1961, one of their two villages had been reduced to a population of just eight. The anthropologist, not unreasonably, assumed that the tribe had already lost its cultural identity and was doomed to extinction. In his account, he wrote: 'It was in that phase that the Gavião disappeared as a group. From then on, they were to be a mere collection of Indians, totally dependent on the national society.'

However, the Gavião made a dramatic recovery in the following 15 years. Their population increased from 30 in 1961 to 108 in 1976. Brazil nuts, the collection of which has been for many decades one of the main activities practised by subsistence peasant families in the area, played a key role in this remarkable recuperation. It provided them with a valuable market commodity which allowed them to achieve economic independence. It is only by chance that the Gavião's lands are rich in Brazil nuts, which had previously been a foodstuff of only minor importance for them. The SPI introduced the collection of Brazil nuts among the Gavião, not in an attempt to rebuild the shattered Indian community, but because it spotted a good chance to boost its own funds. Under the SPI and later Funai, the Gavião were paid only a fifth of the value of the nuts they collected.

However, in 1975 Funai launched a community development project for the Gavião. An anthropology student, Iara Ferraz, was contracted to run it. Showing great initiative, she encouraged the Indians to take control of their own production and to stop selling to Funai. She advised them to manage by themselves the entire operation of collecting, transporting and marketing the product. The project was very successful, but it clearly weakened Funai's control over the Indians. Not surprisingly, Iara Ferraz was dismissed from her post in December 1976 for alleged indiscipline. But by then the Indians were well able to run the business by themselves. By 1977, they were employing Brazilians to assist in the administration and were contracting bank loans so that they could improve their infrastructure. In August 1977, they expelled from their village the Funai official who had been sent in to replace Iara Ferraz.

Though the Indians had achieved economic independence, other dangers still threatened them. In a classic case of bungling, Funai had to move one of the Gavião's villages twice so that it would not be flooded by the Tucuruí reservoir. Then, after their second move, the Indians were told by Eletronorte that the transmission lines from the power station would cut across a part of their land rich in Brazil nut trees and that a large number (1,150) would have to be felled. As we have seen, these lines also crossed the lands of the Parakanã Indians.

After much haggling, Eletronorte agreed in July 1980 to pay Crs 40m (£315,000) in compensation. When the Indians were paid the money later in the year, they immediately deposited three-quarters of it in the national savings bank, which pays a good rate of return duly indexed for inflation. They used the rest to buy 150 cattle and a lorry and to start construction work on a new village designed by an architect from Brasília.

Just a few months later, the Indians discovered that they would lose another part of their land for the construction of the railway to take minerals from the Carajás mining complex to the port of Itaquí on the coastline of the state of Maranhão. The area they were to lose was precisely where they had built a large new village. The constant noise, dirt and pollution, caused first by the construction work and later by the trains, would be a serious disruption for the Indians. After haggling, the state-owned mining company, Companhia Vale do Rio Doce, finally paid the Indians Crs 56.5m (£210,000) in April 1982. Once again, the Indians deposited most of the money in the national savings bank.

This business acumen was not developed without some loss to the Indians' traditional values and life-style. Though they have retained a clear ethnic identity, they have given up many of their old customs in favour of practices learned from non-Indians. The Gavião have been criticised by some anthropologists both for contracting non-Indians to work for them and for bringing in the architect from Brasília to design the new village for them and to teach them how to make brick houses. More seriously, perhaps, their chief has been accused of changing the traditional relations in the group to give himself more dominance.

The Gavião have defended themselves against these charges. Their chief, Kokrenum, reacted angrily to the criticisms made of the new village, which went as far as an endeavour by Funai to halt construction work. In November 1980, Kokrenum sent a letter to the president of Funai in which he challenged him 'to come to the village and speak to me, face to face, like a man' if he wanted to stop the construction. Kokrenum asked:

Why is it that only Funai, and not the Indians, can live well, have television, all paid for with the Indians' money? Other Indians are having a rough time, but I don't want this for us. I want things to get better, to sleep well, to have pretty houses. The President can come here, but the construction will go on. I have decided that and no one goes against what I decide, what I do.

The Gavião have achieved a great deal. They have pulled their group back from the brink of extinction and have worked out a successful form of economic integration. Yet the process is fraught with dangers, for only a few Indian groups have yet managed to take advantage of what the encroaching society has to offer while preserving the essential values of their society.

The Yanomami

The Yanomami, who live in an immense area of tropical forest in south Venezuela and north Brazil, are the only remaining large group of relatively isolated Indians in Brazil. They are thought to number 17,000, more or less equally divided between the two countries. Though most have never been in contact with non-Indians, the government has known about them for several centuries. Their presence was registered in a survey carried out by the Portuguese imperial government in 1707.

For most of the groups which have maintained contact with non-Indians, the experience has been tragic. In the 1950s and 1960s, there were the first indications that the occupation frontier was finally reaching their region. A migratory current of pelt hunters, woodmen and peasant families began to penetrate the area from the south. One group moved along the Apiaú river, a tributary of the Mucajaí, and established contact with some Yanomami Indians. The result was predictable: many died and others finally fled from the region in the early 1970s to infect other groups with the tuberculosis which they had picked up from outsiders. At the same time, diverse missionary groups – the Unevangelised Field Mission, the New Tribes Mission of Brazil, the Catholic Salesian and Consolata missions and others – began to work with various groups of Yanomami.

A savage blow was dealt the Indians with the government's decision in the early 1970s to build a highway, called the Perimetral Norte, to span the frontiers of Brazil like an enormous arc. About 220 kilometres of the road had been built when the government decided to abandon the project because of its prohibitive cost. Funai did very little to prepare the Yanomami and the road went close to 13 of their villages with terrible effect. The Indians met workers from the construction company, Camargo Corrêa, who had not been properly prepared, either psychologically or medically, for the contact. About 60 Indians died in a single measles epidemic. After a year or two all but eight families from these villages had been wiped out. No one knows exactly how many died. In another region, in the upper reaches of the Catrimani river, another 80 Indians died from tuberculosis and others contracted venereal disease. The problem of disease is particularly serious among the Yanomami because the various groups keep in regular contact, intermarrying and exchanging goods. This makes it very easy for diseases to spread. Large numbers of Yanomami, who had never seen a non-Indian, must none the less have died from Western diseases.

The relief felt by anthropologists after the government's decision to halt work on the Perimetral Norte was short-lived. In 1975 cassiterite was discovered in the Serra dos Surucucus. Hundreds of *garimpeiros* moved in. It was a particularly alarming development, for this region had the largest concentration of Indians: 76 villages, containing an estimated 3,800 Indians, most of whom had never been in contact with non-Indians. Serious conflicts broke out and some Indians were killed by *garimpeiros*. In 1976 the federal government finally moved in, banned prospecting and evicted the miners. However, the government did not categorically rule out the possibility of the ore being mined by large companies at a later stage.

Funai's record with the Yanomami has been particularly poor, for it has done very little at all to protect the Indians and has generally acted only when the situation has become highly explosive. It cannot justify its inactivity by saying that it was not aware of what was going on, for it has received a constant bombardment of reports and proposals. As early as 1968, an anthropologist submitted to Funai a proposal for a Yanomami reserve, but no action was taken. Another proposal, sent in by a Roman Catholic mission in March 1969, was lost.

Funai finally came up with its own proposal in 1972, but kept it confidential. A mission from the international body, The Aborigines Protection Society, finally obtained a copy of Funai's proposal. In the report which the Protection Society drew up at the end of its visit it commented: 'It was immediately clear that limits of the proposed reserve were hopelessly inadequate. Almost incredibly, it excludes every single one of the Yanomami villages acknowledged to exist by Funai.' Probably because of the flurry of international protests, this proposal too was eventually shelved.

Finally in June 1977 a Funai team carried out an aerial survey which located over 160 villages. On the basis of these results, Funai issued a series of decrees in which it declared as 'areas of Yanomami occupation' 21 small, scattered areas in Roraima and Amazonas. It seemed that Funai's plan was to convert these areas later into 21 separate reserves. Anthropologists throughout the world were horrified. A spokesman from Survival International in London stated: 'It seems that, far from providing any protection, Funai is seeking to give the Yanomami the maximum of contact, deculturation and disease.' The Commission for the Creation of the Yanomami Park, coordinated by the photographer Cláudia Andujar, led an international campaign against the creation of these small reserves. The commission published a document in which it summarised the reasons for its opposition to Funai's proposal: it would take away from the Indians the large area they needed for their hunting, fishing and gathering activities and it would prevent them from carrying out their periodic moves when the soils around their villages became depleted; it would at best jeopardise, and possibly prevent, the economic, ceremonial and marriage exchanges which were essential to the social dynamics of the groups; and it would greatly increase the contact points with Brazilian society, thus multiplying the risks of infection and disease.

The commission pushed for the creation of a single continuous park, of 6.4 million hectares. It admitted that this was an extensive area, but pointed out that about a third of it was mountainous and, according to Brazil's forestry code, could not be used for farming, and that another 40 per cent had been classified in the government's aerial survey as of inadequate fertility for any farming activity. It thus claimed that only about a quarter of the proposed area could be used for farming by non-Indians. The commission also said that, as the Indians made up 13 per cent of the population of Roraima, it did not seem unfair to be demanding 18 per cent of the territory for them.

Predictably, the proposal was bitterly opposed by many of Roraima's politicians. At the end of 1979, the deputy Hélio Campos, renowned for his hatred of the Indians, indulged in obvious scaremongering, which seemed designed to influence military offiers in the security forces. He said that the Yanomami and other Indian groups practised a type of 'tribal socialism', and that to create large reserves for them on the country's border could be 'the first step towards dismembering these areas from the rest of the country'. He thus proposed that no Indian reserves should be created within 150 kilometres of the frontier and that all Indians living within this zone should be relocated elsewhere in Brazil. Anthropologists and others in Brazil immediately denounced this scheme as 'premeditated genocide' and it was eventually dropped.

For several years the debate over the future of the Yanomami became the key issue in Indian politics. Neither side seems to have been totally honest, which is perhaps to be expected in a struggle of this nature. The commission has stressed the 'fairness' of their demand, given the size of the present population of Roraima. But this is simply a fortuitous aspect of the commission's case. It is difficult to imagine that, if the population of Roraima has increased to five million in 20 years' time – not an unrealistic projection – the members of the commission will be defending the proposal that the size of the Yanomami's reserve be reduced to 41,400 hectares so that all inhabitants in the territory get their fair share. In their turn, the other lobby has tried to make use of the widespread fear of the Indians' differentness by suggesting that the Indians, as they are not 'proper Brazilians', may represent a threat to national security.

When stripped of these camouflages, the debate reveals the deep ideological divisions between the two main adversaries. On one side are the anthropologists and the more radical missionaries, many of them Catholic, who are determined, in the face of their repeated defeats in the past, to do all they can to protect this last group of Indians. Many feel passionately that, whatever mineral riches lie under the Yanomami's lands, the government would never be morally justified in taking away any part of their lands. For them, a truly developed society would do all in its power to preserve the Indians' rich and unique cultures. On the other side are the politicians, mining companies and developmentalists who want to put to productive use the Yanomami's lands. Their motives range from the politicians' wish to build Roraima into a powerful and economically developed state to the anxiety of some of the mining companies to lay their hands on the minerals. Though there are exceptions, most local businessmen believe that it would be ridiculous to hold back the development of Roraima to protect a few allegedly backward Indians.

While the debate raged, the Indians themselves faced further threats. In September and October 1980, Brigadier Ottomar de Souza Pinto, the governor of Roraima and an old friend of Hélio Campos, sent prospectors by plane into the Yanomami's land to mine for gold. Then, after further veins of gold had been discovered by the Couto de Magalhães river, Nobre da Veiga, the president of Funai, said that he might take some of this land away from the Indians so that its gold could be mined. The area is just 50 kilometres away from the Serra dos Surucucus, so its occupation by *garimpeiros* would inevitably lead to the penetration of the Yanomami heartland itself, particularly as there were rumours that fine-quality diamonds had been discovered there. Then, in July 1981, the ministry of mines and energy authorised two big mining companies – Andrade Gutierrez and Paranapanema – to prospect for titanium in the Serra dos Surucucus as traces of the metal had already been found there. The mining front of the encroaching society had reached the Yanomami with a vengeance.

The anthropologists and the commission organised a counter-offensive among public opinion. Under pressure, Funai began in June 1981 to remove some of the 3,000 *garimpeiros* who were mining for gold on the Yanomami's lands. But the measure was taken very late in the day. In July 1981, the Indians caught measles from the prospectors, their sixth epidemic of this lethal disease. The epidemic spread to almost all the villages in the Serra dos Surucucus. Funai eventually sent in a medical team to vaccinate the Indians, but at least 27 died.

The contact with non-Indians was disrupting Yanomami life in other ways. According to press reports in July 1981, the Yanomami in Brazil were receiving firearms in return for jaguar and other skins. The Indians were then using these arms against their traditional enemies, the Yanomami who live in Venezuela. Because of the much greater effectiveness of modern arms, the violence of the clashes had increased at an alarming rate. According to press reports, about 35 Venezuelan Yanomami had died in a clash in early July.

In December 1981 a team from the National Security Council visited the region. This visit was clearly linked to the recent changes in Funai and was the first indication that top members of the government might be getting seriously concerned about the campaign being waged against Funai, at home and abroad. In March 1982, the government took the first step towards establishing a large Yanomami reserve by placing an interdiction order on an area of 7.7 million hectares – an even larger stretch than the 6.4

million hectares demanded by the commission. This measure means that all outsiders are forbidden to enter the area and that all economic activities carried out by anyone other than the Yanomami must be halted. Anthropologists were quick to point out that it was too early for them to celebrate, for not infrequently the size of a final reserve has been much less than that of the area originally interdicted. However, the measure did seem to suggest that the government had given up the idea of scattered reserves and had accepted in principle the idea of a single large reserve. There were grounds for the commission to feel cautiously optimistic.

The government did not, however, follow up its initiative. In mid 1982 Funai put in a request to the federal government for a further Crs 632.5m (£2.1m) so that it could start its Yanomami project with the contracting of 168 new employees. In February 1983, Funai said that it had still not been given the go-ahead by the government. In March, Cláudia Andujar complained to Funai that about 4,000 *garimpeiros* had re-entered the Yanomami's lands and were panning for gold and diamonds. The captain of the army's special frontier battalion, which was supposed to be patrolling the area to keep out intruders, said that because of the mountainous terrain, the thick rain forest and the huge distances involved, he was unable to carry out his task properly with the number of soldiers at his disposal. He suggested that the Yanomami by the river Uraricaá, near the frontier with Venezuela, who were already selling minerals to outside contractors, should take over the whole mining operation and help the army bar the entry of outsiders. The proposal has been enthusiastically received by Funai, always keen to have another source of revenue, but attacked by the more conservative missionary groups, who have long claimed that, to protect their culture, the Yanomami should be shielded from outside contacts and not be allowed to become aware of the problems they face. The members of the commission have, on the whole, welcomed the suggestion, for they are increasingly convinced that, like other Indian groups, the Yanomami will only win secure control over their lands once they themselves are capable of defending them.

But no action was taken. In April 1984 Carlo Zacquini, an Italian missionary who has been living with the Yanomami since 1965, accused the Brazilian government of genocide for not keeping invaders out of the Yanomami lands. He called for the urgent demarcation of the reserve. On 20 July, another missionary priest, Guilherme Damioli, and the bishop of Roraima, Dom Aldo Mongiano, issued a joint statement in which they described the damage that was being done to the Yanomami by the *garimpeiros* – epidemics, alcoholism, sexual abuse of the women, brawls and so on. They called for the immediate closure of the mines, with the expulsion of the *garimpeiros*, and for the setting up of control posts to stop outsiders from entering the reserve.

In February 1985, a group of leading Roraime politicians and businessmen, including apparently the former governor, Brigadier Ottomar de Souza Pinto, sent several hundred *garimpeiros* into the Serra dos

Surucucus. It was an attempt to take advantage of the weakness of the outgoing federal government, headed by General Figueiredo, to speed up the take-over of the Indians' lands.

But the manoeuvre back-fired. Nelson Marabuto, the new president of Funai, who had been greatly criticised by anthropologists at the time of his appointment, reacted with unexpected vigour. He issued a vehement protest and the government of Roraima was eventually forced to send in the police to evict the *garimpeiros*.

Notes

1. Shelton H. Davis, *Victims of the Miracle – Development and the Indians of Brazil* (Cambridge University Press, New York, 1977).
2. Darcy Ribeiro, *A Politica2 Indigenista Brasileira* (Rio de Janeiro, 1962).
3. Paul L. Montgomery, 'Killing of Indians Charged in Brazil', *New York Times*, 21 March 1968, quoted by Davis, *Victims of the Miracle*.
4. Richard Bourne, *Assault on the Amazon* (Gollancz, London, 1978), p.230.
5. Quoted in ibid., p.86.
6. Much of this account is based on articles in *Survival International Review*.
7. Bourne, *Assault on the Amazon*.
8. R.G.A. Goodland, 'Environmental Assessment of the Tucuruí Hydroelectric Project, Rio Tocantins, Amazonia', mimeographed paper, 1978.
9. Much of the information in the earlier part of the discussion comes from Terence Turner, 'The Txukahamae Kayapó are Alive and Well in the Upper Xingu', *Survival International Review*, vol.3, no.22, 1978.
10. Bourne, *Assault on the Amazon*, p.232.
11. Ibid.
12. *O Estado de S. Paulo*, 30 April 1982.
13. *A Folha de S. Paulo*, 10 May 1982.
14. Much of this account is based on a paper given by Alcida Ramos at the Conference on the Development of Amazonia in Seven Countries, Cambridge, 23–26 September 1979.

6. Case Study One: The Battle for Santa Teresinha

Nós de Santa Teresinha	We of Santa Teresinha
Nós todos vamos rezá	We're all going to pray
Vamos pedi a Deus	We're going to ask God
Pro padre Chico voltá	For Father Chico's return
Foi ele quem ajudeu	T'was he who helped us
a nossa terra ganhá.	win our land.
Botaro ele daqui prá fora	They pushed him out of here
Sem direito de voltá	Without right of return
Valei-me Nossa Senhora	Save us, Our Lady
Ai de nós o que será!	Oh what will come of us!

'Roda', a folk ballad by peasant farmer Conceição Lopes Cardoso

A Frontier Settlement

The village of Santa Teresinha, which has been the scene of a long and violent struggle over land, today bears few obvious signs of its traumatic history. It seems a haven of sleepy tranquillity, far distant from the violent clashes which are occurring a few hundred kilometres to the north in the state of Pará. Yet the tale of Santa Teresinha contains very valuable lessons for the present conflicts.

Santa Teresinha, which is situated in the north-eastern tip of Mato Grosso, not far from the border with Pará, grew up around an inlet which provides a natural port in the middle reaches of the Araguaia river. It is a river of exceptional beauty, especially in the dry season when its long white beaches are exposed between the blues and greens of water, forest and sky. Even today, many of the local inhabitants travel by river and it is certainly the most attractive way of arriving. Only at the last moment, as one enters the inlet, does the village appear between the trees. A few brightly painted

225

houses, made up of stores and a boarding house, surround the large triangular village green which opens out from the landing beach. Boys swim in the river, horses graze on the grass, old men sit chatting on benches beneath the large shady trees.

Two main streets lead from the square, one to the school, the cooperative and the pharmacy, and the other to the new church and meeting house which were inaugurated in March 1977. All these are concrete symbols of Santa Teresinha's struggle for survival as a community. The houses become simpler the further they are from the village centre, as the blues, pinks and yellows of paintwork give way to the mud-brown of bricks and adobe. In the grassy back streets there are only the plainest of huts, set in small kitchen gardens, no different from those of the first inhabitants.

Because the river permitted easy access, the region was visited since the earliest days of Portuguese rule by explorers, missionaries, traders and those in search of forest products such as rubber and Brazil nuts. The middle reaches of the river, however, between Barra do Garças and Conceição do Araguaia, were the last to be reached and occupied, partly because they were the most distant from areas of settlement and partly because they were occupied by Indians reputed to be fierce.

In the region there were – and still are – three main groups of Indians: the Carajá, the Kayapó and the Tapirapé, each of which has very different economic and social structures and language. The Carajá are fishermen and live close to the river, many of them inhabiting Bananal island. They have always been considered peaceful and docile by missionaries and settlers. The Kayapó live in the forest and, until the recent shortage of prey caused by the occupation of the region by cattle ranches, they were hunters and gained the reputation among the pioneer settlers of being the fiercest and bravest of the Indians. The third group takes its name from the Tapirapé river, a tributary which joins the Araguaia just north of Santa Teresinha. They were the most isolated, and not only geographically: while the surrounding Indians are mostly of the Gé linguistic group, the Tapirapé are a solitary group speaking a Tupi–Guarani language. Anthropologists believe that they were originally Tupinamba Indians living on the coast who fled inland with the arrival of the Portuguese. Although they have always supplemented their diet by hunting and fishing, they are primarily farmers who traditionally have cleared small areas of the forest by slashing and burning to grow an exceptionally wide variety of crops in addition to the ubiquitous maize and manioc. Because their villages were set back from the rivers, they were also the most isolated from the non-Indian settlers, although Dominican missionaries maintained regular visits after the initial contact in 1914.

These Indians have suffered in different ways from the occupation of their traditional lands by the *tori*, as non-Indians are called by the Tapirapé and Carajá. However, the pioneer peasant families, who were the first *tori* to arrive, coexisted peacefully with the Indians, despite their fear of the Kayapó. Serious conflicts only arose with the arrival of the cattle ranches in the 1960s.

The first settlers reached the area around 1910. They were *sertanejos*, or backswoodmen from the *sertão*, the arid hinterland of Brazil's north-east, hailing mostly from the states of Maranhão and Piauí, although some had temporarily settled in Pará or Goiás. These families founded a small town, called Furo de Pedras, about six kilometres downstream from the present site of Santa Teresinha. The Dominicans from the town of Conceição do Araguaia in Pará, which had been founded in 1897, soon began to visit this region and to make contact with both Indians and frontiersmen. By 1918 there were several families living in the place which was later to become Santa Teresinha but at that time was called Morro de Areia (sandy hill). In 1926 the Dominicans decided to build a small church at the foot of this hill rather than at Furo de Pedras, because the land was higher and so escaped the annual flooding by the Araguaia river.

Despite the difficulties caused by illnesses such as malaria, and encounters with wild animals and Indians, it seems that life for the peasant families was easier and more peaceful during this early period than later on. This was largely because land ownership was uncontested. When we visited Santa Teresinha in January 1979, we talked to Domingo Vieira de Oliveira, known as Domingo Vieira, one of the oldest inhabitants. He told us how his life had changed:

> I'm from Goiás but I came here when I was a boy in '21. There were very few families then, only four families or so. The land was good to work on, there was such abundance of everything, with lots of vegetables. Now we eat rations like a donkey because we don't have land. I have to buy everything, God help me to earn a penny or to find someone who'll sell to me without wanting payment in cash so I can hope to work later to be able to pay. Yesterday I worked, even though I'm sick. Our life has changed so much, there's no comparison with the old times. I'm old now, 75 years old. I'm working so I can buy a little rice, a little manioc flour. Poor people like me don't eat meat. Did you see that meat is 40 cruzeiros a kilo now? We eat fish, but there's only plenty of fish during the dry season. There's very little at the moment.
>
> When I came to this place, it wasn't even called Santa Teresinha. There were no landowners, only smallholders. We had our *roças*, we could clear them wherever we liked in the forest. Everyone had a cow, and all around were deer and capybaras.

In 1931, as the little town of Furo de Pedra had continued to grow and there were also more families living in the surrounding forest, the Bishop of Conceição do Araguaia, Dom Sebastião Tomás, decided to build a larger church as well as a school and a big house on top of the Morro de Areia hill. One of Santa Teresinha's oldest inhabitants told us how he came to the region to work on the construction of the new church:

> My name is Félix de Moraes. I was born in Maranhão in 1903. I left there when I was quite little and came to Conceição in Pará with my mother.

Conceição wasn't much then, just three streets, the old ones. We lived in the village itself, that's to say, we worked in the *roça*, but it was nearby as the forest was very close in the old days. When I was a child, I didn't do much, but later I took charge. We arrived there in '12, I was nine years old. I married there and stayed there nine years with my wife. We had nine children. Then the wife died and I stayed on with four children. I married again, but after a year she died too, so I came here on my own.

I came here in '32. There weren't many people. Quite a few lived in the forest, but hardly anyone lived right here. There was a tiny hamlet downriver called Furo de Pedra, six kilometres away. Then Dom Sebastião, who was Bishop of Conceição – because in the old days the diocese of Conceição in Pará governed the whole region, from the Tapirapé river downstream – he came and, travelling around, he realised that a teacher was needed here, so he arranged for an old woman called Bemvinda [welcome] to come and teach the children. He also arranged for the building of a church, a little chapel, but it was so badly done that he took away the priest who was doing the job and sent in a layman, not a father, to fix things up. Dom Sebastião sent 22 of us masons here. The parochial house was built in '31, then in '32 we came and built the house, the church and the big school. The school is big, not pretty but it's well built. The building was done quite quickly. We worked on it in '32, '33 and '34, and it was ready in '34. It was then that the Bishop gave the name Santa Teresinha to the place, which it didn't have until then.

Félix went on to tell us why he decided to settle in Santa Teresinha, after the construction job was finished:

In Conceição, it was stagnant, quite dead at that time. After the church job here was finished, I went back there, but there were no jobs goings, nothing at all, so I came back here where we could plant, that sort of thing. Then I met this lady here and we got married in '43. I've been living in this house since then.

All my life I've worked on the *roça*, every year, as well as being a mason. It was all peaceful in those days. The only thing that frightened us was the Indians, the Kayapó, but nothing ever happened with them. There was always a Father arriving from Conceição, for baptisms, marriages, then they went back. Only later did Father Francisco come to stay, to live with us.

We heard more about the early days from Conceição Lopes Cardoso, who is also one of Santa Teresinha's local song writers:

I'm from Maranhão but I grew up here in Mato Grosso. I arrived here when I was seven years old. I've been living here for 52 years. People here used to paddle their canoes, there weren't any motor boats, there wasn't anything. We came here because the Father who founded this place was my godfather. We were in Santana do Araguaia and he brought us here and put me, his godson, in the school.

We had our *roça* and sold produce outside, to people from São Félix and Luciara, who came here to buy. We sold rice, maize, *rapadura* [raw brown sugar]. We grew cotton for our own use, to make hammocks. Nobody here worked for landowners.

There were lots of Indians when we came here. In the winter during the floods the Carajá used to move their village to here on top of the hill where we built the school. Everywhere was full of Indians. The Tapirapé stayed upriver, they didn't live with the Carajá, they all lived apart. There were only two tribes here and they still live here. It was peaceful. There was never any problem with the Indians.

The US anthropologist Charles Wagley made his first field trip to visit the Tapirapé Indians in 1939 and stayed at Furo de Pedra on the way. In his book, *Welcome of Tears*, he gives a vivid description of the life of this frontier community:

In 1939 Furo de Pedra was one of the largest non-Indian settlements in the middle Araguaia River region. It contained about thirty-five to forty illiterate frontier families who made a living from grazing a few cattle in the semi-flooded grasslands back from the river and from subsistence gardens. There were two miserably stocked stores which served as trading posts, receiving hides and skins (wild pigskin, alligator, or *jacaré*, and jaguar), as well such products as salted *piracuca* (a fish) in exchange for manufactured goods and tinned foods. Of course, their stock of *cachaça* (a raw sugarcane rum) was always plentiful, but there was a perennial shortage of cloth, agricultural implements, and other more basic items. People were so eager for salt, *rapadura*, tobacco, cloth, bush-knives and hoes that they begged me to sell my meagre supplies. I was a strange visitor and a novelty to them. They had seen few foreigners, except for a Dominican priest who lived over two hundred miles downriver at Conceição do Araguaia and the Scottish missionaries who maintained a ranch at Macaúba, not many miles away, as a refuge for lepers . . . Everyone was friendly and pleasant.

The way of life of the frontier peasants altered little from the time of the first settlements until the disruptions of the late 1950s and the more violent disturbances of the 1960s and 1970s. The main change was a steady growth in the size of Santa Teresinha, as the church and school buildings provided a nucleus around which the houses could cluster, so that gradually Santa Teresinha surpassed Furo de Pedra in size and importance. The Catholic Church has shown a constant concern for the education and welfare of both frontiersmen and Indians in this region and in time its presence became more evident through longer visits by teachers and nurses as well as priests.

The Tapirapé under Threat of Extinction

Durings the 1940s and 1950s, the Tapirapé Indians were threatened with extinction and suffered considerable physical and cultural disintegration from which they recovered to a remarkable degree, particularly in view of the fate of so many other Amazonian tribes (see Chapter 5). Four years before Wagley's trip in 1939, they had been visited by another anthropologist, Herbert Baldus, whose book on the Tapirapé, a classic of comparative ethnology, reflects his rigorous, if narrow, academic training in Germany in the 1920s. Wagley's training and interests differed to those of Baldus. He placed a much greater emphasis on sociology, and this led him to discuss broader issues and to trace out the recent history of the Tapirapé as an example of how an Indian tribe can continue to exist as an ethnic group despite acculturation by the dominant national society.

At the beginning of the 20th Century, the Tapirapé had five villages, which they periodically moved as the surrounding land became exhausted. Their extensive territory was limited only by their fear of possibly hostile Indian groups in the vicinity: the Kayapó in the north, the Xavantes in the south, the Carajá along the Araguaia in the east, and the possibly mythical Ampanea in the west. Nevertheless, the land under their control was more than adequate for the needs of a population of about 1,500 so there was little reason to enter the territories of the other Indian groups.

During the first half of this century, however, they were decimated by new diseases from which they had no immunity: respiratory infections leading to pneumonia, whooping cough, smallpox, yellow fever and the varieties of malaria originally brought over by African slaves. These often fatal diseases were contracted mainly through contact with other infected Indian groups rather than directly from the *tori* and even now are responsible for many deaths among recently contacted groups in the Amazon basin. The shamans' medicine, more often than not extremely effective in the treatment of indigenous illnesses, usually proves to be powerless in the face of these alien diseases.

Because of the deaths caused by these diseases, two villages were abandoned as early as 1905 and 1908, followed by a third in 1930. The survivors joined the two other larger villages. During his visit in 1939, Wagley witnessed the evacuation of yet another village, Chichtawa, with its 40 surviving inhabitants coming to live in the village of Tampiitawa, the only remaining village of the original five. The population continued to decline and Baldus reported a total of only 59 inhabitants during his second visit in 1947.

Shortly afterwards, while most of the men were away in the savannah tending to their gardens, the Tapirapé suffered a devastating attack from a group of Kayapó Indians, who acted with unusual aggressiveness, probably because they were in a state of disarray, as their traditional lands had been invaded by outsiders. The Tapirapé were not strong enough to attempt to reoccupy their village and for three years they were homeless and threatened

Bishop Pedro Casaldáliga talks to peasant farmers

Photo: Lebeck

Tapirapé Indian boys   Photo: António Carlos Moura Ferreira

A Tapirapé Indian boy   Photo: António Carlos Moura Ferreira

with total social disintegration as they scattered all over the region. Most went to live near the SPI post at the confluence of the Tapirapé and Araguaia river which had been set up by Valentim Gomes, Wagley's guide and companion in 1939. Others fled to cattle ranches, some even being fed by Lúcio da Luz whose cattle-raising activities had extended further south towards the Tapirapé river by the time.

However, a small group of 18 or 19 Indians, headed by Kaimará, a strong leader whom Wagley had known well and who was deeply suspicious of the *tori*, chose to trek north through the forest in search of the site of the Chichutawa village, rather than to seek help from the SPI post or the ranches. This group suffered from malnutrition, disease and constant fear of attack from the Kayapó. After a few years, it was assumed that they had all died. However, they were sighted in 1964. Events took a more dramatic turn in 1970 when a hunter met the three survivors from this group – Kaimará, his wife and his son. After 23 years of isolation and hardship, they were persuaded to rejoin the rest of their group near the SPI post.

In 1950 Valentim Gomes and the Dominicans had convinced the families scattered around the SPI post and the cattle ranches to reunite and to create a village near the post. According to Wagley, these Indians were remarkably successful in reconstructing their shattered society. They managed, he said, to retain the rules, ideology and abstract concepts of their culture, and at the same time to adapt to the changed conditions that made necessary an increasingly intense contact with both the *tori* and other Indian groups, notably the Carajá. They were joined in 1952 by the *irmãzinhas*, the Little Sisters of Jesus, a French order of working nuns, who live with them today, and in 1954 by the French worker priest, François (Francisco) Jentel, who stayed with them for ten years.

These religious workers have made a point of respecting Tapirapé society and of adapting to the Tapirapé culture and way of life, rather than trying to impose their own cultural values like so many missionary workers living with other Indian groups. The Little Sisters provide as much rudimentary nursing and teaching as they can within their limited means, and try to help prevent exploitation by traders in money transactions.

They have only tried to make radical changes in the Indian's traditional culture when it has seemed that, in the new circumstances in which the group has to live, the old practices could seriously damage their interests or even threaten their very survival. The most notable example was the practice of infanticide. Traditionally women had been forbidden to have more than three children, or more than two children of the same sex, and unwanted children had been killed at birth. While this practice had earlier been an efficient mechanism for keeping the population at a stable level, it was proving catastrophic under the Indians' dramatically changed circumstances. The nuns persuaded the Indians to give it up and it was one of the key factors accounting for the subsequent population explosion. None the less, as we shall see later, however good the motives, even this infringement of the Indians' earlier customs has created its own problems.

The traditional practice of burying the dead inside their houses was also eventually abandoned. The missionaries felt that this custom had become a health hazard since the Indians had been forced to give up their practice of periodically moving to a new area and building another village. After Jentel had buried outside the village both a visiting Dutch scientist who had died of a snake bite, and her husband who had died of a heart attack several days later, the Indians had been persuaded to adopt the *tori* way of burial and gradually a small cemetery grew up on the outskirts of the village.

Nevertheless, the Tapirapé population continued to decline for some time until it stood at the very low point of about 35 in the early 1960s. One of the continuing obstacles to population expansion was the Tapirapé belief that illness and death were caused by the sorcery of shamans. As a result, not only were additional deaths accompanied by the killing of suspected shamans to avenge the dead, but the Tapirapé refused to believe that the deaths could be caused by other factors, such as dehydration (which killed many children until the mid 1970s); they were thus unwilling either to take preventive measures or to treat the sick. Gradually, however, the missionaries demonstrated the effectiveness of *tori* medicine, particularly in the treatment of alien diseases. By 1972, the Tapirapé population had risen to over 100.

The First Companies

The peaceful life in this isolated frontier community of subsistence peasants and church workers received its first jolt from the encroaching capitalist frontier in 1955, with the arrival of a few relatively big companies. The first to arrive were both airlines: the Companhia Nacional de Transporte Aéreo, known as the Nacional, from São Paulo, and the Companhia Real de Aerofotografia, known as the Real, from Rio de Janeiro. The Real, which eventually bought up the Nacional, began to purchase huge tracts of land in the region. It resold some of this land to another company, Civa, whose main shareholder was Miguel Nasser, of Lebanese descent. Civa – which was known in the region as Silva – set up a small store and a small farm and by 1960 had bought up about 1.2 million hectares. Unlike the airlines, which were responsible for big changes in the region, Civa was fairly inactive. We were unable to find out the full name of the company or its business interests elsewhere even when talking to former employees. It was clear that it bought up the land for speculative reasons and did the bare minimum to ensure that its estate was not invaded by land thieves or peasant families.

The airlines brought Santa Teresinha from the age of river transport into the era of air travel. On a cleared airstrip planes began to arrive from Belém in the north and from Barra do Garças and Goiânia in the south. The airlines also built a sawmill and cleared a small area for farming, where, among other crops, coffee was grown on an experimental scale. For about ten years, the companies rented the school and the house on top of Morro de Areia from the Dominicans and used them as a base for their pilots and as a small hotel, complete with running water and a bathroom, for potential land purchasers and tourists.

Civa pulled out of its commercial activities in Santa Teresinha in the early 1960s, though it did not sell its land until the 1970s. The workers it had contracted locally went back to peasant farming and a few of its employees brought in from outside, including the company administrator, Edival dos Reis from Rio de Janeiro, decided to stay on in Santa Teresinha. The latter took over the company's small store, one of the few shops in the village, and has since become an established resident with a fashionable, contemporarily furnished house on the central green.

Despite its new links with the rest of Brazil, Santa Teresinha was still too isolated from the mainstream of national political life to feel any immediate repercussions from the military *coup* of 1964 which overthrew the civilian government of President João Goulart. It was more affected by the structural changes which were taking place in Brazil as its economy was modernised and it became more integrated into the world economy. Thus in 1964 and 1965 Santa Teresinha received a large influx of migrant families, partly as an indirect result of the land statute which had been drawn up by the Goulart government (although in fact made law by the military regime). This statute, which set by law minimum conditions for labourers living on large estates, was clearly intended to improve the lot of the rural population but, paradoxically, led to large-scale evictions as landowners preferred to contract day labourers rather than comply with the rigorous requirements established. The statute became a pretext for landowners to get rid of resident labourers who were no longer required as the result of the increasing mechanisation of agriculture. Some of the migrants who arrived in Santa Teresinha had formerly been labourers on large estates. Many had tried first to settle on Bananal Island but had been forbidden to cut down trees and make clearings by the *Floresta* (Forest), as the settlers called the officials in charge of the Araguaia national park which had been set up on this island. So the peasants had moved on to Santa Teresinha.

One local resident who arrived at this time was Franciso Manoel da Costa, known as Chicão. At our first meeting, he treated us with the courtesy traditional in the Brazilian hinterland, but seemed mistrustful of our reasons for asking him questions. He was interested in our work but said little himself, probably because of his bitter experience during the conflict. When we went back for a second visit, he had clearly discussed our visit with his neighbours and was far freer in his comments. He told us:

> I'm from Piauí. I left there already married, with three children. I used to work on the *roça* there and here I work on the *roça*, except that now I'm off sick and my wife is planting the manioc. I left Piauí for Maranhão, for there wasn't enough rain. I reached the island on the other side of the river in 1958, but left there because of the *Floresta* – the guard wouldn't let us have our *roças*, as he

didn't want the trees cut down. Quite a few people left the island and came here, or went elsewhere. I came here in 1964 and I've stayed here ever since.

In the same year, the first parish priest, Jean (João) Chaffarod, fell sick and returned to France. He was succeeded by François Jentel, who had been living with the Tapirapé since before Father João arrived in Santa Teresinha. Though he continued to visit the Indians, Jentel became increasingly immersed in the life of this peasant community. No other individual from outside has given so much to Santa Teresinha or had such an impact on its life and history. Rarely has an outsider won such love and respect in an adoptive community. A man of humanity, intelligence, determination and seemingly unlimited energy, his name has become inseparable from that of his Araguaian home.

Jentel was determined to bring progress to this village of subsistence peasants and believed that they could improve their lot by a united effort. Despite later endeavours by leading members of the government and by cattle company executives to paint Jentel as a 'Marxist revolutionary', committed to the 'subversion of the established order', the priest's efforts were in fact directed towards a greater integration of the community into the modern world. From all accounts, Jentel had a tremendous trust in the benefits of technological progress. His overriding objective throughout the years of struggle was simply to provide the peasant families with access to these advances, so that they could break out of the relentless grip of grinding poverty.

His first idea was to set up a cooperative, a suggestion which was immediately accepted by some of the frontiersmen, such as Concieção Lopes Cardoso, who was a founder member, and Félix de Moraes. Together with Edival dos Reis, Jentel helped them organise the Araguaia Valley Mixed Cooperative, which was legalised in May 1965 and soon had more than 100 members. The cooperative functioned at the distribution level by buying in bulk basic supplies for the peasants' use at the lowest possible rates, and at the marketing level by selling their surplus produce, mainly rice, beans and manioc, either locally or in Goiás where higher prices could be obtained. Previously, the small farmers had found it difficult to find a market for their rice.

Jentel then brought in the region's first tractor, for the peasants' use, and helped them build roads to their clearings in the forest. He also installed a husking machine for rice, the peasants' main crop both for their own consumption and for sale. As the best prices could be obtained in Anápolis, which was about 800 kilometres to the south, on the other side of the Araguaia river in the state of Goiás, freight charges accounted for a large proportion of production costs. The 'rice machine', as it is called by the peasant families, allowed the peasants to increase their income substantially, as it both reduced outlay on freight and cut out exploitation by third parties for husking. Jentel was a practical man with a good understanding of mechanics and he taught some of the young men in the village how to drive the tractor and work the machine. Jentel also brought in teachers and a nurse on a more permanent basis than had previously been the case.

In these early years, Jentel gave a few inklings of the courage and determination for which he was later to become renowned. During the first few months of his life in Santa Teresinha, the school buildings on the top of the hill were still being used as a hotel by Civa. The Bishop of Conceição do Araguaia asked the company to leave, but it refused, so he authorised Jentel to go in and take over the buildings. Together with several peasant farmers armed with old hunting muskets and machete knives, Jentel climbed the hill to reclaim the school-house for the use for which it was originally constructed. The Civa officials, who had earlier laughed at the very idea that they could be forced to leave by the priest, quickly backed down and left when they realised how determined the group was.

This was the first incident of open conflict between the community and a company, a foretaste of what was to come. Old Conceição put it as follows:

> The first companies to come, Real and Nacional, started up the sawmill and began farming, but they didn't have anything to do with cattle. They helped us work and never meddled. The only company to stir things up was Codeara. This Codeara arrived in 1965.

The Cattle Ranches

The first two big companies to move into the region both came, typically enough, from São Paulo – the Banco de Crédito Nacional, a large banking institution in which Barclays Bank has a small stake, and the Medeiros group. Attracted to the region by Sudam's tax incentive scheme, both these companies bought land from Civa in the mid 1960s.

The BCN set up a subsidiary, the Araguaia Development Company which was to become known as Codeara. Its directors were Armando Conde, Carlos Alves Seixas and Luiz Gonzaga Murat. Its cattle project, which was to occupy 150,000 of the 196,500 hectares of land which had been purchased by BCN, was approved by Sudam in March 1967.

The Medeiros group bought land from several other dealers such as Nasser, in a strip running along the north bank of the Tapirapé river, on which they set up a number of cattle projects which received Sudam approval during the late 1960s and early 1970s. The first and smallest of this group's projects was Tapiraguaia ranch, owned jointly by José Augusto Leite de Medeiros, the head of the group, José Carlos Pires Carneiro and José Lúcio Neves Medeiros. Its owners began to visit Santa Teresinha in 1965, though the Tapiraguaia project was not approved by Sudam until June 1967. The ranch was to occupy 15,000 hectares at the confluence of the Tapirapé and Araguaia rivers, the traditional lands of the Tapirapé Indians. Despite this,

Tapiraguaia received a certificate from Funai to attest that there were no Indians on its land. While the setting up of Tapiraguaia ranch spelt problems for the Indians, it was the arrival of Codeara that was to create serious difficulties for the peasant families. A long and bitter struggle was to ensue.

To cut down the forest and to plant grass seed, Codeara needed to bring in hundreds of unskilled labourers, for the local labour force was clearly inadequate. It hired contractors, *gatos*, to bring in labourers from other states, particularly Goiás, Maranhão and even Piauí in the impoverished north-east.

Codeara was unhappy about the prospect of opening up the region and bringing in hundreds of labourers while peasant families were occupying areas, albeit small ones, which it claimed to own. It was keen for a little town to spring up around the ranch, but it wanted it to be a community which it dominated from the beginning. It was anxious to evict the peasant families, not so much to take over their land, which was a relatively small area, but so as to gain a monopoly of power and to control the subsequent occupation process.

As a result, Codeara began from the outset to put pressure on the peasant families to move out. Shortly after Codeara arrived, a small police station was opened in Santa Teresinha. It seemed to the peasant families that the police had been brought in merely to provide official backing for Codeara's attempts to evict them.

Codeara had part of its land measured out in 1966 and in early 1967 put labourers to work, clearing the forest. It was no coincidence that, out of the huge area of its ranch, it chose to start clearance precisely where several peasant families had their *roças*. When the peasants complained, they were told that they had no right to be occupying this land and that they must leave. Codeara said that as a gesture of goodwill it was prepared to pay compensation for the work that the peasants had carried out on their land. When the peasants replied that they wanted land – and preferably the land where some of them had been living for decades – rather than money, they were told that this was not possible.

Chicão put it in these terms:

> The first company planted rice and manioc and didn't say anything when we opened up clearings. Then the other company came in, the ranch, and told us not to work on our *roças* any more. They wanted us all out – the land wasn't for building houses, it wasn't for crop farming, it was all to be planted with grass. They paid a pittance in compensation. Some people went away, the ones who were most afraid, but they were only a few.

Félix de Moraes told us what happened to him:

> My little clearing was in the middle of a forest. It was just a small one. I didn't have the wherewithal to open up a big plot. They came along and threw huge

sticks over the wire on to my crops and then they broke up everything. I lost the lot: the wire, the bananas, the cane, the manioc, every single thing that had been planted there. I complained and the man said that they would pay compensation, but I never heard another word. I lost it all for good and to this day I've never been back there. But I didn't move out as they wanted. I started to open up a clearing elsewhere.

Pedro Alves da Costa, known as Pedro Cego (Blind Pedro), gave us a full account of events in Santa Teresinha after Codeara's arrival. When he was 15, he had been playing with a bright, colourful object without knowing that it was an explosive. It had blown up in his face, leaving him blind and unable to work of the *roça* with the rest of his family. As a result, he had developed other skills. He has an excellent memory and has become a kind of unofficial archivist for the people of Santa Teresinha. He is a good musician and earns his living by playing the accordion at parties. He had come to Santa Teresinha in 1957 with his father, Joaquim da Mata (Joaquim of the Forest) and his five brothers and sisters. He told us how they got their *roça*:

When we arrived here my father and the rest of us worked for other people for two months, because we arrived without any resources; the little money we had we paid out for our journey on the boat. We helped to harvest rice: for every three sacks harvested, we earned one. We also made manioc flour, for which they would give us half shares: if we made two sackfuls, we would earn one and the other would be for the landowner.

Then these people, the company, who had cleared land to plant some coffee, had a young employee. They had let him clear his own plot on their land for nothing and they had let him have a lot of things on credit. He couldn't pay so in the end the company took over his *roça*, already cleared and burnt, instead of payment. The owner then asked my father if he would like this *roça*, to take it over in exchange for some of his produce, and my father said yes he would, that that's what his profession had always been. Then the man said, 'Well, you can plant then and consider this to be your property. If ever the land here is sold, you keep this plot for yourself. It's your land, because no one has any land here yet. We're trying out this plantation here, but we're not yet the owners of this land.' They were from São Paulo and only had a small farm, but then they fell out with each other and went away, leaving all the coffee shoots which went to ruin for they were never planted out.

We're still in the same place after 20 years. We only moved the house because we'd planted a lot of fruit trees and the orange trees were too close, so the place became too shady and we built a new house.

In 1967 a group of labourers from Codeara made two camps near our house and another one further on, in a *roça* of ours. Then they started clearing everything in our *roça*, levelling everything we'd planted: manioc, beans, bananas, cane, cotton, the lot was cut down. When my father saw what they were up to, he went and complained, but they said that they were just obeying the ranch's orders. My father said: 'But look, if you're working for the ranch, they contracted you to clear the forest, but this bit here is already planted, it isn't forest, I planted it. I refuse to let you clear land here.' Then they said that he had to go and sort it out with the manager.

My father went off to talk to the manager, at that time Rubião, who said: 'We bought this land and we can't stop doing this job because of half a dozen peasants who happening to be living in the middle.' He told all the labourers to go on clearing the land.

The peasants held a meeting to discuss the situation, which was going to affect them all sooner or later, and decided to go and talk to the labourers to ask them to stop destroying the *roças* as, after all, they were mainly from peasant families themselves and would want a *roça* of their own one day. For more than 30 days, about 150 labourers effectively went on strike, and the clearing of the peasants' *roças* stopped. But the company retaliated by contracting more labourers, bringing in boatload after boatload.

The company also called in the police and accused the peasant families of being 'invaders'. The regional police delegate, accompanied by two soldiers, came by boat from São Félix but failed to sort out the dispute. The peasant families asked the advice of Jentel who told them to keep united, as that was the only way in which they would achieve some strength, and to make sure that they did not do anything illegal. Meantime, he embarked on the first of a long series of trips to see lawyers and government officials to see whether a solution could be found.

Early on he won an important round in the battle. He obtained a signed document from Miguel Nasser in Campo Grande in which he stated that he had sold the land to Codeara with a 5,000-hectare reserve for the village and local residents. This strongly suggested that Codeara had no right to interfere in the running of the little town of Santa Teresinha, at least. And, as Jentel pointed out to the peasant families, even if Nasser had sold some of the land occupied by the peasant families to Codeara, the latter still had a strong legal claim to ownership under the *lei do usucapião*.

According to Edival dos Reis, to whom we talked in January 1979, Codeara in the beginning tacitly admitted that the peasant families had some legal rights, for it made some effort to accommodate their needs. He told us that Codeara held a meeting in October 1967 at which it offered the peasant families new plots about 25 kilometres away on the other side of Morro de Areia. The peasants decided to turn down the offer, because they wanted to remain close to the village and to the river, which was important to them for marketing their crop surpluses and as a source of fish. Furthermore, they did not believe that the company was offering adequate compensation for the land they had already cleared, their houses, the fruit trees they had planted and so on.

As no agreement had been reached, labourers began to clear the *roças* once again in November 1967. Once again, the ranch chose to invade Joaquim da Mata's plot. His son, Blind Pedro, took up the story:

When we stopped the labourers from working the other time, they had cleared the land as far as our house there. The company was angry about what my father had done before so this second time, when they sent the labourers back to our house, they sent the police in with them. My father heard them working away in the middle of the forest and went to have a look. Though he didn't do anything, they arrested him, because, they said, he had held up the work that other time and he wasn't the owner of the land. So my father said that he'd stopped their work because they were destroying everything he had planted there. It would have been different, he said, if they had only cut down forest, but they'd gone on to his *roça* and cut down his sugarcane, cotton, anything that was his. 'And I won't accept it', he said. 'I have the right of possession as a peasant farmer and I won't accept it.' So they arrested my father, and they went to our house and arrested one of my brothers, a boy still, only 14 years old. They took my father to Luciara where he spent nine days in prison. He had a really bad time there because he was ill. He had flu, with a fever, and was sleeping on that cold cement floor. He even started to have asthma. Ever since then he complained about his asthma and when he died he was still complaining about it.

The pressure from Codeara continued, not only in the forest but in the village itself. Dona Juvenilha Pereira da Silva, who, with her large family, had been living in Santa Teresinha since 1960, told us what happened to them in November and December 1967:

Life was really dangerous. They knocked down my hosue – it wasn't the police but Codeara that destroyed it. At that time I lived by the river and they knocked down four houses in our street and burnt down another house opposite. Then we lived in an awful little shack. They gave us 600 cruzeiros in compensation which was nothing, for it was a lovely place. Within two months there wasn't a cruzeiro left. All the children were with us then for only one had married.

Towards the end of that year, some of Chicão's donkeys wandered on to Codeara's lands to graze and were rounded up with the ranch's animals. Chicão went into the ranch's corral without asking permission and retrieved his animals. He was arrested by the police. Chicão told us what happened:

They threatened me and then arrested me. They seized me on Thursday and let me go on Saturday. I was taken to Luciara. Just because some of my donkeys had been put in the corral, so I'd gone and taken them. They arrested me because I'd taken them without asking. They were mine, so why should I have asked permission to take what was mine?

Though Chicão was not keen to give us the details, some of his neighbours told us, laughing, that Chicão had lost his temper and had begun to punch one of the policemen. Another policeman, they said, had taken a pot shot at Chicão, but had hit the first policeman's foot instead. Chicão had been beaten up as a result, but had eventually been released.

In January 1968, the conflict between Joaquim da Mata and Codeara flared up again. Blind Pedro told us what happened after his father had been released from prison:

> When he got back, he went to put up a fence around our yard because he'd lost some of his pigs that had gone off to graze on the ranch's grass. He bought the wire and all and when he'd finished the people at the ranch got to know about it and sent over the police to arrest him again. They said that he had no right to put up the fence because the land wasn't his. But they didn't find him. They came to our house and talked to my mother who said he'd gone away. They said that he was obstinate, that they would arrest him later and really beat him up. They said that they were going over to the ranch, there and then, to fetch the tractor and knock down the fence, that it had been a waste of time putting it up in the first place. They went off, fetched the tractor, drove it over the wire, knocked down the whole fence. They kept on saying that the day my father arrived home, they would take him. My father hid at his sister Josefa's house for a few days.

After knocking down Joaquim da Mata's fence, Codeara put up its own fences right across the tracks leading to the peasants' plots. It was the first time that the ranch had taken measures to stop all the peasant families from farming their plots. José Leandro de Macedo, known locally as Zé Piauí, one of the most outspoken and militant of the peasants, helped organise the peasants' reaction to this act to provocation. His plot was situated on land claimed by Tapiraguaia, not Codeara, so we asked him, when we were in Santa Teresinha for the first time in November 1976, how he had got involved:

> I moved to Tapiraguaia mountains after Codeara arrived, because my old *roça* was worn out and they wouldn't let us clear any more land. But no sooner had I finished clearing a *roça* then this other company, the Tapiraguaia, arrived and said that they were the owners.
>
> I can't live without eating, so I have to work on the *roça* whoever's land it's on, even if they kill me, so I did my planting there and there I am to this day. It's been really hard. My fight's really with Tapiraguaia, not with Codeara, but Father Francisco told us everyone had to unite, those fighting Tapiraguaia with those fighting Codeara, to defend our rights, because what happens here today will happen there tomorrow or later. And I wanted to be united with them, because if they lost, we'd lose, as we were on our own, but if they won, we would too.

Zé Piauí had this to say about the events of January 1968:

Then Codeara attacked the whole village, they surrounded it with wire and came to say that nobody could go in or out any more. Codeara put up the wire and parts of it are still there today, but we cut the wire, it was me who started it. I lived on the other side of the village so I used to have to come through the village on the way to my *roça*. I could get to my *roça* without going through the village, but it put another half league [about 3 kilometres] on my walk. They put the wire up just to annoy people, so I came with my big knife and cut the wire and then went off to my *roça*.

Three days later, the news went round that they were going to arrest me there where I was hidden with Zé Fala Fino [José Fine Talk, the son of Joaquim da Mata] and Luiz, the three of us. A man came and warned me that the police were coming to arrest me, to castrate me! So I went off to this other neighbour's and warned him, for the man had told me that the police thought that he had cut the wire too. And I said to him: 'We too are going to be arrested, castrated. Let's go home and wait for the men to castrate us there!' So I brought him back and we spent the night at my home. I bought a box of bangers and we hid them in the road so that they would go off when the police trod on them so we would know and could wait in a trench we built. But when they came as far as some caves near here, they sent word back that they hadn't found us. They were really afraid, they only came so far and then went back. Six days went by and nobody came, so I went and called on Joaquim da Mata, the one who's dead now, his son José Fala Fino, Big Luiz and his brother-in-law and others. We got 21 men together and we waited. 'Here we're going to defend our rights, everyone has rights here and is a worker', we said. I told Father Francisco that we meant serious business and that we were going to sort it all out, once and for all. We waited another two days and still nobody from the ranch showed up, just news that they'd come today, they'd come tomorrow – but they never came.

Fearful of reprisals, the peasant families began to work more closely together, not only to defend themselves, but also to carry out farming tasks. The friendship and the trust which were built up during this period were very important during a later phase of the conflict. They worked together on Zé Piauí's *roça* and then they all went to Joaquim da Mata's home to help him put up his fence again. His son, Blind Pedro, took up the story:

My father sent a message to the manager, saying that he'd come home again, that he was putting up the fence again and that he didn't want them to knock it down any more, that they should note that he was only fencing in his own land, not anyone else's, and that he could only keep his animals in if he closed off his land.

The manager took this to be an outrage and sent for the police again, from Luciara and São Félix. Someone warned us and everyone was afraid. A lot of men had come to help with the fence so they all stayed together at our house. No one came, but we heard that the ranch had sent a radio message to Cuiabá saying that we were planning to attack the ranch from Santa Teresinha. It was a lie.

Then the secretary of public security, Colonel José de Menezes, came to Santa Teresinha. The Colonel said that he'd come because Codeara was asking every day for police reinforcements, saying that the village was building up a stock of weapons to attack the ranch. He went from house to house and thought it very peculiar as nothing like this was happening at all. Then the Colonel said that he wanted to see the men, as he'd come to sort out all this business, that he'd come to fix things up in peace, that there wasn't going to be any of this prison business or anything like that. So then Father Francisco sent a message to our house to find out where the men were, so we told him that they were all at our place. The Colonel and Father Francisco went there and my father explained, properly, how it had all happened and the Colonel invited everyone to a meeting in Santa Teresinha with the people from the ranch to decide what should be done. So everyone had a meeting. The Colonel said that the ranch had been wrong to knock down the fence. 'I saw with my own eyes that he'd only fenced in his own crops', said the Colonel. He gave the order that my father should put up the fence. He even gave his address and said that, if anything should happen, it was just a matter of writing to him. It seemed that everything was being sorted out. This was in '68, around January. All the families went back to working on their *roças* again.

Colonel Menezes made a thorough investigation. He talked and, perhaps more important, he listened to all concerned. Though Codeara had accused the peasant families of 'subversive activities' and of building up an arsenal of Czech weapons, he only found one Czech weapon among the frontiersmen's hunting weapons. It was a .22 rifle, manufactured before 1947, so it could hardly be seen as evidence of 'communist infiltration'. Menezes publicly backed the peasant families in their claims and is believed to have privately warned the local police force not to carry on siding with the ranch.

Thanks in part to Jentel's persistent efforts, help also appeared to be coming from another source at this time. Since 1967, Jentel had been making trips, mostly to Brasília, to try to bring the conflict to the attention of people in IBRA (the Brazilian Institute for Agrarian Reform, the forerunner of INCRA), the SNI (the intelligence service), the federal police, federal ministries and even the President of the Republic. As early as 12 April 1967, at Jentel's request Bishop Tomás Balduíno, of Conceição do Araguaia, had sent a long report to President Arthur da Costa e Silva in which he outlined the history of Santa Teresinha and made the following proposals for the solution of its problems:

(a) the creation of the district of Santa Teresinha with its respective urban area under the jurisdiction of the mayor of Luciara;

(b) the concession of land titles to the residents and to the peasant families registered by IBRA;

(c) the expropriation of a further 10,000 ha. of land for colonization;

(d)   the land to be chosen and the colonization project to be organized by
       the cooperative and not by the government, and the plan to be duly
       submitted to the competent government organ.

On 29 November President Costa e Silva finally forwarded this report to
the minister of agriculture, Ivo Arzua Pereira, with a covering note in which
he requested the rapid implementation of the proposals. The matter was
referred to IBRA as a question of 'the greatest urgency' on 4 December of
the same year, almost a full nine months after Bishop Tomás Balduíno had
sent in his report. Even then, despite the President's request, the matter was
subjected to further long delays in the quagmire of government bureaucracy.
However, probably because Colonel Menezes alerted it to the deteriorating
situation, IBRA finally sent in a team in February 1968. They showed the
peasant families which plots of farming land were theirs and promised to
provide titles.
    Confident that they would enjoy a long period of peace, the peasant
families recommenced work. With Jentel's encouragement, they continued
to work collectively, not now because they were afraid to work alone, but as
an expression of their increasing unity and solidarity. They put particular
effort into a new collective *roça* which they had opened on land recognised
as theirs by IBRA.

Conflict in the Village

However, the peace proved short lived. In a serious oversight, IBRA had
taken no measures to solve the dispute over the urban area of Santa
Teresinha. Codeara drew up its own urbanisation plan for which it received
authorisation from the mayor of Luciara, José de Barros Lima. Amazingly,
this plan, which it presented to the land registration office in Barra do
Garças, had been drawn up as if the land were unoccupied, without any sort
of community, let alone one with more than 1,000 inhabitants. It was
illegal, for all the town plans had to show existing houses, fences, farm land,
roads and other works.
    In March 1969, Codeara tried to persuade the peasant families to sign a
document in which they would admit to being 'invaders' and promise to
vacate their urban plots in exchange for others, 15 metres by 33 metres, to
be donated by the company. After consulting Jentel, the peasants refused to
sign. In reprisal, on 14 April, some gunmen, led by the then ranch manager,
Solomão Proence dos Santos, accompanied by the assistant manager and
the company topographer, invaded several houses in the centre of Santa
Teresinha. Edival dos Reis, already considered by the company to be one of
the leaders of the peasant families, had his fence knocked down. This
particular confrontation was brought to an abrupt end by the unexpected
arrival of federal police officers. Paradoxically, they had been sent in after
Codeara had complained about the peasant families' refusal to collaborate

in its 'official' urbanisation plan, but the ranch was clearly embarrassed at having being caught red-handed using violence against the local inhabitants.

Codeara pushed ahead with its plan, despite the problems. It began to sell urban lots, at Crs 1,300 (£124) each, on the outskirts of the village. After great pressure, a few of the families sold out to Codeara, though they were paid paltry sums in compensation. The urbanisation plan is still in evidence today in the larger lots and wider streets beyond the village centre. Many of the inhabitants agree that the plan as such was not without its merits for those areas that were then uninhabited.

However, the violent destruction of property and the terrorisation of the local population made the good points in the plan irrelevant to the inhabitants. While concentrating their efforts on the urban plots, Codeara still sent gunmen out to the *roças*. It was at this time that Jentel made his special trip to Conceição do Araguaia to consult Paulo Botelho de Almeida Prado, the São Paulo lawyer who had come to the Amazon to administer a Sudam ranch but, deeply shocked by what he had seen, had stayed to provide legal assistance to peasant families and labourers.

Both men were passionate defenders of justice, who wished only to see the law enforced. When we spoke to Dr Paulo – as he was known throughout the region – it was evident that an immediate bond had sprung up between the two men. Dr Paulo told us that Jentel had been very anxious to know whether peasant families had the legal right to resort to violence to prevent themselves from being evicted. Dr Paulo had replied that only the authorities had to right to carry out evictions and that, if a landowner was attempting illegally to evict a family, then that family had the right to use force, not only to prevent its eviction, but also to regain possession of its plot if it had been unable to prevent the eviction. The law did not demand that the peasant family had the legal title to its land, he had added.

When talking to us, Dr Paulo pulled down a thick tome from one of the shelves in his simple wattle-and-daub hut and showed us the relevant article in the civil code. He said that he had done the same with Jentel who, like us, had copied the article down in his notebook. The article read:

> The perturbed or evicted dweller can use his own force to maintain possession or reinstate himself, provided he acts quickly. Acts of defence or reinstatement cannot go beyond the minimum indispensable for maintenance or restoration of possession.[3]

Confident of the legality of the peasants' actions, Jentel stepped up his campaign. In April he and Reis wrote joint letters of protest to the agriculture minister, the director of the state police, the justice minister and the president of the SNI, having written to the President in February. Chicão told us: 'Father Francisco did not want us to fight. He always said that we'd got to get the law to help us.' Reis told us that he had had to help Jentel with the letters, because his written Portuguese contained errors and because he tended to be too outspoken and honest, 'too objective', as Reis put it. 'I knew much better what *not* to say', he explained.

Another bone of contention was the collective *roça*. Though IBRA had told the peasant families that this land was theirs, it had provided them with no land title and Codeara refused to accept IBRA's judgement. In June 1969, it took the peasants to court with the help of its new, astute lawyer, Olímpio Jaime, whose skill in obtaining court injunctions to evict peasant families was already well known in the region. The judge in Barra do Garças duly gave a judgement in Codeara's favour without so much as consulting IBRA, and instructed the families to hand over the collective *roça* to Codeara. Jentel immediately wrote to the justice minister to ask for the suspension of the judgement so that IBRA could be consulted. In October 1969, the federal government overruled the earlier judgement and sent in IBRA to demarcate the land in the name of the peasant families. Delighted that at last they had achieved by peaceful methods the victory that Jentel had long hoped for, the families recommenced work on the land which had by then been given the nickname of *roça da confusão* (confusion *roça*).

Codeara, however, was not content to accept this decision, particularly as the courts had earlier decided in its favour. In January 1970 the company sent in bulldozers to destroy the crops on the *roça da confusão*. It was clear that to dare to undertake such an act of aggression Codeara had won the backing of a powerful sector of the government. This initiative had been favoured by important political changes at a national level, for at the end of August 1969, President Costa e Silva had been replaced by a tough military junta, which in its turn had handed over power to the hard-liner, General Emílio Garrastazu Médici. Codeara had leapfrogged the specialist government bodies, such as IBRA, and had alerted the top military leaders to Jentel's 'subversive' activities. From then onwards, Codeara skilfully used the spectre of 'communist infiltration' to win the government over to its side in its battle against the peasant families. Its task was made easier by the replacement of Colonel Menezes at the Mato Grosso department of public security by Colonel José Ferreira Diniz, who showed little of his predecessor's objectivity and accessibility.

Many of the peasant families spoke to us of the particular animosity shown by Codeara to Jentel. Chicão said to us:

> When Father Francisco lived with us, the company harassed him. It didn't want him to make any progress for us. Everything the Father did it destroyed. When the Father was paving the road with stones to harden the ground, the company sent in a tractor to ruin it. The Father got everyone to open up a large *roça*, then just when it was full of manioc, it sent in its tractor to ruin it again. Codeara arrived, but it didn't ask, 'Are you the owner here?' No, it just sent its men straight in.

In 1970 Codeara began a careful campaign against Jentel and Edival dos Reis, whom they began to consider almost as important a leader and instigator as Jentel. Olímpio Jaime, Codeara's lawyer, drew up a report in which he claimed that, not only Jentel and Reis, but also Tadeu and Teresinha, a young couple who had recently arrived in Santa Teresinha as lay workers, were subversives. He is said to have suggested that they were working together to establish, little by little, a base for a rural guerrilla offensive and that they were linked to the urban guerrilla groups which were active at that time in the south of the country. In this report, which was later sent to top members of the federal government, Jaime said that he felt it his duty to alert the government to the danger to national security that this initiative represented, while at the same time stressing Codeara's willingness to make concessions to the real peasant families in the region. He said that Codeara was so anxious to resolve the conflict that it was willing to donate to the mayor of Luciara a large area that could be used to create a new and well-planned Santa Teresinha. Codeara's only condition, he said, was that the peasant families handed over their present plots, both in the village and in the countryside, and accepted new areas.

The report was discussed at a private meeting held at Suiá-Missu ranch on 1 May between the interior minister, General José Costa Cavalcanti, the governor of the state of Mato Grosso, José Fragelli, the Mato Grosso secretary for public security, Colonel José Ferreira Diniz, the president of Sudam, General Bandeira Coelho and several businessmen with interests in the region, including Codeara director Luiz Gonzaga Murat and Ariosto da Riva. The participants at the meeting are reported to have expressed their support in principle for Codeara and their concern at the danger that Jentel and the lay workers represented for national security. This expression of solidarity was to have very important consequences, for, by ringing the alarm bells at this early stage, Codeara was later in a very strong position to claim that a small group of subversives was behind any conflict. At the same time, members of the government at the meeting requested Codeara to take care to avoid any open confrontation with the peasant families because of the negative repercussions among the general public. Colonel Diniz was also authorised to take whatever measures he considered necessary to maintain law and order in the region.

On the following day several of those at the meeting, including the interior minister, the governor of Mato Grosso, the president of Sudam and Gonzaga Murat, attended the official opening of Codeara's hospital. Colonel Diniz began his offensive against Jentel that very morning. He arrested Reis and took him to Cuiabá where he was held for 72 days without being charged. Reis told us that he was well treated and even made friends with some of his guards. He was eventually released for lack of evidence.

Though the scene was now set for the later conflict, no immediate confrontation occurred and an uneasy peace settled on Santa Teresinha. Mindful of the government's request to avoid bloodshed, Codeara continued with its tactics of attrition without outright violence. It constantly harassed the peasant families by sending in employees to warn them of what could happen if they insisted on 'illegally' occupying the land and offering them small sums in compensation if they left. At the same time, it pushed ahead quietly with its urbanisation project.

Slave Camps in the Forest

The plight of the labourers on Codeara ranch was brought to the attention of the public during this period. On 3 August 1970, the *O Globo* newspaper in Rio de Janeiro reported that the federal police were investigating allegations that a ranch in Santa Teresinha was running a 'forced labour camp'. It said that a young labourer had managed to escape from the ranch and, after spending 20 days in the jungle fleeing from a group of gunmen who had been sent in to capture him, he had arrived in Brasília, about 1,700 kilometres away. He had then got in contact with the federal police to tell them of the hundreds of labourers who were being held like slaves in the forest.

O Globo, which has very good contacts with the authorities and often reflects official thinking, then continued:

> This is not the first time a forced labour camp has been reported to the federal police. Other camps in Mato Grosso have already been dismantled by the federal police. On each occasion the federal police has acted with efficiency, but until now it has kept its activity a close secret so as to avoid distortion of the facts by the international press which, instead of showing that the Brazilian authorities are moving swiftly to put an end to these camps where the workers live in real slavery, attempts to show the negative side of the problem to international public opinion.[4]

At first sight, it may seem strange that the federal police should choose to publicise their investigation into conditions on Codeara shortly after the ranch's directors had won the tacit support of the authorities in their struggle against the peasant families. The paradox is largely to be explained by the tensions between the various government bodies. Codeara had won the backing of leading Mato Grosso state bodies, along with the federal government's interior ministry. But the federal police, which had been called in on several occasions – and had even witnessed acts of aggression by Codeara employees – had been excluded from the talks. The federal police may thus have acted partly out of vindictiveness. But it is also true that they are widely regarded by the peasant families to be much more honest and open-minded than the local police and the military police. So they may have been barred from the earlier meeting because the other participants believed that they would not be sympathetic to the discussions.

The federal police began their investigation on 8 August. A group of police agents, accompanied by the young labourer, travelled to Codeara and ordered the ranch to release about 500 workers who were being held as virtual prisoners in the jungle. The police then heard the evidence of about 400 people and concluded that this was the most serious case of semi-slavery that it had ever investigated. On 16 February 1971 it sent in its report to the department of federal justice. Though no charges were ever made against Codeara, parts of the report were leaked to the press and caused the ranch considerable embarrassment. The following is a summary of the main findings in the report, as given in the press.

In 1970, Codeara was employing about 1,200 men, most of whom had been brought into the ranch by *gatos*. Because the ranch could only be reached by river or air, the labourers remained isolated from the outside world and were not even provided with transport to visit Santa Teresinha. None of the temporary labourers had work contracts. They earned about Crs 7 (50p) a day, or Crs 230 (£16.40) for each *alqueire* (4.84 hectares) of jungle they cleared. Payment was not made directly to the labourers, but to the *gatos* who deducted transport costs – it took three months to pay back the fare if they had been brought in by plane.

The labourers could only buy food supplies at the company store and their purchases of rice, beans and dried meat were controlled by the *gatos* who then made further deductions from their wages. The labourers never knew how much they had earned or spent, especially as accounts were not settled when they moved on to a new work front in the malaria-infested forest. The labourers were generally working at least 30 kilometres from the village and did not usually receive any medical treatment when they fell ill, though it was estimated that about 70 per cent contracted malaria during the time they spent at the ranch. If they were lucky, they were provided with medicines by Codeara's hospital staff, but inflated prices were then charged for the remedies, leading to further heavy deductions from their wages. It was for this reason that the labourers themselves made little effort to obtain medical treatment unless it was a case of life or death.

Armed guards watched over the forest trails. They hunted down any labourers who attempted to escape and either shot them dead as a warning to the others or forced them to return to the work front after a beating. Many labourers claimed to have been 'barbarously beaten'. It was not known how many had died, either from malaria and other diseases, or from work accidents, or from the gunmen's bullets. There were rumours (still repeated today) of cemeteries deep in the jungle, some of the graves containing more than one corpse.

If the labourers survived the hardship, illness and violence and had anything at all left after the deductions, the *gatos* gave them coupons, to be redeemed against the *gatos*' own accounts with the company. Not infrequently, however, Codeara refused to give the *gato* further credit and sent the labourers away with nothing. It was common for labourers to be caught in a web of indebtedness and be forced to work on indefinitely with little hope of breaking out of the vicious circle of debts. In these conditions, the labourers were often willing to risk their lives in a hazardous attempt to escape.

At the end of 1971, Bishop Pedro Casaldáliga, who had been deeply shocked by what he had seen during the three years he had spent in the north of Mato Grosso, published a book about life in his diocese. He spoke to labourers from many of the ranches in the area, including Codeara. The following are extracts of his findings from conversations with Codeara labourers:

— José Borges, resident of São Félix, in his early twenties, recently married, fell ill while working in the forest for Codeara. He was carried in a hammock by his friends for several days, but he died, without receiving any treatment from those in charge of the ranch.[5]

— Honofre Pires – 32 years old, from Goiânia – was 'tricked', he said, by the labour contractor Riverino, of São Miguel do Araguaia. He went to Codeara in January [1971] and left in July. He cleared 25 *alqueires* of forest. Ill with malaria, he managed to escape from the camp and walked for 22 leagues [132 kilometres], seven of them without a drop of water. When he reached São Félix, he was a skeleton. He had a heart attack and was taken by motor-boat to the Indian hospital on Bananal Island where Dr Sanchez saved his life by giving him a transfusion of his own blood.[6]

— Antônio Pedro Santos – 23 years old, from Natal, Rio Grande do Norte – arrived at our [i.e. the Bishop's] house on 8 August. He broke into tears. He had come from Codeara, where he had been working for 60 days. João Gerente [João the manager] had contracted Antônio and 49 other labourers in Santa Helena in the south of Goiás. They had caught a plane in Gurupi. As usual, they had been forced to work for 90 days to pay back the plane fare. Antônio had worked for 60 days and then had caught 'fever' – malaria – and had asked permission to leave. This was not given and he had been obliged to work for another 30 days to pay off his debt for the fare.

No adequate assistance is given at Codeara. The chemists, Ari and Chiquinho, are tipplers of *pinga* [cheap white rum].

Antônio spoke of the way the labourers were persecuted. He said that on Sunday, 12 July, he and another 12 labourers had fled. The *capangas* and *jaguncos* [both words for gunmen] had gone after them. One of the labourers, an old man, had a .20 calibre gun, their only weapon. The *jaguncos* attacked them. Ari shot at the old man with the gun and he had shot back, wounding Ari. Then all the *jaguncos* had opened fire. Three of the labourers, including Antônio, fell into a trap – tripping over a creeper laid across their path – and were caught. They were barbarously beaten. Antônio showed his scars.

Says Antônio: 'It's a butcher's shop in that jungle.'[7]

— Claudio Borges, from Paraiba, married with two small children, shows two gun wounds. He received them on Codeara ranch. One from João Gerente. It went through his chest to his back. 'I had such a high fever. It was Saturday. I really couldn't work. So João Gerente shot me with a .38 . . . The other shot was with a .22.' He knows of 100 or so men buried on the Codeara ranch. João Gerente once said to a labourer: 'I don't kill men standing up. Squat on all fours, like a cat.' The man did what he was told and then was shot. Another colleague, killed by the ranch's gunmen, was not buried. 'We passed close by him on our way to work, with that terrible smell. We had to throw banana leaves on top of the corpse . . .'[8]

— João, 33 years old, from Colina, went to Codeara with his wife and six-month-old son. He was taken then by a *gato* and suffered all kinds of humiliation. Seeing that he was likely to die, he decided to leave as soon as he could and he sold his things to his colleagues. He ended up with only the clothes on his back. He, his wife and his child, were waiting for the boat for two days, in the sun and without food. His wife with fever. 'I was due to receive Crs 500 (£35). It went to settle accounts with João Gerente. He promised to pay me the following Saturday . . .' On the Saturday, when he went for his pay, João Gerente told him: 'I don't owe you anything. If you persist, you'll get a whipping.'

35 men had come with him to Codeara, of whom 15 had already died. He himself said: 'I'm not afraid of the hunger, but of dying from disease in the jungle. It's horrible. You die forgotten, burning with fever and knowing that you will be buried like the others without a coffin, and that your family will never know what happened to you.'[8]

— One young man from São Félix, profoundly shocked, told me that he had seen some of the labourers, some of them married, with children, weeping on the banks of the Araguaia, in Santa Teresinha, and asking for pity's sake to be given the boat fare so that they could get far away from the companies.[10]

The labourers said that they were badly treated, not only by the gunmen, but also by the ranch's ordinary employees, including managers and medical staff. In its report, the federal police singled out the following people as responsible for the worst treatment: João de Paula Siqueira, known as João Gerente, who hid in the jungle when the police visited the ranch; Luis Sales de Oliveira, known as Luisão, who had been accused of many murders; and Salomão Proence dos Santos, who had been manager until June 1970 when he was succeeded by José Norberto Silveira. The latter is considered by the labourers to be 'less inhuman' because he removed some of the guards and thus made it easier for them to escape.

After parts of the police report had been leaked to the press, journalists interviewed the São Paulo directors of Codeara – Murat, Seixas and Conde. They all denied any knowledge of, or responsibility for, events on the ranch. Explaining that they only looked after the technical and administrative side of the company, they referred the journalists to their representatives on the ranch who, they claimed, were solely responsible for the recruitment of workers.

The 'Battle of the Pharmacy'

Codeara continued its attempts to wear down the peasant families in 1971. Though it avoided direct confrontation, it tried to stop the peasant families working on their *roças* and pushed ahead with its urbanisation project, selling lots and offering small sums in compensation to the families who would agree to leave the village and build new houses in the forest. Though Jentel and most of the peasant families continued to oppose Codeara's plans for the centre, they accepted its claim to own and to sell the unoccupied land on the outskirts of the village.

Blind Pedro explained what it was like:

> The ranch kept on sending in new people, to abuse the local inhabitants and to tell them to stop work on their *roças*. It went on and on in just the same way . . . I think that they did this on purpose to provoke a fight, to see if they could gain the upper hand in this way. Then they divided up the village into lots. People said that Codeara had bought the land from the local council, had divided it up and was now selling it. Father Francisco went to speak to the manager. He said that he needed three lots. He already had one for the cooperative, but he needed two more, one for the pharmacy and one for the school. The company said that it would sell the lots he needed but told him that it was not giving any legal document. He was offered a little bit of paper, knocked out on a typewriter, but it was nothing official. Father Francisco said 'no', he wasn't buying like this. He had the money to pay, but he wanted the whole thing legalised. They said no.
>
> So Father Francisco bought a house from a family which wanted to leave because of this whole business. It was a good site which he decided to use for the pharmacy. Father Francisco decided to knock down the old building and make a bigger one, but Codeara said no, they wouldn't let him. Father Francisco said that the plot was his and that he wasn't doing anything on the ranch's land. Well, can you believe it, he started on the building and the ranch went with its bulldozer and knocked down what he had built, choosing a time when he wasn't there. It was the manager who sent the bulldozer in. The men grabbed hold of Salvador (who was looking after the site), cuffed him, took away the camera he had brought with him to take some pictures and broke it.

The demolition took place on 10 February 1972. Codeara claimed that the pharmacy – in fact, to be a combined chemist's shop and clinic – would not fit in with its plans for a new street, even though it was being built on the foundations of the previous house. Jentel sent a letter of protest to the judge at Barra do Garças. He also got in touch with his superior, Bishop Pedro Casaldáliga, who gave him his full support and told him to instruct the labourers to resume work.

The company again tried to hold up the construction, even obtaining a court order from the local judge to halt work for three days. However, Jentel and the villagers were not to be deterred. They were determined to set up the pharmacy, which was desperately needed as the town had no proper medical centre.

It was gradually becoming clear to the villagers that the whole future of Santa Teresinha was at stake in this apparently minor confrontation. If they backed down on this issue, Codeara would take advantage of the breach in their defences and push ahead with its whole plan. And, if they let Codeara take control of the planning of the little town, it would clearly dominate all future developments.

Zé Piauí told us of the firm support the villagers received from the church when they took the decision to dig in their heels:

> Bishop Pedro came here and said: 'You mustn't lose courage . . . We must win the battle of this village.' Father Francisco called round again and told me that we must go on another of those 'strikes' because that house of his really belonged to everybody and we must defend the village. So I said: 'Let's all meet up there on the day they are planning to come and knock down the house again and stop them.' So we got together on 3 March, some 36 of us, all armed.

Blind Pedro carried on the story:

> The people at the site knew that the people from the ranch were tough. They'd already come once and beaten up the man looking after the building. So they prepared themselves. They cut themselves small wooden clubs.

That afternoon, three company vehicles drove into Santa Teresinha, bringing two captains and five soldiers from the military police, José Norberto Silveira and 10 or 12 armed employees from the ranch. Elypídio Florenço Rocha, one of the peasant farmers at the site, described what happened then:

> The Codeara lot came at about four o'clock in the afternoon . . . We were expecting them and were ready. We had built trenches in the ground and most of us went in them, while I and some others stayed inside the half-built house.

Piauí went on:

> At three o'clock, they arrived. They were going to knock the house down. They came in a van to arrest everybody first. Only after doing that would they come in with their bulldozer. In the beginning, the ones inside the building were at risk. They ran and the police ran after them to catch them and tie them up. Big Silveira and the others from the ranch surrounded the house so that they could round us up if we were inside.

Elypídio continued:

> We'd put wire across the entrance of the building, because they had always said that wire had to be 'respected' – Codeara puts up fences across other people's plots and then says that 'justice' means 'respecting the wire'. So we put up the wire in front of the building to show it was ours and that anyone who entered was an invader, just as they'd claimed we were invaders.

252

As we'd arranged, the builders all left the site as soon as they arrived and the police went after them. And then Silveira crossed the wire, went in and, standing there, beat his chest and said: 'You said I wouldn't come, didn't you? Well, I'm here!' And then all the others crossed the wire – and the shooting started. Shots flew out from all sides, in all directions.

Zé Piauí said:

When they got near us, we were already sending bullets – it was us who started. The policemen let go of the men they'd caught and came back, but it was too late. They ended up with seven wounded on their side, while we had none.

The police had come with an order to arrest Jentel and some of the peasant farmers who had been accused, yet again, of being invaders and infringing the national security law. As the police had not been directly involved in the shooting, all the wounded men, two of whom later died, were ranch employees. Silveira himself had been hit. By this time, the company was convinced that it was facing an armed uprising.

The policemen and ranch employees withdrew, to fetch reinforcements. Zé Piauí told us what the peasant farmers did:

We stayed there until nightfall. Then we left our position and went over to the Father's house, to spend the night there. Father Canuto arrived and suggested that it would be better if we all left because more police might arrive and things would get worse. So we left. We hurried to the *roça* and we stayed there.

The 'Persecution'

The next day two Brazilian air force Búfalo aircraft brought in Colonel José Ferreira Diniz and about 80 military policemen who began to hunt down the male peasants – all of them, not just the 36 involved in the shooting. Most of the men in Santa Teresinha fled, the peasant farmers into the forest and Edival dos Reis and Jentel to Brasília. More than 100 peasants hid in the jungle for 105 days, while many of those who had decided not to flee, because they had not been directly involved in the incident, were arrested.

Zé Piauí told us what happened:

The day after the shooting the Búfalos arrived with a hundred or so policemen, to get us. Someone told them where we were so they went there. I'd already made a trench so we could defend ourselves. But as there were only four of us in that part of the forest we took to our heels. I arranged with my wife, if they came to our house, to say that I was on the other side of Bananal Island, so that they would go in the opposite direction to us. We hid in the forest. They next day they did go to my house. One of my wife's brothers-in-law was there and, though he had had nothing to do with it, they arrested him straightaway. His name was Valdo Ferreira Tito, known as Maroto. They took him to Cuiabá and he spent more than a month in prison there.

So then I went to warn the others that the whole business was really dangerous. Altair [the local school-teacher] and I went to the Tapirapé river where there were some people hidden. There were more than a hundred people because, though there were only 36 in the fighting, everyone had scattered. They were picking up anyone who was a peasant farmer. They weren't choosy. They wanted to get me, to kill me, because they said I was the leader of the fighting; I was the commander, they said.

Later I went with two companions to harvest rice on one of the *roças*. There was a girl at the house, so we said to her: 'If the police come here, you warn us so we can get away'. When the police came, Altair by bad luck was at the house. They took him straightaway and really thrashed him. I got away because this girl shouted: 'The police are here.' It was this fellow Pedro who brought them – that's why we used to say at our meetings that there were people in our own families, poor people, who received money for helping to pursue the others. Pedro Gualdino was one of these, a pursuer. He knew me. They brought him, so that he could say: 'This is Zé Piauí'. He's still living here to this day. So when we started to run, he spoke up like this: 'Hey! Stop, because I want to talk to you.' 'We've got nothing to say to you', I said and we ran. 'Don't run or I'll shoot!' Bang! Then I drew out my revolver and they all fell on the ground there and I went into the forest and called my companions. Then I stayed hidden in the jungle in a little hut.

Elypídio related his experiences during this period:

They came after us into the forest, right up to this house. We had to spread out, one group here, another there. One day I was at Cícero's house, his wife cooked some food and I was just starting to eat when his little son came in saying: 'Run! The police have come.' We got to the house of a cousin of mine and they'd already arrested his wife and another man who was there. So then we ran to where the others were, to warn them about what had happened. Then we had to stay right in the jungle.

About 40 days after the 'confusion', they took one of my brothers. He was sleeping at five in the morning when they kicked him and knifed him, here on this part of the shoulder – he lost a lot of blood. Then they made him walk from his house carrying some really huge bunches of bananas and a chicken that the police took from this man's *roça* – chicken and a pumpkin, all the way to Papa Mel's house, where they made him take off his clothes and fired shots at him, forcing him to run backwards. The one who did all this was Sergeant Jacob, from Barra do Garças.

We had to live for more than 30 days on an island where there were no huts, we had to build shelters. It rained and rained and rained and rained while we were there. We had to make this shelter of banana leaves – in the jungle you can find banana trees, wild banana. Some had hammocks and others had to sleep on the ground. Only a few let it get them down. I myself didn't get at all upset.

We ate anything, there were so many people. I even ate monkey. And we went hungry a lot of the time as there wasn't much poultry or livestock at home and anyway we couldn't get home very often.

I had been living up at my parents' house just before it happened. So a few days later, they arrested my father and took him to Cuiabá, then to Campo Grande, and kept him in prison for quite a time. My father was an old man, nearly 80 years old, and he was in prison for more than 60 days. He hadn't done anything but just happened to be there, so they took him away. And then he got ill. A man of his age, he'd caught a chill sleeping on the floor – he had a thin mattress but even so, the floor was cement. He died not a fortnight after getting back on 4 May 1973.

Dona Josefa Alves da Costa, Blind Pedro's aunt, a lively old lady who follows all the local events with passionate interest, told us: 'He was only freed because of this illness of his. They said that if someone died in prison it would look bad for them. So they let him go. They took a doctor there to see him and he gave him some medicine so that he was strong enough to leave.'

Dona Josefa's family, which has been living in the region since 1957, suffered a great deal throughout the conflict with Codeara, ever since the company had first harassed her brother, Joaquim da Mata, in 1967. All the members of the family to whom we talked were forthright, clear-thinking, warm and generous people. They were all effective speakers, who knew how to present their case, and Codeara seems to have regarded them as a key family, a powerful centre of resistance. During the period of repression after the 'confusion', the police shot at one of Blind Pedro's brothers. His sister, Maria, began the story:

If we tried to tell all the stories about this Codeara we wouldn't even be able to remember properly what they've done. They did everything, against men, against women, against everyone because they were mad with rage. A sister-in-law of mine was ill at the very time that everyone was fighting in the street. My brother was here with her and every day he went into the village to buy meat. He was going to buy some meat but there wasn't any that day, so a cousin of his told him to leave the money with her and she would buy the meat the next day and he could go and fetch it. He left the money there and came home.

Blind Pedro continued:

So he went back the next day. He was on his pony and, when he passed in front of Codeara's headquarters, which was near his home, there was a battalion of labourers and police there and they called him over. He drew up and the police ordered his arrest. He asked why. The police said he was a gunman. He said he wasn't, he'd never fought with anyone. 'I'm on my way to buy medicine and meat because my folks are at home sick. I'm not going to be arrested, I don't owe anything to anyone.' When he spoke like this, the big sergeant pulled out his .38 and shot at him. The horse took fright and bolted. They then fired lots of shots, but God helped him and not one of them hit him. He got away safely.

Maria carried on:

They sent a car after him and he realised that, if he carried on along the road, they'd knock him down for sure, so he went into the grass and rode like mad. They kept running to see if they could catch up with him, but they didn't manage it. His wife heard all this noise and wanted to go and see what was happening. Antônio, who was passing by, said 'Don't go, they won't let you through.' She started to cry, going mad with nerves and fear, so he had to let her go. Off she went. The men at the ranch told her to go back home or they'd arrest her. She went home, crying, scared out of her wits that they'd killed him. But he'd fled into the forest and came out here to our house. We told him to leave because if he stayed they'd arrest him and beat him up.

One of Félix de Moraes's sons was also arrested. Maria Martin de Olveira, Félix's wife, told us about it:

There was no motive for his arrest at all. My son left his wife at the *roça* in the morning because she was sick and he was going to buy her some medicine. He told her he'd be back at one o'clock. When he arrived here, he bought medicines, sugar, coffee, milk – then they arrested him along with a friend of his leaving the two animals tied up with nothing to eat. They shouted at him: 'You're a trouble-maker!' 'No, I'm a worker.' 'You're a trouble-maker, a peasant, you're under arrest!' 'I only came here to buy medicine for my wife and a child who are sick.' 'That's a lie! You're under arrest!' Then the news reached me and at four o'clock in the afternoon I sent the boy, in the rain, to fetch his wife and the children. So he went and got there with the sedatives which he gave her, and then they travelled back at night. Lots of mosquitoes, heavy rain, 12 kilometres, she with fever and her head aching, holding one child by the hand, another on her hip, and the boy with the other child. They arrived the next day, and at eleven o'clock they let her husband go.

Meanwhile, during these weeks of hiding in the forest, the rice crop had ripened and had to be harvested. Chicão explained how they were able to reap it despite the problems:

There was a lot of ripe rice, so I and a few of the other men went to harvest it. Most of the men were too scared to go, but the police didn't go either, though they knew we were there, because they were scared too. Just a few of the women came out to the *roças* to help in the harvest, but they were afraid to stay there, afraid of being caught. None the less, we managed to reap all the rice.

However, the women to whom we spoke gave a different picture of what happened and it appears that – not untypically – some of the men have underestimated the role of the women peasants. Maria Alves da Costa, Blind Pedro's sister, and some of her neighbours told us about the harvest and some of the hardships the women suffered during the 'persecution':

> Then the planes touched down, filled up with policemen who went round the houses to force the women to say where the men were hiding. They came twice to our home. One day they came and there was only a girl here and this brother of mine, who's blind. They surrounded all the doors and came with all those weapons to get us to say where the men were so they could arrest them. We said we didn't know – they argued and said they would beat up Pedro, beat us all up. Then they went away but there were a lot of them.

A woman neighbour added: 'They harassed the women in lots of ways, making them sit on anthills so they'd get bitten.' Maria went on:

> And another time, they took all the women in this house and lined them up like this and said: 'If you don't talk, we'll kill you, all of you at once.' So we were all there, with the children in our arms beginning to cry. 'Sit down on the ground!' So we sat down. 'You'll talk or you'll die!' So we were all terrified. When the men saw that we were really dead scared but were not going to talk, they said: 'We won't kill these wretches this time. Stop all this bullying!' and they let us go. It was the same story in every house they went to.

Another woman commented: 'At this time a man died and the other men couldn't even come to fetch the body to bury him. We had to ask for a tractor to take him away to be buried. And none of us was allowed to attend the funeral.' Maria went on:

> The rice in the *roças* was all ripe for harvest and the men were unable to do it. So it was the women who went. There was a lot of rice, so Father Canuto came and helped. There was just a bit lost, because women don't really have the knack, but we were able to get in a whole load. The work was hard for us, but we knew if we got discouraged and ran off, everything would be lost. The men from the ranch were a real nuisance. They were very unpleasant. They didn't let the women go along this road to do their shopping. We had to go a long way round so as not to pass nearby. They'd put the company buildings up right on our road which was already there and didn't want us to go either that way or this way. But things went on until the men were freed and began to come back to their homes and things got better.

It was not, however, the peasant families but the people brought in by the Catholic Church – the school-teacher Altair, and the young couple, Tadeu and Teresinha – who suffered the worst treatment during this period, though none of them had been directly involved in the 'battle of the pharmacy' or was centrally involved in the struggle against Codeara. Teresinha was treated worse than anyone. Dona Juvenilha told us about it:

> There weren't any women arrested, though some were beaten up, except for Teresinha. She was held for three months. They even put electricity in her to make her jump and say all she knew. Altair was kept even longer, four months. Altair, Tadeu and Teresinha were the ones who were in prison for the longest time.

The viciousness with which the authorities treated the church workers is partly to be explained by particular political events which were occurring at a national level. A couple of years earlier the internal security forces had crushed an urban guerrilla movement in the industrialised south. It was known that some of the survivors from this movement had fled to the north of Goiás and, tracked down by the security forces, had been forced to launch a rural guerrilla offensive. At the meeting in May 1970, Olímpio Jaime is believed to have claimed that Jentel and his lay workers were linked to the urban guerrillas. As a result, the authorities were quick to accept Codeara's suggestion that the 'battle of the pharmacy' had been masterminded by the guerrillas, though no evidence ever seems to have been produced to support this allegation.

But the speed with which the authorities moved against the lay workers also reflects the suspicion and fear with which the authorities regard educated outsiders, particularly those linked to the Catholic Church who choose to live in a backward peasant community such as Santa Teresinha. These outsiders, whether priests, teachers or nurses, play a crucial role as intermediaries between the community and the outside world. They bring with them knowledge of all aspects of the social system which is penetrating the countryside and forests and is impinging on both peasant and Indian communities. Anthropologists who live with Indian groups also often act as mediators in this way.

Many individuals who choose to live in these communities do so, at least partly, because they are concerned to help those whom they see as oppressed and exploited. They assume the role of shock absorbers as more primitive forms of social production and organisation first confront – and then are dominated by – the more powerful encroaching society.

Government officials, military officers and businessmen tend to perceive the outsiders rather differently. They often have difficulty in understanding that some people may be driven primarily by altruistic ideals and be prepared to give up high salaries and the benefits of the modern, urban way of life. They find it much easier to believe that these people have been sent there by a political party as part of a plot to 'overthrow the capitalist system'. If any of the outsiders show any political interest, be it no more than a concern that the peasant families or Indians organise on a national scale to defend their collective interests, they are immediately classified as subversives or communists. 'Reds-under-the-bed' become 'reds-in-the-jungle', a similarly harmful distortion of the motives of those who defend the interests of the poor.

By classifying Jentel and his co-workers as communist, the government stopped the work of a man who, paradoxically, was a passionate defender of the very forces of modernity which the government claimed to be anxious to bring to the region. It would seem that the government wanted to bring up-to-date capitalism to the Amazon but, unlike Jentel, who wanted to give the peasant families access to its benefits, it wished only to benefit the small social elite to which it was linked. Jentel and the church workers were hounded with particular ferocity because they defended, with far greater coherence than the peasant families and Indians to whom they were linked, an alternative way of developing the Amazon. They had to be stopped and the easiest way of halting them was to brand them as subversives, thus encouraging the powerful *comunidade de informações* (see Chapter 4) to move against them.

Codeara's Version

We visited Codeara ranch for the first time in November 1976, and spoke to the then manager, Amílcar Rodrigues Gameiro, who gave his account of what had happened. He had not worked for Codeara from the earliest days but he had witnessed events in the early 1970s, though he did not take part directly in the pharmacy incident. He and the peasant farmers agreed on the essential facts, but – as was to be expected – Gameiro attributed a very different significance to the events.

Gameiro saw his ranch as a spearhead of modern, industrialised society. He spoke with enthusiasim of the technological challenge presented by the Amazon region for cattle-rearers. Though his ranch was clearly facing serious problems of soil leaching, bush invasion and cattle mortality from poisonous plants, he told us optimistically that considerable progress had been made, particularly in the field of artificial insemination. The ranch's motto, he proclaimed proudly, was: '*nascer sempre mais, nascer sempre melhor, morrer sempre menos*; more births, better births, fewer deaths'. He was talking about cattle. Gameiro's obsessive concern for cattle made it clear why peasant families in the region have coined the ironic saying: 'Calves are more important than children. Grass is more important than families.'

Gameiro constantly emphasised his concern to produce fine-quality beef. Not without a touch of moral indignation, he recognised that his ranch could not compete with the peasant families in terms of cost. He quoted the findings of a study carried out by the Association of Young Calf Producers: 'Amazing as it may appear, we cannot produce cheaper beef than the peasant farmer. His production costs are so low. To compete, we have to have a better product than his.'

Gameiro showed an initial unwillingness to talk about the 'confusion', a reluctance which slowly melted away with three-quarters of a bottle of Campari. He spoke reproachfully of the general misunderstanding of the ranch's intentions with respect to the resettlement plan. 'We only wanted to move the peasants off their present poor soil on to good land. We all know that a community does not develop successfully on bad land.'

He talked bitterly of the church, which, he claimed, had acted in bad faith from the beginning. This did not surprise him as he believed that, except for a few important bulwarks of 'true faith', the Catholic Church was a subversive force: '80 per cent of Brazil's bishops are communist.' He maintained that the church workers had arrived in the region with the specific intention of setting the peasant families against the cattle ranch and referred to Jentel as 'a very clever man'. He recalled seeing an army major in Cuiabá knock Jentel down in exasperation after the priest had won an argument. 'I always avoided any discussion with the priest after that', Gameiro confessed. 'I knew he would beat me.' Indeed, although he was a great believer in dialogue, Gameiro saw little point in trying to reason with 'Jentel, Casaldáliga or any other of the priests, as they are so prejudiced against us'.

Gameiro admitted that the church had been very successful in winning over the peasants to its point of view.

> The peasants were 100 per cent against me. In the early 1970s, they would spit in my face as I went by. If I protested, they threatened me with a knife. Things got so bad that I didn't dare go out alone.

Gameiro claimed that the pharmacy conflict was deliberately provoked by Jentel. 'He wanted to make the headlines in the foreign press.' He further asserted that in 1973 there were 15 former urban guerrillas in the region, subversives who had taken part in the kidnapping of the West German ambassador to Brazil in 1970 and had then returned clandestinely to the country. Some of them must have received guerrilla training in Cuba, he added, as the peasants had adopted the 'Cuban way' of digging trenches. As 'definitive proof' of his allegations, Gameiro said that after the famous urban guerrilla leader Carlos Marighela had been killed in São Paulo in the early 1970s, documents concerning the 'illegal activities' of church workers in Santa Teresinha had been discovered among the possessions of some of the Dominican priests who had acted as his accomplices.

We later investigated Gameiro's allegations as best we could, but found little evidence to support them. It seems that some of the church workers had been involved in left-wing politics in the south of Brazil before going to Santa Teresinha, but this did not seem to us proof that they had engineered the whole confrontation. We were unable to discover what precisely were the Cuban features of the trenches the peasants had built. It is possible that the Dominican priests may have been in contact with some of the church workers in the region, but no evidence has ever been produced to suggest that they had possessed reports of 'illegal activities'. It is highly likely that, if such accounts had existed, the government would have publicised them to justify its harsh treatment of Jentel, which, as we shall see, was vehemently criticised inside Brazil and abroad.

Gameiro said that the pharmacy incident had shaken the government. 'Before then, the government ignored this region, despite our warnings. But after that the security organisations swarmed in.' He said that various secret investigations had been made. He recalled in particular a summons he received late in 1973 to go to the Third Air Base in São Paulo. There he was informed that three men, masquerading as land dealers from the state of Paraná, would soon be appearing on his ranch. He was told to give them all the assistance he could without attracting attention. To be sure, Gameiro added, the 'dealers' duly appeared shortly after his return. Pretending that they required full information for their work, they made enquiries into land ownership, work conditions on the ranch, the activities of the local priests and lay workers. One of them told Gameiro to sack one of his cattle-hands who was suspected of subversive activities. The advice was taken, though Gameiro was never given any explanation as to the nature of the mysterious subversion.

Though he admitted that relations between Codeara and the government had greatly improved, Gameiro believed that the government was still too lax with church workers. 'The government still only carries out curative treatment, after the situation has been allowed to get bad. It is clear that preventive treatment is required.' When we asked whether this preventive treatment should extend to the assassination of Bishop Pedro Casaldáliga, as several cattle-ranchers wanted, Gameiro replied: 'No. Not his murder, but his expulsion from the country as a foreign agitator, yes.'

Gameiro's views were fairly typical of Amazon cattle-rearers. Throughout our conversations, we were impressed by his evident sincerity and could only marvel at the profound influence that his initial entrenched set of values had exerted on his interpretation. After our talks with the peasant families, we found it impossible to give much credence to his view of events. To us it seemed self-evident that the conflict had built up over a long period and that it stemmed from a basic disagreement with the peasant families over the way in which the land should be occupied. Though Jentel and the lay workers may have influenced the shape of events, some form of confrontation had become inevitable. To a large extent it seemed irrelevant whether or not former guerrillas were in the region. It seemed remarkable to us that Gameiro and some government officials could, apparently in good faith, attribute blame for the conflict to the work of a small group of political fanatics.

The 'Liberation'

The 'battle of the pharmacy' had repercussions far beyond the confines of Santa Teresinha or even Amazonia itself. With the attention that the national and international press was paying to the conflict, the federal government had little option but to intervene in this embarrassing case of what they referred to as 'social tension' and to impose a solution in which justice was at least seen to be done. Though the church played a crucial role in publicising the events, it was the organised and united resistance of the peasant families which was responsible for the breakthrough.

After 105 days of hiding in the jungle by the men, of struggle to keep the *roças* going by the women and of continued harassment of all the peasant families by the military police, the army intervened on 15 June 1972. The local population still refers to this event as its 'liberation'.

Antônio Canuto, a priest from southern Brazil who had joined Jentel in the parish of Santa Teresinha shortly before the 'battle of the pharmacy', and the village nurse, Suzanne Robin, a young French woman, visited the *roças* almost daily during these three months to maintain contact with the fugitives and to attend to their needs. Canuto also acted as intermediary between the army and the peasant farmers. After consulting the peasants, he told the army officers that they would only agree to come out of hiding if they received a signed guarantee from the armed forces, the police and Codeara that the peasant families would be left in peace and that no arrests would be made. The army officers agreed to this condition. Elypídio told us how it happened:

> On the day of liberation, we were up at a place called Roça Grande, and there were many who didn't want to go – this crowd from the army and this military battalion had sent us an official letter, but there were many among us who didn't trust them, because they really weren't to be trusted. After all, on the day of the happening, the police had been the first to attack. So among our lot there were many who got nervous, yet that official letter they'd sent had to be followed up as they'd made lots of guarantees that they had put down in writing. It was Canuto who brought it there and, as so many didn't want to go, I said: 'I'll go; if none of you want to go, I will', and I went with two others. The next day everybody went, but on that first day only the three of us presented ourselves. I was tired of being in the jungle.

Zé Piauí, who was known to be the peasant farmer most hated by Codeara, was the most reluctant to give himself up. Later events showed that he had been right to be suspicious. He told us what happened:

> I decided first of all not to show up there because they wanted my revolver and I didn't want to give it up. 'Tell them I'm not here!', I said and I didn't go that night when a lot of them went. They liberated all those who went and didn't take their weapons, just registered them. So after several days had gone by, the rest went and presented themselves at the police station. In the end I went too. They looked up my name, didn't do anything to me, searched for my revolver and I said: 'I sold it – I was hungry so I sold it so I could eat.' Afterwards I wasn't worried as I thought they weren't going to harass me any more. I went home when the colonel from INCRA, this Clovis, arrived and, I

think, went to the police station saying that I was a criminal. All I know for sure is that later they came here full of lies saying that the colonel had sent for me to make sure that I got my rights in the Tapiraguaia. They seemed to trust me as they came without a revolver or anything. So I got in the car and thought it would be about precisely that, my rights in the Tapiraguaia. But I was wrong. Some bloke had shown them the way to my house, earning 100 cruzeiros, knowing that they were going to arrest me . . . They took me to Barra do Garças.

There we had a real fight because of a pistol of theirs that had disappeared and they accused me of taking it. I hadn't taken it, but they really beat me up and gave me hell all the same.

I spent five days there in Barra do Garças. From there they put me on a plane and didn't tell me where they were going to take me – 'Hey! You're going away now!' – and they took me from Barra to Cuiabá. The whole thing was stupid. I wasn't what they thought I was. I wasn't a criminal. The police had known me for so many years, they first got to know me 18 years ago. If I was a criminal, I would have shown that I was long before then.

He went on to tell what happened to him in Cuiabá:

The bishop got me free in Cuiabá. First I was taken to the police station by the same lot that were here on the day of the shoot-out. Then the bishop saw to it that I was sent over to the army barracks. When I got there, I felt much happier – there weren't going to beat me up for nothing. They searched me all over, they even searched my shoes. They found the money I had and kept it, and on the day I left they gave it back. The next day, the army captain sent for me and asked me: 'Do you know who you're talking to?' 'No, Sir.' 'You're talking to an army captain.' 'Then I'm amongst good folks, I feel at home.' He started asking me questions. I arrived there on Saturday and on Monday they took me to the judge. Canuto was there, and the judge told the soldier who'd taken me there to go away. He soon let me go free.

Elypídio explained why he thought that the military police had picked on Zé Piauí:

He'd stayed in the jungle. After we were all liberated, he didn't want to present himself because the Codeara gang had him marked, thinking he was the leader. They hated him because he was someone who wouldn't yield to their justice. When they did something that was unjust, he would point it out and stay firm and wouldn't let them invade our lands. So they really had it in for him. They kept him marked and the battalion left this Jacob from Barra do Garças to bring Zé Piauí back there. He was kept in prison a while there and even in the Barra do Garças jail the police argued with him and they fought, exchanging blows. I don't think he was put on trial. He was the only person arrested after the liberation.

He was just someone who stood firm because of the injustice, and so because of his firmness the others stood firm too, but not because he tried to make others do as he said. He was always firm and wouldn't yield to their justice because sometimes the authorities were also injust. He said he didn't want anything to do with the justice of the police because they came here with injustice.

Thus, despite the written guarantee, the peasants were not wholly immune from reprisals. Significantly, the police sergeant from Barra do Garças who arrested Zé Piauí had also been responsible for the hounding of Elypídio's brother. He may well have been acting without the authorisation of the federal police for Bishop Pedro Casaldáliga had little difficulty in arranging for his release once he was in the hands of the army. From then on, the peasants of Santa Teresinha suffered no more imprisonment or even harassment.

The 'liberation' by federal troops was eventually followed by the distribution of land to nearly 120 peasant families by INCRA. Blind Pedro told us how this came about:

> After this fight, Codeara was forced to sign the contract to give the land to the peasants. They didn't want to, but they had to. Finally, the manager signed and ordered the land to be handed over. There were families who didn't receive anything because they'd run away and on the day of the deed they weren't there so they lost their right. Everyone got 20 *alqueires* [96.8 hectares].

The peasant families did not win an outright victory, for Codeara got its way on some issues. Not all the families were given the land that they had cleared and on which they had been living for many years. Many months passed before Codeara handed over the titles, probably because it realised that it still had considerable support among some government sectors, even in INCRA, and for a long time did not give up hope of reversing the earlier decision. The land was finally marked out in 1973, and the titles for 115 plots were distributed in 1974 and 1975. In 1976 there were still a few families who had been allocated land but had not yet received their titles. When we spoke to Amilcar Rodrigues Gameiro, he told us that the company would not hand over any titles to a representative, but only personally to the head of the family, and that this strict ruling had caused some delays, particularly when the head of the family was ill or had been called away urgently to another part of the country. There seemed to be no justification for this requirement and it seemed that at this late stage Codeara was trying to rob a few families of their plots.

INCRA decided that only families who had been living on their plots for ten years or more, and thus had clear legal rights, should be given titles. Several of the families who had been heavily involved in the struggle ended up with nothing. But, from the peasants' point of view, the greatest cost of their partial victory was the loss of Jentel. After the 'battle of the pharmacy', he and Edival dos Reis had rushed to Brasília to mobilise support for the peasant families. It was largely as the result of their efforts that the incident received such publicity. However, Jentel's strenuous efforts worked against his own individual interests for they were taken by the military hard-liners as further evidence of his 'subversive' desire to 'disturb public order'. They decided to make an example of Jentel and to use him to warn left-wing members of the church that the hard-line faction within the armed forces and the government would not tolerate this type of political involvement. Jentel was duly arrested at the Tapirapé village on 28 May 1972, while the peasant farmers were still in hiding.

He was tried later in the year on charges of infringing the national security law. No pretence of a fair trial was made by the military tribunal in Campo Grande. The military judges were unanimous in their verdict and Jentel was sentenced to ten years' imprisonment. The only discordant note came from the single civilian judge, Plínio Barbosa Martins. In an outspoken and impassioned speech, he said that Jentel 'deserves an award, not punishment' for his exemplary Christian behaviour and for all his efforts on behalf of Santa Teresinha. He said later: 'I am not affected by the pressures from those who try to dictate the paths to be followed. We must take the way to independence, subject only to the strength of our conscience.' It was also an eloquent comment on the way in which the trial had been conducted.

An appeal to the Supreme Military Tribunal in Brasília by Jentel's lawyer, Heleno Cláudio Fragoso, was heard on 15 June 1973. In his speech, Fragoso pointed to numerous irregularities. He said that the Mato Grosso policemen who carried out the inquiry had been brought to Santa Teresinha in a Codeara plane and had been accompanied by two Codeara lawyers while they obtained their evidence from the villagers. This had clearly made it impossible for them to carry out an objective inquiry and had even been criticised by the public prosecutor during the trial. Fragoso described Jentel as 'superlegalistic' in the way he had meticulously reported every incident of aggression and conflict to numerous government bodies, including the National Security Council. Nor was there any evidence that Jentel was left-wing. At the end of his interrogation, Jentel had declared that he believed in the 'good intentions of the government' and said that he had struggled to 'improve the social level' of the people in the region, who, he said, were not taking part in a 'class war' but had 'great aspirations of social justice'. Fragoso claimed to have proof that a meeting had been held in Campo Grande by the military judges and other military officers a week before the trial and that this and other evidence suggested that the verdict had been arranged in advance.

Jentel was unexpectedly acquitted. Though considerable mystery still surrounds the case, some leading members of the church believe that Jentel made a secret deal with the authorities before the appeal was heard, in which he agreed to leave the country as the condition for his acquittal. Whether by prior arrangement or not, Jentel surprised the peasant families by travelling to France immediately after his release to visit his mother and to study.

However, Jentel found it difficult to settle in France. In December 1975, he returned to Brazil to live once again in his beloved Araguaian home. He spent a week in Brasília before travelling on 10 December to Fortaleza in the north-east at the invitation of the local bishop, Aloisio Lorscheider. Two days later Jentel was kidnapped in the street by soldiers in civilian clothing and taken to the federal police for 'interrogation about his passport'. It was evident from the confidence with which the soldiers acted that they were obeying orders from a top authority, possibly General Silvio Frota, the army minister.

Jentel was taken by military aircraft to the maritime police in Rio de Janeiro. On 15 December, President Ernesto Geisel signed a decree for his explusion. He left the next day, never to return. He died in France of cancer of the kidneys on 2 January 1979. The villagers of Santa Teresinha say that Father Francisco died of a broken heart because he had not been allowed to returned to his adopted and rightful home with them and that, although his body is in France, his soul is in Brazil.

The Tapirapé's Struggle for Their Land

The Tapirapé also undertook a long and difficult struggle to win possession of their lands. Like many other Indian groups, the Tapirapé had found it difficult in the early years first of all to understand the capitalist idea of land as private property, and then later on to realise that they must fight to defend their lands as they were essential for their survival. The Tapirapé made mistakes in the early days when they were struggling to grasp these alien concepts, but, unlike many other groups, they were given a chance later on to recoup what they had lost through their initial blunders.

Their main error, they realised later, was not to have stood up to the ranches from the beginning. The Tapirapé, who had traditionally occupied a large area near the confluence of the Araguaia and Tapirapé rivers, came under great pressure from the cattle companies in the late 1960s to give up part of this land. Reluctantly, they agreed to limit their claim to 9,000 hectares. However, even this concession did not satisfy the cattle companies, particularly Tapiraguaia, which maintained that it had bought part of the land claimed by the Indians from Nasser and other land dealers.

Despite his heavy involvement with the peasant families, Jentel continued to visit the Indians a great deal. It was partly through his efforts and those of other church workers that the Tapirapé became aware of the overwhelming dangers that they faced through the gradual encroachment of the cattle companies on their land. By the mid 1970s the Tapirapé were adopting a much tougher position. They attended the assemblies of Indian chiefs organised by Cimi and, through these discussions, they strengthened their resolve to fight for their lands and also influenced other groups by their ideas.

The Tapirapé chief Txibae Ewororo attended the first assembly of Indian chiefs at Diamantino in Mato Grosso in April 1974. The following is part of the speech he made:

> We come from the Tapirapé post at the invitation of the Bororo tribe. Here all of us who are Indians come together. We would like to tell you something about the way we live. The ranches are surrounding us. The Codeara, the Tapiraguaia are taking away all our land. Why did the whites want to pacify us? Afterwards what is going to happen to us in the middle of whites, working for the whites who want to take away our land? Is it meant that the Indians should have nothing and that an end should be made to the Indians? The whites arrived and decided that the Indian could find another place to live. Where shall we go? The Indian lives in the place which he knows. If he moves to another place on the river bank, in the hills, in the lowlands, this is not good.
>
> There was a Father who lived with us. He was a poor man. He was young, between twenty and twenty-five years of age when he arrived. He stayed with us. We carried things for him and he also carried loads at the same time. He could not speak Portuguese; he was a foreigner and did not understand anything. Each time a Brazilian came, he spoke all mixed up. Then he studied Portuguese and in five years he spoke well. Everyone liked him. The Tapiraguaia company wants to take all of our land. It wants to give us a small piece of *cerrado* [bush land] which is not worth anything. Where we plant is good forest. The whites say, 'Look, the Indian is not equal to us. Let's take away their land because they do not have guns nor machine guns, nor bombs, nor money. All they have are bows and arrows and clubs. Only these are for the Indian to use.' Because of this they took away Father Francisco. The police arrived while the men were away and there were only women in the village. The women were afraid of the police and they took the Father away. We feel his absence to this day because he was as poor as we are. We miss him greatly.[11]

Not all the young Tapirapé men were keen to become involved in political discussions about the future of the Indian nations. Txywãeri, who was their representative at the second assembly of Indian chiefs held in May 1975 at the Cururu mission in Pará, was inexperienced and evidently unwilling to participate. He said during the first session of this assembly:

> I didn't want to come. I have to build my house. Who will do it now? I was making flour. I said: 'I don't think I will go.' But Marco, our chief, said: 'It's been arranged. You're going'. 'But I don't know how to speak!' He told me to talk about our land which has not been marked off.[12]

Txywãeri was accurate in his assessment of his speech-making skills: he was probably the least articulate of the participants. None the less, he gave an idea of the dilemma faced by his tribe:

Funai was there. Then it went away. It didn't help. We asked Funai to order wire for us. It didn't order any, for by keeping the wire they keep the land for themselves. So we are wondering what to do. We were coming to an end. A long while ago, there were only two huts. Now there are many more. We need land.[13]

Txywãeri was also the Tapirapé representative at the sixth assembly of Indian chiefs, held at Diamantino in December 1976. By then he was speaking with much more confidence and he gave a coherent account of their dissatisfaction with Funai: it had inexplicably threatened to send the Little Sisters away and to sack their lay teacher, Luís, and it had said that it was planning to move the Tapirapé to Bananal Island in a joint reserve with the Carajá. Txywãeri said that this proposal was completely unacceptable: while the Carajá were fishermen and some of them already lived on the island, the Tapirapé had never lived there and their slash-and-burn farming methods were impossible on lands that were seasonally flooded. Txywãeri said incisively: 'Indians are not animals to be moved to another place.'[14] At about this time, the Tapirapé decided to increase their claim to 30,000 hectares.

Unhappy with the help they received from Funai, the Tapirapé decided to act on their own initiative and to mark out themselves the boundaries to their land by cutting trails through the forest. They were fortunate in receiving the visit of an unusually supportive Funai official who encouraged them in their offensive against the cattle companies. Probably without the authorisation of Funai head office, he sent in a land surveyor who helped them mark out what they considered to be their traditional lands. The demarcation, which enclosed an area of about 30,000 hectares, was completed by the end of the dry season in 1978. By then Funai had been officially informed of what was happening and, the Indians told us, they appeared to give their approval.

The ranch owners were greatly angered by this new development. They believed that they had solved the Indian problem by 'donating' an area of 9,000 hectares on the island of Bananal to Funai to set up a joint reserve for the two groups. They were further startled on 30 August 1978 by the announcement by the then president of Funai, Colonel Nobre da Veiga, that about 28,000 hectares of land in the northern part of the island of Bananal was to be turned into a reserve for the Carajá Indians.

However, Funai did nothing to set up this new Indian reserve, except to close down the forest reserve previously established on that part of the island. By 19 December 1978, by which date, according to the timetable set out in the Indian Statute in 1973, Funai should have demarcated all Indian reserves throughout the country, the Tapirapé were among a minority of groups which had had their reserves marked out – and they were only in this fortunate position because they themselves had taken the initiative.

However, the Tapirapé did not win their battle so easily. In 1979 Porto Velho and Tapiraguaia ranches, both of whom had lost land by the Tapirapé's unilateral action, began a long and bitter struggle to regain the land. When in January 1979 we spoke to Hildebrando de Campos Bicudo, at that time administrator of Porto Velho ranch, he told us that his company was going to take Funai to court for stealing its land. He believed that it would have been more just to sue the Indians themselves, but, as they were under the guardianship of the state, this could not be done. Hildebrando said that the Indians were behaving like spoilt children, in that the more you gave them the more they wanted. It was evident that in his opinion an area of about 10,000 hectares was more than enough for them. We pointed out that Porto Velho itself only employed 85 people on its 101,000 hectares and thus, along with the other cattle companies, was scarcely in a position to use the criterion of population density against the Indians. He was irritated by our remark and said that the comparison was quite improper as his ranch, unlike the Indians, was producing goods for the market and thus contributing to the country's gross national product.

Though Hildebrando would undoubtedly have rejected his arguments, Charles Wagley, in his book, *Welcome of Tears* gave the reasons why the Tapirapé needed a large area of land:

> Without doubt, the shortage of suitable agricultural land within a reasonable distance of their village may ultimately prove to be the major impediment of Tapirapé adaptation to their new circumstances. It might seem that a reservation of slightly more than 9,000 hectares would provide enough land for just over 100 people. But much of this land is not suitable for tropical-forest, slash-and-burn farming. In the years to come that portion of the area which is covered by high forest will have been cleared and planted, at least during one growing season . . . They are fully aware that a garden site planted two years in succession loses much of its fertility as measured by production. They are also aware that planting in secondary growth which has been fallow for only a few years is about half as productive as gardens planted in high forest . . . In the past, the Tapirapé rarely made use of forest land that had not lain fallow for 20 years or more.[15]

For Wagley, adequate land for their slash-and-burn farming techniques is the first of three conditions necessary for the continued growth of the Tapirapé population and their persistence as an ethnic group. The other two are: that they continue their formal rules of tribal endogamy by which outside marriages are forbidden except on a limited scale with the Carajá; and that they retain enough elements of their native culture to provide tribal identity *vis-à-vis* national culture.

The ranches saw that they were becoming bogged down in a long and messy legal battle, so, following the example of the Tapirapé, they decided to take the law into their own hands. In August 1980 Tapiraguaia ranch began to mark out what it considered to be the limits of the Indians' reserve. It even bribed some Carajá Indians to help in the work.

The Tapirapé reacted angrily. To prevent a violent confrontation, Funai persuaded the ranch to stop work on its demarcation and told both sides not to enter the area under dispute until an agreement had been reached. Part of this area was made up of rich pasture which had been formed by the ranch in the late 1960s. Unwilling to give up this land, even temporarily, Tapiraguaia continued to graze cattle on it. The ranch was warned on two occasions by the Tapirapé not to carry on with this practice in open infringement of Funai's ruling, but the ranch ignored them. On 15 January 1981 the Tapirapé killed 27 out of the 2,000 head of cattle on the land in dispute.

Funai officials rushed to the area, clearly afraid that open warfare could develop between the two sides. Colonel Nobre da Veiga, president of Funai, assured the Tapirapé that he would support their claim and that by 30 July 1981 their reserve would be officially demarcated. He said that he would also arrange for the transfer of ten of the peasant families living on land claimed by the Indians. There were 13 families on this land, but the Tapirapé had agreed to allow three of the families, all of which had been living on their plots for over 20 years, to remain where they were.

By the end of July Funai had not marked out this land. Worse still, it appeared to be going back on its commitment to honour the limits established by the Indians. It suggested to the Indians that they gave the area of pasture to the ranch and, in compensation, received an area of the same size to the south of their reserve. The Indians firmly rejected this proposal for, they said, the new area was flooded half the year and could not be used for slash-and-burn agriculture.

In early August, the Mato Grosso state government sent 30 soldiers from the military police to Santa Teresinha to keep the peace between the Indians and the ranch. Dom Tomás Balduíno, vice-president of Cimi, bitterly attacked Funai's 'double-dealing'. He said: 'After ten years of lies and procrastinations, Funai is forcing the Tapirapé, with the help even of military policemen, to accept a demarcation which is harmful to their interests and which has been unanimously rejected by the whole group.'[16] Colonel Nobre da Veiga retorted that he would not 'allow the Indians to give him orders'.

The tide seemed to have turned against the Tapirapé. A unit from the army's geographical service was sent in to demarcate the reserve, without the disputed area of pasture. A group of angry Tapirapé warriors forced the unit to stop work. A leading Funai official in Brasília, Inimar Nascimento da Silva, reacted furiously, saying: 'The army should have fired a few shots into the Tapirapé to teach them a lesson.'[17]

When we visited the village in early November, the Indians were on a war footing. They were united and very determined to regain what their considered their rightful lands. They showed none of their earlier doubts and hesitations. By then the Indians numbered 187 and several mothers had five or six children, in marked contrast with their earlier practice of limiting the size of a family to three children. This in itself had created problems for, though they had planted a much larger *roça* in 1980, they had run out of manioc flour at the end of the year and had been forced reluctantly to sell fish in the streets of Santa Teresinha to raise money to buy more.

The Indians were preparing for a special festivity. All the girls who had had their first menstruation were dressing themselves up in duck and parrot feathers. Others were painting traditional designs on their bodies with a dye made from *genipapo* berries. After this feast, the young girls who had through the ceremony shown themselves to be women would be allowed to experiment with various suitors until they found a suitable partner. They would only marry after they became pregnant. The girls would all marry Tapirapé men, though Tapirapé men did occasionally marry Carajá women. In these cases, the Tapirapé man went to live in a Carajá village.

The Tapirapé had started burying their dead in their huts once again. They dug a very deep hole, wrapped the corpse in a hammock and suspended it in a little room they built at the bottom of the hole. A small mound inside the hut indicated the site of the grave.

Though life was carrying on much as usual, the Tapirapé were clearly in a state of extreme tension. I left their village full of foreboding, apprehensive that at any moment the conflict could explode into horrific violence. I was convinced that the Tapirapé would die rather than relinquish any part of their lands.

Later in November the Tapirapé sent an urgent message to Colonel Paulo Leal, the new president of Funai, in which they warned him that the army had recommenced demarcation and they were preparing to take violent action to halt the work. As a result, Leal visited the Tapirapé village in early December. He agreed to the Tapirapé's request that he bring with him Marcos Terena, the president of the newly-formed Union of Indian Nations, though the latter had been *persona non grata* under the previous Funai administration.

After carefully considering all the evidence, Leal agreed to respect the Indians' own demarcation and to include the pasture in their reserve. Funai began talks with Tapiraguaia over the compensation to be paid. The Indians were exultant. After years of struggle, they appeared to have won. When the official demarcation was finally completed, they said, they would be in a strong position to face the future. Other Indian groups have not been slow to draw the obvious conclusion: the Tapirapé were victorious in this struggle because they were united, persistent and forceful.

The Fruits of Victory

In August 1975, Unicas, the village health association set up by Jentel, carried out a census. It found the population of Santa Teresinha to be 1,443 adults (753 men and 690 women) and 483 children (under ten years old). About half (750) of the adults had had one or more attacks of malaria. About 80 per cent of those over 16 years old said that they were literate. Though it should be borne in mind that anyone who can write his or her name and can read with difficulty simple texts is called literate, it is clear that there had been a big improvement since Wagley's first visit in 1939, when nearly everyone was completely illiterate. (This does not mean, however, that the educational level of the population had risen, for many of the old skills, such as spinning, weaving and basketry, were dying out.)

Many of the tables in the report were based on incomplete data. This is scarcely surprising, given the practical difficulties in carrying out this type of research. None the less, the study gives us a valuable indication of the type of society which Santa Teresinha had become by then. Some of the findings are set out below:

Occupation:

peasant farmers	186	drivers	21
labourers	74	builders & masons	14
traders & salesmen	30	seamstresses	12
employees	25	boatmen	10
maids	25	teachers	10
washerwomen	20		

Year of family's arrival:

Main states of origin of families

1930–40	7	Goiás	200
1941–50	15	Maranhão	98
1951–60	110	Piauí	33
1961–4	54	Pará	26
1965–70	97	Bahia	19
1971–3	75	Ceará	17
1974–5	55	Minas Gerais	14
		São Paulo	11

The state of Mato Grosso itself, in which Santa Teresinha is situated, is not included in the states of origin, because very few of the town's adult inhabitants were born in it. The results of the survey backed up what we had been told: that most of the settlers reached Santa Teresinha as part of an early and slow wave of migration in which families moved slowly westward from the north-east (mainly Piauí, Ceará and Bahia), first to Maranhão and Goiás and then to Mato Grosso and Pará.

Though there was no earlier survey with which to compare the results, it seems clear that the range of occupations had extended with the growth of the village itself. By 1975 about a third of the jobs were in the service sector. Probably because hardship had forced many more women to find a paid job, the list included a number of traditional female occupations. Though peasant farming continued to form the largest single occupation group, it had undoubtedly lost ground as a proportion of the total. Moreover, the survey did not provide clear definitions of the various occupations and it is probable that the loose term peasant farming included many share-croppers, working on other people's land.

The diversification of jobs reflected the increasing social stratification in Santa Teresinha. Whereas in the early days almost everyone belonged to a poor peasant family, the town had by 1975 a middle class of tradespeople and farmers rich enough to buy the services of other people. But the swelling of the service sector was also an indication of another change: the difficulties faced by newcomers in finding a plot of land to farm. For the victory of the peasant families in their conflict with Codeara did not solve the land question in the village. INCRA provided titles for those who had lived there longest. It failed to resolve adequately the problem existing at that time, for many more families were looking for land, and made no provisions whatsoever for the future influx of families. INCRA did the minimum necessary to defuse the tense situation in the village. Its brief was to eliminate a threat to national security, not to work out a lasting solution to a social problem.

By the 1971–5 period, 24 families were arriving each year, which was twice the rate in the 1950s. Most were looking for land on which to open up their *roças*, but very few found it. Dona Juvenilha talked to us about the new settlers:

> There are lots of people arriving from outside. They don't have *roças* of their own, so they work for an income on other people's. Working for an income means this: if I have some cleared land and put someone to work there, he gets a third of the produce, if there are 100 sacks of rice, he gets 33. It's the same proportion for manioc, maize and beans. Water-melons are done in half shares. Now, when someone has to clear and burn the land before he can work on it, he gets a bigger share, usually half.

This system tides over the impoverished families for a few years, but provides no permanent solution.

Many of the families which obtained plots have not prospered. When I was back in the village in November 1981, I was told that at least half of the 120 families had sold their plots. A variety of reasons was given for these surprising sales. A few of the families had been faced by a sudden emergency, such as a serious illness, and the land had been the only thing available for them to sell. At times these families had received absurdly low prices, as little as Crs 2,000–4,000 (£10–£20) for these plots for which they had fought for so long.

Other peasant farmers had been very old when they obtained their land, and their children had shown no interest in farming it, preferring to work for a wage in the village or even to get a job on the ranch, where working conditions had improved substantially. Though he had not sold his plot, Félix de Moraes was not making use of it. When we spoke to him in January 1979, he said:

Now I've got the little plot of land that INCRA fixed up for me in 1972. It's 20 *alqueires* (96.8 hectares), about nine kilometres away. I'm not planting much these days, just one or two hectares – and that's including what my sons do as well. They're grown up now, one married already and the others soon will be, but they don't like farming, they don't feel the need to produce. They eat every day, but they don't know where the food comes from. They are working though, here in the village.

One of his sons was employed as the driver of the cooperative's tractor. He had been taught how to drive by Jentel. Félix said that he had not sold his plot, or even rented it out, because he liked to think of it there, for one day they might need it. But it was sad to see that, after all the long struggle to win his plot of land, Félix was not making use of it.

Other peasant farmers had been forced to sell their plots because they had got entangled in financial difficulties. In 1979 the big state-owned Bank of Brazil had opened up an agency in nearby São Félix and for the first time in their life some of the farmers had obtained bank loans to cover planting costs. Though these loans were provided on highly advantageous conditions, the farmers were not used to handling money and for many the experiment ended in disaster. A few spent the money on clothes, household goods, a radio – consumer goods which they had never been able to afford before. Some had tried to raise their output, but without farm machinery (except for the cooperative's tractor) it had been very difficult. Some employed extra workers, paying out a cash wage for the first time in their lives. But they found that, without farm machinery, the additional output produced by the labourer was so small that it did not even cover his wages. These farmers learnt to their cost a basic economic truth: that unmechanised crop-farming only makes economic sense on the basis of unpaid family labour. Others found it difficult to realise that to pay back their loans they must greatly increase their produce sold on the market. Many of them, brought up in the closed economy of the *sertão*, still practised itinerant cattle-rearing and regarded crop-farming as a secondary activity. They were not prepared, psychologically or technically, to embark overnight on capitalist farming.

All these problems were exacerbated by marketing difficulties. Many of the farmers were forced in 1979 and 1980 to sell their rice to unscrupulous middlemen who, enjoying a virtual monopoly, were able to pay very low prices. After the cooperative had repeatedly complained to the government, a state agency (Production Financing Company – CFP) finally sent in its own buyers in 1981. This was a great boon to the farmers, for the CFP paid the minimum prices guaranteed by the government, which were considerably higher than those they had been receiving from the middlemen.

However, this improvement came too late for some of the peasant farmers. To pay back their bank loans, a few of them were forced to sell their plots and join the mass of landless peasants in Santa Teresinha. Others managed to cling on to their plots by rescheduling their debts. But once bitten, twice shy: these peasants reverted to their old practice of subsistence farming.

These problems were partly responsible for the gradual collapse of the cooperative set up with such enthusiasm by Jentel in 1965. Many of the members became caught up in their own financial problems and had little time or energy left for the cooperative. Though it sporadically springs to life, as when it requested marketing assistance from the government, its functions have become largely limited to selling its members foodstuffs and farm inputs at slightly cheaper prices.

Antônio Canuto, the priest who arrived in Santa Teresinha shortly before Jentel's arrest, has been living there every since. He never shared Jentel's passionate desire to bring modern farming methods to the farmers, but has made great efforts to build up a local community around the principles of communal action. Whereas Jentel wished to speed up the incorporation of the peasant families into the modern, capitalist world, Canuto has attempted to build up a socialist alternative to capitalism.

In keeping with his ideological position, Canuto made several attempts to set up communal systems of work in the second half of the 1970s. The most ambitious was an endeavour to set up a *roça comunitária* (a communal *roça*) in which a group of men, including Canuto, would work together on the land. The idea was to divide the crop between the men, the share of each depending on how much work he had put in. In defiance of normal capitalist practice, but in keeping with the peasants' old traditions, it was to be accepted by the participants that land was part of common wealth and no rent would be paid to the member who provided it. Canuto hoped that this pilot scheme would later be copied on a much bigger scale as the peasant farmers saw the advantages of collective farming.

The project was a complete failure. In a frank paper he gave at a seminar on collectivisation held by the Catholic Church's Ecumenical Centre of Documentation and Information (CEDI), Canuto gave his explanation. It had been difficult in the beginning to find enough farmers to take part in the experiment. Some had been wary of Canuto's own intentions, suspecting that he might be taking advantage of the free labour. The set-up had seemed to please no one: while some of the small landowners thought it unjust that they would not be paid rent, some of the landless peasants thought it wrong that they should be clearing someone's land for nothing. Squabbles had broken out, and the time taken to resolve them was one of the reasons why the experiment had not proved an economic success.

Canuto had become disillusioned with the whole project. He said:

> Even if the economic results had been worthwhile, we would only have managed to increase the living standards of a small group of people, while the vast majority would have gained nothing. The most that would have been achieved would have been islands of prosperity and no greater transformations.

Hardship was on the increase in Santa Teresinha in the late 1970s and early 1980s. Unemployment had become a very serious problem and, with so many families without land, many people were going hungry. To keep their families from starving, women were increasingly working as maids, washerwomen and seamstresses. But, by 1981, few jobs were available even in these traditionally badly-paid occupations. I noticed a marked increase in hardship, compared with our first visit in 1976.

On our trips we liked to talk to the washerwomen and to listen to them talking between themselves. Though women seemed to wash on most days of the week, Friday was official wash-day in Santa Teresinha. Early that morning many women used to wend their way down to the Araguaia, the elder women clothed in long-sleeved and full-skirted dresses, all of them with huge bundles of laundry on their heads or on their bicycle seats. Most of the women were just doing the family wash, but some of them had enormous piles of washing they were doing to earn a few cruzeiros. The women told us that they preferred to wash in the river, rather than in the sinks in their backyards, because the water was more plentiful as they did not have to pull it up in buckets from the well and because they could beat the clothes and the linen clean on wooden planks.

Moreover, as elsewhere in the Amazon, this weekly wash-day is a social occasion. Women meet together down by the local river to talk over family and village affairs, their conversation accompanied by the rhythmic slapping of the wet clothes.

We talked on one occasion to a lively 75-year-old who was washing for one of the small boarding houses to help her daughter and numerous grandchildren as her 'no-good' son-in-law had abandoned them. Sitting on her haunches at the end of a plank above the river water, she talked to us of the difficulties of making ends meet, with ever-rising prices. There are countless women in the Amazon, who, like this old woman, have to fend for themselves as widows or even more frequently as abandoned wives and mothers, though the difficulties they face are so commonplace that they rarely attract attention.

Illness is a serious problem in Santa Teresinha, displaced only by land and employment as a source of worry. According to church workers, there is not a healthy child in the village during the rainy season because the flooding brings worms, skin infections, flu and lung complaints. Though Santa Teresinha finally has a doctor, the medical service is still inadequate and far too expensive. All too often people end up buying drugs – often unsuitable and exorbitantly priced antibiotics – at the local pharmacy, without any medical supervision.

In January 1979, we visited Maria, Dona Josefa's 22-year-old granddaughter, who had just given birth to her first child. Maria had been abandoned by her husband during the early days of her pregnancy and had suffered intense pains during the last three months. The baby was born with a malformed head and died within hours. The mother was still in pain after the birth and her abdomen and leg were inflamed. During all this time, Maria had stayed in a back room of her family's mud-brick house, attended by her mother. When we visited her, she was taking medicine prescribed by the woman who works at the pharmacy. According to the written instructions

– which only we could read – the medicine was for the treatment of typhoid, paratyphoid and whooping cough, none of which illnesses she appeared to be suffering from; there was no mention of post-natal conditions.

It struck us forcibly on our return visit in January 1979 that Santa Teresinha had become a backwater. Though it was by then linked by river, road and air to the rest of Brazil, there was relatively little traffic of any kind. Santa Teresinha had suffered from the swing away from rivers to roads as the main axis of penetration. For the road to Santa Teresinha is a dead end, an offshoot of the main road which links Conceição do Araguaia, Marabá and other towns in Pará to the south.

Santa Teresinha seems sleepy and stagnant. Its inhabitants are dissatisfied and latch on to any rumour which could mean that Santa Teresinha could once more become a thriving regional centre. When we were there in January 1979, many people told us with great delight that large deposits of gold had been discovered on Codeara's land. Conceição Lopes Cardoso expressed the general excitement:

> The other day I was conversing with the men from over there, from Codeara – they're really going to hit the big time. They've already discovered one *garimpo* [mine] and are exploring another, all on their land. This way, Santa Teresinha will grow rapidly. The moment they set up a panning post here, there will be a bank, an office for registering land sales. Everyone is excited about it. Soon the company won't be able to find any workers for their ranch because everyone will be in the mine.

We became infected with the general climate of euphoria. Though the Codeara manager denied that any discoveries had been made, he confirmed that a detailed geological survey was being carried out. We began to wonder whether they were keeping information from us, as the people in the village seemed so certain . . .

In the event, the bubble burst as quickly as it had blown up. When I returned in November 1981, most people had completely forgotten about the earlier rumours. Large gold deposits had been found in the region but much further to the north, in the state of Pará.

Another incident in 1980 illustrated the pent-up frustration felt by many peasant families at being deprived of land in such a sparsely populated region where much fertile soil has not been brought into productive use. It also showed how land speculators were able to take advantage of the desperation felt by the families.

Early in 1980 a group of 28 peasant families decided to occupy a neck of land lying between the plots won by the peasant families in 1972 and the boundary of the Tapiraguaia ranch. Codeara claimed to be the owner of this land, though serious doubts existed over the legality of its documents. Although the land was cut off from the rest of the ranch and, as was freely admitted by some ranch employees, was of no great value to it, it was clear that Codeara would not take kindly to this 'invasion'.

Most of the families were very poor, on the verge of starvation, but the occupation was led by two better-off peasants who did not need the land to ensure their livelihood. It seems that the two leaders were land speculators who, as so frequently happens in the Amazon, were taking advantage of the desperation felt by the families. If they had not been in such a hopeless situation, caught in the poverty trap of Santa Teresinha, these peace-loving and law-abiding families would never have agreed to this dangerous and possibly illegal venture.

After some discussion, the peasants decided to work together to clear part of the forest and to divide the harvest later, according to each one's contribution to the work. A few weeks after they moved in, Codeara sent armed security guards to speak to them. They were told that Codeara was not interested in selling the land to them and advised them to leave at once if they wanted to avoid bloodshed. The peasants replied bluntly that they would not budge. After the guards had gone, the peasants built trenches across the only pathway leading to the land. Fearful that Codeara might send in gunmen at any moment to evict them, they mounted a constant watch, though this seriously interrupted their work on the land. They made a house-to-house collection in Santa Teresinha to raise money to buy ammunition.

After a few weeks news came that Codeara was planning its feared attack. At the beginning of May employees at the ranch told the peasant farmers that Codeara was collecting together a group of experienced gunmen to send in very early one morning. Then on 3 May the doctor in Santa Teresinha was called to the ranch in the middle of the night to attend a wounded man. He found a group of 12 gunmen who told him that they were waiting to be taken early the following morning to evict a group of peasant families. The gunmen had had their guns taken away from them and had been put up in a communal dormitory. A fight had broken out among them and Parazinho, a much-feared gunman from Pará, had managed to inflict a serious knife wound on another gunman.

On hearing that the attack was definitely planned, some of the inhabitants in Santa Teresinha began to take vigorous action. Raimundo Moreira Costa, acting president of the local branch of Contag, was woken up in the middle of the night and told what was happening. He immediately wrote a letter, addressed to the head of the federal police in Brasília, in which he strongly protested about the presence of gunmen at the ranch. He also claimed that the ranch had built up a big arsenal of arms and ammunition. He gave a brief account of the recent troubles and said that the peasant families were expecting an attack at any moment. He called for immediate action by the police. The letter was taken by road that very night to Santa Isabel do Morro, on Bananal Island, and handed over to officers from Brazil's air force which had a base there. Other inhabitants of Santa Teresinha went to warn the families that an attack from the gunmen was imminent.

In the event, the attack never took place. After the doctor had left, another fight had broken out between Parazinho and another of the gunmen. The ranch manager had finally called in the local police and Parazinho had been arrested. By now the presence of the gunmen on the ranch was public knowledge and the ranch manager must have thought it more prudent to call off the whole plan. Soon after, Codeara began negotiations with the peasant families. With the union acting as mediator, an agreement was finally worked out by which Codeara agreed to sell 32 plots, only 25 hectares each in size, to the peasant families. Some people in Santa Teresinha thought that the families should have stuck out for much larger plots, of at least 100 hectares, but others felt that in the circumstances they were wise to settle for what the company was willing to offer.

Once again this tiny victory did nothing to solve the basic problems of land shortage and unemployment. When I went back in November 1981, the prevalent mood was more despondent than ever. Though neighbours still helped out whenever they could, some of the poorest families were on the verge of starvation. When the gold fever had passed, many inhabitants had fixed their hopes on a new project – the building of a road across the north of Bananal Island to link up Santa Teresinha, and thus the whole of the north of Mato Grosso, with the important, asphalted Belém–Brasília highway. The project was strongly backed by the cattle companies. Though it is undoubtedly true that the construction of this road would put Santa Teresinha back on the map, it was dispiriting to see the importance that this as yet vague proposal was assuming for the families. Overwhelmed by the problems, the once resourceful inhabitants of Santa Teresinha were doing little themselves to sort out their problems but were desperately clutching at any straw.

Church workers in Santa Teresinha, some of whom lived through the turbulent period of the 'battle of the pharmacy' were clearly worried by the new trends. 'The peasant farmers may have won the war, but they're losing the peace', commented one lay worker wryly. The sparkle had gone out of Santa Teresinha. The peasant families were able to organise effective resistance against a clearly recognisable enemy, such as Codeara, but it was far more difficult to join battle with a faceless occupation process which was working against them in so many ways. The historical moment for revolutionary change appeared to have come and gone.

At the height of their conflict, the peasant families were prepared to lose all or to gain all. Perhaps through tension and excitment of the action, most of those involved had a heightened awareness and, some lay workers felt, were on the way to gaining a new political consciousness. Once the thrill had gone, many families had retreated into a defensive, cautious attitude. It was a matter of dispute whether the old fervour could be rekindled by a new conflict.

In October 1982 the government announced its decision to build the new road, to be called the Transaraguaia. It said that construction work should begin at the end of the rainy season in June or July 1983. Several public figures, including Bishop Pedro Casaldáliga and Mário Juruna, the first

Indian to become a federal deputy, were highly critical of the decision, because of the disruptive impact the road would have on the Carajá Indians, through whose lands it would pass. In November 1982, a church lay worker who had been in Santa Teresinha for more than a decade was elected mayor for the opposition PMDB party. Several months later came the announcement that Codeara, in conjunction with Goodyear, was to set up a large rubber plantation. Then in 1984 came news of a plan to build two hydroelectric power stations along the Araguaia river, at Santa Isabel and São Félix. The two projects, which are estimated to cost about $2 billion, will be largely financed by the USA, which is to provide most of the equipment. They should come on stream in 1992. Santa Teresinha is clearly in for some big changes.

Notes

1. The capybara is the largest extant rodent. It looks something like a giant guinea pig.
2. Wagley, *Welcome of Tears*, pp.11 and 12.
3. Código Civil Brasileiro, Direito das Coisas, note V, article 377, from the *Código de Procedência Civil*, article 502.
4. *O Globo*, 3 August 1970.
5. Pedro Casaldáliga, 'Uma igreja da Amazônia em conflito com o latifúndio e a marginalização social', p.107.
6. Ibid.
7. Ibid., p.108.
8. Ibid., p.109.
9. Ibid.
10. Ibid., p.108.
11. Wagley, *Welcome of Tears*, p.125.
12. Yves Matarne (ed.), *The Indian Awakening in Latin America* (An Original Paperback, Friendship Press, New York, 1980).
13. *Boletim do Cimi*, no.35, pp.8-9.
14. Ibid., p.10.
15. Wagley, *Welcome of Tears*, p.78.
16. *O Estado de S. Paulo*, 7 August 1981.
17. Ibid.

7. Case Study Two: Fazenda União Wages War on the 'Japanese'

The women burnt the truck and the corral. They were at it for six days. When Satoshi's plane flew over to have a look, the place was overrun with women. When Satoshi and his men came to the ranch, they were heard to say: 'There's nothing we can do, because it's the women who are burning everything down.'

Introduction

Our second community, called Fazenda União, lies to the centre-west of the state of Mato Grosso, about 800 kilometres to the south-west of São Félix. Though, as we were to discover, there are striking similarities with Santa Teresinha in the tale of land conflict its inhabitants tell, it was the differences from the Araguaia region, particularly in climate and history, which first attracted our attention.

Fazenda União lies on a mountain ridge, called Chapada dos Parecis, to the west of the BR–364 highway which runs from Cuiabá, the capital of Mato Grosso, to Porto Velho, the capital of the newly-created state of Rondônia. The Chapada dos Parecis acts as a watershed between South America's two great river basins: to the north the waters flow into the Amazon and out to sea in the north of Brazil; to the south they flow into the Paraguay river and then into the River Plate, the huge estuary which lies between Uruguay and Argentina. The head-waters of rivers that reach the Atlantic as far apart as Belém and Montevideo – a distance of about 3,500 kilometres – are only a few kilometres apart in this ridge. Although the altitude of the ridge is no more than 1,000 metres, it is sufficient to change the climate and thus the type of forest. The nights can be very cold, sometimes close to freezing point, though the daytime temperature can be very high. Such extremes of temperature are unheard of in the Araguaia river valley, almost all of which lies below 200 metres.

Discoveries of diamonds and gold were made in this mountain ridge during colonial times. Though the finds were far less extensive than those made in Minas Gerais and elsewhere in Brazil, they were bait enough for prospectors to undertake a long and difficult journey. Diamantino, the largest town in this region, is about 200 kilometres from Cuiabá. Like its sister town Diamantina in Minas Gerais, it was founded by prospectors. Its careful, colonial design, with the 200-year-old church and the houses built around the central square, forms a vivid contrast to the disorderly, straggling frontier towns which are being built in Amazonia today, and makes the town more akin to the beautiful 'Brazilian baroque' mining towns in Minas Gerais.

Until recently, the region was very isolated and sparsely populated. Around Diamantino itself there was a small cluster of mining towns which grew up in the same period: Alto Paraguai (near the source of the great Paraguay river, at this stage a tiny stream), Nortelândia, Arenápolis and others. Even with the stagnation of the mining activities, these towns continued to attract a trickle of migrants searching either for a plot of land or for work in one of the mines. Most of these migrants came from Goiás, Minas Gerais or other areas of Mato Grosso, or, via these states, from Espírito Santo or Bahia. Diamantino became a diocese town early in its history and until 1982 its diocese covered a huge region of 354,000 square kilometres, an area larger than Italy.[1]

This isolation began to be broken in the late 1960s when, largely as the result of the government-sponsored 'march to the Amazon', cattle companies and land speculators began to arrive, mainly from São Paulo. Little by little the advancing occupation frontier overtook both the isolated mining communities and the hamlets of subsistence backwoodsman peasants. As elsewhere, this change brought trouble to the hitherto peaceful region, with conflicts arising both between the peasants and the landowners and between the landowners themselves. One such tussle broke out between about 250 peasant families and various alleged landowners over an area of fertile land called Fazenda União (Union Ranch), about 16 kilometres from the little town of Afonso, in the district of Arenápolis, which is in its turn about 80 kilometres from Diamantino.

We paid our longest visit to this region in August 1978, the month with least rain, when the trees and plants which have been cut down earlier in the year are burnt. It was on this trip that we were struck most forcibly by the extent of the forest destruction, at least in this part of Amazonia. During our entire bus journey across Mato Grosso, from its border with São Paulo state in the south to Diamantino – a distance of about 1,000 kilometres – the sky was hazy with smoke and the sun looked like a huge red disc, even at the height of the day.

Some of the cattle companies let the fires on their lands run their course until they finally burnt out, checked by some river. They took no precautions to ensure that their fires did not harm the peasants' crops or houses. The peasants did what they could. Before the fires reached them, they made their own smaller fires to burn the dead vegetation on their *roças* and thus to create a fire check. At times they got together to clear a larger area, which they hoped would protect all their homes. Even so, the families were always fearful that their efforts had been insufficient and, not infrequently, huts were burnt down. Throughout our visit in 1978, while the peasants told us the remarkable tale of their long struggle, we could hear the crackling noise of fire in the distance and we were aware of a constant fear that the fires would get out of control or be brought their way by a strong wind.

Fazenda União (Union Ranch) – or, as it is called today, Gleba União (Union Glebe) – is made up of four plots, covering an area of about 27,000 hectares: Garça (heron), Agua Branca (white water), Abolição (abolition) and Bosque da Saudade (wood of longings).[2] The peasant families have occupied only three of these plots, for the largest – Garça – already had an owner from the peasants' first days in the area. When we were there in 1976 and 1978, Fazenda União was still an isolated frontier community. Whereas in Santa Teresinha, the peasants had founded a little town in the early days of the occupation, in Fazenda União they had scattered out over the region. Even as late as 1978 there was no village whatsoever. The families had to travel the 16 kilometres to Afonso to make all their purchases.

The Early Settlement

The peasant families at Fazenda União showed an unusual degree of unity and solidarity even in the first days of their settlement. As we have seen, migrants generally travel and settle in family units or as lone individuals. However, in Fazenda União it was different. Because the soil was known to be particularly fertile, its occupation had been much discussed in the region. A few families had thought of moving in, but had been deterred by rumours that the land already belonged to a landowner. Some families said that the supposed landowner was no more than a 'Japanese land thief' who had 'no rights' and that there was nothing to stop peasant families from moving in. Others claimed that the whole situation was very confused and it was far too risky to occupy plots there. We were told that for months people in the little towns in the region – Nortelândia, Progresso and elsewhere – had talked over the question.

Finally a group of about 30 families got together in Afonso in April 1974 and decided to try to find out if there was any real chance of them obtaining plots. There was no reliable way in which they could clearly establish the legal status of the land involved, but they did what they could with their limited resources and sent a representative to the nearest land registration office in Diamantino. He was told that Satoshi Kuroyanagi, a Brazilian of Japanese descent, had registered 10,000 of the 27,000 hectares – the Garça plot – but that the rest of the land appeared to be *terra devoluta* and thus available for the peasants.

Their delegate obtained a 'negative certificate' (that is, a written statement from the office stating that, as far as it knew, the land in question did not have an owner) for the rest of the land. Although many of the families appeared not to realise it, this certificate was not a watertight guarantee in Brazilian law as, given the complexity of the registration system, it was possible for a landowner to have legally registered the land elsewhere. However, it was a valiant attempt and, in the circumstances, as much as could reasonably be expected. On the basis of these hopeful findings the families moved into the area in May 1974.

Amongst the first settlers were Amado Ferreira da Silva and his wife, Dona Geralda. When we stayed with them in 1978, they were living with their three youngest children in an adobe house which, by peasants' standards, was very spacious – it had three bedrooms, two living rooms and a kitchen, where the wood stove burnt all day, with food and weak, sweet coffee on the hob for all comers. The couple had had 12 children, but two had married and left home and seven had died in infancy.

Like most peasants at the time, this family was virtually self-sufficient. On their *roça*, they grew rice, beans, maize and other food crops, as well as cotton which Dona Geralda spun and wove into the blankets which were needed during the cold nights. Pigs and chickens – as well as cats and dogs – roamed freely around the yard and in the house itself. The family did not have any cattle of their own, but received fresh milk every day – a rare luxury – in return for the use of their pasture by a neighbour's cattle.

Maria, their 13-year-old daughter, did the washing up and the laundry in the little river at the end of the yard, using soap made by her mother. Dona Geralda used to take ashes from the fire, pack them tightly in a tin with a perforated bottom and pour water through it. She then mixed the alkaline water she obtained in this way with pig fat to make the soap. As we could see, this method was laborious and, even in 1978, most of the women in the region preferred to use caustic soda purchased from a shop rather than the home-prepared alkaline water. This family only needed regularly to buy kerosene, coffee, salt and sugar. They were self-sufficient in almost everything else and could survive for months without money.

Dona Geralda told us how they had come to live in Fazenda União:

> All my life I've worked on the *roça*. I was born and raised in Goiás and spent another 18 years there, married. It's five years now since I came to Mato Grosso. I arrived here with my husband, who's from Goiás too. We've moved lots of times, from ranch to ranch, from *roça* to *roça*, always working on other people's land, paying rent all our lives. When we weren't paying 25 or 30 per cent of our crops as rent, we were paying half. We kept on moving because we thought each time that we'd get a better deal elsewhere and earn our daily bread more easily. But every time things got more difficult, until it got to the point when we couldn't make ends meet any more. We worked as hard as we could on the *roça*, but hardly anything was left over for ourselves.
>
> So we said: 'Let's go to the town. Who knows, the town might be better for us, we might be able to lead a life that's more or less all right.' So we went to Córrego do Ouro, in Goiás still, our local town. There Amado opened a butcher's shop, but in the end this left us with nothing for everyone bought on credit and, when their time was due, they didn't pay. As we'd already spent

everything we had on the shop, we lost everything, we ended up with nothing. So we decided to move to Mato Grosso.

We from Goiás, we knew about Mato Gross, because people said that you could get land very cheaply there and that there was a lot of work to be had. In Goiás there wasn't any more land left and the only work to be found was on farms where it was all mechanised, so they didn't really want us. So we had this idea: 'Let's go to Mato Grosso, because perhaps we can sharecrop there and then have enough over to buy a little plot of land.' So we came here. We've been in Mato Grosso for five years now and it's nearly beaten us.

We spent two months back there, near Afonso, working for someone else so we could have enough money to come on here. There was a lad from Pernambuco there, who'd worked a lot with us in Goiás, and he told Amado: 'Uh, Amado, I know a place which a Japanese is looking after, but it's not his ranch, he's just trying to grab the land.' When everyone was thinking of moving in here, they went to the office in Diamantino to hunt for documents about these lands, just to make sure that it didn't have a real owner. But they didn't find any, because it was public land.

So a group of about 30 men decided to go in. At that time, there wasn't any road at all, it was just pure jungle, so they hacked their way through with big knives and carried what they needed for eating and sleeping on their backs. They got to realise how good the land was, digging it with the point of their knives. They spent eight days in the jungle and then came home. Afterwards they went in again with their farm implements to start work there.

So the men set up a little hamlet there, with 18 huts. At that time there were lots and lots of wild animals, but now the forest has been burnt down and the animals have fled deeper into the jungle. At that time we women were still in Afonso, only the men were working there.

Another peasant, Maximiano Bispo da Silva (or Massu) had come to Fazenda União on his own, before the others. He told us that Satoshi Kuroyanagi, usually referred to as Satoshi (or just 'the Japanese'), was already farming a small part of the land when he arrived:

When I left Minas, I came here because there wasn't any land left there to work on. So I came to Mato Grosso in 1970 and arrived at Fazenda União. The boss, Satoshi, the Japanese, gave me work as a share-cropper. But the contract we made said that he wasn't responsible for any damage done to my crops, even if it was his employees who did it. Now, when my crops were ripe, ready to be harvested, his men decided to knock down all the tree stumps in the fields where I'd planted my crops. I went to complain that his men were trampling down my crops and he told me to go and hunt for land which didn't have a ranch or anything there, because here it was ranch land. Then he said that I'd come to grab the land for a land thief. I didn't even know what he was talking about. I'd heard about this land, because hunters had talked about it. But I knew that I'd have to leave. Then everyone decided to come into this area, saying that it was public land, so I stayed with the group.

Another of the group was universally known as Boca Rica, or Rich Mouth, as he had eight gold crowns on his teeth. (We never discovered his real name.) He told us how he became involved:

> I'm from Governador Valadares in Minas Gerais. First I left for Paraná state, where I worked on other people's lands, mainly on coffee plantations, and then in a sawmill. On the *roças* I always worked like this – sharecropping by halves, thirds, by every way possible. The best thing was to pay them by percentage, about 30 per cent. Then I'd harvest 200 bags or rice, give them 60 bags and keep 140 for myself. Just imagine if it had all been mine and I could have sold all those bags!
>
> In the sawmill I worked by the month, for a wage. I spent 17 years there but it was really difficult. I always wanted to fix up a plot of land but there was no way, so I moved here to Mato Grosso. In Paraná there are too many people, so life's more difficult.
>
> So I arrived in this place, Progresso, and there were some lads having a beer there and they were talking together: 'Over near Afonso there's some land in dispute and it is lovely land.' I got off my bicycle and heard them talking like this. So I kept quiet and then I took my bike and went off to Afonso to see if I could discover where this land was. When I got to Afonso, an old lady there showed me the road and I came here, only arriving when it was dark, on my own, just jungle, all jungle!

The First Conflicts

After the initial expedition by the group of 30 in April 1974, about 200 peasants went back in May to occupy the land and clear their first plots. They were all excited by the opportunity that had opened up for them. Many of them told us that they had spotted *bacuri* trees growing on the land, which was a sure indication to them that the soil was extremely fertile. They left the Garça plot, already occupied by Satoshi, well alone and divided up another virgin area, giving each other plots with 500 metres of riverbank.

Immediately after they had moved in, they received a visit from Agostinho Corrêa, the ranch manager, who told them that the whole area was owned by Satoshi and his associates, and warned them that, if they did not leave at once, he would bring in the police. Confident of their legal right to the land, the peasants told him in no uncertain terms that they were staying. On 1 June, the police duly appeared in the form of Major Zuzi Alves da Silva, police commissioner for the state of Mato Grosso, and several assistant officers. Dona Geralda told us what happened: 'Major Zizi [*sic*] came here to take everyone out of the jungle. They even took one of the 30 comrades off to Cuiabá where he was imprisoned for five days.'

The arrested man, called Geraldo Módulo, was accused of being the 'leader of the invading group'. On the day after his arrest, the other peasants hired a lorry to take them to Cuiabá so that they could demand the release of their companion. They were stopped at Arenápolis by the local mayor, who promised to put their case to the authorities and asked them to return home. Somewhat reluctantly they agreed.

After five days, Geraldo was released. No formal charges were brought against him, which was seen by the peasant families as further evidence that their occupation was not illegal. It soon became clear, however, that Geraldo had paid a high price for his freedom. Dona Geralda explained: 'He was told that he couldn't come back here under any circumstances. I think that they made him sign a document saying that he wouldn't ever return.' Thoroughly scared, Geraldo immediately left the region, never to be seen again by the peasant families. Even more serious than this defection was the loss of the 'negative certificate' that they had obtained from the land registration office in Diamantino. Major Zuzi had taken this certificate when he had arrested Geraldo. Though he had promised to return it to them later, he never did. It was felt to be a serious loss, for the peasants had attached great (and undoubtedly excessive) importance to this 'proof' of the legitimacy of their occupation.

Aware that the conflict could readily escalate into a serious confrontation, members of the Catholic Church began to take an interest in the case and to investigate the possibilities of a peaceful settlement. Isidoro Schneider, the local priest, began to visit the families and on 13 June Dom Henrique Froehlich, the Bishop of Diamantino, sent a letter to INCRA's land commission[3] in which he requested information and asked INCRA to sort out the legal status of the land in question. In reply, Altamir Wollmann, president of Mato Grosso branch of the commission, promised to send in a team to inspect the area and to sort out the problem of land titles. But no immediate action was taken.

Satoshi was irritated by the growing involvement of the Catholic Church. On 15 October he sent an extraordinary letter to Dom Henrique in which he thanked the bishop for his 'friendly dialogue' and reminded him that in an earlier conversation he had admitted that Satoshi and his associates were 'completely right'. He then proceeded to warn the bishop that 'his sheep persist in running along dangerous paths', by which he appeared to be referring to the work being carried out among the peasant families by Isidoro Schneider and other church members. In a contorted mixture of veiled threats and obsequious flattery, he told the bishop that these members of the church were helping 'opportunist elements' who harboured 'criminal intents'. Quoting various laws, including the National Security Law, he cautioned the bishop that, unless firm action was taken to put an end to these activities, he would be taking legal action to defend his rights.

Even before the letter was sent, Satoshi had resorted to extra-legal pressures to evict the families. He had sent in gunmen in August, though they did not immediately use force. Dona Geralda told us about the first act of violence committed by these gunmen:

> The Japanese sent in a group of gunmen headed by a so-called Jurandir.
> People here have the custom of celebrating All Souls' Day on 2 November, so
> on that day all the men left their plots and went to Afonso to be with their
> families. No one stayed behind. So the gunman Jurandir went in with two
> other gunmen, chopped everything with an axe, knocked down everything.

The gunmen also destroyed the men's huts, setting fire to some of
them.

The peasants reported what had happened to the local police force in
Afonso, who, unlike their superiors in Cuiabá, the state capital, showed
considerable sympathy for the peasants' cause. Dona Geralda continued:

> It must be the mercy of God, because the police finally caught Jurandir and the
> two other gunmen in Afonso. They almost beat them to death. We didn't bring
> any accusations against them. We stood there, with our arms crossed, not
> knowing what to do. Nobody knew how to work the law, as they'd had no
> experience.

Jurandir and his companions were freed after only a few days in jail,
apparently after Satoshi's manager, Agostinho Corrêa, had intervened on
their behalf with the police authorities in Cuiabá.

The Harassment Increases

It was about this time that the peasants began to come under pressure from a
new source. At the very end of 1974, another self-proclaimed landowner,
Luís Jorge da Silva, from Diamantino, appeared at Fazenda União. He
claimed to own 1,200 *alqueires* (about 2,900 hectares),[4] some of which was
already occupied by the peasants. He and his men built huts in the 'invaded'
area, using wood from the peasants' destroyed homes. He was already well
known in the region as a *grileiro* (land grabber) and it seemed likely that he
was working in league with Satoshi to get the peasants out. Luís Jorge
offered to sell the peasants the land on terms which were impossibly high for
them: Crs 4,000 (£227) an *alqueire*, with 30 per cent down payment.

Some members of the church thought that, as the situation had become so
tense, it was essential to end the conflict as soon as possible, even if it meant
the peasant families buying from Satoshi and Luís Jorge land that they
probably did not own. So Dom Henrique approached Satoshi to see
whether he would accept terms similar to those offered by Luís Jorge. As he
agreed in principle, the bishop then approached several government
agencies in January 1975 to see if they would finance the transaction. After
some hesitation, Sudeco (the centre-west development agency) and the
agriculture ministry agreed jointly to put up the money provided that the
peasants committed themselves to paying it back over a period of years.
The scheme then ran into opposition from INCRA, which said that it could

not authorise plots of less than 60 hectares in size, as this had been fixed as the minimum area that could support a family in that region.[5] However, INCRA eventually agreed to a way round this ruling (which in any case was not appropriate for such fertile land): three families would be allowed to join together to purchase a 60-hectare plot. It seemed that everything was going to be resolved amicably and the peasant families were delighted, though some resented the idea of paying for land which they believed they already owned. A meeting was arranged for 4 February at which the final details would be hammered out. Satoshi and his lawyer, the peasants, representatives of the Arenápolis branch of Fetagri, the Mato Grosso rural workers' union, INCRA representatives and members of the Catholic Church – a total of about 250 people – attended.

José Pego da Cruz, known as Zé Pego, Amado's neighbour and his constant companion during the long struggle, told us about the meeting:

> The bishop, Dom Henrique, suffering the pain of the poor, had spoken to the Japanese who had said that he would sell the land, so the bishop had gone to the bank with a proposal and they had agreed, provided we paid them back later. So he chose the day for us all to meet in Afonso to resolve the case. When the day came, we were so pleased that at last there'd be a real solution. The bishop explained everything to us, but when the Japanese arrived, he told the bishop that the land was mortgaged, so he couldn't sell it, that he could only sell land by a certain stream. But that land is useless, it's like a lake.
>
> So the peasants refused. The land there wouldn't produce enough even to pay for itself. We were all fed up, but what could we do? We wouldn't have minded paying. I think when most of us moved in, we had accepted that we wouldn't get the land free, that we would have to pay someone for it, the government or whoever.

After the peasants had unanimously turned down Satoshi's offer to sell them lands that were virtually useless – and had then refused a second option, to buy land over 100 kilometres away – he gave them six months to leave the area without compensation, 'or else'. The meeting had reached deadlock. The peasant families were very depressed by the results of the meeting, but they went back to their plots determined not be to bullied into leaving. It soon became clear that Satoshi had decided to take the offensive and to make a concerted attempt at various levels to drive them out.

First of all, Luís Jorge, who had begun to harass the peasant families before the meeting, kept up the pressure. Dona Geralda told us what it was like:

> Luís Jorge began to move against us in January 1975. His surveyor came in and divided the land into plots, though there were peasants already living there. He then sold off this land to ranch owners from São Paulo, Paraná,

all over. He brought these people in and sold them the land with false documents – he never had any good, legal documents. Then they opened a road, took out the timber, beat people up.

Then Satoshi mounted another offensive, with the backing of the state authorities. On 17 February some military policemen, headed by Major Zuzi, arrived from Cuiabá and installed themselves on Simão Barroso's ranch, near Fazenda União. The region became alive with rumours as to their intentions. The local inhabitants did not have to wait long: on the following day Major Zuzi sent two armed military policemen, with farm manager Agostinho Corrêa, to bring in those whom they considered to be the leaders of the peasant families so that they could be questioned. It was during this interrogation that the peasant families realised for the first time that the authorities wanted to use them to incriminate members of the Catholic Church. Several of the peasants were clearly bewildered, since until then, except in the efforts at mediation, the church had played a very secondary role.

Massu was one of the eleven peasants arrested and he told us what happened:

In February 1975, the police came. Two policemen took us over to Simão's ranch and, when we got there, there were five policemen with a machine gun, revolvers, the lot. Then we were taken to see Satoshi's manager, Simão and Zizi in a room with a desk. The police stayed at the door with their revolvers and they kept on ordering us to say that it was the bishop and the father who'd sent us in to invade the land in the first place. I said: 'No. No one told us to go in. It was sheer need that sent us in.' Zizi then said: 'But everyone's saying that it was the father and the bishop who ordered you to go in there, and you're the only one to say that it wasn't them.' 'Well, I'm the only one telling the truth then, and all the rest are lying, because I don't know of any father or bishop doing this.'

So then he said he was going to have some statement or other typed out for me to sign, but I said: 'I'm not going to sign anything that's not true, that's just lies.' But then they threatened me and I was forced to sign – the poor have no choice. The police had taken ten or eleven of us and we all signed, though only one or two had really criticised the father and the bishop, and then only because they were afraid of the revolvers. But, as we all signed, the authorities said that we had all condemned them.

The 11 peasants later regretted that they had given in to the pressure and felt that they had betrayed the bishop. On 27 March they went to Diamantino to see the local judge, Agnelo Bezerra Neto, to see if they could retract their statements. Massu told us what happened:

The secretary came out and said: 'If it's about the Japanese, we can't do business with you. You can count without us, because we can't interfere.' So

I said: 'Well, I'm going to tell you something, all of you – we're being turned out, dying of hunger, to spread out all over Brazil, dying of hunger, because we've not even been able to speak to the authorities.' 'But why don't you go and see a lawyer? I know a lawyer in Várzea Grande, near Cuiabá. She's well informed about the case.' 'Why?' 'She's Satoshi's niece.' 'What are you trying to do? Get us into more of a mess.'

Feeling very angry, the peasants visited Father Renato Roque Barth, who had become the parish priest in Diamantino in December 1974, to ask his advice. He took them to a public office and, according to Massu, they signed a declaration saying: 'Major Zizi and five policemen have been forcing us to say that it was the father and the bishop who ordered us to enter that land.'

It was about this time that two local priests – Renato Barth and José Pedro Lisboa, known as Zé Pedro, the parish priest at Alto Paraguai – began to take a keen interest in the conflict. Both priests were shocked by the accounts they heard from the peasant families and began to see what they could do to help resolve the conflict. As a first step towards putting pressure on the authorities, these two priests suggested that the peasant families should ask the local union, Fetagri, to help them to carry out a survey into the exact number of families involved and the location of their plots. About 200 peasants attended a meeting in April 1975 at which this proposal was made and unanimously accepted.

Like the peasant families, we were at first puzzled by the authorities' attitude towards the Catholic Church. It was admittedly clear that throughout the struggle church members had played an increasingly important role, particularly in the way they were able to put the peasants in touch with organisations, such as Fetagri, which could provide invaluable assistance, and in publicising the conflict. By attracting nationwide attention to the conflict, the church made it much more difficult for Satoshi, in alliance with the state police, to get away with the use of outright violence against the families. But it was also evident to anyone who talked to the families that the church only supplied help and advice and it was the peasant families themselves who decided on what course of action to take. Nevertheless, as we shall see, the Mato Grosso police went to extraordinary lengths to fabricate evidence against the church workers. Their objective seems to have been to accumulate sufficient evidence to accuse them of 'subversion' and of acting as the 'intellectual mentors' of the acts of violence perpetrated by the peasants. There is no indication that the state authorities ever tried to carry out an honest, unbiased investigation into exactly what had happened.

This witch-hunt against the church is partly to be explained by the tense church–state relations at a national level (see Chapter 4). However, equally important must have been the wish of the state authorities to cover their tracks and to hide their own dubious involvement in this affair. While it would be extremely difficult, even in the corrupt local courts, to argue that the illiterate and scrupulously honest peasant families had 'plotted against the state', the charge would gain a minimum of plausibility if it was levelled against progressive, educated church members. Moreover, the state authorities knew that they could count on considerable support from the powerful hard-liners in the armed forces, if they claimed to be fighting an ideological war with the progressive wing of the church.

The constant support given by the state authorities to Satoshi, on occasions when he was clearly acting in a completely illegal fashion, was remarkable even in a corrupt state like Mato Grosso. It continued after the Fazenda União dispute had become a political embarrassment to the government. It should be realised that Satoshi himself was a leading official in this government. He ran the finance department of the state's electricity board from 1968 to 1971 and then Matemat, the state's mining company, from 1971 to 1973. He worked in the state's planning department from 1974 until the first half of 1976.

The First Death

While terrifying the peasant families, Satoshi also sought to drive them out by legal means. On 9 May his lawyers sent a document to judge Agnelo Bezerra Neto in which they requested a court order for the 'reintegration' of the Agua Branca and Bosque de Saudade plots, in the name of Satoshi and his wife and other alleged owners, against 29 peasant families, who, it was claimed, had 'perpetrated a mass invasion' of these properties. The bishop and the priests were accused of being the 'instigators'.

It was clear, however, that the court case could drag on for years. Towards the middle of 1975, Satoshi and Luís Jorge grew impatient and stepped up the violence of their harassment. On 5 July the peasant farmer João Antônio Gonçalves, known as João Barvino, was walking down the road to Afonso when he had his way blocked by two cars: one was driven by a *paranaense* (a man from Paraná), accompanied by his son and Jucelino Miranda, the police officer in charge of the Arenápolis police station; and the other by Marcos Nunes Almeida, Luís Jorge's surveyor, accompanied by two more policemen from Arenápolis, and two gunmen, known as Baianinho and Angelim. João Barvino was told that his plot was included in the land that had been sold by Luís Jorge to the *paranaense* and that he must move out immediately, accepting the trivial compensation of Crs 1,000 (£54). He was forced to pack up his belongings and taken by car to Arenápolis.

The next day the first killing took place, but it was not, as everyone had been expecting, one of the peasant farmers who died. Dona Geralda told us what happened:

> They killed a man whom they'd brought from Paraná to work for them as a gunman. He told them that he didn't want to work as a gunman any more, that

he wanted a plot of land to work as a peasant farmer, so they shot him, in that house over there. The man who was killed was called Dionísio Julião. He was visiting one of the peasant farmers whom he had got friendly with when the gunmen Baianinho and Angelim came up to the house. The peasant farmer invited him in for a coffee. Baianinho went in and immediately fired two shots at Dionísio. He managed to run outside, but the gunmen continued to fire shots at him until he dropped down dead.

The 'investigation' into this crime was carried out by Marcos Nunes Almeida, Luís Jorge's surveyor, and the two policemen who had been travelling with him on 5 July. Not surprisingly, no arrests were made or charges brought. A leaflet denouncing the crime and accusing the authorities of corruption soon circulated in the region. On the following Sunday Barth briefly spoke about the crime at his evening mass. Two days later he was arrested by Itamar Fernandes Costa, a police officer from Diamantino, and taken to Rosário Oeste for interrogation by the regional police chief, Benedito Bruno. He was questioned about his activities, asked why he had chosen to work in such a backward region and then released.

The pressure increased. In August six peasant families were woken up in the middle of the night by the sound of cars arriving and shots being fired into the air. They were forcibly evicted from their houses and taken, protesting, with their possessions to Arenápolis. Though they filed a complaint with the police, they had no redress.

Another group of peasant families went to Arenápolis at the end of September to complain that the gunman known as Baianinho had invaded their *roças* and destroyed their crops. They also said that he was bragging that he had killed Dionísio but was still free. A police officer, Antenor Gonçalves, went to investigate their complaints. As he failed to find Baianinho, he arrested Marcos, Luís Jorge's surveyor, who had become the *de facto* leader of the gunmen. However, Marcos did not languish in jail for long; within days he was visited by Luís Jorge's uncle and released shortly afterwards.

Until then, though they had destroyed crops and homes, the gunmen had not harmed the peasants. But this now changed. On 5 October a small group of well-armed gunmen, led by Marcos, attacked several peasant families, choosing very isolated huts. Nine peasants were seriously wounded with machetes and clubs. The gunmen took all the peasants' arms, including penknives used to cut tobacco, and warned the families that they would all be killed if they did not leave within 24 hours.

It seemed the beginning of the end. Amado told us of the anguish and despair felt by the peasants at this time:

> Luís Jorge seemed to have everything in the palm of his hand. His gunmen told us that he had 200 men ready to fight, so that there wasn't any point in resisting. Luís Jorge, they said, was big enough to put an end to the lot of us. So we were left, afraid, wondering about our situation here in Mato Grosso.

> We'd come from afar to find a little plot of land to work on and we'd thought that we were safe and sound, but now there was a storm going on around us. When we'd arrived, these lands belonged to the state – we checked that – but afterwards all these sharks had turned up, claiming that they were the owners and sending in gunmen to throw us out. And the authorities were no help. They earned money by turning the screw on us.

Panic-stricken, the peasant families could only turn to the police, though by now they had little hope that it would do any good. They sent a representative, Gonçalo Clemente de Assis, to complain to the police in Afonso. Word of the peasant families' predicament soon spread around the village. The local inhabitants decided that, if the police were incapable of taking decisive action, they had better fill the breach: a lorry left for Fazenda União with 30 armed men, offering their support to the peasants. Dona Geralda told us:

> A little later a whole lot of people came from Afonso to help, people who felt sorry for us and brought food, drink, medicine for the children, even bedclothes, as some of the huts had been destroyed and the children got ill from sleeping on the cold ground.

The Peasants' 'Rebellion'

Up to now the peasants had scrupulously respected the law and, when in trouble, had sought help from the authorities with what seemed to us remarkable faith that justice would eventually be done. But now the situation had become so desperate that they decided to combat violence with violence. The peasants got organised on 6 October. The peasant farmers and the men from Afonso divided themselves into groups: some built trenches beside the roads, while others kept guard outside the houses where the women and children had gathered. Amado's and Geralda's house was overflowing with people afraid to stay alone in their isolated houses. But very few people lost their nerve. Nearly all the families decided to stay at Fazenda União to fight for their lands. As far as we could ascertain, practically the only people who left the area were nine pregnant women, who, it was agreed by common consent, had to move out temporarily.

On the afternoon of 7 October, a blue Volkswagen drove down the road and was shot at by the entrenched peasants who recognised it as one of Luís Jorge's cars, often used by his gunmen. Dona Geralda told us: 'They shot at a VW, shot it to pieces. It looked like lace, it was so riddled with bullet holes.' Remarkably the two passengers in the car were not hurt by the bullets, but they were slightly injured when their car crashed into a tree. They got out and fled into the forest, abandoning the car. Later on, another car, also known to belong to Luís Jorge, was found in the area and the peasants knifed the tyres to stop its occupants making a getaway. The peasants found out later that on 6 October Luís Jorge had sold the blue

Volkswagen to a *paranaense*, Braz Martins, and that the new owner and a colleague – not gunmen – had been in the car when they shot at it. Braz Martins, who had just bought land occupied by the peasant families from Luís Jorge, was thoroughly scared by what had happened and tried unsuccessfully to sell back both his land and his car to Luís Jorge.

Meanwhile the church workers in the region had met in Diamantino to see what else they could do to prevent further violence. A group, including Dom Henrique and Zé Pedro, visited the local judge, Bezerra Neto, to tell him what had happened and to ask for help. But the judge merely advised them not to meddle in peasants' affairs. A couple of days later a group from the diocese, including Dom Henrique, Zé Pedro and the peasants Zé Pego and Lídio Pereira, travelled to Cuiabá, where they put the peasants' case to Fetagri and to Colonel José Ferreira Diniz, the secretary for public security in Mato Grosso.

As the result of their visit, a lawyer in the public security department, known simply as Dr Haroldo by the peasants, was sent to Fazenda União at the head of a group of goverment officials and policemen to carry out an inquiry. The gunmen were warned of the visit and, by the time the group arrived, they had all disappeared. Dr Haroldo took all the peasants to Afonso for questioning. After making them hand over their weapons, he told them to go back home and to continue to work on their *roças*. Massu said that he told them: 'We haven't come here to give you land. We don't even know who this land belongs to. But you keep on working, united, until a decision is made about the land, because Brazil needs hard workers like you.' The peasants returned home, feeling cautiously optimistic.

The next few months were relatively peaceful. The Catholic Church's Pastoral Land Commission (CPT) published two documents[6] which helped to attract national attention to the situation of the peasant farmers. On 30 October Luís Jorge had a meeting with the bishop in which he sought the latter's help, but at the same time complained of the peasants' 'aggressiveness'. He was also very critical of the priests Zé Pedro and Renato, claiming that they had been behind the peasants' uncharacteristic use of violence in their attack on the car. Luís Jorge said that he had written, but not yet sent, a letter of protest to General João Baptista Figueiredo, at that time head of the SNI, in which he accused the priests of acts of 'subversion' and 'inciting the peasant families to invade private property'.

Dom Henrique strongly defended the priests from the accusations and said that he thought that the peasants' 'aggressiveness' was natural, given the treatment they had received. The bishop also questioned the authenticity of Luís Jorge's land documents and asked him why he had not registered them with INCRA, if they were valid as he claimed. The bishop said that he would only be willing to hold further talks with Luís Jorge once he had taken this step. Luís Jorge had no answer to the bishop's question. He appears to have realised that he was facing a powerful and determined opponent in the Catholic Church and, from then on, nothing more was heard of his documents or seen of his gunmen.

Satoshi Reappears

The peasants were greatly relieved to see the back of Luís Jorge, but their unexpected victory was short lived. Dona Geralda explained: 'During the year or so that Luís Jorge was in here, the Japanese kept very quiet. But after Luís Jorge disappeared, he started up again.' Satoshi's first reminder of his presence came in December 1975 when over 900 bags of guinea grass were sown on the peasant families' *roças* from planes flying overhead. As the peasants had no weed killers, they could do nothing, only wait for the grass to grow and then laboriously pull it up by hand before it had rooted. Despite their efforts, they told us three years later that it was still sprouting on their plots. There seemed to be no way of eliminating it completely.

Satoshi then left them alone until March 1976 when he sent in labourers to clear the land, including their *roças*. Dona Geralda said:

> He brought in labour contractors to clear the land, to take out the wood and to turn everything into pasture. But we, the peasants, met together and went to ask the workers to stop the job. And they did. They went away.

This incident is similar to one that took place in Santa Teresinha (see Chapter 6).

Satoshi was extremely angry and quickly planned to unleash his toughest offensive yet against the peasant families. It was at this time that João Kauling, a Jesuit, arrived at Fazenda União to work as a schoolteacher. He was thus deeply involved in the conflict from the very beginning of his stay. At the end of April Satoshi contracted Severiano Soares de Oliveira, known as Lourival, to clear 100 *alqueires* (242 hectares) of the peasants' land for Crs 70,000 (£3,300). Lourival, who was a professional labour contractor or *gato*, was renowned for his violence. He brought in 50 labourers and a group of gunmen to work for him on the job. Dona Geralda told us:

> Satoshi kept sending in *gatos*. Finally this man Lourival came in, telling us that he'd got rid of the peasants from three ranches and he'd make sure that here too there wouldn't be any peasants left, as he was to hand the land over to the Japanese 'all clean'. He said that he'd kill any peasants with pretty wives and carry their women away, and that he'd kill those with ugly wives too, but he'd drive their women off into the forest.

Lourival started to cut down the peasants' crops and set alight some of their huts. Amado and some other peasants told Lourival several times to stop harassing them, but he took no notice. At last their patience was exhausted and they decided to 'get rid of the *gatos*', as they put it. Amado told us what happened on 27 April:

> In the end, they sent in gunmen to put pressure on everyone, burning our homes, with us all running and fighting for justice, without rebelling. Lourival sent word to us that we 'little peasants' weren't worth anything, that he was

used to being in a real conflict, not in these little ones, that there were eight men there in his hut, ready to come and beat us up. They'd kill all the men, he said, and carry off the pretty women. This really made our blood boil, so we went over there, 56 of us, to give them some of their own medicine, to tie them up, put them in the car and send them away, once and for all.

We did it like this. We went along the trail, a little path cut out with a machete, and five of their men were coming our way, so we all lay on the ground, except for two men who stood in the middle of the path, with their revolvers ready. When the other men came up, these two pointed their revolvers at them and told them to put up their hands, otherwise they'd die.

Then the rest of us stood up with our shotguns and they went quiet. We took all their weapons and tied their hands behind their backs and sent them all off back to their hut. Lourival's labourers warned us: 'Be careful, this man is really tough, he's not going to give himself up.' So we went off to face him. We got there and were pointing our weapons at him, when he pulled out a revolver, so shots flew out from the whole group. He didn't make it and ended up dying. And then our suffering really started...

Though Amado's description of the death is perfectly straightforward as far as it goes, some aspects of the affair have never been completely clarified. Several of the peasants told us that the meeting at which it was decided to 'get rid of the *gatos*' was called by four strangers, who had not even got land in the region, led by someone called Irair. After the five labourers had their hands tied up, they were told to leave the area, which they did. Then, apparently, Irair and his companions were quick to persuade the peasants that they must follow up their first victory by confronting Lourival himself. Several peasants told us that Irair and his companions were at the head of the group of peasants and that Irair was the one who gave the order to kill Lourival, firing 12 shots himself. Not one of these four men was ever arrested by the police. While not denying that they were all very angry and prepared to do what was necessary to get rid of the *gatos*, some of the peasants now believe that Irair was in fact sent in by Satoshi 'to create an incident' and thus give him a pretext for calling in the authorities. However, no conclusive evidence has ever been produced to support this interpretation.

'The Suffering Began'

Whether or not Lourival's death was deliberately engineered, the incident certainly rebounded in Satoshi's favour. On 3 May Gonçalo Clemente de Assis, the local policeman at Afonso, who was known to be sympathetic to the peasant families, was arrested and taken to Nortelândia for questioning by the regional police head, Benedito Bruno. He was detained for several days and then released with a warning not to the give peasant families any kind of assistance. Then, on 7 May, José Garcia Neto, the state governor, visited Afonso to open the new school and the new road between Afonso and Arenápolis. Many of the peasants attended the ceremonies in the vain hope of talking to the governor and securing his assistance. The local priest, Isidoro Schneider, was 'escorted' all day by Major Zuzi Alves da Silva, though at that time he only occasionally visited Fazenda União.

Two days later the police went to Fazenda União and made several arrests. The peasants themselves give conflicting numbers but, as far as we could ascertain, eight peasant farmers plus João Kauling were detained. Boca Rica was one of those arrested and he gave us a vivid account of what happened:

> I was arrested. This prison business was the result of a problem to do with the gunmen. They attacked us lots of times. You see that gap over there? They stayed there with their rifles, 15 of them shooting by that big mango tree, to get everyone to run. They were going to end up killing us, so we had to do something. After the killing of Lourival, everyone left their *roças* and I found myself on my own here, planting maize and rice, my little boy with my gun, standing behind me and watching out for gunmen, and my wife behind me too, with the other little child and another gun, all of us working. They didn't come into this house, but they attacked all round, saying that they'd kill us, they'd burn the houses and so on. They were armed with revolvers on their belts, with the holster tied to their thighs, like this. And so I worked for four days, without eating, nervous, my mouth all bitter, my head aching. It went on like this.
>
> When they took me off to prison, on the way they broke my teeth with the point of a rifle. I had eight gold crowns and they broke them. They laughed, saying: 'You'd better change your name now, to Boca Pobre [poor mouth].' So you see, they hadn't come to do justice. They took us, tied us up with ropes, seven of us with our hands tied one to the other, and we had to walk 18 kilometres on foot, in the rain. After they'd taken me, the police went to my house and pointed a revolver at my wife. The police have created so much injustice! Really pestering her, swearing at her, until she was crying, at all the things they did. They went into that room and took my revolver and the shotgun, as well as all our forks, spoons and knives, all the table knives and the bread knife. They stole my little daughter's sweater. They stole soap, a hoe, a clock, everything they could. I feel ashamed telling how the police robbed such nonsense.
>
> They didn't want to know if I'd killed anyone or not. They didn't ask me anything about that. After they took me, they took an old man over there, another down there. They took three children and they asked them if Boca Rica had killed the man. At first they said yes, but then one of them said no, it wasn't Boca Rica. Then they asked Eduardo, and he said no, and they asked João Gato, and he said no. But they took me prisoner anyway and they beat us all the way. There was a teacher of ours, Brother João, who they beat up so badly that they broke one of his ribs. He was tied by a rope to the rest of us. It seems that they were most angry with me and him. They beat us the most.
>
> They left us all Friday and right through to Sunday without any food. We woke up on Monday and still no food. They released us on Tuesday, still

without food, not even a piece of bread. That was in Nortelândia. We were sleeping in the police jeep, seven of us in that tiny space – just like pigs – with our hands tied up so tight they turned blue. On Monday the statements started, at dawn, about four in the morning. Major Zizi was so unjust with me, a man in such a position doing such injustice! He kept asking me what Father Isidoro did, if he gave us classes, if he gave us arms, bullets. It was so strange as the father never went there. I'd been there two years and never seen him there.

I was sitting like this and he took the handle of a sickle and beat it up against my leg so this huge lump swelled up. I thought that he'd broken my leg. And there I was, thinking about all the crops I had to harvest – now he's broken my leg, so how will I thresh that rice? Then he grabbed hold of me, asking me again if I knew the priest. 'No! I don't!' I passed my hand over my leg to see if I could feel the bone, but it had all gone numb so I took the leg and put it on top of the other. He asked again: 'Do you know this priest?' I said: 'No! You can kill me if you want, because I don't know him.' The man asked me how tall the priest is, what colour and so on. 'If you ask me what he looks like, I can't tell you because I don't know him! You can beat me but I'm not lying!' Then he had another go, the sickle on top of me again, causing another huge bump, so I thought that this time he'd really broken my leg, though in fact he hadn't.

Dona Geralda gave us more details:

Poor Father João was the one who suffered most. The police took him and almost killed him, breaking his rib. They took nine men altogether, tied their hands together with rope and made this string of people walk about 18 kilometres through the mud, at night. Then they came back and took 17 more men, nearly all heads of family. They kept on coming back to take yet more. Though they managed to get a lawyer, they spent 90 days in prison. They had to put up with every kind of punishment. There's one man here, from Pernambuco, they slapped him on the ears and broke his eardrum so he's had trouble with it ever since. His head still hurts.

This man was Severino Joaquím da Silva, whose left eardrum was burst by a policeman called Ataide.

Two young boys were also taken with their fathers: 12-year-old João Roberto and 8-year-old Luís Carlos. They were both released after a few hours. Boca Rica and João Kauling were unexpectedly released first, on 11 May, but the other men were taken to the prison in Rosário Oeste.

Amado was one of the 17 men arrested during the second round of imprisonments:

Five cops came, taking those they had already arrested to Arenápolis and Diamantino. And then word went out that they wanted to arrest all of us. Ataide arrived with eight other policemen to hunt down the rest of us. They found me when I was on my way to Afonso. They all looked frightened when they realised that I was Amado and pulled out their weapons. They looked to see if I was armed. Ataide said to me: 'We've heard a lot about you in these parts, but it's not as people say, because I haven't found any arms on you.' They'd only found a penknife. He took it and kept it and said: 'Come, help us catch the others, for that might be your way out. For you're marked as the leader, though I don't think you are.'

We went further down and they found other comrades, until 17 of us were brought back to this house. We had lunch and then went on with him on foot, taking food with us, not knowing where we were heading. We were all wondering what these people wanted from us. There was even a gunman with an unknown weapon, one we'd never seen before. We were put in a truck and at night we reached the jail at Rosário Oeste, where we were imprisoned in a cubicle, humiliated and beaten. One of us was hit on the ears by Ataide because he'd been telling the story in a different way from what he wanted. The suffering was terrible. We thought we'd only be giving our statements and would then all be freed, but it didn't turn out like that.

Then the others gave themselves up. They had a meeting, realised how much we were suffering and decided to join us to try to sort things out more quickly. So they came and gave themselves up, in groups of six, eight, four, leaving their families all alone.

Lídio was one of those who gave themselves up:

When the police came, they seized seven people straight away and really gave them a very rough time. So we here thought that, if we gave ourselves up, it would help free the others. So we decided, the whole group, to give ourselves up in Afonso, thinking that we'd be free in five days. But we weren't – we spent 76 days there, in Rosário Oeste. They asked us so many things, if the priest had given us orders – that's what they most wanted to find out. They wanted to know if the priest was our leader, if he supplied us with arms, and so on.

The peasants were appalled by their prison experience. Zé Pego told us:

We were all badly shaken up in prison. We'd never been arrested before. We'd never even been to a police station to make a statement. There were comrades who wanted to commit suicide there and then, they were so scared. They'd say: 'We've had it anyway, so I'm going to fall head first on this concrete bed in the cell, I'm not going to put up with being beaten any more.' I said: 'Hold firm, friend. This is just pressure they're putting on us. They're not going to kill us really.' 'But they *are* going to kill us!' 'Then there's no need to commit suicide then.'

Through this experience Amado lost much of his earlier confidence that justice would eventually be done:

We were beaten for hours, and then left without food, until we felt crazy, that they could get us to say what they wanted, because what we said about what we knew had happened wasn't good enough for them – they'd only accept our condemning the priest and the bishop. They called them 'subversives'. Nowadays, anyone who speaks in favour of the poor is accused of treason and is persecuted by the sharks. The big authorities live in this way, persecuting people who work to help the poor. They make these accusations to throw them out of their jobs. There have even been cases of people being exported because they've been fighting for justice.

Meanwhile the women were left on their own to look after the children, to take care of the *roças* and, at the same time, to face constant harassment and threats from the gunmen. As in Porto Alegre, they coped extremely well. Many of them spoke of the support they received from Rovena Kuhn, a teacher from southern Brazil, brought in by the Catholic Church in 1975. She had set up a little primary school in a wooden hut, with no walls and a roof made from *sapé*, a thick-leaved grass much used for roofing by the peasant families. Rovena proved to be an excellent teacher and soon won a place in the hearts of her pupils and their parents. Though she never interfered in the peasants' decisions, she provided constant loyal support and became a key figure in the community.

Dona Maria, Lídio's wife, told us what it was like while the men were away in prison: 'Off Lídio went and was held in prison and, as everything had to be done here, I was forced to do it all on my own, including harvesting 17 bags of beans. That's a lot to pick and beat, with three children.'

Zé Pego added:

When I was in prison, they were still exerting pressure. The gunmen, with their gang of labourers, who were clearing the land right up to our doors, were saying that the brave ones were all in prison, that those who had stayed at home were all feeble, that they could do what they liked with them. The gunmen killed lots of pigs, even belonging to people who didn't live on Fazenda União. They caused a lot of damage.

Dona Geralda's house was the one with most women and children and, as a result, was the one visited most frequently by the gunmen. She told us how she was able to outwit the gunmen on one occasion:

Fazenda União filled up with gunmen again. A lorry came with 14 of them, they all came to this house. I'd just killed a piglet. 'I've come with an order from the judge to evict all the families from here, so as to leave the Japanese's ranch all clean. Everyone has to leave within 24 hours.' So I asked him to show me the judge's order and he answered that he didn't have it, that he'd left it at the ranch with the colonel. I told him that, when we labourers go to the *roça*, we carry our hoe or axe or whatever tool we're going to need, and that, if he'd come to do this job here, he needed his tool, his judge's order. But he wouldn't have any of it and told us to get everything ready to leave. I said that I wouldn't go, not until I'd fried my piglet. He told me to take the piglet raw and fry it wherever we stopped off, but I said no, because all our supplies are on the *roças*. The rice is in the trough, the beans pulled up and spread all over the place, not even beaten yet. And he said that we couldn't take any chicken, we couldn't take any pigs. So what are my children going to eat? I have family to look after. 'You can fry the piglet and serve it to your children to eat with manioc flour.' So I told him that I'd fry my piglet first and that, as they were going to push us out of here, they'd better take us to the judge's door. The judge would have to be responsible for all these children while their fathers were in prison. 'Here we have everything they need to eat: papaya, sugar-cane, bananas, maize, manioc, rice, beans. But if I go out into the world with my children, what am I going to give them to eat? I haven't any money to buy them food and I've never had the courage to steal, nor do I want my children to learn to rob. Let's all go and eat at the judge's expense.'

Four of the gunmen stayed to keep watch and wouldn't even let us go to the toilet as they were afraid to let us out of their sight in case we fled. And my women friends were here to help me with the pig as my finger was bruised and swollen. Then one of the gunmen went over to where the piglet was and threw chunks of meat on the ground for the dogs, just to upset us.

In the evening the lorry came back with the other men to take us to town, but because it was so cold and we had nothing to wrap the children in, they decided that we'd leave the next morning at 5 o'clock. So they stayed the night. They were well armed, with two revolvers each and at least one rifle between them. Then they decided to take my son-in-law and three other neighbours off to the ranch. So there we were, kneeling on the ground, praying, but at about half past ten they brought the boys back. Nothing had happened to them, but they'd been asked who'd sent the peasants in. 'We know it was the bishop and Father Isidoro who sent you all in and that the bishop supplied you with firearms.' They said that they were making an investigation. But the men said that it wasn't like that at all, they had just been working here and, if there had been some shots, it was just some rusty old shotgun that the men had bought to kill animals with, but nobody supplied them with it and, anyway, where would the bishop and the father get such things from.

Dona Geralda's delaying tactics worked well. Just as they were about to be evicted, some policemen from Afonso arrived and arrested three of the lorry drivers and two gunmen. Though he had been warned not to give the peasant families any more support, Gonçalo Clemente de Assis, head of the Afonso police station, had responded to the peasant families' near desperate pleas for help. But he was soon overruled: on the very next day, Benedito Bruno, head officer at Nortelândia, gave an order for the release of those arrested.

By now, with the help of the church, the arrested peasants had acquired a lawyer, João Guarino. He went to Rosário Oeste to file requests for habeas corpus and complained to the judge that it was absurd that 42 men had been arrested for the murder of a single man. The requests for habeas corpus were turned down, but certain concessions were made by the judge: the police would make no more arrests unless a new conflict occurred; the six peasants most recently arrested, whose imprisonment order had not yet been decreed, would be released immediately; and the other peasants under arrest would have their case heard as soon as possible. On 15 June, the six peasants were duly released. They returned immediately to Fazenda União, bringing the families their first good news for many weeks.

Once again the let-up did not last for long: on 25 June Satoshi sent in 60 men who began to cut down the peasants' crops and intimidate the population. The peasants reacted quickly, appealing to both the local branch of Fetagri and the Catholic Church for help. The next day the CPT sent an open letter – called an SOS – to the government in which it strongly criticised the tactics Satoshi was using against the families and called for the release of the other families.

Probably in response to this widely publicised letter, the agriculture department from the Mato Grosso government sent in a team to assess the damage inflicted by the gunmen. It was estimated that the peasants had lost 7,398 bags of various types of grains, a heavy loss for a small community. Soon after, Colonel Aloysio Madeira Evora, the secretary for public security in the Mato Grosso government, said that Satoshi would be made to pay compensation to the peasant families.

But the harassment continued: on 18 July, despite the earlier promise made by the judge, yet another peasant – Joaquím Ramos – was arrested, bringing the total number of detained to 37. However, on 27 July, the seven men who had been arrested first, were brought to Rosário Oeste and then, on the following day, transferred to the jail in their home town of Afonso. It appeared to the peasants, both those in prison and those at home, that the deadlock had been broken and that the prisoners were edging their way back to Fazenda União.

The End of their 'Holiday'

Finally, in August, the peasants were tried. By this time the notoriously corrupt Agnelo Bezerra Neto had been replaced as judge in Diamantino by Crescentino Sisti. It was the peasant families' good luck that the new judge turned out to be incorruptible and objective. After a short session, Sisti dismissed all the charges against the peasants, on the grounds that there was no concrete evidence that any of them had been directly responsible for the death of Lourival. All the peasants were released.

The 37 men returned home on 6 August, known in the region as Good Jesus day, amidst festive celebrations. In animated fashion they soon started to harvest what would have been good crops had it not been for the destruction by the gunmen and the time lost in jail. The work was particularly difficult for those who had just spent two and a half months in jail. Zé Pego explained why:

> Afterwards we were taken aback at how soft we'd become. We came back with fine hands and we were fat and swollen after our time in jail. And we'd got quite white. We're used to being in the sun all day and in there we didn't see the sun. So it was really hard getting back to work again.

Today the peasants jokingly refer to their imprisonment as their 'holiday'. Certainly it was the only time in their lives that they had not been working six days a week.

Yet again their jubilation was short lived. A week later Colonel Aloysio Madeira Evora sent two cars to Fazenda União with a team to carry out a fact-finding mission. As one of the members of the team was Ataide – who had broken Severino's eardrum – the peasants refused to give any information whatsoever. Then, just a few days later, the gunmen moved back in, with renewed threats. This time they gave what they called their 'final ultimatum': either the peasants left by 20 August or there would be an 'accidental' fire during this period of annual forest burning.

By now the peasants had had their weapons taken away from them on three separate occasions, so with no adequate means of defence they were more vulnerable than ever. They sent another letter of protest to the authorities and at last the state governor, José Garcia Neto, took action. He sent a message to the peasants, saying that he personally would make sure that nothing happened to them or their possessions until a definitive decision was taken in the courts about their lands. A detachment from the military police was sent in during the harvest to prevent the outbreak of any 'accidental' fire.

We visited Fazenda União for the first time in August 1976.[7] We found the peasant families determined, but apprehensive. Despite the problems, they were pushing ahead with their endeavours to farm the land. They told us that Father Isidoro and Rovena, the schoolteacher, were providing them with a great deal of support. They said that Father Isidoro was encouraging them to persist with crop farming, for he considered the land too fertile to be used for cattle-rearing. Most of them were following his advice and some of them proudly took us to see their crops.

Though, as a result of the action taken by the state government, Satoshi reduced his direct harassment of the peasant families, he still seemed determined to take over their land. By September he had brought in 20,000 head of cattle, built a corral and constructed an airstrip – all of this on the peasants' land. The CPT issued another document, entitled 'The Second and Possibly Last SOS'.

Setbacks for Satoshi

On 13 September, Crescentino Sisti, the new judge at Diamantino, began further hearings to sort out the conflict. After initial investigations, he signed an order authorising 73 peasant families to occupy their plots at Fazenda União until the question was finally sorted out in the courts. Satoshi was furious. In a desperate attempt to have the order annulled, he tried to bribe the judge by sending him a bottle stuffed with Crs 10,000 (£420) in notes. This was Satoshi's first serious blunder: either he was a hopeless judge of character, or he simply found it impossible to imagine an incorruptible judge. Sisti reacted with predictable indignation, suing Satoshi in the courts in Cuiabá for attempting to bribe an officer of the law.

At the same time, Satoshi was dealt another blow. Early in 1976 he had left his job with the Mato Grosso state government to take up the post of regional director of the US volunteer organisation, the Peace Corps. In August 1976, he spoke to us in Cuiabá about his work with the Peace Corps, though he became immediately hostile when we started to question him about Fazenda União.[8] About the same time, the bishop, Dom Henrique, wrote to John Crimmins, the US ambassador to Brazil, to complain that a man such as Satoshi should be employed by the US government. Very soon after, Satoshi was sacked, though the official reason for his dismissal was not his involvement in Fazenda União but a minor infringement of an internal Peace Corps regulation: at one period Satoshi had broken the regulations by employing his wife in the office in Cuiabá. Though these were serious setbacks for Satoshi, they were not sufficient to make him give up his attempt to evict the peasant families forcibly. He appears to have been so confident of his support at the top of the state government that he was sure that he would suffer no reprisals for continuing to send in his gunmen to bully the families into leaving, provided he acted with discretion.

After the detachment of military policemen had left, Satoshi's gunmen, including Ataide, renewed their threats and violence against the peasants. In October grass seed was once again scattered on the *roças* by plane. The CPT published two documents in November in which it strongly attacked Satoshi for renewing the aggression and called on the authorities to take urgent action. The peasants themselves sent a petition to Sisti. In reply, the judge ruled that everything that had been erected by Satoshi's men since his earlier order should be knocked down.

Four days later nearly 100 peasants, with police protection, pulled down the 15 kilometres of fencing that had been put up cutting across several of their *roças*. They made a good job of it, chopping up the wooden stakes and unwinding the wire completely before cutting it into small pieces. Just as they were pulling down the last stake, Satoshi himself arrived on the scene, accompanied by two carloads of gunmen, including the ubiquitous Ataide. Satoshi demanded to see the judge's order, which was immediately presented to him by a police officer. After he had carefully read it, he told his men to get back in their cars and they drove away.

Though the peasants were fearful of retaliations, Satoshi took no action until the new year. He then let some of his cattle loose on the peasants' land and started to build another fence across their land. The peasants sent a written complaint to the authorities. Sisti was away on holiday, so the case was referred to the judge in Cuiabá. On 14 January, this judge ruled in the peasants' favour and despatched a police detachment to spend 20 days in the troubled area to enforce the occupation order issued earlier by Sisti.

Though the peasants had won another victory – for now Sisti's order had been upheld by the judge in Cuiabá – their patience began to run out. Three years of continuous harassment by the gunmen and a long spell of imprisonment had worn down their earlier faith in the authorities and in the efficacy of passive forms of resistance. On the day after the verdict by the Cuiabá judge, the courts received another document in which the peasants explained that they themselves had knocked down the new fence on their land for they no longer had the patience to wait for action from the authorities. They said that on the following day Ataide had visited the peasant families whose *roças* had been most affected by the construction of the fence and had warned that he would kill them all if they dared to knock down a fence ever again. Finally another police detachment was sent to enforce the law, but once again the gunmen disappeared before it arrived. It stayed until mid February and, just as before, the gunmen returned as soon as it had left and began to threaten families with eviction once again.

The pressure escalated. On 20 April, two peasants travelled to Diamantino to complain of assassination threats from Satoshi's gunmen. Then, on 2 May, the courts received another letter from the peasants in which they complained that Satoshi had let loose horses, donkeys and cattle on to their plots. A week later came another complaint: timber was being taken from their land. The following week, yet another letter: more fences were being built across their *roças*. A fortnight later, 48 peasants signed a joint letter of protest: gunmen had again let livestock loose on their crops. By then the courts had a thick file of complaints, a remarkable achievement for a barely literate community.

The Destruction of the 'Nest'

Unexpectedly, the harassments stopped in August. But it proved to be the calm before the storm. On 5 September, the conflict erupted into unprecedented violence. Zé Pego told us what happened:

> So there we are, struggling to work, when gunmen appeared all over the place again, telling everyone to leave or else this and that would happen. Then one day a comrade of ours was putting a fence around his house with the help of some friends, when gunmen opened fire on them. They arrived unseen, the

nine of them, and surprised the seven comrades at work. The seven of them ran, one here, another there. One of them, called Geraldo, tried to run but his leg gave way. He sat down on a log and a gunman came up and shot him. He shot him as he was sitting there.

Geraldo Santana and four other peasants wounded during this attack were taken to hospital in Nortelândia. The doctors said that they could do little for Geraldo with their limited equipment, so he was taken by taxi-plane to Cuiabá on 6 September. He died there on the following day. The wanton brutality shown by the gunmen in shooting Geraldo, defenceless, as he sat on a log, seems to have been the final straw. Even before the news of Geraldo's death reached them, the whole community – men, women and children – reacted with unprecedented fury. Massu and Amado together described what happened:

[Amado:] About ten of us went over to where the lad had been shot and then we spread the news around the whole area. Everybody was horrified and gathered together, saying: 'Let's put an end to this group's nest for once and for all.'

[Massu:] By one o'clock about 500 people had gathered together and they all said: 'Only by totally destroying their nest will we get rid of them. Otherwise they'll come back again.'

[Amado:] So we decided to set fire to the place where they stayed, as that would put an end to their coming here. We started the fire with petrol – there were some petrol drums there. So we went all round their place and set light to everything: their lorry, the sawmill, their radio, the light generator. There were more than a 100 of us – old people, children, everyone. We had a proper strike.

[Massu:] The women burnt the truck and the corral. They were at it for six days. Satoshi's plane flew over to have a look, the place was overrun with women. Satoshi and his men came to the ranch, they were heard to say: 'There's nothing we can do, because it's the women who are burning everything down.'

During the six days of the 'great fire', as it is called, the peasant families burnt everything they could find that belonged to Satoshi or his men. In part, it was a tribute to Geraldo. The peasants told us that they felt deeply both his death and the fact that they could not pay their last respects to him. (Geraldo was buried in Cuiabá, his funeral attended only by the local representatives of the CPT.) Through their determined action, the peasants achieved what even Sisti had been unable to do: they brought Satoshi's violence against them to an end. He sent no more gunmen to threaten the families. By November the rains had come and the grass grew over the remains of the ranch buildings. All that is left of Satoshi's ranch today is an overgrown heap of ruins, scarcely discernible to the casual visitor.

307

Fazenda União Today[9]

Life calmed down after the gunmen had left. The peasant families settled down to farming the rich land which it had taken them so much effort to win. They worked hard: according to a survey carried out by the Mato Grosso state government at the beginning of 1981, over a third (3,339 hectares) of the total area occupied by the peasant families (9,843 hectares) was in use. In 1980 the area – now known as Gleba União – produced 473,520 tonnes of maize, 352,850 tonnes of rice, 88,354 tonnes of beans and 2,600 tonnes of manioc.[10] The families had also planted 164,410 coffee bushes, 88,509 sugarcane shoots and 27,026 pineapple plants, as well as many orange, guava, cashew, mango, and avocado pear trees, and passion fruit vines. Most of the families had some pigs and poultry. An increasing number was starting to rear cattle.

The switch to cattle-rearing has not been fortuitous. Despite efforts to eradicate it, the grass sown by Satoshi continued to spread. Without farm machinery the peasant families have found it difficult to get rid of it and many have taken the line of least resistance. Amado now has no crops, just pasture. Though he has few cattle of his own, he has done well financially. He earns about Crs 100,000 (£360), letting out pastures. He also buys calves, fattens them and then re-sells them three or four months later, with a profit of Crs 5,000–10,000 (£18–36) per animal.

A few of the settlers, however, remember Father Isidoro's belief that the land is too good for cattle. An early settler, Vitório Ferreira da Silva, known as Velho Vitório, is of this opinion:

> I will admit that a piece of land can later be used for few cattle, after it has first been used for crops. But what I don't approve of is people cutting down good jungle straight for pasture – this I don't tolerate. My intuition tells me to cultivate crops. When I got here, they sowed grass seed all over my plot, from the air. But I pulled it up. It's hard work, but it can be done.

His plot bears out the truth of his words. He is reaping good crops of maize, manioc, rice, beans, bananas and sugar-cane on the 24 hectares he is cultivating with his 21-year-old son. Velho Vitório has also built a watermill to husk his rice, and is setting up a mill to manufacture manioc flour, to be driven by animal traction. He is lubricating his machinery with oil crushed from castor beans grown on his plot.

The community has changed in other ways. A little village, called Boa Esperança (Good Hope), had finally been formed. It consists of about 40 wooden houses, including three general stores-cum-bars, a school (a room of which is used by the Catholic Church for its services), a chemist's shop, a butcher's, a diesel-fuelled rice-husking machine and three Protestant chapels. The peasant families no longer have to go to Afonso for their shopping.

The first tradesman to arrive was José Julío dos Santos, from the north-east state of Alagoas. He said that people laughed at him when he arrived in 1979 with all his wares, saying: 'You're mad, friend. Who are you going to sell all these things to, the jaguars?' Though he has survived, despite the sceptics, José Julio has not done as well as another tradesman, Fidelcino Mendes de Brito, known as Quincas, from Bahía, another state in the north-east. Quincas has been prepared to take more risks than José Julío and his gambles appear to have paid off. He has accepted many credit purchases and has received payment in rice and other crops during the harvest. He said that the peasant families only regularly purchased about five or six products: kerosene, salt, sugar, caustic soda, *cachaça* and tobacco. In this respect, the families do not appear to have changed greatly from the early days.

Quincas has been quick to spot a chance for making money and brought the first husking machine into the area. He said: 'I am a kind of Christ. My function is to help everyone, whether they have money or not.' Many peasant families would not agree with this analogy: they claim that he always makes sure that his bills are finally paid and charges very high prices to husk rice. They say that some people even prefer to transport their rice to Afonso, as the prices are so much lower. Another newcomer is the butcher, Sebastião Andrade dos Santos, known as Tatão. He kills a cow each fortnight and a pig more frequently, whenever there is enough demand. He said: 'I would kill more if the demand were greater. People here don't have cash, so I have to sell on credit, to be paid during the harvest.'

However, despite the progress, Fazenda União is not the paradise the peasants dreamed of. In April 1982 Dona Geralda explained one of the problems:

> We still haven't got our land titles, so we still haven't any security. We've been here for nine years but we're still not sure that we'll be allowed to stay. And, as we haven't land titles, we can't get bank loans and that's a terrible thing. We have to do what we can with the little bit of money we have, obtained through the sweat of our brows.

The only document that the peasant families have to indicate that they are the owners is a registration paper, issued by the Mato Grosso department of social development in February 1981. Officials from this department simply filled in the forms with information supplied by the families and made no attempt to check the figures. As a result, some of the families professed to own a much larger area than the one they were actually occupying and there were a few cases of overlapping claims. Since then the officials have made no attempt to sort out the confusions. According to Dona Neli de Melo, an INCRA official in Cuiabá, the registration was undertaken, not as the first step towards the eventual issuing of definitive land titles, but as a means of stopping further families from moving in and buying up sub-plots from the families already there. For this reason, she said, the form had been stamped in large red letters with the term *INTRANSFERIVEL* (non-transferable).

The families, however, were not told that the documents had no value as land titles. One of them, called João Francisco da Silva, known as Tobías, travelled to Cuiabá where he tried to use the document as proof of ownership to raise a loan with the Banco da Amazônia. He said: 'I was told that the document was worthless. So I came back and told the rest that we'd been hoodwinked.' Tobías's experience greatly alarmed the other families and the state government was forced to send in another official to reassure them that there had been no attempt to deceive them and that they would eventually get their titles once all the complex legal questions had been resolved. However, the peasant families are still fearful that Satoshi could manipulate the authorities behind the scenes and that they could suddenly be presented with eviction notices. This fear will only disappear once the families have received official definitive titles.

When asked, state government officials in Cuiabá were adamant that the families had no real cause for alarm. Both Marcos Martinelli, president of the Mato Grosso Land Department (Intermat), and Paulo Pitaluga, head of INCRA's Mato Grosso division, said in April 1982 that there was no doubt that the families would eventually obtain their titles. The delays stemmed from the legal complexities, as Satoshi was the legitimate owner of the Garça plot and possibly had some rights over part of the other plots, and for this reason had to receive compensation. Martinelli claimed that the problem was being sorted out on the basis of state law no. 4,003, of 29 June 1978, which empowered the state government to exchange one plot for another within the state to resolve a social problem. Martinelli said that Satoshi himself had asked for an exchange and that an equivalent area (14,724 hectares) would be given to him in the district of Aripuanã.

Despite the assurance with which Martinelli spoke, his information was later contradicted by Dona Neli, who said that, in compensation for losing Fazenda União, Satoshi would be given the legal rights to a property of roughly the same size which he had already occupied, semi-illegally, in the district of Diamantino. It was impossible to discover which version was correct and both options were probably still being discussed. It seemed very likely, however, that one way or another the peasants at Fazenda União would eventually be given their titles. Martinelli said that the families would have to pay for their titles when they got them, 'if only a symbolic sum'. According to him, the families occupied an area of 9,844 hectares and he was unable to say what would happen to the rest of the land at Fazenda União.

The delay in receiving their land titles was not the only dissatisfaction voiced by the peasant families. Several of the older settlers complained that their community had lost its earlier cohesiveness and unity. This had happened, they thought, because in the late 1970s they had relaxed their earlier rigour in carefully vetting all newcomers and had thus allowed in strangers who had later turned out to be land thieves. Several of the peasants commented: 'We won the battle against the shark, but now we are having to face the piranhas.'

Velho Vitório spoke about one of these piranhas:

> José Borges, known as Borginha, got in here through a trick. He asked Brother João [João Kauling] if he could buy Isaias's plot. We didn't want to let him, for he was an outsider and we'd had a bad time with outsiders. But he persuaded Brother João that he was a very active Christian, so Brother João asked us to make an exception, as Borginha was one of us. We let him convince us, because we need people with community spirit. But what community spirit? He's been a disaster, Borginha has.
>
> The first time I spoke to him, he told me that he likes to get on well with his neighbours. Then he saw my pigsty and he said that it was stupid to keep pigs shut up in a sty, that you could rear pigs much better if you let them loose. I said no, that I'd come here to cultivate crops and that the pigs would destroy them if I let them loose. Well, to cut a long tale short, he said that he was going to let his pigs loose, that if any of these pigs got on my land then I should tell him. Well, the only thing that divides his land from mine is this little stream, that dries up in the summer. I already began to feel afraid.
>
> Well it didn't take long for Borginha to show his claws. He refused to become part of the community and began to rear even more pigs. They began to invade my crops and, when I went to complain, he used to say to me in the beginning: 'Oh dear, Vitório, I'll take them out straightaway. I'd rather lose my pigs than a good neighbour.' But his pigs still came in. It was then that I began to turn my dogs onto them, to scare them away. One of my dogs even learnt how to bite off a pig's ear.
>
> One day I got so angry that I went to the union [the local branch of the rural workers' union] to make a complaint. I told them all about it and they gave me the authority to kill his pigs, as he was refusing to fence them off. So the situation calmed down for some time.
>
> Then one day I arrived home at about eleven o'clock at night and found a pig in my maize. As I'd been told that I could kill them, I set my dogs on it and it ended up drowning in the stream. However, it turned out that it wasn't Borginha's pig, but belonged to another newcomer, called Zé-do-Rolo. It turned into a big mess, because I didn't want to pay the price that Zé-do-Rolo demanded in compensation. I was called to the police station in Arenápolis, where I explained what had happened and we sorted out the question. The police officer told me that, despite the present problem, I had the right to kill Borginha's pigs if they invaded my *roça*. Borginha learned what had happened at the police station and he told anyone who wanted to listen: 'If Vitório puts his dogs on to my pigs, I shall send in someone to kill him, if I don't kill him myself.' So, you see, I've been threatened by this man, who has also threatened to kill Núncio, from the union.

Velho Vitório got very upset while telling his tale. He said that Borginha had used his pigs in this way with others of his neighbours, to force them to sell up their plots very cheaply, and that Borginha had managed to buy up five plots in this way and would have bought up another two, if the peasant farmers hadn't got together and decided to stop it. Velho Vitório said: 'I myself feel like selling, because I can't bear all this fuss and bother. Amado has tried to get people to swop with me, but no one wants to, everyone is afraid of Borginha.' João Costa, another of Borginha's neighbours who has refused to sell up, told a similar tale. The soil in his plot is particularly fertile and he didn't know how many times Borginha had offered to buy him out. He said that Borginha was particularly keen to buy his land, regardless of its fertility, because it lay between two of Borginha's plots and, if he bought it, he would be able to bring the plots together into a single farm.

Dona Geralda explained that they were not opposed to the entry of new peasants, only to land thieves:

> What we don't like is people selling land to outsiders, people we don't know, who might be landowners. If we can be sure that a family are poor peasants like us, we welcome them, because they will join us. For look, we are getting surrounded by landowners, by sharks – Lincoln Torres, Salim, Baiano, Boca Torta [Twisted Mouth], Aliança ranch, Buffulin ranch. Now, if we keep this land just for the first settlers, all the land that is over will go to these landowners. Just take the case of Lincoln Torres. Didn't we all see that he stole a big piece of land, just because we, peasants, hadn't occupied it yet? A lot of peasant families could have lived there.
>
> So we need new peasants to stop the sharks. For we, poor people, what do we want in the world? We just want a small plot of land. We don't want to take over a big area. We wouldn't be able to manage it, at any rate. We haven't the money. And, without money, the axis of the world, you can't get anything moving.
>
> So we don't want ambitious, greedy people, who want to take over other people's land when it's all been prepared, who want to set up big estates. We want people like us, who can make us stronger.

Apart from Borginha's threats, another scandal which had shaken Gleba União concerned Boca Rica. Sebastião da Ponte described what happened:

> It was Sunday, 17 January 1981. I was alone at home when Boca Rica arrived. He wanted to swap some beans with me. I invited him in, made some sugarcane syrup for us to drink, and we had a good chat. I didn't agree to his proposal, because I didn't want the beans he was offering, but I told him that he could have as many of mine as he needed. I leant down to pick up some beans. Then, as I lifted up my head, he fired his gun at me, a 0.28, double-barrelled. If I hadn't lifted my head at that moment, he'd have got me in the head. As it was, the shot got me in the neck. I was completely taken aback. I shouted out and then he shot me again, in my chest.
>
> Boca Rica thought that he'd finished me off and fled. I saw him jump over the fence into Torres's farm. Though I was bleeding a lot, I got to a

neighbour's house. Then I was taken to Diamantino and then, by plane, to Cuiabá. Thanks to God I survived, but my left arm's useless now. And I've got bits of lead in various parts of my body.

The families in Gleba União were amazed at what had happened. Boca Rica had always been a good friend of Sebastião da Ponte and there seemed to be no reason why he should have wanted to kill him. Boca Rica was one of the most successful of the settlers: he had planted 4,000 coffee bushes; he had a big herd of cattle, with a large corral; and he had built himself the only brick and plaster house in Gleba União. After chewing it over for some time, the families have come to the conclusion that Boca Rica was persuaded – and no doubt bribed – by the neighbouring farmer, Lincoln Torres, into making the assassination attempt. Though their explanation has never been fully substantiated, the peasant families recall that Boca Rica had become a close friend of Lincoln Torres and Sebastião da Ponte had seen him heading for his ranch after he carried out his murder attempt. Sebastião da Ponte had been involved in a dispute with Lincoln Torres, for he had filed a complaint with the police after cattle from Torres's ranch had got on to his land and eaten up 75 bags of rice and other grains.

Several days after the crime, Boca Rica gave himself up to the police, but he was soon released. Tobias wrote a petition which demanded that Boca Rica be punished and warned: 'If this man is allowed to come back, he will take away our peace of mind. So we have decided not to allow him back so that he does not do us this great damage.' After it had been signed by 23 other farmers, Tobias delivered it to the local judge. As a result, Boca Rica decided not to return, but he let it be known that he had vowed to kill Sebastião da Ponte, Tobias, Amâdo, Zé Pego, Francisco Pereira da Silva and even his own brother, Manuel, who had not supported him.

Though in moments of crisis like this, the families show that they can still take effective, collective action, the unity between the settlers – which used to make them proud of the word *união* (union) in the name of the area they were occupying – has clearly grown weaker. The peasants point to one factor in their decreasing unity: the less effective support they are receiving from the Catholic Church. Though at times he showed considerable support for the peasant families at Fazenda União, Dom Henrique Froelich, the local bishop, believed that by the mid 1970s the Catholic church workers had become too involved and too partisan. In what can only be seen as a deliberate attempt to break up an effective and highly politicised team of priests he transferred them out of the area: Renato Barth was removed from Diamantino in 1976; in the following year Zé Pedro Lisboa was sent away to Acre; and then finally in 1979 Isidoro Schneider was sent to Juara in Rondônia. No one was sent to replace Father Isidoro at the parish of Afonso. Zé Pego commented in 1982: 'We are like sheep without a shepherd.'

Rovena Kuhn, the school-teacher, was still there in April 1982, though in 1981 she had been sacked as a Mato Grosso state teacher, probably because she was a well known supporter of the PMDB opposition party and was thus strongly disliked by the PDS party members who dominated the state machinery. But Rovena admitted that she was feeling dispirited.

If she were to leave, Rovena would be sorely missed, for she is greatly loved. Said Velho Vitório:

> Rovena is the mother of the people. I stand up for her in Arenápolis against the PDS people. For me she is the very best type of person. When my children came here, they were all illiterate and they all learnt to read and write in Rovena's school. The PDS people say: 'But she is in the PMDB'. But I say: 'I'm more in favour of her than any political party.'

Though the breaking up of the Catholic Church's team in the region was undoubtedly a contributory factor, it seemed to us that to a large extent the decrease in unity and in militancy among the peasant families was the result of a much wider economic and social process. Having in effect won control over their lands, the peasant families in Fazenda União – just as in Santa Teresinha – have become involved in the day-to-day details of farming. They are all keen to increase their productivity, to have access to bank loans, to make money, to break out of the grinding poverty of subsistence farming. Though almost all the families still feel a strong dislike of landowners of all sizes, and are quick to provide assistance to other peasant families in difficulty, these are no longer the essential issues of their lives.

Notes

1. On 5 May 1982, the diocese of Diamantino was divided into two: one new diocese, centred in Sinop beside the Cuiabá–Santarém road, covered the westerly region of the old diocese; another, still centred in Diamantino, looked after the eastern part. Bishop Henrique Froehlich, formerly bishop of the whole diocese, became bishop of the diocese of Sinop.

2. Our version of the struggle is based largely on our own taped conversations with the peasant families. However, we have also freely used a fascinating account, entitled 'Os Pequenos Se Unem', which was written by members of the Catholic Church working in the area. Much of this account was written during the struggle and contains precise dates. As a result, we have been able to be much more specific about the dates of the incidents referred to by the peasant families here than in the other case study.

3. The commission's full name was Comissão de Discriminação de Terras Devolutas (CDTD).

4. In Fazenda União, the peasant families use the *alqueire paulista*, the São Paulo *alqueire*, which is equivalent to 2.42 hectares. In Santa Teresinha they use the *alqueire goiano*, the Goiás *alqueire*, which is exactly double: 4.84 hectares.

5. INCRA's minimum area, known as the *módulo*, was later decreased to 25 hectares.

6. The documents were entitled: *Os Ultimos Acontecimentos na Area da Fazenda União, municipio de Arenápolis, Mato Grosso,* and *Solidaridade–Gesto Concreto de Cristianismo.*

7. This trip was undertaken by Sue Branford with another British journalist, Jan Rocha.

8. This interview was carried out by Sue Branford and Jan Rocha.

9. Most of the information in this section was kindly supplied by Antônio Carlos Queiroz, who visited Fazenda União in April 1982.

10. According to a survey carried out by Eudson de Castro Ferreira, from the Universidade Federal de Mato Grosso.

8. Conclusion

First of all we must answer for ourselves the question: why are we seeking the 'development' of other regions at all, especially of thinly populated humid tropical forest zones like Amazonia? The concept of 'development' has become a widespread belief which almost nobody in the 'highly developed' countries dares to question. It is being introduced to tropical countries from outside, like a new religion brought by foreign missionaries, once again viewed to be their only hope of 'salvation' . . . Although it is not an easy task, I think the observance of at least basic ecological principles is a prerequisite to the rational utilisation of any region. This is the only path to follow if we do not wish to lead the so-called 'developing' regions, such as Amazonia, into the same impasse into which our modern world-encompassing civilisation has been driven, through the regardless consumption of the riches, resources and beauties of the earth.

(Harald Sioli, September 1979)

One of the constant themes in this book has been the hostility of the authorities towards the peasant families and the Indians. The big government offensive in the mid 1960s, with the creation of Sudam and the beginning of an ambitious road-building programme, arose to a large extent in response to the threat represented by thousands of peasant families who were moving in on their own initiative and starting to take over large areas. To halt this influx, the government, in alliance with the powerful elite of landowners and industrialists in the south, carried out what we have called preemptive occupation, for the region was still too isolated for commercial farming to be viable. The government paid out fat bribes, dressed up as tax rebates, and the companies, with a few notable exceptions, suppressed any doubts as to the economic viability of the ranches they were setting up.

But the offensive was carried out too late to be merely preemptive; about a quarter of a million peasant families were already living in the region, not to mention the Indian population of about 100,000. So the government turned a blind eye while the companies evicted many of the people already in the region, both peasant families and Indians.

To carry out this large-scale expropriation, the companies brought in a barrage of material from the modern industrialised world: aircraft to transport goods and to sow seed (or to fly in dozens of hired gunmen or police in the case of trouble with the peasant families); herbicides to eradicate weeds in the pasture (or to poison waterplaces used by the peasants' animals); huge tractors to carry out jungle clearance (or to destroy peasants' crops); and arms for hunting (or for terrorising labourers and peasant families).

Though for the most past the ranches failed as commercial enterprises, the businessmen made a handsome profit and much of the land was duly reserved for capitalist farming. However, in a few areas, groups of peasant families and Indians have won partial victories and retained possession of some of their land. As our case studies have shown, they have only been successful when they have been united in their resistance and have tenaciously clung on, against all odds. Very often, however, courage, solidarity and dogged determination have not been enough in themselves. The peasant families and the Indians have also needed to publicise their conflicts and turn their struggle into a political issue of regional, national or even international importance. It is here that the role of the Catholic Church has been important, and possibly crucial. When the conflict has taken on this dimension, the cattle companies have become defensive and have felt unable to resort to outright violence as in the past. It is no coincidence that the worst violence – be it against Indians or peasant families – has occurred at the most remote outposts of the occupation frontier, where the cattle-rearers feel confident that no hard evidence of their conduct can ever be produced. The construction of roads, and the rapid establishment of bus services on them, forces the cattle companies to become more cautious.

But the victories have been isolated. Much more frequently the families have been evicted. From this point of view, our case studies are clearly unrepresentative. The practical difficulties of tracing families who have scattered all over Brazil after eviction deterred us from attempting to tell the more typical tale of a defeated peasant community. We felt that this dimension was not completely lost, however, for at one point at least in both of the tales it is easy to imagine a very different outcome, with the complete success of the cattle company.

Though effective in its political objectives, this early offensive did not prove an adequate long-term strategy for the economic occupation of the region. Most of the rearers, ill-prepared for the peculiar risks of Amazon farming, soon faced frightening prospects of ecological disaster. Fearful that the ranches might ruin the land permanently, the government reduced the flow of subsidies. As a result, the undertaking lost much of its attractiveness for the companies. Some decided to pull out. Many others preferred to scale down their operations and to await the hefty profit that they could eventually expect through the appreciation of their lands. Yet others turned to the much safer business of land colonisation, in which the company manages both to make a big profit and to hand on to the settlers the responsibility of proving the economic viability of the undertaking. And a few, particularly large Brazilian and transnational groups which had moved into the region with serious farming intentions, not only in response to the bait of tax rebates, accepted the challenge and pushed on, despite the heavy investment. They are learning by trial and error, experimenting with crop-farming as well as different ways of cattle-rearing. Some of these may eventually demonstrate that, given sufficient investment and patience, farming can be made both profitable and permanent in the Amazon. Despite the government's disenchantment with cattle-farming in general, these companies are still receiving considerable financial support.

The government meanwhile has turned to mining as the main focus of its developmental thrust. Some of the big new projects have been delayed by the serious recession through which Brazil is currently passing, but in the medium term they are likely to go ahead. The government is confident that they are the key to the future of the Amazon. In an interview with a group of journalists from Belém in December 1982, planning minister Antônio Delfim Neto acknowledged for the first time, with unexpected frankness, that the government's attempt to open up the region through farming had failed. 'We must recognise with all humility, so that something can be learnt from the experience, that we have failed so far with farming in the Amazon.' He then spoke in extraordinarily enthusiastic terms of the great future that lay ahead for the region through the setting up of the giant mining projects:

> Carajás is going to revolutionise the north of Brazil. There is no doubt about that . . . When it is working at full steam, it will be exporting US$9bn–10bn a year . . . Amazonia is going to develop very rapidly and intensely over the next decade . . . The moment has come when the axis of national development is moving, visibly, to the north. The Amazon will become a new world. It is the new frontier of Brazil.

Today the government's Amazon policy is geared to very big projects, in both mining and agriculture. It seems a desperate effort to vindicate a development model which has failed in the industrialised south. Scarcely any effort is being made today to use the region to solve pressing social problems which have emerged elsewhere in the country. Since the failure of the official colonisation projects along the Transamazônica, the federal government has given up its grandiose plans for organised mass migrations. The only part of the Amazon with large-scale official colonisation projects is Rondônia, where they are being set up by the state government in conjunction with INCRA. Elsewhere, the private colonisation projects cream off the relatively wealthy small farmers, but little provision is made for the rest. The peasant families are largely seen, not as potentially important producers, but as a threat to the government's development plans and, as such, to be kept out of the region or, if they are already firmly entrenched, to be kept in order through firm, repressive action. As we have seen, the main reason for setting up GETAT under military control was to ensure that peasant families, in alliance with church workers, did not disturb this 'new world' and, through unseemly agitation, put off foreign investors.

There is little doubt that the government has been successful in the short term through the militarisation of its land policy. Peasant families, rural unionists, priests and lay workers cannot compete militarily with the armed forces. But the long-term viability of the government's strategy seems far more doubtful. Two aspects – national migratory patterns and the environment – seem particularly questionable.

Building up the Pressure on the Cities

The government's insistence on regarding the peasant families as a military problem and in refusing to provide them with land in the Amazon is short sighted from both a political and an economic point of view. We found that the peasants who successfully won possession of their lands soon turned their attention to gaining bank loans, to increasing their productivity, to mechanising their farming methods, and so on. The families want to become integrated into the market economy, to increase their money incomes and to enjoy the benefits of consumer society. They could form a stable – and conservative – political force, as well as becoming key producers of crops, such as maize, that the government hopes to export in growing quantities.

As it is, the displaced families will exacerbate social problems elsewhere in the country. Some, mainly those with resources, are joining the massive influx into Rondônia. Others, who do not have the money to make the down payment for a plot in Rondônia, are pushing on westwards to Acre or, far up to the north, to Roraima to try to find cheaper land. But many of the poorer families are too dispirited to take this difficult option. They know that almost all land in Brazil has an owner, on paper at least, and that, wherever they go, unless they have the resouces to buy a plot, they are unlikely to find available land; even if they do, they may eventually face eviction.

So many of the families will migrate to the cities, though they know that their chances of employment are not good. They will thus add to the serious problems which are arising from the swelling of the urban areas. It is possible that some of these families, who arrive in the cities after long years of conflict in the Amazon, may contribute to the radicalisation of the shanty-town dwellers. There have already been reports of this in the shanty-towns of Cuiabá, the first stopping place of many peasant families moving south.

Yet other families will stay on their plots despite the pressure, resorting to violence to protect their land and, like some of the peasant farmers in the communities we visited, being increasingly prepared to be killed rather than evicted. As the families have become better informed of the grim options they face if they leave their plots, their reluctance to move out has grown.

The creation of GETAT seems to have increased the violence in these conflicts, for it has deprived the families of the moderating influence of the church workers, who almost invariably advise the families to do everything to avoid a violent confrontation which they are almost certain to lose.

The Ecological Threat

The government has long refused to draw up an ecologically sound programme for the occupation of the Amazon region. Its policies have been makeshift and improvised. It has reacted to problems, rather than planned to avoid them.

In the early 1970s the pace of destruction by the cattle companies was so fast that it seemed that the forest would be obliterated within a decade or two. However, as we have seen, serious ecological problems arose on many of the ranches, jeopardising the long-term viability of farming in the region. The government was forced to rethink its policy and, as a result, it reduced the supply of 'free money' to the ranches. It began to turn its attention to mining, an activity which does much less ecological damage.

However, it still failed to draw up an effective plan for the whole occupation. While the threat to the ecology receded on one front, it advanced on another. Because there is so little land available for small farmers, not only in the Amazon, but in the whole of Brazil, families have rushed to the few areas where they believe they can obtain a plot. Rondônia in particular has become an overspill for the whole country. Families are arriving in absurdly large waves, and the authorities are unable to cope. The settlers are becoming caught in an irrational form of occupation which, while it is socially more acceptable than the earlier phase, dominated by the cattle companies – for at least it has settled thousands of families on the land – is equally destructive in its long-term impact on the ecology.

It is a savage indictment of contemporary society that the greatest harm to the forest has been caused by those closely integrated into the market and using fairly sophisticated farming methods. To date, the only groups of inhabitants who have managed to live in ecological harmony with the Amazon have been the Indians. Until their life-styles were disrupted by outsiders, Indian groups maintained a remarkably sensitive relationship with their environment. Many of them, like the Tapirapé, took measures to control the size of their families so as not to overload the support capacity of the region they inhabited. The first migratory wave of peasant families from the north-east also caused relatively little ecological damage. The families spread out over a large area and practised shifting agriculture. According to Harald Sioli:

> Provided the population density remains low, the old-style, slash-and-burn, shifting cultivation is within the 'buffering capacity' of the Amazonian ecosystem. The temporary, small clearings are only pin pricks in the forest,

which soon heal again and do not leave permanent wounds or scars. After 30 or 40 years only a botanist could still distinguish this secondary forest from the primary forest around it.[1]

By far the greatest damage has been caused by the most recent arrivals, be they cattle companies or settlers from the south.

No one quite knows what proportion of the forest has been destroyed, as existing methods of measurement, including the images from the Landsat satellite, have proved unreliable. But it is known to be small, probably no more than about a tenth. But what is worrying scientists is the pace of the destruction. In a recent article, Philip Fearnside, a scientist working at INPA in Manaus, drew attention to the explosive rate of forest clearance in many parts of the Amazon.[2] In three states at least, he warned, the area of cleared land was no longer increasing in steady linear fashion, but had entered a dangerous exponential curve in which the rate of increase grew each year. If these exponential curves are projected, they suggest that Mato Grosso will have lost all its forest by 1989, Rondônia by 1990 and Acre by 1993. Ecologists believe that the whole of the forest could be wiped out within 30 or 40 years. What would be the impact on the world environment, if this were to happen?

It is now recognised by most ecologists that the destruction of the Amazon forest would not have as dramatic an effect on the global climate as has at times been suggested. It is not true to claim that the Amazon forest is responsible for the production of half of the world's oxygen, as has been reported. Harald Sioli has explained: 'The Amazon forest is in climax. Its biomass is constant and it thus produces as much oxygen by its photo-synthesis as it consumes again by the oxidation of the dead matter.'

However, this does not mean that the destruction of the forest would not have very serious consequences. The most harmful global result would be a marked increase in the pollution of the atmosphere. Sioli believes that, if all the forest were to be displaced by grassland, only a small fraction of its carbon content would be retained in the new vegetation. The rest would be oxidised, by fire or natural decomposition, to carbon dioxide, which would go into the atmosphere and increase its carbon dioxide content, probably by at least 16 per cent. Half of the increase might well be absorbed into the oceans, but there would remain a net increase of 8 per cent.

The carbon dioxide content of the atmosphere has already risen by 16 per cent during the last 100 years, as a result of the burning of fossil fuels and the destruction of many of the world's forests. A further rise would increase the 'greenhouse effect', that is, the process by which the carbon dioxide, like the glass panes in a greenhouse, traps the sun's radiated heat in the earth's atmosphere and causes warmer climates throughout the world, with unknown long-term consequences.

It is difficult to assess with any precision the consequences of the total destruction of the forest on the local environment. According to Sioli, it would reduce annual rainfall, as it would break the pattern of water recycling and would create a much longer and more intense dry season. It would also provoke a less stable river regime, with a much quicker rise in the river levels during the rainy season and much lower levels during the dry season. In all, the wholesale destruction of the forest would be likely to jeopardise the long-term agricultural future of the region.

Another serious consequence would be the impact of the destruction on human knowledge. The Amazon jungle is thought to contain about a tenth of the plant, insect and animal species on earth. This means a figure of between 500,000 and 800,000 species. The vast majority have not been studied and it is impossible to imagine what contribution they could make to medicine and technology.

Ghillean Prance, senior vice-president for science at the New York Botanical Garden, gives one reason for protecting these species: 'Our survival depends on diversity. The world today is fed by fewer than 20 major food crops. If one of these is extensively damaged by pests or disease, part of the world faces famine.'[3] He cites cocoa, only one species of which is harvested commercially, while 20 others are found in the Amazon. It is alarming to think that a few species may have already been wiped out from the Amazon, before they were even discovered by the scientific community.

Sioli takes the discussion an important step forward:

> Amazonia has an immensely extensive stock of vegetable and animal genes and gene-combinations, which has evolved in Amazonia during its long history, never interrupted by a glacial period. Its experience is probably unique on earth and the majority of its species only occur there. It is therefore not only a practical question of whether it be opportune for humanity to extinguish, through deforestation, such a reservoir, with the unthought-of possibilities it contains for the future, and to do so for eventual, and highly-dubious, momentary economic profit. But above this question there stands in every case the ethical problem of whether man can answer, not only before himself and his descendants, but also before the whole creation handed down to him, for the total and definite annihilation, in a few decades and only for his own egoistic purposes, of a life so rich and colourful as that of the Amazonian forest, which needed millions of years for its formation.[4]

It is not a comforting exercise to bring together prospects at an ecological and political level. It seems likely that, once Rondônia has been completely settled – and partly destroyed – the wave of occupation will move on into Acre and then, possibly, into the largely unoccupied state of Amazonas. Settlers have already begun to travel to the remote territory of Roraima, on the border with Venezuela. If precedent is any guide, the occupation will be disorderly, intense and lawless. The driving force will be profit maximisation, not the establishment of rational, long-term farming. Few effective measures to protect the fertility of the soils will be taken. The worst of both worlds is likely: the forest, with all it has to offer, will be destroyed; but the opportunity to settle permanently some of Brazil's landless families will be lost.

The real solution requires a profound and complex shake-up in the system of land tenure throughout the country, so that many more families can be settled on small plots and the pressure relieved both on the shanty-towns on the outskirts of the cities and on the few states, like Rondônia, which are accepting small farmers. These types of reform are most likely to occur under a democratic form of government in which popular organisations can be mobilised to give the government the power to stand up to the big landowners whose interests would be hurt by land distribution.

The process of political liberalisation is advancing, particularly in the wake of the mass demonstrations in early 1984 in favour of a return to direct elections for President. In January 1985 Tancredo Neves, a moderate politician from the main opposition party, the PMDB, was chosen in the electoral college as the president to succeed Figueiredo. Even though Neves himself was taken ill on the eve of his inauguration and died before taking office, his government came to power. Despite enormous political uncertainty, a big step in the process of political liberalisation has been taken.

But even so, the problems facing the Amazon region remain daunting. As a result of GETAT and the land ministry, the armed forces are firmly established as the main authority in the region. The military leaders, in alliance with technocrats and big landowners, will oppose any fundamental change in the way the Amazon is being occupied. It will be a formidable alliance in favour of the maintenance of the *status quo*. The new government, which only reached power by the PMDB forming an alliance with a breakaway faction of the PDS party, faces enormous problems, not least of which are the foreign debt crisis and the widespread underemployment and starvation in the cities. It will be tempted to ignore the Amazon region, which is not yet an important source of political pressure.

Yet there are pressing reasons why the Amazon question cannot be postponed. In the first place, if Fearnside's projections prove correct, three Amazon states will be on the road to desertification by the end of the new government's term of office. There is no time to be lost. And secondly, what has been happening in the Amazon over the last decades cannot be summarily divorced from what has been going on in the rest of Brazil, for it is largely a reflection of a much broader development process. For it is the authoritarian, unequal form of development in Brazil over the last 20 years which has been largely responsible for the catastrophic nature of Amazon occupation. By permitting further concentration in land tenure, so that Brazil has ended up with what is probably the most unequal system of land distribution in the world, the military regime permitted millions of families to be driven from the land and indirectly provoked an unmanageably heavy flow of migrants to the Amazon region. By outrageously favouring in all its policies an elite of very big national and foreign companies, the military government permitted a highly unjust division of land in the Amazon and, by providing generous tax rebates, encouraged an ecologically harmful use of the land. If over the last 20 years land throughout Brazil had been distributed more equitably and the elite of big companies had enjoyed far fewer privileges, the Amazon would not find itself in the present mess.

By the same logic, the present chaotic and irrational form of Amazon occupation will only be eased if agrarian reform is carried out and the power of the big companies is curtailed. These changes are essential, not only for the Amazon, but to resolve other of Brazil's crucial problems, particularly the heavy migration to the cities which is creating widespread underemployment, starvation and crime. If the government fails in the Amazon, it will be a clear indication that it is failing in the rest of the country. The whole of Brazil, not just the Amazon region, is calling out for a new, humane and more rational form of development, in which the welfare of the people is put before growth in economic output for its own sake. Any government which fails to move the country in this direction will betray the hopes of the millions of ordinary Brazilians who took to the streets in early 1984 to express in the only effective way at their disposal their heartfelt rejection of the kind of society created in the name of development by the successive military governments over the previous 21 years.

This seems to have been well understood by Tancredo Neves, the man who should have become the present president. According to the Brazilian news magazine *Isto É,*[5] he was once asked what were the country's main problems. He answered: 'Hunger, unemployment, illness, housing and violence, in that order of importance'. And the solution? 'Democratisation and agrarian reform'.

Notes

1. In an address given at the Conference on the Development of Amazonia in Seven Countries, Cambridge, 23–26 September 1979.

2. Philip M. Fearnside, 'A Floresta Vai Acabar?', *Ciência Hoje*, Vol.2, No.10 (Jan/Feb 1984).

3. *Time*, 18 October 1982.

4. Address to Conference on the Development of Amazonia in Seven Countries.

5. *Isto É*, 24 April 1985.

Chronology

1500	The 'discovery' of Brazil by Portuguese explorer Pedro Alvares Cabral.
1532	First sugar mill built in the north-east, marking the beginning of Brazil's role as leading sugar exporter.
1695	Gold discovered in state of Minas Gerais, sparking off gold rush.
1727	Introduction of coffee into Brazil.
1808	Portuguese royal family, headed by King João VI, moves to Brazil during Peninsular Wars.
1821	João VI returns to Portugal after Napoleon's defeat.
1822	Prince Pedro declares Brazil's independence and receives title of Emperor Pedro I.
1858	Coffee becomes Brazil's main export.
1888	Abolition of slavery.
1889	Emperor Pedro II dethroned and the republic established.
1890	Separation of Church and State.
1917	Brazil declares war on Germany.
1930	Getúlio Vargas comes to power in coup.
1937	Vargas establishes authoritarian regime called Estado Novo.
1942	Brazil declares war on Axis powers.
1944	Brazilian Expeditionary Force sent to Europe, containing numerous young officers who were to take power 20 years later.
1945	Vargas regime deposed by military anxious to reestablish democratic government in Brazil.
1950	Vargas elected President.
1954	Worried by Vargas's nationalist policies, military threaten coup. Vargas commits suicide.
1955	Juscelino Kubitschek elected president by an alliance of the two parties set up by Vargas – Partido Trabalhista Brasileiro (PTB) and the Partido Social Democratico (PSD).
1955-60	Rapid growth, with the setting up of car and shipbuilding industries, development of steel industry and building of big network of roads. Construction of new federal capital, Brasília.
1960	Jânio Quadros, standing for the conservative União Democrática Nacional (UDN), is elected president by large majority. João Goulart, from the leftish PTB, is elected vice-president.
1961	After just seven months in office, Quadros unexpectedly resigns. Despite military disquiet, Goulart takes over as president.
1964	*March*: In deteriorating economic situation and after growing signs of

middle class disquiet over the left-wing rhetoric of the government, Goulart is overthrown by military coup.

April: The three military ministers decree Institutional Act no. 1, which vests them with power to legislate and to create an authoritarian state. General Humberto de Alencar Castelo Branco, formerly head of the army general staff, is chosen as president.

1965 Planning minister Roberto Campos imposes harsh economic squeeze and carries out basic economic reforms. The living standards of the poorer sectors fall significantly.

Castelo Branco bans all former political parties and sets up an artificial system with just two parties – the pro-government Arena and the MDB for the opposition.

1967 General Arthur da Costa e Silva, war minister under Castelo Branco, is selected by the military rulers as Castelo Branco's successor. He takes over in March. Antônio Delfim Neto becomes finance minister, a position he is to hold until 1974.

1968 Large student demonstrations, re-emergence of the labour movement and the first public criticisms of the government by the bishops of the Catholic Church.

December: Costa e Silva decrees Institutional Act no. 5, the most repressive of the new Acts, and uses it to close down Congress. The economy emerges from recession. The first of five years of high growth, about 10% a year, known as Brazil's 'economic miracle'.

1969 *August*: Costa e Silva is taken ill and the government is taken over by a military junta. General Emílio Garrastazu Médici is chosen by the military rulers to become the next president.

1970 Period of highly authoritarian government. Urban guerrilla groups become active, kidnapping the US ambassador, Burke Elbrick. All political activists are hounded by army, which sets up special repressive units, such as Operação Bandeirantes (Oban).

1974 *March*: General Ernesto Geisel, selected by the military rulers, becomes president. The new finance minister, Mário Henrique Simonsen, encourages the second phase of import substitution by providing generous incentives for investments in steel, capital goods, hydro-electric power and roadbuilding.

1976 Under the guidance of his top adviser, General Golbery do Couto e Silva, Geisel begins a cautious process of political liberalisation, to be known later as *abertura* (opening).

1978 After ten-year lull, labour movement re-emerges with important strike among car-workers in São Paulo's industrial suburbs.

1979 *March*: After bitter infighting among the military leaders, General João Baptista Figueiredo takes over as president.

August: Planning minister Mário Henrique Simonsen resigns. He is replaced by Antônio Delfim Neto, who begins second term as economic supremo.

November: As part of *abertura*, the artificial two party system is abolished. Six new parties are formed, the most important of which are: PDS, which replaces Arena as the pro-government party; PMDB, taking over from MDB, which continues to be by far the largest opposition party; and the PT, the Worker's Party, which is set up by Luis Inácio da Silva, 'Lula', the country's most important labour leader, and other independent trade unionists.

1980   *January*: Karlos Rischbieter resigns as finance minister, after criticising the goverment for allowing the foreign debt to snowball out of control. He is replaced by Ernane Galvêas.

May: Military occupy industrial suburbs of São Paulo to end car-workers' strike.

1981   *August*: General Golbery resigns as top presidential aide. Electoral reform package, geared to improving PDS's electoral chances, is passed.

September: Figueiredo has heart attack and goes to USA for heart treatment. He is replaced temporarily by vice-president Aureliano Chaves.

1982   *November*: In the elections for Congress, opposition parties win 57% of the vote, but, because of the skewed electoral system, do not control the Senate and have only a tiny majority in the Chamber of Deputies.

December: After running out of foreign currency in September and October, the government turns to International Monetary Fund (IMF) and begins to reschedule foreign debt.

1983   At the behest of the IMF, the government imposes a tough austerity programme, which leads to a 3.5% fall in gross national product.

April: Rioting by unemployed in São Paulo.

1984   *April*: Despite enormous popular campaign, the opposition parties fail by a few votes to obtain the necessary two-thirds majority in Congress to pass a constitutional amendment bringing back direct elections for president. All the opposition parties, except the PT, decide none the less to put forward a candidate in the electoral college which is to select Figueiredo's successor.

1985   *January*: Tancredo Neves, the opposition's candidate, is selected as president by the electoral college.

March: The civilian government takes over, ending 21 years of military rule, though Tancredo Neves himself is prevented by illness from taking office.

April: Tancredo Neves dies, and José Sarney becomes president.

Bibliography

Alves, Maria Helena Moreira, *Brazil: Structures of Repression*, Latin American Working Group Letter, vol.VII, no.3/4, Toronto, Jan.-April 1982.
——— *Estado e Oposição no Brasil (1964-1984)*, Editora Vozes, Petrópolis, 1984.
Amnesty International, *Relatório do Julgamento dos Padres Aristides Camio e Francisco Gouriou*, September 1982.
Asselin, Victor, *Grilagem – Corrupção e Violência em Terras do Carajás*, Editora Vozes and Comissão Pastoral da Terra, Petrópolis, 1982.
Banco da Amazònia, *Desenvolvimento Econòmico da Amazònia*, Editòra da Universidade Federal do Pará, Belém do Pará, 1967.
Barbara-Scazzocchio, Françoise (ed.), *Land People and Planning in Contemporary Amazonia*, Proceedings of the Conference on the Development of Amazonia in Seven Countries, Cambridge, 23-26 September 1979, Centre of Latin American Studies, Occasional Publication no.3, Cambridge University, 1980.
Bourne, Richard, *Assault on the Amazon*, Victor Gollancz Ltd, London, 1978.
Càmara, Diógenes Arruda & others, *Guerrilha do Araguaia 1972-82*, Anita Garibaldi, São Paulo, no date.
Càmara dos Deputados, Projeto de Resolução no.85, 1979, *Relatório e Conclusões da Comissão Parlamentar de Inquérito Destinado a Investigar as Atividades Ligadas ao Sistema Fundiário em Todo Território Nacional*, Diário do Congresso Nacional, Suplemento ao no.121, Brasília.
Casaldáliga, D. Pedro, *Uma Igreja da Amazònia em Conflito com o Latifúndio e a Marginalização Social*, São Félix (MT), 1971.
CEDI (Centro Ecumênico de Documentação e Informação), *Aconteceu – Povos Indigenas no Brasil/1980*, Especial, April 1981.
——— *Aconteceu – Povos Indigenas no Brasil/1981*, Especial, April, 1982.
——— *Aconteceu – Povos Indigenas no Brasil/1982*, Especial, April, 1983.
——— *Aconteceu – Povos Indigenas no Brasil/1983*, Especial, April, 1984.
——— *Peões e Garimpeiros – Terra e Trabalho no Araguaia*, Cadernos do CEDI 11, June 1983.
Comissão Arquidiocesana de Pastoral dos Direitos Humanos e Marginalizados da Arquidiocese de São Paulo, *Repressão no Brasil – Reflexo de uma Situação de Opressão (1968-1978)*, São Paulo, no date.
Comissão Pastoral da Terra, *Denúncia: Caso Araguaia-Tocantins*, Goiània, no date.
Comissão Pastoral da Terra/Alto Paraguai Mato Grosso, *Os Pequenos se Unem*, mimeo., no date.

Confederação Nacional dos Trabalhadores na Agricultura (CONTAG), *As Lutas Camponesas no Brasil*, Editora Marco Zero, Rio de Janeiro, 1980.

Coutinho, Luiz Paulo & Barbosa, Rubens, *Desamparo, a Recompensa ao Peão Escravo da Amazônia*, in A Amazônia Brasileira em Foco, Boletim no.8, CNDA, Rio de Janeiro, 1973.

Davis, Shelton H., *Victims of the Miracle – Development and the Indians of Brazil*, Cambridge University Press, New York, 1977.

Diluca, Zé, *Peleja da Piaba do Araguaia com o Tubarão Besta Fera*, Prelazia de São Féliz do Araguaia, August 1981.

Falesi, Italo Cláudio, *Solos da Rodovia Transamazônica*, Boletim Técnico do Instituto de Pesquisa Agropecuária do Norte (IPEAN), Belém, 55, July 1972.

Filochowski, Julian and others, *Reflections on Puebla*, Catholic Institute for International Relations, London, 1980.

Foweraker, Joe, *The Struggle for Land – A Political Economy of the Pioneer Frontier in Brazil from 1930 to the Present Day*, Cambridge University Press, Cambridge, 1981.

Goodland, R.J.A. & Irwin, H.S., *Amazon Jungle: From Green Hell to Red Desert?*, Elsevier Scientific, Amsterdam, 1975.

Goodman, David, & Redclift, Michael, *From Peasant to Proletarian – Capitalist Development and Agrarian Transitions*, Basil Blackwell, Oxford, 1981.

Ianni, Octávio, *Colonização e Contra-Reforma Agrária na Amazônia*, Editora Vozes, Petrópolis, 1979.

Ianni, Octávio (introduction), *Projeto Jari – A Invasão Americana*, Brasil Debates, São Paulo, 1980.

IBASE, *Os Donos da Terra e a Luta pela Reforma Agrária*, Editôra Codecri, Rio de Janeiro, 1984.

———— *Carajás, o Brasil Hipoteca Seu Futuro*, Achiamé, Rio de Janeiro, 1983.

Katzman, Martin T., *The Evaluation of the Brazilian Model of Regional Planning*, mimeo., no date.

Kotoscho, Ricardo, *O Massacre dos Posseiros – Conflito de Terras no Araguaia-Tocantins*, Editora Brasiliense, São Paulo, 1981.

Kucinski, Bernardo, *Abertura, a História de uma Crise*, Brasil Hoje no.5, Brasil Debates, São Paulo, 1982.

Leão, Velloso, *Euclides da Cunha na Amazônia*, Livraria São José, 1966.

Lopes, Eliano Sérgio Azevedo, *Frentes de Expansão e Conflitos Sociais na Amazônia (Rondônia como Objeto de Reflexões)*, PIPSA/CPDA/EIA, Fundação Getúlio Vargas, 1979.

———— *Colonização Oficial na Amazônia: a Reprodução das Desigualdades*, Boletim do CEPES, Porto Velho, vol.1, no.1, Oct.-Dec. 1981.

Margolis, Maxine L., *The Moving Frontier – Social and Economic Change in a Southern Brazilian Community*, University of Florida Press, Gainsville, 1973.

Martine, George, *Recent Colonisation Experiences in Brazil: Expectations Versus Reality*, mimeo., 1978.

Martins, Edilson, *Nós, do Araguaia*, Editora Graal, Rio de Janeiro, 1979.

Martins, José de Souza, *Capitalismo e Tradicionalismo*, Livraria Pioneira Editora, São Paulo, 1975.

———— *Expropriação e Violência – A Questão Política no Campo*, Hucitec, São Paulo, 1980.

———— *O Cativeiro da Terra*, second edition, Livraria Editora Ciências Humanas,

São Paulo, 1981.

————— *Os Camponeses e a Política no Brasil*, second edition, Editora Vozes, Petrópolis, 1983.

————— *A Militarização da Questão Agrária no Brasil*, Editora Vozes, Petrópolis, 1984.

Mata, M., Carvalho, E.U.R., & Castro e Silva, M.T., *Migrações Internas no Brasil: Aspectos Econômicos e Demográficos*, IPEA/INPES, Rio de Janeiro, 1973.

Moura, Clóvis (introduction), *Diário da Guerrilha do Araguaia*, Editora Alfa-Omega, São Paulo, 1979.

Pinto, Lúcio Flávio, *Amazônia – O Anteato da Destruição*, Grafisa, Belém, 1977.

————— *Amazônia: No Rastro do Saque*, Hucitec, São Paulo, 1980.

————— *Carajás, O Ataque ao Coração da Amazônia*, Marco Zero, 1982.

Prado Junior, Caio, *Formação do Brasil Contemporâneo*, Editora Brasiliense, São Paulo, 1942.

————— *História Econômica do Brasil*, Editora Brasiliense, São Paulo, 1962.

Ramos, Alcida R., and Taylor, Kenneth I., *The Yanoama in Brazil – 1979*, and The Committee for the Creation of the Yanomami Park, *Yanomami Indian Park, Proposal and Justification*, IWGIA Document 37, Copenhagen, 1979.

Rêgo Reis, Gustavo Moraes, *A Cabanagem – Um Episódio Histórico de Guerra Insurrecional na Amazônia (1835-1839)*, Série Torquato Tapajós, Edições Govêrno do Estado do Amazonas, Manaus, 1965.

Salem, Helena (ed), *A Igreja dos Oprimidos*, Coleção Brasil Hoje no.3, Editora Brasil Debates, São Paulo, 1981.

Silva, General Golbery do Couto e, *Conjuntura Política Nacional – o Poder Executivo a Geopolítica do Brasil*, second edition, Livraria José Olympio Editora, Rio de Janeiro, 1981.

Singelmann, Peter, *Structures of Domination and Peasant Movements in Latin America*, University of Missouri Press, Columbia and London, 1981.

Valverde, Orlando & Dias, Catharina, *A Rodovia Belém-Brasília*, IBGE, Rio de Janeiro, 1976.

Valverde, Orlando & Freitas, Tácito Lívio Reis de, *O Problema Florestal da Amazônia Brasileira*, Editora Vozes, Petrópolis, 1980.

Velho, Otávio Guilherme, *Frentes de Expansão e Estrutura Agrária*, Zahar Editores, Rio de Janeiro, 1972.

Index